Communications
in Computer and Information Science   1771

Rationale

The CCIS series is devoted to the publication of proceedings of computer science conferences. Its aim is to efficiently disseminate original research results in informatics in printed and electronic form. While the focus is on publication of peer-reviewed full papers presenting mature work, inclusion of reviewed short papers reporting on work in progress is welcome, too. Besides globally relevant meetings with internationally representative program committees guaranteeing a strict peer-reviewing and paper selection process, conferences run by societies or of high regional or national relevance are also considered for publication.

Topics

The topical scope of CCIS spans the entire spectrum of informatics ranging from foundational topics in the theory of computing to information and communications science and technology and a broad variety of interdisciplinary application fields.

Information for Volume Editors and Authors

Publication in CCIS is free of charge. No royalties are paid, however, we offer registered conference participants temporary free access to the online version of the conference proceedings on SpringerLink (http://link.springer.com) by means of an http referrer from the conference website and/or a number of complimentary printed copies, as specified in the official acceptance email of the event.

CCIS proceedings can be published in time for distribution at conferences or as post-proceedings, and delivered in the form of printed books and/or electronically as USBs and/or e-content licenses for accessing proceedings at SpringerLink. Furthermore, CCIS proceedings are included in the CCIS electronic book series hosted in the SpringerLink digital library at http://link.springer.com/bookseries/7899. Conferences publishing in CCIS are allowed to use Online Conference Service (OCS) for managing the whole proceedings lifecycle (from submission and reviewing to preparing for publication) free of charge.

Publication process

The language of publication is exclusively English. Authors publishing in CCIS have to sign the Springer CCIS copyright transfer form, however, they are free to use their material published in CCIS for substantially changed, more elaborate subsequent publications elsewhere. For the preparation of the camera-ready papers/files, authors have to strictly adhere to the Springer CCIS Authors' Instructions and are strongly encouraged to use the CCIS LaTeX style files or templates.

Abstracting/Indexing

CCIS is abstracted/indexed in DBLP, Google Scholar, EI-Compendex, Mathematical Reviews, SCImago, Scopus. CCIS volumes are also submitted for the inclusion in ISI Proceedings.

How to start

To start the evaluation of your proposal for inclusion in the CCIS series, please send an e-mail to ccis@springer.com.

Marina Yusoff · Tao Hai · Murizah Kassim ·
Azlinah Mohamed · Eisuke Kita

Editors

Soft Computing in Data Science

7th International Conference, SCDS 2023
Virtual Event, January 24–25, 2023
Proceedings

Editors
Marina Yusoff ⓘ
Universiti Teknologi MARA
Shah Alam, Malaysia

Tao Hai ⓘ
Baoji University of Arts and Sciences
Baoji, China

Murizah Kassim ⓘ
Universiti Teknologi MARA
Shah Alam, Malaysia

Azlinah Mohamed ⓘ
Universiti Teknologi MARA
Shah Alam, Malaysia

Eisuke Kita ⓘ
Institute of Liberal Arts and Sciences
Nagoya, Japan

ISSN 1865-0929   ISSN 1865-0937 (electronic)
Communications in Computer and Information Science
ISBN 978-981-99-0404-4   ISBN 978-981-99-0405-1 (eBook)
https://doi.org/10.1007/978-981-99-0405-1

This Springer imprint is published by the registered company Springer Nature Singapore Pte Ltd.
The registered company address is: 152 Beach Road, #21-01/04 Gateway East, Singapore 189721, Singapore

Preface

Welcome to the proceedings of the Seventh International Conference on Soft Computing in Data Science (SCDS 2023). SCDS 2023 was a virtual conference co-hosted by China's Baoji University of Arts and Sciences. 'Science in Analytics: Harnessing Data and Simplifying Solutions' was the conference's theme. SCDS 2023 aimed to provide a knowledge-sharing platform for Big Data Analytics and Artificial Intelligence theory and applications. Big Data Analytics enables businesses to better leverage data for data-driven decisions and AI for optimal performance. The world is shifting toward automation and innovation through Artificial Intelligence. Experts in industry are capitalizing on emerging technologies such as artificial intelligence, big data, and cloud computing.

The papers in these proceedings address issues, challenges, theory, and novel applications of big data analytics and artificial intelligence, including but not limited to Artificial Intelligence techniques and applications, Computing and Optimization, Data Mining and Image Processing, and Machine and Statistical Learning.

In the advanced society of the twenty-first century, knowledge and technology on Big Data and Artificial Intelligence must be transferred to industrial applications and used to solve real-world problems that benefit the global community. Collaborations between academia and industry in research can result in novel, innovative computing applications that enable real-time insights and solutions.

We are thrilled to have received paper submissions from a diverse group of national and international researchers this year. We received 61 paper submissions, with 31 of them being accepted. The SCDS 2023 review process was double-blind. All accepted submissions were assigned to at least two independent reviewers to ensure a rigorous, thorough, and convincing evaluation process. The review process included 15 international and 30 local reviewers. The conference proceeding volume editors and the Springer CCIS Editorial Board made the final acceptance decisions, with 24 of the 61 submissions (39.34%) published in the conference proceedings.

We would like to express our gratitude to the authors who submitted manuscripts to SCDS 2023. We appreciate the reviewers taking the time to read the papers. We gratefully acknowledge all conference committee members for their valuable time, ideas, and efforts in ensuring the success of SCDS 2023. We would also like to thank the Springer CCIS Editorial Board, organizations, and sponsors for their ongoing support. We sincerely hope SCDS 2023 has provided a forum for sharing knowledge, publishing promising research findings, and forming new research collaborations. We hope everyone took something away from the Keynote and Parallel Sessions and enjoyed interacting with other researchers via this virtual conference.

January 2023

Marina Yusoff
Tao Hai
Murizah Kassim
Azlinah Mohamed
Eisuke Kita

Organization

Advisor

Jasni Mohamad Zain   Universiti Teknologi MARA, Malaysia

Conference Chair

Marina Yusoff   Universiti Teknologi MARA, Malaysia

Co-chair

Hai Tao   Baoji University of Arts and Sciences, China

Secretaries

Nurain Ibrahim (Head)   Universiti Teknologi MARA, Malaysia
Siti Afiqah Muhamad Jamil   Universiti Teknologi MARA, Malaysia

Registration and Presentation

Lu Ye   Baoji University of Arts and Sciences, China
Fang Xu   Baoji University of Arts and Sciences, China
Yang Xuelan   Baoji University of Arts and Sciences, China
Wan Fairos Wan Yaacob   Universiti Teknologi MARA, Malaysia

Finance Committee

Nurbaizura Borhan (Head)   Universiti Teknologi MARA, Malaysia
Nur Asyikin Abdullah   Universiti Teknologi MARA, Malaysia
Azira Mohamed Amin   Universiti Teknologi MARA, Malaysia

Technical Program Committee

Murizah Kassim (Head)	Universiti Teknologi MARA, Malaysia
Abdul Kadir Jumaat	Universiti Teknologi MARA, Malaysia
Mohd Abdul Talib Mat Yusoh	Universiti Teknologi MARA, Malaysia
Nurain Ibrahim	Universiti Teknologi MARA, Malaysia

Publicity & Sponsorship Committee

Memiyanty Abdul Rahim (Head)	Universiti Teknologi MARA, Malaysia
Nooritawati Md Tahir	Universiti Teknologi MARA, Malaysia
Muhammad Imran Mohd Tamrin	Universiti Teknologi MARA, Malaysia
Siti Nurul Aslinda Mohd Nahrowei	Universiti Teknologi MARA, Malaysia
Nur Yasmin Sofiya Ahmad Kamal	Universiti Teknologi MARA, Malaysia

Publication Committee (Program/Book of Abstracts)

Siti Afiqah Muhamad Jamil (Head)	Universiti Teknologi MARA, Malaysia
Mohammed Adam Kunna Azrag	Universiti Teknologi MARA, Malaysia
Saiful Farik Mat Yatim	Universiti Teknologi MARA, Malaysia
Yang Xuelan	Baoji University of Arts and Sciences, China
Nur Aliah Khairina Mohd Haris	UiTM Technoventure Sdn. Bhd, Malaysia
Putri Azmira R Azmi	UiTM Technoventure Sdn. Bhd, Malaysia

Website & Online Committee

Mohamad Asyraf Abdul Latif	Universiti Teknologi MARA, Malaysia
Muhamad Ridhwan Mohamad Razali	Universiti Teknologi MARA, Malaysia

International Scientific Committee

Mario Köppen	Kyutech Institute of Technology, Japan
Sri Hartati	Universitas Gadjah Mada, Indonesia
Chidchanok Lursinsap	Chulalongkorn University, Thailand
Hizir Sofyan	Syiah Kuala University, Indonesia

Aiden Doherty	University of Oxford, UK
Hamid R. Rabiee	Sharif University of Technology, Iran
Ruhana Ku Mahamud	Universiti Utara Malaysia, Malaysia
Nur Iriawan	Institut Teknologi Sepuluh Nopember, Indonesia
Rajalida Lipikorn	Chulalongkorn University, Thailand
Agus Harjoko	Universitas Gadjah Mada, Indonesia
Min Chen	University of Oxford, UK
Simon Fong	University of Macau, China
Mohammed Bennamoun	University of Western Australia, Australia
Yasue Mitsukura	Keio University, Japan
Dhiya Al-Jumeily	Liverpool John Moores University, UK
Dariusz Krol	Wroclaw University of Science and Technology, Poland
Richard Weber	University of Chile, Chile
Jose Maria Pena	Technical University of Madrid, Spain
Yusuke Nojima	Osaka Prefecture University, Japan
Siddhivinayak Kulkarni	University of Ballarat, Australia
Tahir Ahmad	Universiti Teknologi Malaysia, Malaysia
Daud Mohamed	Universiti Teknologi MARA, Malaysia
Wahyu Wibowo	Institut Teknologi Sepuluh Nopember, Indonesia
Edi Winarko	Universitas Gadjah Mada, Indonesia
Retantyo Wardoyo	Universitas Gadjah Mada, Indonesia
Rayner Alfred	Universiti Malaysia Sabah, Malaysia
Faiz Ahmed	.
Mohamed Elfaki	Qatar University, Qatar
Mohamed Chaouch	Qatar University, Qatar
Abdul Haris Rangkuti, S.	BINUS University, Indonesia
Eisuke Kita	Nagoya University, Japan
Waheb Abdullah	.
Abduljabbar Shaif	Birmingham City University, UK
Achmad Choiruddin	Institut Teknologi Sepuluh Nopember, Indonesia
Jerry Dwi Purnomo	Institut Teknologi Sepuluh Nopember, Indonesia

Reviewers SCDS 2023

Abdul Kadir Jumaat	Universiti Teknologi MARA, Malaysia
Albert Guvenis	Boğaziçi University, Turkey
Azlan Iqbal	Universiti Tenaga Nasional & College of Information Technology, Malaysia
Dipti Prakash Theng	G. H. Raisoni College of Engineering, India
Ensar Gul	Maltepe University, Turkey

Weng Siew Lam	Universiti Tunku Abdul Rahman (UTAR), Malaysia
Yusnani Mohd Yusoff	Universiti Teknologi MARA, Malaysia
Yuzi Mahmud	Universiti Teknologi MARA, Malaysia
Zainura Idrus	Universiti Teknologi MARA, Malaysia

Organized by

Industry and International Collaboration

Contents

Data Analytics and Technologies

Data Mining and Image Processing

Mathematical and Statistical Learning

Artificial Intelligence Techniques
and Applications

Explainability for Clustering Models

Mahima Arora$^{(\boxtimes)}$ ⓘ and Ankush Chopra ⓘ

Tredence Inc., Bengaluru 560048, India
mahima.arora@tredence.com

Abstract. The field of Artificial Intelligence is growing at a very high pace. Application of bigger and complex algorithms have become commonplace, thus making them harder to understand. The explainability of the algorithms and models in practice has become a necessity as these models are being widely adopted to make significant and consequential decisions. It makes it even more important for us to keep our understanding of the decisions and results of AI up to date. Explainable AI methods are currently addressing the interpretability, explainability, and fairness in supervised learning methods. There has been very less focus on explaining the results of unsupervised learning methods. This paper proposes an extension of the supervised explainability methods to deal with the unsupervised methods as well. We have researched and experimented with widely used clustering models to show the applicability of the proposed solution on most practiced unsupervised problems. We also have thoroughly investigated the methods to validate the results of both supervised and unsupervised explainability modules.

Keywords: Clustering · Explainability · Explanations · Interpretability · Unsupervised methods · XAI

1 Introduction

1.1 Explainable AI

Explainability in machine learning is the process of explaining the decision made by the model to an end-user. Explainable AI (XAI) is a set of algorithms, methods, tools, and frameworks which enable users to understand and interpret the results of complex AI models. Explainable AI algorithms are considered to follow the three principles of transparency, interpretability, and explainability. It helps in finding answers to the critical how? and why? questions about AI systems and can be used to address rising ethical and legal concerns. As a result, AI researchers have identified XAI as a necessary feature of trustworthy (Responsible) AI, and explainability has experienced a recent surge in attention. The explanations provided by XAI tools help users in interpreting the predictions generated as the output by the black-box ML models, which further helps them in taking informed decisions efficiently. The output generated by XAI tools is referred to as explanations. Explanations can be understood as a weight to each feature proportional to its contribution to the sample prediction. Various models inherently provide the explanation of the output. GAM [1], GLM [2], decision tree etc. are examples of such models. These models are often simpler and do not provide the level of performance many black-box models offer. Explanations for black box supervised models can be generated using model agnostic methods. LIME [3] and SHAP [4] are both good choices for explaining black-box models. As these tools are model agnostic, they do not directly peak into the model. They treat the model as a function which maps the input feature set to model prediction values. To figure out what parts of the interpretable input are contributing to these predictions; they perturb the input around its neighborhood and see how the model's predictions behave. These methods then weigh these perturbed data points by their proximity to the original example and learn an interpretable model on those and the associated predictions.

1.2   Limitations of Explainability AI

XAI methods are feature attribution methods, which means they attribute to a set of input features(X) responsible for the output (predictions, Y) of a function $F(X) = Y$ that depends on those features. This function does not have to be a supervised machine learning model, but it needs to give numeric output in a specific format. In the case of Regression, the output value is continuous, i.e., the output is a numeric value and can be explained using XAI methods. In the case of a classification task, it explains the contribution of each feature toward the resultant probabilities for each class. The model agnostic implementation of the XAI tools (for classification tasks) only supports probabilistic models and is designed to work with the output probabilities of the given model. This restricts users to compute explanations for Unsupervised approaches (clustering algorithms) which unlike supervised classification models are not probabilistic models. Instead of returning a numeric value as output, they only return the cluster name as its output.

1.3   Probabilistic Clustering

There is already some work done towards building probabilistic clustering model. Gaussian Mixture Model is one such model which is probabilistic in nature. It is a generative probabilistic model, and its algorithm works on the concept of density estimation. The core theme of this paper is not to propose any probabilistic clustering methods, rather it deals with the existing clustering methods (non-probabilistic) and the methods to compute its explainability. It proposes a method which introduces probability to non-probabilistic clustering methods in order to explain them.

1.4   Unsupervised Explainability

This paper proposes a solution to explain the output of unsupervised algorithms using current or newer model interpretability techniques. The current model agnostic implementation of the explainable methods can support explanations for any given probabilistic model/function (mapping input to output). If we are somehow able to get probabilities of observations for any clustering method, we can use these model agnostic approaches for unsupervised methods as well. This paper introduces a method to get probability values for the most commonly used clustering algorithms which include K-Means [5], DBSCAN [6], BIRCH [7], Hierarchical clustering [8] and mini-batch K-Means. Also, we have worked on validating the explanations obtained from supervised and clustering methods.

2   Related Works

The explainability of black-box models has become an essential requirement as ML models are being widely accepted and adopted in multiple domains, thus demanding to be understandable and interpretable. In recent years, there has been a lot of active work and research done towards explainable AI and it is mainly focused on classification and regression problems. Ribeiro et al. (2016) [3] have proposed a tool called LIME which learns an interpretable model locally around a prediction and explains the predictions of any classifier. Lundberg and Lee (2017) [4] have presented a unified framework for interpreting predictions called SHAP, which is based on the game-theoretic approach of shapely values. It assigns each feature a contribution value for a particular prediction. Both SHAP and LIME are commonly adopted frameworks in the field of supervised explainability.

Unsupervised explainability is still an unexplored area with very less work done in this segment. Wickramasinghe et al. (2021) [9] have presented a Self-Organizing Maps based explainable clustering methodology which generates global and local explanations. Kauffmann et al. (2019) [10] have proposed a method to compute explanations which is based on the idea that clustering models can be neuralized, i.e., it can be rewritten as neural networks. They reviewed this 'neuralization-propagation' (NEON) approach in Montavon et al. (2022) [11] and worked on bringing explainability to unsupervised learning such as k-means clustering and kernel density estimation. Morichetta et al. (2020) [12] discusses a methodology which deals with unlabeled data by building a supervised data splitting model out of the clustering results. Dasgupta et al. (2020) [13], Bandyapadhyay et al. (2021) [14] and Gamlath et al. (2021) [15] design and discuss an algorithm that produces explainable clusters using decision tree with k leaves. In this paper, we focused on existing non-probabilistic clustering algorithms and proposes a solution to provide explainability for different clustering methods by extending the work done in supervised explainability.

3   Methodology

This section focuses on the core method responsible for deriving explanations for different clustering methods. It also discusses the use and interpretation of explanations in classification problems and how we can extend their application to explain clustering methods as well. Since the explanation methods for unsupervised algorithms are built upon the explanation computed for supervised algorithm explainability, this section initially discusses about the supervised explanations, the proposed method for clustering algorithms followed by a validation process involving both supervised and unsupervised methods.

3.1 Supervised Explanations

SHAP and LIME are surrogate models, i.e., they are model agnostic in nature. They tend to tweak the input features and use different combinations of input features to observe the changes in prediction values. The changes made in the input are very small so that the data point is still around the vicinity of that particular instance (local region). For the particular instance, the interpretability tool models the observed changes in the predictions due to the variation in input values. Higher the change in prediction, the more influential is the tweaked feature. For classification task, they explain the contribution of each input feature towards the output probability of the model.

3.2 Proposed Unsupervised Explainable AI (UXAI) Method

The input requirements include the input data (X) and a clustering model (Z) trained on the input data.

Step 1: The first step includes extracting the clustering labels of input data from the given model. This returns the predicted cluster label set Y.

$$Z(X) = Y \tag{1}$$

Clustering methods generally belong to two categories, first where the centroid is an essential part of the clustering process, and clustering is driven by calculated centroids. K-means and Birch belong to this category. Hierarchical clustering methods are part of the second category where the pair-wise distance between the data points is the main deciding criteria for clustering.

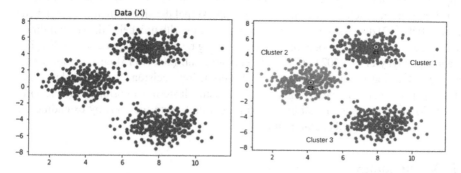

Fig. 1. The figure shows an example data set X and clustering labels for the data.

Step 2: Using the input data and labels obtained from the model, the next step is to compute the centroid for each cluster. A centroid is a vector of length equal to the number of input features, where each number is the mean of a feature for the observations in that cluster. Figure 1 shows the centroids of each cluster for given data X. The centroid can be thought of as the dimension-wise average of the cluster constituents.

$$C(k) = \sum_{i=1}^{n} \frac{x_i}{n}, (y_{label} == k) \tag{2}$$

Step 3: After we get the centroids for each cluster $C(k)$, for methods in the first category, we use these centroids as the representation for the clusters. For each data point x_i, we then calculate the distance from each centroid ($Dist[x, C(k)]$). The distance value between a data point and each cluster's centroid helps to determine the relationship between that point and the cluster. The distance metric is the same as the distance measure chosen in the clustering model.

For methods like Agglomerative or Divisive clustering which belong to the second category, the distance between a data point and clusters can be computed by mimicking the linkage method that was used in the original clustering model. In such a scenario, instead of using the centroid as the cluster representation, a distance matrix is computed for data points. For Single-Link clustering, the distance between a point and a cluster is computed by considering the closest point from that cluster. For Complete-Link clustering, the distance between a point and a cluster is computed by considering the farthest point from that cluster. For Ward-Link and Average-Link clustering, the centroid is used as the cluster representative. The different methods to compute distances are shown in Fig. 2.

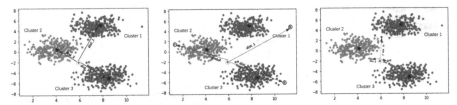

Fig. 2. For instance x_i, the figures show the distances from cluster centroids, farthest point of each cluster (Linkage = Complete) and nearest point of each cluster (Linkage = Single) respectively.

Table 1. Example for a 3-cluster problem: distance computed from cluster centroids. Model: k-means, data set: Iris data set [16]

X_i index	Dist 1	Dist 2	Dist 3	y labels
0	1.880	3.346	0.269	3
1	5.597	0.644	3.931	2
2	4.845	0.207	3.179	2
3	1.289	3.741	0.764	3
4	1.121	4.506	1.232	1
5	1.438	5.997	3.073	1
6	4.681	0.379	3.012	2

For the k-cluster problem, this step gives us k-distance values for each data point as shown in Table 1.

Step 4: We hypothesize that these calculated distances indicate the relative similarity of the data point in hand with all the other points in the cluster. A point that is closer to a cluster and it does not originally belong to that cluster may have a higher similarity to the points within this cluster. The next step of this method is to convert the distance values obtained from the previous step to probability values. We compute probabilities based on the distance values as all the clustering methods considered use distance between points as their primary measure while forming clusters.

The method introduces a supervised model referred to as the probability model. The probability model is a classification model where the input features are the k-distance values across each point and the ground truth is the predicted clustering labels.

Training Data Features: Dist 1, Dist 2, . . . Dist k, Target Column: y labels.

Any of the multi-class classification models can be used to convert the distance into probabilities and be selected as the probability model. The probability model learns to classify the cluster labels using the distance values of the data points from cluster representation. Table 2 shows the probability values for a data sample using a probability model over distances. These steps (Method 1) map the input feature set to final prediction probabilities. Here the feature set will remain the original feature set X.

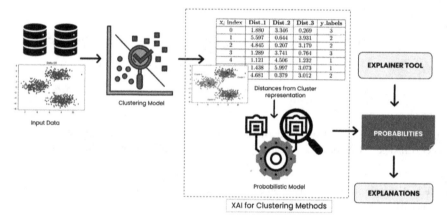

Fig. 3. XAI for clustering models

Table 2. Probabilities for computed distance values

X_i index	Dist 1	Dist 2	Dist 3	y labels	Prob_1	Prob_2	Prob_3
0	1.880	3.346	0.269	3	0.0030	0.0006	0.9964
1	5.597	0.644	3.931	2	0.0000	0.9980	0.0020
2	4.845	0.207	3.179	2	0.0000	0.9837	0.0163
3	1.289	3.741	0.764	3	0.0752	0.0015	0.9233
4	1.121	4.506	1.232	1	0.5919	0.0014	0.4068
5	1.438	5.997	3.073	1	0.9993	0.0001	0.0006
6	4.681	0.379	3.012	2	0.0000	0.9692	0.0308

The final step is to explain this final mapping method using explainability tools. Here the features on which the explanations would be computed will be the original feature set X, not the distance values on which the classification modeling is performed. Figure 3 depicts a summarized version of the proposed method.

Algorithm 1 UXAI Method

Input: Data X (n rows, m features), Model Z, clusters count = k
Output: Explanations
Function GetProbabilities(X):
    y_labels = Z(X)
    Centroids = **[]**$_k$
    for i = 1 to k **do**
      | Centroids[i] = mean(x) where y_labels==i
    end
    distances = **[]**$_{n*k}$
    for i = 1 to n **do**
      for j = 1 to k **do**
        | distances[i][j] = compute distance(X[i], Centroids[j])
      end
    end
    Probability_Model = train_classification_model (input = distances, target = y_labels,
    train_test_split = 85:15)
    probabilities = Probability_Model(X)
    return probabilities
Explanations = use_explainability_tool(data = X, method = GetProbabilities)

Method 1

3.3 Explanations

In the case of classification problems, the explainability tools present explanations at the class level. In unsupervised explainability which is analogous to classification explainability, we compute explanations at the cluster level.

Table 3. Local explanation for data index = 3. Model: k-means, Data set: Iris data [16], Explainability tool: SHAP

Features	Cluster 1	Cluster 2	Cluster 3
petallength	−0.201	−0.311	0.513
sepallength	−0.038	−0.006	0.045
petalwidth	−0.026	−0.010	0.037
sepalwidth	0.009	−0.001	−0.009

Local explanations obtained from interpretation method attempt to explain how a model operates in a certain area of interest. It focuses on explanation of an individual prediction. Table 3 represents local explanation of an instance. It gives explanation value, i.e., contribution to output probability from each feature towards each cluster.

To get explainability for the entire model behavior, global explanations are computed using the local explanations of all the data points. One such method is proposed in the implementation of SHAP library [4]. For each cluster, local explanations for each entity are averaged out across each feature. These averages are computed on absolute values so that the feature impact does not cancel each other. Global explanation is used to get the average influence of features and is able to attribute which of the input feature contributed the most to the decisions made by the model. Table 4 represents global explanation for a clustering model. It gives the average explanation value across all the predictions.

Table 4. Global explanations. Model: k-means, data set: Iris Data set [16], Explainability tool: SHAP

Features	Cluster 1	Cluster 2	Cluster 3
petallength	0.267	0.409	0.369
sepallength	0.070	0.009	0.065
petalwidth	0.040	0.015	0.035
sepalwidth	0.006	0.004	0.009

3.4 Validation Process

We perform a comparative study to validate the explanations obtained by employing the proposed method. We select a few data sets that have ground truth for the dependent variable. Next, we build few supervised classification models (by considering dependent variable) and a few unsupervised (clustering) algorithms (by discarding the dependent variable). After the model training, we rank and compare the global explanations obtained for these models. If explanations match then we can consider the proposed method to be working.

Steps for validating the explanations:
For a given data set (with target column):

1. We use commonly used supervised methods and one or more clustering methods that we want to run the validation for.
2. We generate explanations for all the models. We directly use SHAP on supervised algorithm outputs. For clustering methods, we first compute the probabilities and then use SHAP as explained in the proposed method.
3. For each model, features are ranked based on global absolute average feature contribution values from these explanations.
4. Compare these feature rankings using ranking correlation coefficient methods.
    (Similar steps are performed for LIME as well.)

We use multiple ranking correlation methods:

- Spearman Rank Correlation [19]: It is a non-parametric measure of rank correlation that is used to measure the strength and degree of association between two ranked variables.

$$\rho = 1 - \frac{6 \sum d_i^2}{n(n^2 - 1)} \tag{3}$$

- Weighted Spearman Rank Correlation: Add weight equal to 1/rank as a parameter while computing Spearman correlation coefficient. This is done to give higher importance to top features as their ranking measures should have a higher impact on correlation value than features with lower importance.

$$\rho = 1 - \frac{6 \sum w_i * d_i^2}{n(n^2 - 1)} \tag{4}$$

5. Pair-wise Correlation between the feature ranking is calculated for all the supervised and unsupervised methods employed.
6. High correlation values would indicate the similarity in the explanations provided by supervised and unsupervised methods.

4 Experiments

In order to test and evaluate the proposed method, we ran extensive experiments on three datasets for both supervised and unsupervised explanations.

For computing explanations for unsupervised methods, we experimented the model used for probability conversion with Logistic Regression (Linear Model), Random Forest Classifier [17] (Tree Model), and Support Vector Classification (Kernel-Based Model). For training the probability model, data first needs to be divided into training and validation set in the ratio of 85:15 using stratified sampling, and a model is trained while monitoring the validation performance. The probability model with the overall best recall score is selected. Here, the labels predicted from the clustering model are used as the true labels since all the explainability methods try and explain the model and not the ground truth.

4.1 Datasets

We selected three datasets for experimentation purpose. These include

1. Wine Data Set [20] (Features: 12, Classes/Clusters: 3)
2. Rice Data [21] (Features: 7, Classes/Clusters: 2)
3. Random Isotropic Gaussian blobs for clustering (Features: 5, Classes/Clusters: 3)

4.2 Validating UXAI

Initially, we hypothesized that a set of supervised algorithms shall produce similar explanations if they are performing the same in terms of metrics like precision, recall, accuracy, etc. For both supervised and unsupervised models, models should perform well since both classification and clustering methods with large error may have non-overlapping problematic area, and explanations may not match. Additionally, if a clustering method is able to cluster the original classes well, then the explanations for these too shall match the explanations from the supervised methods. After experimenting with multiple data sets, we found this to be incorrect as the correlation among the features seems to be affecting the relative feature importance and in turn the explanations produced by SHAP/LIME.

We also observed that having many input features with similar predictive contribution also resulted in different explanations even amongst supervised algorithms. Since this results in many variations in which these competing features can be picked by models. These explanations were alternate explanations that did not agree with each other completely but were correct explanations. Additionally, if a model is not performing well compared to its counterparts, then their explanations would also not match.

To overcome these issues while validating the proposed method, we selected models which were performing at par with each other. We then performed PCA over the data set. The explanations were computed using this transformed data for different supervised and unsupervised models and were then compared. We performed two variations of experiments. In the first, we used all the principal components and for the second, we selected only the top ones which were able to explain the cumulative variance of around 90% of the data. These steps were performed on multiple data sets to validate the results of the proposed method. The use of feature ranking comparison is one of the ways where we could validate for a data set, that the critical features which are an important aspect of decision making are identified by the UXAI method.

4.3 Observations and Results

Table 5 shows a detailed analysis of the experiment performed on a data set. For this example, the data set used was Wine Data Set [20] (Features: 12, Classes/Clusters: 3), ranking correlation method was Spearman Ranking Correlation with the Probability Model as Logistic Regression. The number of components explaining 90% variance were 6 for this data set. Here, multiple models were trained using this data as input, and the explanations were computed over them. Feature ranking of each model was compared with all the other supervised and unsupervised model's feature ranking using rank correlation measure.

For the purpose of comparison, the average correlation value was calculated. "With Supervised" and "With Unsupervised" columns show the average correlation value obtained for the given model when compared to the supervised and unsupervised models respectively. For example, for the model LightGBM "with Supervised" cell shows the average of the ranking correlation value from the rest of the supervised models and the "with Unsupervised" cell shows the average of the ranking correlation value from the four unsupervised models used in the experiment. This experiment was performed on different input settings: (a) using original feature space of the input data, (b) Performing

PCA on the input data and using all the components as input to the method, and (c) Performing PCA on the input data and using only the top components.

Table 5. This table shows the average ranking correlation for each model when compared with rest of the supervised and unsupervised models under different input data settings, which include original feature space, transformed data, and transformed data with top components. Data set: Wine Data Set [20] (Classes/Clusters: 3)

Using original features of the data set				
Models	Learning	Accuracy	With supervised	With unsupervised
Logistic regression	Supervised	0.983	0.696	0.301
Light GBM	Supervised	0.994	0.62	0.528
Multi-layer perceptron	Supervised	0.934	0.696	0.365
Random forest classifier	Supervised	0.978	0.711	0.703
K-means	Unsupervised	0.944	0.428	0.924
Mini-batch k-means	Unsupervised	0.944	0.489	0.937
BIRCH	Unsupervised	0.904	0.526	0.946
Hierarchical clustering	Unsupervised	0.904	0.502	0.864
Using transformed values from PCA (all components) number of components = number of features in the data set)				
Models	Learning	Accuracy	With supervised	With unsupervised
Logistic regression	Supervised	0.994	0.832	0.785
Light GBM	Supervised	0.989	0.755	0.705
Multi-layer perceptron	Supervised	0.989	0.826	0.821
Random forest classifier	Supervised	0.989	0.702	0.637
K-means	Unsupervised	0.944	0.792	0.881
Mini-batch k-means	Unsupervised	0.944	0.79	0.875
BIRCH	Unsupervised	0.904	0.79	0.873
Hierarchical clustering	Unsupervised	0.933	0.79	0.845
Using transformed values from PCA (Components with high explained variance) Top components cumulatively explaining 90% variance				
Models	Learning	Accuracy	With supervised	With unsupervised
Logistic regression	Supervised	0.978	0.896	0.876
Light GBM	Supervised	0.989	0.9	0.893
Multi-layer perceptron	Supervised	0.994	0.91	0.855
Random forest classifier	Supervised	0.994	0.905	0.844
K-means	Unsupervised	0.944	0.833	0.889

(*continued*)

Table 5. (*continued*)

Using original features of the data set

Models	Learning	Accuracy	With supervised	With unsupervised
Mini-batch k-means	Unsupervised	0.944	0.872	0.921
BIRCH	Unsupervised	0.888	0.881	0.909
Hierarchical clustering	Unsupervised	0.916	0.867	0.906

It can be observed that the average correlation value for models with transformed data with only top components is higher than with all the components and original features. This is because the input features are uncorrelated and the least contributing features which were adding noise are not considered. This creates a clear ranking structure for the most influential features, thus giving a higher-ranking correlation value. When transformed data with all the components is used, in few cases, the average correlation is even less than the one in original features setting. This is because the least contributing features are adding noise, thus dropping the overall average correlation value. Weighted ranking correlation methods were used to give higher weights to the top contributing ranks.

Table 6. This table shows the average ranking correlation value compared among supervised-supervised, supervised-unsupervised, and unsupervised-unsupervised models under different input data settings. Data set: Wine Data Set [20] (Classes/Clusters: 3)

Spearman ranking correlation

	Original feature set	PCA	PCA (top features)
Supervised-supervised	0.681	0.779	0.903
Supervised-unsupervised	0.474	0.737	0.867
Unsupervised-unsupervised	0.893	0.824	0.918

Weighted spearman ranking correlation

	Original feature set	PCA	PCA (top features)
Supervised-supervised	0.644	0.949	0.972
Supervised-unsupervised	0.428	0.932	0.958
Unsupervised-unsupervised	0.897	0.952	0.960

Table 6 shows summarized results for the experiment shown in Table 5. It considers the average of the average ranking correlation values. For the supervised-supervised setting, it takes the average of the correlation values for the cases where a supervised model is compared to the rest of the supervised models. For the supervised-unsupervised setting, it takes the average of the correlation values for the cases where a supervised model is compared to the rest of the unsupervised models and vice-versa. Similarly, for

Table 7. This table shows the average ranking correlation value compared among supervised-supervised, supervised-unsupervised, and unsupervised-unsupervised models under different input data settings. Data set: Random Isotropic Gaussian blobs for clustering (Classes/Clusters: 3). Here, we observe lower correlation values in weighted because in this example the top 2 features had similar contribution value and last 3 features also had similar contribution value, thus giving higher penalty in weighted ranking correlation, hence resulting in lower correlation value.

Spearman ranking correlation

	Original feature set	PCA
Supervised-supervised	0.496	0.950
Supervised-unsupervised	0.276	0.888
Unsupervised-unsupervised	0.864	0.908

Weighted spearman ranking correlation

	Original feature set	PCA
Supervised-supervised	0.358	0.790
Supervised-unsupervised	0.212	0.719
Unsupervised-unsupervised	0.745	0.719

the unsupervised-unsupervised, similar steps are performed. Table 7 and Table 8 show the summarized results on Random Isotropic Gaussian blobs data set and Rice data set [21].

From this experiment, it can be observed that again the ranking correlation coefficient for these transformed data sets has a higher value as the top features were identifiable in this case. Also, the average weighted correlation gives a higher value than the non-weighted one as it is giving more importance to the top contributors and giving less importance to jumbled ranks of least contributors. When comparing supervised-supervised values to unsupervised-unsupervised values, it is observed that the overall average in unsupervised is higher than in the supervised setting. This shows more consistency and stability in the explanation results of clustering methods and identification of top contributing features. This shows that the proposed method can be used to successfully explain the non-probabilistic clustering methods.

Table 8. This table shows the average ranking correlation value compared among supervised-supervised, supervised-unsupervised and unsupervised-unsupervised models under different input data settings. Data set: Rice Data [21] (Classes/Clusters: 2)

Spearman ranking correlation

	Original feature set	PCA	PCA (top features)
Supervised-supervised	0.510	0.799	0.900
Supervised-unsupervised	0.096	0.750	0.900

(continued)

Table 8. (*continued*)

Spearman ranking correlation

	Original feature set	PCA	PCA (top features)
Unsupervised-unsupervised	0.498	0.831	1.000

Weighted spearman ranking correlation

	Original feature set	PCA	PCA (top features)
Supervised-supervised	0.398	0.998	1.000
Supervised-unsupervised	0.147	0.654	0.998
Unsupervised-unsupervised	0.383	0.471	1.000

5   Conclusion

Explainability has become an important aspect of machine learning modeling as it helps in understanding the decisions made by the model. Enabling true explainability for the unsupervised task requires a lot more research and experimentation. In this paper, we proposed a method to explain the results of clustering models by converting the distance measures into probabilities. We observed that explainability for any black-box model, be it supervised or unsupervised, depends on various factors. Its reliability is influenced by different aspects including model performance and size of feature space. For the proposed method, the quality and reliability of explanations generated by the unsupervised explainability method are directly proportional to the performance of the clustering model on the input data set. Also, we observed that when supervised and unsupervised models perform at the same level and their input features are uncorrelated then the explanations for supervised models and unsupervised models (derived by the proposed method) match to a very high degree. This in turn proves that the proposed method was able to generate meaningful and correct explanations.

This work mainly focused on the clustering methods of the unsupervised learning domain. The work can be extended to other methods of unsupervised learning and also to the nonstructured data. The proposed method can be redesigned accordingly as a wrapper for different unsupervised methods and data types.

References

1. Hastie, T., Tibshirani, R.: Generalized additive models: some applications. J. Am. Stat. Assoc. **82**(398), 371–386 (1987)
2. Müller, M.: Generalized linear models. In: Gentle, J., Härdle, W., Mori, Y. (eds.) Handbook of Computational Statistics. Springer Handbooks of Computational Statistics. Springer, Heidelberg (2012). https://doi.org/10.1007/978-3-642-21551-3_24
3. Ribeiro, M.T., Singh, S., Guestrin, C.: "why should I trust you?": Explaining the predictions of any classifier. CoRR abs/1602.04938 (2016)

4. Lundberg, S.M., Lee, S.-I.: A unified approach to interpreting model predictions. In: Guyon, I., et al. (eds.) Advances in Neural Information Processing Systems 30: Annual Conference on Neural Information Processing Systems 2017, December 4–9, 2017, Long Beach, CA, USA, pp. 4765–4774 (2017)

5. Kanungo, T., et al.: An efficient k-means clustering algorithm: analysis and implementation. IEEE Trans. Pattern Anal. Mach. Intell. **24**(7), 881–892 (2002). https://doi.org/10.1109/TPAMI.2002.1017616

6. Ester, M., Kriegel, H.-P., Sander, J., Xu, X.: A density-based algorithm for discovering clusters in large spatial databases with noise. In: Proceedings of the Second International Conference on Knowledge Discovery and Data Mining, KDD 1996, pp. 226–231. AAAI Press (1996)

7. Zhang, T., Ramakrishnan, R., Livny, M.: Birch: an efficient data clustering method for very large databases. ACM SIGMOD Rec. **25**(2), 103–114 (1996)

8. Sasirekha, K., Baby, P.: Agglomerative hierarchical clustering algorithm-a. Int. J. Sci. Res. Publ. **83**(3), 83 (2013)

9. Wickramasinghe, C.S., Amarasinghe, K., Marino, D.L., Rieger, C., Manic, M.: Explainable unsupervised machine learning for cyber-physical systems. IEEE Access **9**, 131824–131843 (2021). https://doi.org/10.1109/ACCESS.2021.3112397

10. Kauffmann, J.R., Esders, M., Montavon, G., Samek, W., Müller, K.-R.: From clustering to cluster explanations via neural networks. CoRR abs/1906.07633 (2019)

11. Montavon, G., Kauffmann, J., Samek, W., Müller, K.R.: Explaining the predictions of unsupervised learning models. In: Holzinger, A., Goebel, R., Fong, R., Moon, T., Müller, KR., Samek, W. (eds.) xxAI - Beyond Explainable AI, xxAI 2020. Lecture Notes in Computer Science(), vol. 13200. Springer, Cham (2022). https://doi.org/10.1007/978-3-031-04083-2_7, ISBN 978-3-031-04083-2

12. Morichetta, A., Casas, P., Mellia, M.: EXPLAIN-IT: towards explainable AI for unsupervised network traffic analysis. CoRR abs/2003.01670 (2020)

13. Dasgupta, S., Frost, N., Moshkovitz, M., Rashtchian, C.: Explainable k- means and k-medians clustering. CoRR abs/2002.12538 (2020)

14. Bandyapadhyay, S., Fomin, F.V., Golovach, P.A., Lochet, W., Purohit, N., Simonov, K.: How to find a good explanation for clustering? CoRR abs/2112.06580 (2021)

15. Gamlath, B., Jia, X., Polak, A., Svensson, O.: Nearly-tight and oblivious algorithms for explainable clustering. CoRR abs/2106.16147 (2021). https://arxiv.org/abs/2106.16147

16. Fisher, R.A.: Iris. UCI Machine Learning Repository (1988). https://archive.ics.uci.edu/ml/index.php

17. Breiman, L.: Random forests. Mach. Learn. **45**, 5–32 (2001). https://doi.org/10.1023/A:1010950718922

18. Ke, G., et al.: Lightgbm: a highly efficient gradient boosting decision tree. In: Guyon, I., et al. (eds.) Advances in Neural Information Processing Systems, vol. 30. Curran Associates, Inc. (2017)

19. Zwillinger, D., Kokoska, S.: CRC Standard Probability and Statistics Tables and Formulae. CRC Press, USA (1999)

20. Wine UCI. Wine. UCI Machine Learning Repository (1991). https://archive.ics.uci.edu/ml/index.php

21. Cinar, I., Koklu, M.: Classification of rice varieties using artificial intelligence methods. Int. J. Intell. Syst. Appl. Eng. **7**(3), 188–194 (2019). https://doi.org/10.18201/ijisae.2019355381

Fault Diagnosis Methods of Deep Convolutional Dynamic Adversarial Networks

Tao Hai[1,3]([✉]) and Fuhao Zhang[1,2]

[1] School of Computer and Information, Qiannan Normal University for Nationalities,
Duyun 558000, Guizhou, China
haitao@bjwlxy.edu.cn
[2] School of Computer Sciences, Baoji University of Arts and Sciences, Baoji 721007, China
[3] Key Laboratory of Complex Systems and Intelligent Optimization of Guizhou,
Duyun 558000, Guizhou, China

Abstract. A DCDAN is proposed for intelligent fault diagnosis to address the issue that it is easy to obtain a large amount of labeled fault-type data in a laboratory environment but difficult or impossible to obtain a large amount of labeled data under actual working conditions. This method transfers the fault diagnosis knowledge acquired in the laboratory environment to the actual engineering equipment, obtains more comprehensive fault information by fusing the time domain and frequency domain data, employs the residual network to deeply extract fault features in the feature extraction layer, and makes use of the extracted fault features to improve fault diagnosis. To achieve unsupervised transfer learning, the marginal distributions and conditional probability distributions of the source and target domains are aligned by maximizing the domain classification loss, while the failure classification of mechanical equipment is achieved by minimizing the class prediction loss. The experimental results demonstrate that this model has a high classification accuracy in the unlabeled target data set and can effectively solve the problem of the lack of labels in the data set, i.e., realize intelligent mechanical fault diagnosis, under certain conditions.

Keywords: Transfer diagnosis · Deep learning · Adversarial network · Unsupervised learning

1 Introduction

As storage capacity and processing power increase, the significance of data science in industrial engineering becomes more obvious [1, 20]. Currently, the majority of businesses employ routine maintenance for equipment management of rotating machinery. The growth of artificial intelligence, machine learning, smart manufacturing, and deep learning in industrial engineering has exploded in recent years [2, 21, 22]. With the extensive development of cutting-edge technologies such as novel sensing, the Internet of Things, big data, edge computing, and artificial intelligence, rotating equipment fault detection and predictive maintenance are progressing into the future. Rapid progress is

M. Yusoff et al. (Eds.): SCDS 2023, CCIS 1771, pp. 18–31, 2023.
https://doi.org/10.1007/978-981-99-0405-1_2

being made toward digitalization and intelligence [3, 10]. We can construct deep learning models for mechanical failure diagnostics using vast amounts of data. The greatest challenge in using deep learning to perform fault diagnosis in engineering practice is that the presence of problem data makes it impossible to independently develop a useful fault diagnostic model. Consequently, transfer learning [4] was developed. As a novel paradigm for machine learning, transfer learning uses information from one or more unrelated but related disciplines to help solve problems in new settings, hence boosting the model's generalization. Transformational capacity.

Shen Fei et al. [5] devised a system for motor bearing defect diagnostics that combines singular value decomposition and transfer learning. Lei Yaguo [6] used laboratory data to address the issue that it is difficult to obtain high-precision intelligent diagnostic models in engineering practice; Guo et al. [7] proposed a deep convolutional transfer learning network (DCTLN), which is a combination of one-dimension convolutional neural networks (1D-CNN) [8] and maximum mean discrepancy (MMD) to achieve transfer between different data sets. In the migration process, however, the aforementioned technique only analyzes the marginal distribution of the data, not the conditional distribution [3]. Due to the varied degrees of similarity between samples in different source domains and samples in the destination domain, the relevance of marginal distribution and conditional distribution differs [10] in the process of knowledge transfer [9]. When the overall data distribution between two operating conditions is relatively similar, that is, when the inter-class spacing is small, the condition distribution is relatively significant for mechanical equipment failure; on the other hand, when the overall data distribution between two operating conditions is distinct, the condition distribution is less significant. When the inter-class spacing is considerable and the intra-class spacing is modest, the edge distribution should account for a greater proportion [11].

In response to previous research, this study suggests the use of a deep convolutional adversarial network (DCDAN) to detect mechanical equipment failures. The proposed DCDAN utilizes a dynamic adversarial learning technique and dynamically calculates the percentage of the two marginal distributions and conditional distributions in the transfer process based on the similarity of the two operating conditions, thus enhancing diagnostic accuracy.

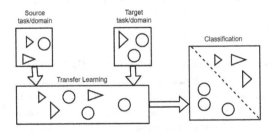

Fig. 1. Schematic diagram of transfer learning

2 Transfer Learning

The task of adversarial transfer learning is to obtain a failure dataset of mechanical equipment under laboratory conditions, assuming that the laboratory labeled source domain is $D_s = \{x_i, y_i\}_{i=1}^{n}$, due to the complexity of the actual working conditions, there is a big difference in the generation of data between the two. It is assumed that the unlabeled target domain data of the actual operating condition is $D_t = \{x_j\}_{j=n+1}^{n+m}$. The distributions of these two domains are different due to the influence of the data generation mechanism [12], $P(x_s) \neq P(x_t)$.

But they have the same feature space $X_s = X_t$, assuming their classes are also the same $Y_s = Y_t$. Therefore, the purpose of transfer learning is to use labeled data to learn a classifier $f : x_s \rightarrow y_t$ to predict D_t the label $y_t \in Y_t$ of the target domain, as shown in Fig. 1.

3 Deep Convolutional Dynamic Adversarial Networks

Aiming at the problem of "effective fault diagnosis for unlabeled data in different working conditions" in the process of transfer learning, a DCDAN is proposed for intelligent fault diagnosis of spindle bearings of CNC machine tools. Figure 2 depicts the overall diagram of the established DCDAN approach. Two major components make up the network: feature extraction and dynamic domain adaption. In the feature extraction part, 1D-CNN is used to automatically extract the feature sets of the source and target domains from the processed signals; in the dynamic domain adaptation part, the dynamic domain adversarial learning strategy is adopted to reasonably calculate the similarity between the working conditions. Adjust the proportion of marginal distribution and conditional distribution in the transfer learning process and decrease the distribution difference between the source domain and the target domain in order to achieve the goal of transferring "prior knowledge" from the source domain to the target domain. To efficiently train the model parameters, a gradient reversal layer (GRL) [13] is added to the conditional distribution discriminator and the marginal distribution discriminator to implement the automated inversion of the gradient direction in backpropagation and forward propagation. The gradient direction remains unchanged.

3.1 Feature Extraction

The developed 1D-CNN model is illustrated in Fig. 3. 1D-CNN includes an input layer, a convolutional layer, a pooling layer, and a fully connected layer. ReLU is utilized as the activation function in the convolutional layer, the maximum pooling layer is used for downsampling, and LeakyReLU is used as the activation function in the last two fully connected layers. The particular parameter settings are provided in Table 1.

3.2 Dynamic Adversarial Learning Strategies

Based on the adversarial learning strategy, a dynamic confrontation element is incorporated to build a dynamic adversarial learning method. Among them, the dynamic adversarial factor directly adopts the domain discriminator's loss to automatically fine-tune the value and utilizes the proxy A distance [14] to compute the marginal distribution and the conditional distribution [15]. Consequently, based on the definition of A distance, the marginal distribution may be determined as follows:

$$d_{A,g}(D_s, D_t) = 2(1 - 2L_g) \tag{1}$$

where L_g is the marginal distribution discriminator loss function. Similarly, the conditional distribution can be calculated as:

$$d_{A,l}(D_s^c, D_t^c) = 2(1 - 2L_l^c) \tag{2}$$

where D_s^c and D_t^c represent the c-th samples in the source domain and the target domain, L_l^c respectively; and are the conditional distribution discriminator loss of the c-th samples.

The dynamic confrontation factor is defined ω as:

$$\hat{\omega} = \frac{d_{A,g}(D_s, D_t)}{d_{A,g}(D_s, D_t) + \frac{1}{C}\sum_{c=1}^{C} d_{A,l}(D_s^c, D_t^c)} \tag{3}$$

At training initialization, set $\omega = 1$, and pseudo-labels fr samples in the target domain will be automatically generated as training iterates.

Because the loss function is the cross-entropy function, the conditional distribution of the cth failure can be calculated as follows:

$$L_l^c = \text{CrossEntropy}(\hat{y}^c, d^c) \tag{4}$$

where is $\hat{y}^c = \left[\hat{d}_s^c, \hat{d}_i^c\right]$ the predicted output set d^c of the cth sub - discriminator; d^c is the set of actual labels. Likewise, marginal distributions can also be calculated. Therefore, the dynamic adversarial factor can be dynamically adjusted in each iteration, and the corresponding value is calculated.

3.3 Loss Function

As depicted in Fig. 1, the loss function of the proposed model is composed of three components: the label classifier loss function, the conditional distribution discriminator loss function, and the marginal distribution discriminator loss function. Consequently, the global training loss function can be defined as follows:

$$L\left(\theta_G, \theta_P, \theta_D^c|_{c=1}^c\right) = L_P - \delta\left[(1 - \omega)L_g + \omega L_l\right] \tag{5}$$

where δ is the trade-off coefficient; L_l is the loss function of the conditional distribution discriminator, and each part of the function is described in detail below.

Label Classifier Loss Function. The label classifier's function is to perform fault identification on source domain samples. Since the source domain contains labels, the label classifier is trained under supervision using the cross-entropy function as the loss function.

$$L_P = -\frac{1}{n_s}\sum_{x_i \in D_s}\sum_{c=1}^{C} P_{x_i \to c} \lg G_P(G_G(x_i)) \tag{6}$$

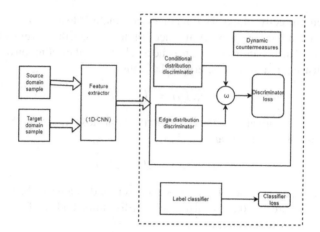

Fig. 2. Deep convolutional dynamic adversarial network

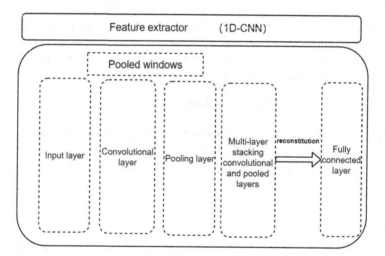

Fig. 3. Schematic diagram of one-dimensional convolutional neural network

where is $P_{x_i \to c}$ the probability G_P of belonging to class c, and x_i is the Category Label Classifier.

Conditional Distribution Discriminator Loss Function. During migration between the source and target domains, the conditional distribution discriminator is used to compute the conditional distribution. Comparatively to the marginal distribution discriminator, the conditional distribution discriminator employs a multi-model structure that enables transfer learning to be carried out in greater detail. In particular, the conditional distribution discriminator G Din includes C sub-discriminators, G Dc, and each sub-discriminator is responsible for calculating the degree of matching between the c-th source domain samples and the target domain samples. Similarly, the number of samples contributing to the training of the sub-discriminator is equal to the product of the c-th output probability of the label classifier and the overall data. G_D^c Therefore, the loss function of the conditional distribution discriminator is defined as:

$$L_1 = \frac{1}{n_s + n_t} \sum_{x_i \in (D_s \cup D_t)} \sum_{c=1}^{C} L_D^c \left(G_D^c \left(\hat{y}_i^c G_G(x_i) \right), d_i \right) \tag{7}$$

where G_D^c and L_D^c are the sub-discriminator of class c and its corresponding cross-entropy loss function, respectively; $\hat{y}_i^c$ and are the predicted probability distribution of data samples in class $c.x_i$.

Table 1. Parameter settings of feature extractor GG

Layer type	Activation function	Nuclear size	Step parameter	Output dimension
Enter	/	/	/	(1024, 1)
Convolutional Layer 1	Relu	6 4	1 6	(61, 60)
Batch Normalization	/	/	/	(61, 60)
Convolutional Layer 2	Relu	3	1	(61, 32)
Batch Normalization	/	/	/	(61, 32)
Max Pooling Layer	/	2	/	(30, 16)
Convolutional Layer 3	Relu	3	1	(30, 16)
Batch Normalization	/	/	/	(30, 16)
Convolutional Layer 4	Relu	3	1	(30, 8)
Batch Normalization	/	/	/	(30, 8)
Max Pooling Layer	/	2	/	(15, 8)
Refactor	/	/	/	(120, 1)
Fully Connected Layer 1	Leakyrelu	/	/	(50, 1)
Fully Connected Layer 2	Leakyrelu	/	/	(50, 1)

Marginal Distribution Discriminator Loss Function. The edge distribution discriminator determines the edge distribution between the source and destination domains. With the knowledge of the adversarial learning technique, the loss function of the marginal distribution discriminator is determined as follows:

$$L_g = \frac{1}{n_s + n_t} \sum_{x_i \in (D_s \cup D_t)} L_D(G_D(G_G(x_i)), d_i) \tag{8}$$

3.4 Proposed Method Steps and Flow Chart

Figure 4 depicts the flowchart of the proposed DCDAN approach. The particular experimental procedures are as follows:

Step 1: Use sensors to gather vibration signals under various operating conditions from high-speed defective equipment and preprocess the data using the fast Fourier transform (FFT) [16];

Step 2: Randomly divide the processed data into training set samples and test set samples. The samples in the training set are labeled data, whereas the samples in the test set are unlabeled data.

Step 3: Use 1D-CNN to automatically extract feature sets from source domain and target domain samples;

Step 4: Utilize the dynamic confrontation learning approach to dynamically calculate the weights of the marginal distribution and the conditional distribution to generate a trained model throughout the transfer learning process;

Step 5: Put the test set samples into the model that has been trained to get the diagnosis of migration.

4 Test Verification

4.1 Source of Data

The migration diagnosis data set used in the test consists of the XJTU-SU rolling bearing acceleration life test data set and the CWRU test bench data set.

1) Xi'an Jiaotong University's accelerated life test bench [17] is the XJTU-SU data set. The data parameters are provided in Table 2. The test bearing model is an LDK UER204 rolling bearing, and the support bearing under 11 kN radial force is employed as the test data set. The sampling frequency is 25.6 kHz, and the rotating speed is 2250 r/min.

Table 2. Technical parameters and specification information of XJTU-SU bearing

Inner ring diameter/Mm	Outer ring diameter/Mm	Rolling body diameter/Mm	Contact angle/(°)	Rolling body number
29.30	39.80	7.94	0	8

2) The CWRU bearing dataset is Case Western Reserve University's bearing test bed. Table 3 lists the data parameter values. The rolling bearing model for testing is a SKF6205, and the sampling frequency is 12 kHz. The test loads are 0 HP, 1 HP, 2 HP, and 3 HP, and vibration signals are collected under four operating conditions corresponding to the rotational speeds of 1979, 1772, 1750, and 1730 rpm.

Table 3. Technical parameters and specification information of CWRU bearings

Inner ring diameter/mm	Outer ring diameter/mm	Rolling body diameter/mm	Contact angle/(°)	Rolling body number
25.00	52.00	7.94	0	9

4.2 Comparative Analysis of Experiments

The experimental data set is subdivided into a training set, a test set, and a validation set in the proportion of 7:2:1. Due to the high demand for experimental data sets, the data sets are oversampled to increase the number of samples and satisfy the demand.

The test sample is the original vibration signal of the bearing, the sampling length is 1024, and the effective spectrum length of the frequency domain signal is 400. Among them, the model has been analyzed for many times, and the learning rate $l_r = 0.01$, hyperparameters $\alpha = 0.05$, $\beta = 0.25$, the model has the highest accuracy. The damage parameters are 0.18, 0.36, 0.5, and 0.72 mm. In order to simulate the environment of the actual working condition, the experiment adds noise to the target data to simulate the noise effect of the actual working condition. The added noise signal is Gaussian white noise.

Data Fusion Layer Test. Experiments verify the impact of time domain, frequency domain and fused data on model transfer learning. The data set is shown in Table 4. The data input is input by the convolution of the first layer of the model, and experiments are carried out for the migration diagnosis task A → B to verify the influence of the data type on the migration effect.

Table 4. Bearing dataset

Rolling bearing data	Load	Health status	Number of samples
XJTU-SU(A)	11kn _	Inner ring failure	1 000
		Outer ring failure	1 000
		Normal	1 000
		Inner ring failure	1 000
CWRU(B)	0	Outer ring failure	1 000
(0.18)		Normal	1 000

The test results are shown in Table 5, and the average accuracy rate over numerous training sessions is calculated. The model migration accuracy is 85% when the time domain signal is used as the input and 87% when the frequency domain signal is used as the input; when the fused data is used as the input, it is 95%, which has a high migration accuracy Rate. Therefore, the fused data can be used as model input to obtain more comprehensive fault information and effectively improve the effect of model migration.

Verification of Transfer Learning from Different Data Sources. The experiments are divided into two groups. The first group of experiments uses data set A → B for model validation; the second group uses B → A for model validation (data sets are shown in Table 4). In order to simulate the actual working conditions, Add Gaussian white noise with SNR = 30 dB to the target domain data. The test results are shown in Table 6. The accuracy of the model in the figure is based on the average of twenty training cycles. The accuracy of adversarial transfer learning for the transfer diagnostic task AB is 95% with a standard deviation of 3%. For task BA, adversarial transfer learning achieves an accuracy of 82% with a standard deviation of 4%. Under specific settings, it is evident that the suggested approach (DCDAN) may transfer the defect diagnostic knowledge acquired in the laboratory environment to the health status diagnosis of real-world working conditions.

Add Gaussian white noise with SNR = 30 dB to the target domain data. The test results are shown in Table 6. The accuracy of the model in the figure is based on the average of twenty training cycles. The accuracy of adversarial transfer learning for the transfer diagnostic task AB is 95% with a standard deviation of 3%. For task BA, adversarial experiments were undertaken to evaluate and examine the transfer learning ability of the ResNet network itself, the transfer learning ability of TCA [18], and the transfer learning ability of DDC [19] in order to further show the benefits of the proposed strategy.

1) ResNet. This technique has the same structural characteristics as the proposed method, with the exception of the transfer-fault feature domain adversarial layer. For the migration diagnostic task AB, the accuracy of the migration diagnosis of the approach for data set B is 61%, but for the migration diagnostic task BA, the accuracy is 42%. Due to disparities in the distribution of data from various sources, the recognition accuracy for target data is low.

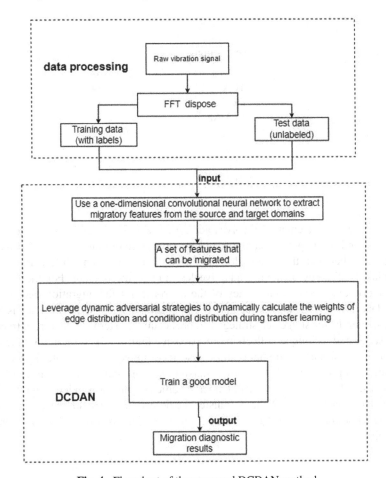

Fig. 4. Flowchart of the proposed DCDAN method

Table 5. Time domain, frequency domain, and fusion data migration accuracy comparison table

A → B	Time domain	Frequency domain	Data field
Accuracy	84	88	94

2) TCA. The TCA method involves mapping the data from both domains into a high-dimensional, regenerated Hilbert space. In this space, the data distance between the source and destination is reduced while their respective internal qualities are preserved to the greatest extent possible. For the migration diagnostic task AB, the accuracy rate of the approach for the migration diagnosis of dataset B is 35%, whereas for the migration diagnostic task BA, the accuracy rate is 34%. Compared to standard ResNet, TCA has a reduced capacity for transfer learning. The problem is that TCA lacks the ability to identify features using deep transfer learning.

Table 6. Comparison of migration diagnosis results of different data sources

Test serial number	Instructions	Accuracy
Trial 1 A → B	ResNet	62
	TCA	34
	DDC	85
	DCDAN	93
Test 2 B → A	ResNet	43
	TCA	34
	DDC	68
	DCDAN	83

3) DDC. The DDC technique involves adding an adaptive layer between the source domain and the target domain so that the network may minimize the distribution difference between the source domain and the target domain while learning how to classify, thereby achieving adaptive learning of the domain. For the task AB migration diagnosis, the accuracy of the approach for the migration diagnosis of the dataset B is 82%, but for the task BA migration diagnosis, the accuracy is 69%. Consequently, the suggested strategy is more accurate. In terms of feature extraction, the suggested technique collects more extensive fault information in the fault time domain and frequency domain, and it also incorporates the adaptation process of conditional probability distribution. Transfer learning achieves an accuracy of 82% with a standard deviation of 4%. Under specific settings, it is evident that the suggested approach (DCDAN) may transfer the defect diagnostic knowledge acquired in the laboratory environment to the health status diagnosis of real-world working conditions.

Table 7. CWRU bearing failure dataset

Load/HP	Damage diameter/Mm	Health status	Number of samples
0/1/2/3	0	Normal	1 000
		Inner ring failure	1 000
	0.07 _	Outer ring failure	1 000
		Rolling element failure	1 000
		Inner ring failure	1 000
	0.14 _	Outer ring failure	1 000
		Rolling element failure	1 000
		Inner ring failure	1 000
	0.21 _	Outer ring failure	1 000
		Rolling element failure	1 000

Transfer learning studies under varying settings of application. To further test the transfer learning capability of the proposed approach under various working settings, three sets of transfer learning verifications are compared under various working conditions. The sample data set is shown in Table 7. The test utilizes 0 as the source data and applies transfer learning under the settings of 1 HP, 2 HP, and 3 HP, respectively, to validate the migration accuracy under varying situations.

To imitate the environment of real working circumstances, SNR = 35 dB Gaussian white noise is introduced to the bearing data of 1 HP, 2 HP, and 3 HP in the target domain to simulate the noise effect under actual working conditions. Table 8 outlines the test outcomes. The accuracy of the model in the table is based on the mean of twenty training instances. For the first set of experiments 0–1 HP, the accuracy of adversarial transfer learning is 77%, with a standard deviation of 4%; for the second set of experiments 0–2 HP, it is 80%, with a standard deviation of 3%; and for the second set of experiments 0–3 HP, it is 78%, with a standard deviation of 4%.

In addition, the experiment compares and examines the transfer learning abilities of the created ResNet network, TCA, DDC, and the suggested technique (DCDAN). Evidently, the strategy described in this research may also result in improved transfer learning in a variety of working situations.

Table 8. Comparison of migration diagnosis results under different loads

Test serial number	Instructions	Accuracy
Test 1 0 → 1HP	ResNet	53
	TCA	37
	DDC	71
	DCDAN	73
Test 2 0 → 2HP	ResNet	53
	TCA	35
	DDC	72
	DCDAN	81
Test 3 0 → 3HP	ResNet	44
	TCA	38
	DDC	68
	DCDAN	77

4.3 Analysis of Test Results

The effectiveness of the proposed method is validated by examining the effects of migration on various data sources and working conditions. In the meantime, comparing ResNet, TCA and deep transfer DDC, the experiment proves that the proposed deep adversarial transfer learning (DCDAN) has higher classification accuracy than other methods.

5 Conclusion

A For the practical engineering application of intelligent diagnosis, this paper develops an adversarial transfer learning diagnosis model for the non-stationarity and nonlinearity of mechanical equipment faults under different loads and complex working conditions. Transfer learning is performed from the sample space of mechanical equipment failure under laboratory conditions to the sample space of actual project operation, and then a migration diagnosis model is established from the sample space of the laboratory to the actual sample space of the project. The following is a summary of this paper's principal conclusions:

1) Regarding data processing and the extraction of features Utilize various facets of homologous data to obtain more exhaustive fault information. In order to address the issue of insufficient data volume, overlapping sampling is used to increase the number of training samples in order to gather more effective data for training the model.
2) The proposed technique is used for the changeable working condition fault diagnosis job of spindle bearings; compared to the current ResNet, TCA, and DDC transfer learning methods, the experimental findings demonstrate that the suggested method has superior diagnostic accuracy and performance. Excellent generational performance.

Acknowledgement. This research was made possible with funding from the National Natural Science Foundation of China (No. 61862051), the Science and Technology Foundation of Guizhou Province (No. ZK[2022]549, No. [2019]1299), the Top-notch Talent Program of Guizhou Province (No. KY[2018]080), the Natural Science Foundation of Education of Guizhou Province (No. [2019]203), and the Funds of Qiannan Normal University for Nationalities (No. qnsy2018003, No. qnsy2019rc09, No. qnsy2018JS013, No. qnsyrc201715).

References

1. Hai, T., Zhou, J., Muranaka, K.: An efficient fuzzy-logic based MPPT controller for grid-connected PV systems by Farmland Fertility Optimization algorithm. Optik **267**, 169636 (2022)
2. Tao, H., et al.: SDN-assisted technique for traffic control and information execution in vehicular adhoc networks. Comput. Electr. Eng. **102**, 108108 (2022)
3. Hai, T., Alsharif, S., Dhahad, H.A., Attia, E.A., Shamseldin, M.A., Ahmed, A.N.: The evolutionary artificial intelligence-based algorithm to find the minimum GHG emission via the integrated energy system using the MSW as fuel in a waste heat recovery plant. Sustain. Energy Technol. Assess. **53**, 102531 (2022)
4. Yosinski, J., Clune, J., Bengio, Y., Lipson, H.: How transferable are features in deep neural networks?. In: Advances in Neural Information Processing Systems, vol. 27 (2014)
5. Shen, F., Chen, C., Yan, R.: Application of SVD and transfer learning strategy on motor fault diagnosis. J. Vib. Eng. **30**(01), 118–126 (2017)
6. Lei, Y., Yang, B., Du, Z., Lv, N.: Deep transfer diagnosis method for machinery in big data era. J. Mech. Eng. **55**(7), 1–8 (2019)

7. Guo, L., Lei, Y., Xing, S., Yan, T., Li, N.: Deep convolutional transfer learning network: a new method for intelligent fault diagnosis of machines with unlabeled data. IEEE Trans. Ind. Electron. **66**(9), 7316–7325 (2018)
8. Krizhevsky, A., Sutskever, I., Hinton, G.E.: ImageNet classification with deep convolutional neural networks. In: Advances in Neural Information Processing Systems, vol. 25 (2012)
9. Wang, J., Chen, Y., Hao, S., Feng, W., Shen, Z.: Balanced distribution adaptation for transfer learning. In: 2017 IEEE International Conference on Data Mining (ICDM), pp. 1129–1134. IEEE (2017)
10. Hai, T., et al.: An archetypal determination of mobile cloud computing for emergency applications using decision tree algorithm. J. Cloud Comput. (2022)
11. Hai, T., Abidi, A., Abed, A.M., Zhou, J., Malekshah, E.H., Aybar, H.Ş: Three-dimensional numerical study of the effect of an air-cooled system on thermal management of a cylindrical lithium-ion battery pack with two different arrangements of battery cells. J. Power Sources **550**, 232117 (2022)
12. Pan, S.J., Yang, Q.: A survey on transfer learning. IEEE Trans. Knowl. Data Eng. **22**(10), 1345 (2009)
13. Ganin, Y., Lempitsky, V.: Unsupervised domain adaptation by backpropagation. In: International Conference on Machine Learning, pp. 1180–1189. PMLR (2015)
14. Ben-David, S., Blitzer, J., Crammer, K., Pereira, F.: Analysis of representations for domain adaptation. In: Advances in Neural Information Processing Systems, vol. 19 (2006)
15. Wang, J., Feng, W., Chen, Y., Yu, H., Huang, M., Yu, P.S.: Visual domain adaptation with manifold embedded distribution alignment. In: Proceedings of the 26th ACM International Conference on Multimedia, pp. 402–410 (2018)
16. Sorensen, H.V., Jones, D., Heideman, M., Burrus, C.: Real-valued fast Fourier transform algorithms. IEEE Trans. Acoust. Speech Signal Process. **35**(6), 849–863 (1987)
17. Lei, Y., Han, T., Wang, B., Li, N., Yan, T., Yang, J.: XJTU-SY rolling element bearing accelerated life test datasets: a tutorial. J. Mech. Eng. **55**(2019), 1–6 (2019)
18. Tzeng, E., Hoffman, J., Zhang, N., Saenko, K., Darrell, T.: Deep domain confusion: maximizing for domain invariance. arXiv preprint arXiv:1412.3474 (2014)
19. Ganin, Y., et al.: Domain-adversarial training of neural networks. J. Mach. Learn. Res. **17**(1), 2096–2130 (2016)
20. Hai, T., et al.: Thermal analysis of building benefits from PCM and heat recovery-installing PCM to boost energy consumption reduction. J. Build. Eng. **58**, 104982 (2022)
21. Hai, T., Wang, D., Muranaka, T.: An improved MPPT control-based ANFIS method to maximize power tracking of PEM fuel cell system. Sustain. Energy Technol. Assess. **54**, 102629 (2022)
22. Hai, T., Zhou, J., Muranaka, K.: Energy management and operational planning of renewable energy resources-based microgrid with energy saving. Electr. Power Syst. Res. **214**, 108792 (2023)

Carbon-Energy Composite Flow for Transferred Multi-searcher Q-Learning Algorithm with Reactive Power Optimization

Jincheng Zhou[1,3(✉)] and Hongyu Xue[1,2]

[1] School of Computer and Information, Qiannan Normal University for Nationalities,
DuyunGuizhou 558000, China
zjc81@sgmtu.edu.cn
[2] School of Computer Sciences, Baoji University of Arts and Sciences, Baoji 721007, China
[3] Key Laboratory of Complex Systems and Intelligent Optimization of Guizhou,
DuyunGuizhou 558000, China

Abstract. In the conventional carbon emission computation paradigm, the primary obligation falls on the electricity-generating side. However, according to the theory of carbon emission flow, the grid side and the user side are the primary producers of carbon emissions and must carry the majority of the obligation. To minimize carbon dioxide emissions, it is required to apply the carbon emission flow analysis approach to move the carbon footprint from the power generation side to the grid side and the user side in order to create more efficient energy saving and emission reduction plans. In order to accomplish the low-carbon, energy-saving, and cost-effective operation of the power system, the carbon-energy composite flow is included in the objective function of reactive power optimization in this study. In order to solve the reactive power optimization model of carbon-energy composite flow and to demonstrate the superiority of the Q-learning algorithm of migration multi-searcher, this paper designs a carbon-energy composite flow optimization model on the IEEE 118 node system and adds six algorithms, such as the genetic algorithm, in order to solve the reactive power optimization model of carbon-energy composite flow. Come in for a simulation exercise, including comparison. The simulation and verification outcomes of an example demonstrate that the suggested model and algorithm may achieve economical, low-carbon, and secure functioning of the power system.

Keywords: Carbon emission · Carbon-energy composite flow · Transfer multi-searcher Q-learning algorithm · Reactive power optimization

1 Introduction

Carbon dioxide ($CO2$) emissions are integrally tied to the growth of extreme weather and global warming trends, which have progressively garnered the attention of a growing number of researchers. In response to the need to cut carbon emissions and combat climate change, power operators, as major $CO2$ emitters, must be given top priority and be required to take action regarding generating dispatch and grid carbon emissions [1–3]. Renewable energy sources such as solar power [4, 5], wind power [5], and hydropower [5] have entered the market in recent years, but fossil fuel power plants continue to represent a threat. Carbon capture and storage is an effective strategy for lowering emissions from the power industry's reliance on fossil fuels [6]. Eco-nomic dispatch plays an important role in the management of power networks by finding the best generating mix within the limits of committed units and operational safety requirements [7]. Researchers and academics have suggested several strategies to reduce carbon emissions during the last decade. The broad integration of wind power and the increased usage of carbon capture facilities on combustion units may substantially reduce CO_2 emissions into the atmosphere. Despite the fact that wind energy capacity is clean and affordable, its volatility places a heavy burden on power system dispatch [2, 8].

State Grid Corporation of China and China Southern Power Grid Corporation have conducted research on energy conservation and emission reduction in accordance with their actual conditions and actively proposed various stages of emission reduction targets, low-carbon production plans, and corresponding technical means. It has assumed responsibility for energy conservation and emission reduction. This study provides a low-carbon economic dispatch model under the constraints of both the electricity and natural gas systems, taking wind power's increasing penetration into account. The proposed model provides mathematical formulations of the post-combustion carbon capture system and power-to-gas facility in order to reduce CO_2 emissions and boost wind energy consumption. In addition, a variable operating mode of the post-combustion carbon capture system and power-to-gas plant is explored in further detail. The provided model's goal function is to minimize total cost, which includes operating costs, CO_2 processing costs, and wind power curtailment penalty costs. Under the constraints of this research, a low-carbon economic dispatch model is presented. This study provides a long-term expansion planning model for power production that incorporates integration costs for renewable energy penetration. This model is used to find the most cost-effective low-carbon transition path for the power sector with a high penetration of renewable energy and to analyze the implications of including short-term integration costs into long-term planning for power generation. Reference No. 13 Diverse energy systems cannot be exploited with great efficiency without integrated energy systems. This study (IPGHS) examines the stochastically optimum functioning of a micro-integrated electric power, natural gas, and heat delivery system. The suggested model provides mathematical formulations of the post-combustion carbon capture system and power-to-gas facility in order to reduce CO_2 emissions and boost wind energy consumption. In this context, this work investigates the optimization of the power system's carbon-energy composite flow reactive power model. Considering the low-carbon needs of the power grid and including carbon emissions in the issue of reactive power optimization, a novel model for reactive power optimization is developed that takes low-carbon, cost-effective, and safe carbon-energy composite flow into consideration. The suggested migrating multi-searcher Q-learning method may provide an optimal carbon emission solution and can be applied to other, more complicated power system optimization models, which has practical significance.

2　Reactive Power Optimization Model of Carbon Energy Composite Flow

2.1　Basis of Carbon-Energy Composite Flow Model

This study adds a "carbon concept" to each device in the grid technology [13] in order to characterize the condition of carbon emissions dispersed in each node and branch. The carbon flow is a virtual network flow, and its flow direction is also from the measurement of power production to the grid side, followed by the user side. Layer-by-layer recursion is used to measure the carbon emission transfer process. Carbon source, carbon loss, and carbon load are analogous to power supply, network loss, and load in the power system in the carbon emission flow theory. Carbon sources are generators that emit carbon dioxide. Wind turbines and solar generators are examples of clean energy units that do not emit carbon emissions and hence cannot be utilized as carbon sources. Carbon load refers to the active power demand of the power system as well as the user side's associated obligation for carbon emissions. Carbon loss refers to the carbon emission liability associated with the transmission of electrical energy via the power grid. Energy flow refers to the movement of active power along the electrical network in a real power system. Figure 1 depicts the carbon energy recombination flow in the power system.

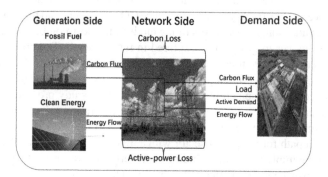

Fig. 1. Carbon energy recombination flow in power system

Suppose a system contains n nodes, b branches, s and generators, L_{ij} representing nodes i and j branches between nodes. According to the superposition theorem, for a node i, m the active power p_{im} flowing into the node from the i generator node and the active power flowing into m the node from the i generator node m and the total active power flowing into the node i are expressed

$$P_{im} = \lambda_{im}P_{Gm} \tag{1}$$

$$\varphi_{im} = \frac{P_{im}}{P_i} = \frac{\lambda_{im}P_{Gm}}{P_i} \tag{2}$$

As: λ_{im} The coefficient is equal to m the ratio of the active power P_{Gm} flowing into the node through i the generator node to the total active power emitted by the generator node;

it is the total active power emitted m by the generator node m; it is P_i the total inflow active power of the node. i For the lossless network of the power system, the power from the node i to j the two ends of the node is the same, that is $P_{ij} = P_{ij}$. However, in the actual power system, due to the heat, impedance and other reasons in the process of electric energy transmission, a certain network loss ΔP_{ij} is often generated in the branch L_{ij}. What happens at this time $P_{ij} \neq P_{ij}$. The branch active power loss formula is

$$\Delta P_{ij} = g_{ij}\left[U_i^2 + U_j^2 - 2U_iU_j co\theta_{ij}\right] \tag{3}$$

where: U_i, U_j are i the voltage amplitude of the node g_{ij} and the node respectively; is j the conductance θ_{ij} of the line; is L_{ij} the phase angle difference between the node i and the node. j Assume that the system contains a total M of 1 generator sets. Then the active power loss generated by the ΔP_{ij} branch can be L_{ij} divided into formula

$$\Delta P_{ij} = \Sigma_{m=1}^M \left(\varphi_{im}\Delta P_{ij}\right) = \sum_{m=1}^M \left(\frac{\lambda_{im}P_{Gm}}{P_i} \times \Delta P_{ij}\right) \tag{4}$$

Which is assumed N^G to be a set of all generator nodes, which is a set Z of branches. Then, the total active power loss per unit time of the entire grid is the sum of the active power losses of all branches.

$$P_{loss} = \sum_{m\in N^G i,j\in Z} \sum_i \left(\frac{\lambda_{im}P_{Gm}}{P_i} \times \Delta P_{ij}\right) \tag{5}$$

Total carbon emissions equal carbon emission intensity multiplied by active power [14, 15]. The intensity of carbon emissions is dependent on the kind of power source. For clean energy power plants like wind power generation and photovoltaic power generation, the carbon emission intensity is zero. For conventional energy power plants like thermal power generation, on the other hand, the carbon emission intensity is the generator set's operation time carbon emission factor. According to the superposition theorem, then for the branch L_{ij}, its carbon emission loss formula is

$$C_{loss} = \sum_{i,j\in Z} \sum_{m\in N^6} \left(\frac{\lambda_{im}P_{Gm}}{P_i} \times \Delta P_{ij} \times \Delta_m\right) \tag{6}$$

where, is Δ_m the carbon emission intensity $(kgCO_2/kW \cdot h)$ of the generator node, and its unit is m, which is used to measure the carbon emission corresponding to the output unit of electricity. Then, the formula for

$$C_{loss} = \sum_{i,j\in Z} \sum_{m\in N^6} \left(\frac{\lambda_{im}P_{Gm}}{P_i} \times \Delta P_{ij} \times \Delta_m\right) \tag{7}$$

The total carbon emissions of C_{loss} the entire grid is.

For the carbon emissions on the power generation side C_G, the value is the sum of the carbon emissions on the grid side and the carbon emissions C_{loss} on

$$C_{loss} = \sum_{i,j\in Z} \sum_{m\in N^6} \left(\frac{\lambda_{im}P_{Gm}}{P_i} \times \Delta P_{ij} \times \Delta_m\right) \tag{8}$$

The C_D user side. According to the carbon emission flow theory, there will be a part of carbon emissions double-counted, and the carbon emission responsibility assumed by each subject will affect the overall carbon emission measurement standard. Therefore, this chapter re-allocates the carbon emission responsibilities on the grid side and the user side according to the

$$C_G = \underbrace{(1 - \eta)C_G}_{Powergenerators} + \underbrace{\eta(C_{loss} + (1 - \mu)\eta C_D}_{Powergrid} + \underbrace{\eta\mu C_D}_{user} \qquad (9)$$

New η allocation mechanism. The carbon emissions with a μ ratio of 1 on the grid side are transferred to the grid side; η it is the responsibility sharing rate on the user side, and its value is between 0 and 1, which means that the carbon emissions with a ratio of 1 on the grid μ side are transferred to the user side. Therefore, for the grid side, the carbon emission C_{gs} formula after apportionment is

$$C_{gs} = \eta C_{loss} + (1 - \mu)\eta C_D \qquad (10)$$

2.2 Reactive Power Optimization Model Considering Carbon Energy Composite Flow

The first paragraph of a section or subsection should not be indented. The first paragraphs that follow a table, figure, or equation are also not indented.

The purpose of the subsequent paragraphs, which are indented, is to reduce the power generation cost and carbon emissions of the unit as much as possible, given that the power grid satisfies various constraints and guarantees the safe and normal operation of the power. In this chapter, the three optimization objectives of active power loss, carbon emissions on the grid side and voltage stability component are selected as the research objects, in order to investigate the economy, environmental protection and safety of the grid [16]. After linear weighting, its objective function formula is

$$min : f = \partial_1 C_{gs} + \partial_2 P_{loss} + \partial_3 U_d \qquad (11)$$

$$U_d = \sum_{i,j \in Z} \left| \frac{2U_i - U_i^{max} - U_j^{min}}{U_i^{max} - U_j^{min}} \right| \qquad (12)$$

where: ∂_1, ∂_2 and ∂_3 are weight coefficients, the ∂_1 value is between 0 ~ 1, the ∂_2 value is between 0 ~ 1, the value is between ∂_3 0 ~ 1 is $\partial_1 + \partial_2 + \partial_3 = 1$ the voltage stability value; P_{loss} is U_d the active power loss value of the system; U_i is i the voltage amplitude of the node, and its maximum value is U_i^{max}; U_j is the node j voltage amplitude, and its minimum value is U_j^{min}. The equation constraints in the reactive power optimization model of carbon energy composite flow mainly include active power balance constraints and reactive power balance constraints, the formula is

$$P_{Gi} - P_{Di} - U_i \sum_{j \in N^i} U_j \left(g_{ij} co\theta_{ij} + b_{ij} si\theta_{ij} \right) = 0 \qquad (13)$$

$$Q_{Gi} - Q_{Di} - U_i \sum_{j \in N^i} U_j \left(g_{ij} sin\theta_{ij} - b_{ij} cos\theta_{ij} \right) \tag{14}$$

In the formula: P_{Gi} is i the active power sent by the Q_{Gi} node; is i the reactive power sent by the P_{Di} node; is i the active power demand Q_{Di} of the node; is i the reactive power demand of the node; N^i is i the set of all nodes in the G_{ij} power j grid; B_{ij} susceptance size. The inequality constraints in the reactive power optimization model of $Q_{Gi}^{min} \leq Q_{Gi} \leq Q_{Gi}^{max} \leq, i \in N^G$ carbon energy composite flow mainly include the upper and lower limit constraints of the reactive power compensation device capacity, the constraints of the on-load voltage regulating transformer, etc. The formula is

$$Q_{Gi}^{min} \leq Q_{Gi} \leq Q_{Gi}^{max}, i \in N^G \tag{15}$$

$$U_i^{min} \leq U_i \leq U_i^{max}, i \in N^i \tag{16}$$

$$Q_{Ci}^{min} \leq Q_{Ci} \leq Q_{Ci}^{max}, i \in N^C \tag{17}$$

$$T_k^{max} \leq T_k \leq T_k^{max}, k \in N^T \tag{18}$$

$$|S_1| \leq S_1^{max}, l \in N^L \tag{19}$$

$$P_{Gi}^{min} \leq P_{Gi} \leq P_{Gi}^{max}, i \in N^G \tag{20}$$

In the formula: is Q_{Ci} the capacity of the reactive power compensation device T_k of node i; is the transformation ratio of the on-load voltage regulating transformer; N^C is the set of all reactive power compensation nodes in the power grid; N^T is the set of all the branches of the on-load voltage regulating transformer; is the set N^L of all branches Set; S_l the apparent capacity of the line.

3 Migrating Multi-searcher Q Learning Algorithms

3.1 Information Matrix State-Action

Similar to the multi-searcher optimization algorithm, the migration multi-searcher Q learning algorithm also has a global searcher and a local searcher. Each global searcher has its own search range. Search. And on this basis, a corresponding information matrix (that is, the Q matrix-valued function of the traditional learning algorithm) is constructed for each global searcher and local searcher Q [17, 18], which are used for global searcher and global searcher or global search. The information transfer and migration between the searcher and the local searcher. Each searcher interacts with the environment in which the searcher is located, as shown in Fig. 2.

The specific interaction mechanism is as follows: First, each searcher learns the state of its environment through the initial information matrix. Then, the transfer multi-searcher Q learning algorithm evaluates the timely rewards obtained by each searcher,

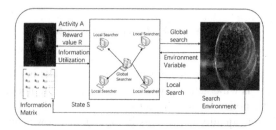

Fig. 2. Learning mechanism for migrating multi-searchers

which is used to update its searcher's information matrix. Finally, each searcher re-selects a new action strategy according to the current newly formed information matrix, so as to continuously learn and update the information, and finally obtain the optimal information matrix of the searcher. The traditional Q learning algorithm uses one subject to Q update the matrix, and each time it is exploratory and trial-and-error, only one element in the information matrix can be updated, and the convergence time is too long. The migration multi-searcher Q learning algorithm uses the searcher group as multiple subjects to search the information matrix in parallel, and all searchers share the same information matrix. In each search iteration process, multiple information elements can be updated at the same time, which greatly shortens the time. Time for optimization.

3.2 Space Dimensionality Reduction

This chapter uses Q the framework of learning algorithms to build the information matrix of multi-searchers. However, learning algorithms do not have Q a mechanism for reducing the dimensionality of the state-action space. When the scale of the power grid becomes larger and the number of variables increases, the size of the information matrix will rapidly increase exponentially, which will easily lead to the "dimension disaster", making it impossible for information to be stored and iteratively calculated. For example, the problem to be solved contains q a variable that needs to be optimized, and the action of the i first variable has a certain situation, then the number of feasible solutions for the action is to $P_i|A| = P_1 P_2 P_3 ... P_q$ use the idea of layering to avoid such a problem of "dimension disaster", but Since the hierarchical design and relationship of the objective cannot be easily determined, the algorithm cannot converge to the global optimal solution. Therefore, this chapter further proposes a dimensionality reduction method based on information transfer based on the idea of layering, so that each searcher can reduce the dimensionality of the state-action space in the process of searching for the environment.

The migration multi-searcher Q learning algorithm divides the high-dimensional action space A into low-dimensional action spaces $[A_1, A_2, ..., A_q]$, so that the large-scale information matrix is Q decomposed into multiple small information matrices $[Q_1, Q_2, ..., Q_q]$, and the variable set is followed by the decomposition of the large-scale information matrix. $[x_1, x_2, ..., x_q]$ Correspondingly, the variables are connected by an information matrix, and the elements in each matrix are the relevant information between each variable [19]

$$x^j = \left[a^{1j}, a^{2j}, \cdots, a^{ij}, \cdots, a^{qj} \right] \tag{21}$$

$$SA^j = \left[\left(s^{1j}, a^{1j} \right), \left(s^{2j}, a^{2j} \right), \cdots, \left(s^{ij}, a^{ij} \right), \cdots, \left(s^{qj}, a^{qj} \right) \right] j \in J; a^{ij} \in A^i = S^{i+1}; s^{ij} \in S^i = A^{i-1} \tag{22}$$

In formula (22), S_{ij} is the state when the i th controllable variable or sub-information matrix is selected by the j th searcher action a_{ij}; J is j the set of searchers. After the action of the previous variable is determined, the next variable can select the action according to the state after the selection of the previous variable, complete an information transfer, and maintain the mutual connection between the variables, and finally achieve the purpose of reducing the dimension of the information matrix. After searching optimization and state-action space dimensionality reduction through the cooperation of multiple searchers, the update method of the sub-matrix is

$$Q^i_{k+1}\left(s^{ij}_k, a^{ij}_k \right) = Q^i_k\left(s^{ij}_k, a^{ij}_k \right) + \alpha \eta^{ij}_k \tag{23}$$

$$\eta^{ij}_k = R^{ij}\left(s^{ij}_k, s^{ij}_{k+1}, a^{ij}_k \right) + \gamma \max_{a^i \in A_i} Q^i_k\left(s^{ij}_{k+1}, a \right) - Q^i_k\left(s^{ij}_k, a^{ij}_k \right) i = 1, 2, \cdots, q; j = 1, 2, \cdots, J; s^{ij} \in S_i; a^{ij} \in A_i \tag{24}$$

where: i is the first i controllable variable or sub-information matrix; j is the first j searcher; J is the searcher group set; is $R^{ij}(S_k, S_{k+1}, a_k)$ the feedback value of the state after the action S_k selection optimization S_{k+1} during the first k iteration. a_k When dealing with continuous variables, the action space becomes extremely large due to the high granularity of actions. The information matrix is difficult to store in limited space, and may face the problem of "curse of dimensionality" again. Therefore, it is necessary to study the problem of continuous variables or the problem of mixed variables containing continuous variables. Considering that the computer system adopts the binary computing mechanism and the data is discrete, this paper intends to introduce binary to discretize the continuous variables for the fast

$$H^i = f(x_i) = de2bi\left(2^m \times \left(\frac{x_i}{x_i^{max} - x_i^{min}} - \frac{x_i^{min}}{x_i^{max} - x_i^{min}} \right) \right) \tag{25}$$

solution $i = 1, 2, \ldots, p, p$ of the problem.

$$x_i = f\left(H^i \right) = x_i^{max} \times \sum_{j=0}^{q-1} \left(2^{q-j} \times H^i_j \right) + x_i^{min} \times \left[1 - \sum_{j=0}^{q-1} \left(2^{q-j} \times H^i_j \right) \right] \tag{26}$$

The dimension of the vector; x_i is the i th continuous variable; X_i^{max} is i the maximum value X_i^{min} of the i th continuous variable; is the minimum value of the the th continuous variable; $H^i = \left[H^i_0, H^i_1, \cdots, H^i_{q-1} \right]$; is H^i the i binary vector set corresponding to the q th continuous variable, which can only be 0 or 1; x_i digits. The binary-coded state-action space also requires state-action dimensionality reduction. For the first i continuous variable x_i, it $H^i = \left[H^i_0, H^i_1, \cdots, H^i_{q-1} \right]$ is a binary coding space. Since there are only two choices of 0 or 1, the binary of the next bit has only 4 cases: 0 to 0, 0 to 1, 1 to 0, and 1 to

1., so a mapping relationship can be established to realize the transformation from binary space to state action space. For the state-action group chain $H^i = \left[H_0^i, H_1^i, \cdots, H_{q-1}^i \right]$ with one-to- $Q^i = \left[Q_0^i, Q_1^i, \cdots, Q_{q-1}^i \right]$ one correspondence and as a variable x_i deeper dimension reduction, the formula

$$
\begin{array}{c}
x_1 \\
x_2 \\
\vdots \\
[x_i] \\
\vdots \\
x_p
\end{array}
=
\left[
\begin{array}{ccccc}
H_0^1 & H_1^1 & H_2^1 & \cdots & H_{q-1}^1 \\
H_0^2 & H_1^2 & H_2^2 & \cdots & H_{q-1}^2 \\
\vdots & \vdots & \vdots & & \vdots \\
H_0^i & H_1^i & H_2^i & \cdots & H_{q-1}^i \\
\vdots & \vdots & \vdots & & \vdots \\
H_0^p & H_1^p & H_2^p & \cdots & H_{q-1}^p
\end{array}
\right]
=
\left[
\begin{array}{ccccc}
Q_0^1 & Q_1^1 & Q_2^1 & \cdots & Q_{q-1}^1 \\
Q_0^2 & Q_1^2 & Q_2^2 & \cdots & Q_{q-1}^2 \\
\vdots & \vdots & \vdots & & \vdots \\
Q_0^i & Q_1^i & Q_2^i & \cdots & Q_{q-1}^i \\
\vdots & \vdots & \vdots & & \vdots \\
Q_0^p & Q_1^p & Q_2^p & \cdots & Q_{q-1}^p
\end{array}
\right]
\tag{27}
$$

$$
Q_{k+1,h}^i \left(s_{kh}^{ij}, a_{kh}^{ij} \right) = (1-\alpha) Q_{kh}^i \left(s_{kh}^{ij}, a_{kh}^{ij} \right) + \alpha \left[R_{kh}^{ij} \left(s_{kh}^{ij}, s_{k+1,h}^{ij}, a_{kh}^{ij} \right) + \gamma \max_{a_k \in A_{ik}} Q_{kh}^i \left(s_{k+1,h}^{ij}, a_{kh}^{i} \right) \right]
\tag{28}
$$

In formula (28): h is the h th binary code; R_{kh}^{ij} is k the reward value given by the environment when the j th subject is in the state of the th binary code S_{kh}^{ij} corresponding to the h variable in the first x_i iteration, and is transformed into a state after action a_{kh}^{ij} selection $S_{k+1,h}^{ij}$.

3.3 Combined Prediction Model

The opening paragraph of a section or subsection should not be indented. The first paragraph The RNN model is composed of an input layer, a hidden layer, and an output layer. The nodes between the hidden layers are interconnected, and its input not only includes the output of the input layer of this layer but also the output of the previous hidden layer, allowing the RNN model to implement the "memory" function of the previous content. Figure 3 displays the RNN model's structural diagram. The paragraph that follows a table, figure, equation, etc. is also not indented.

The purpose of the following indented paragraphs is to reduce the unit's power generation costs and carbon emissions as much as possible, given that the power grid satisfies various limits and ensures the safe and normal operation of the power.

Among them W, is the weight matrix that retains the memory information of the hidden layer, is the weight matrix U of the input sample at this moment, is the weight matrix U of the sample that emerges at this moment, x is the input sample, and the o model output t indicates the current moment, and $t - 1$ indicates the previous moment. The model output at the moment is

$$
\{ h_t = Ux_t + Ws_{t-1} s_t = f(h_t) o_t = g(V_{s_t})
\tag{29}
$$

It can be seen from the above theoretical analysis that the RNN model has a simple structure and high computational efficiency, but the model will learn all the historical information of the sequence during training, and there are problems of gradient explosion and disappearance. LSTM is updated on the basis of RNN, and the input gate,

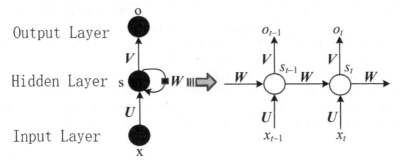

Fig. 3. RNN model structure diagram

forgetting gate and output gate are added to the hidden layer, which can compare the memory information with the current information, and execute information learning by adjusting the size of the valve to regulate the amount of remembering or forgetting. This mitigates the issue of gradient expansion and disappearance during RNN model training. A diagram of the unit structure is given in Fig. 4.

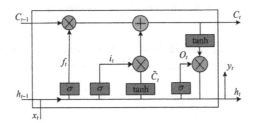

Fig. 4. LSTM model structure diagram

The model contains three inputs, namely the input sample at the current moment x_t, the short-term memory information h_{t-1} at the previous moment, and the long-term memory information at the previous moment C_{t-1}. There are 3 gates inside the structure to control the legacy and discard of memory information and current information, namely forget gate f_t, input gate i_t and output gate Q_t:

$$\{f_t = \sigma\left(w_f \times [h_{t-1}, x_t] + b_f\right) i_t = \sigma\left(w_i \times [h_{t-1}, x_t] + b_i\right) O_t = \sigma\left(w_o \times [h_{t-1}, x_t] + b_o\right) \tag{30}$$

where: w, b is the weight matrix and bias vector of the control gate; σ is the Sigmoid activation function. After the outputs of the three control gates are calculated by the above formula, the long-term memory information C_t, the short-term memory information h_t and the final output of the unit can be further calculated y_t:

$$\{\tilde{C_t} = tanh\left(w_c \times [h_{t-1}, x_t] + b_c\right) C_t = f_t * C_{t-1} + i_t * \{\tilde{C_t} h_t = o_t * tanh(C_t) y_t = w_y h_t + b_y \tag{31}$$

In the formula: *tanh* is the hyperbolic tangent activation function; * is the Hadamard product. Although the LSTM model solves the problem that the RNN model is prone to gradient disappearance and gradient explosion, the number of parameters of the LSTM model is 4 times that of the RNN model, and the network structure is more complex. Therefore, the LSTM model has the risk of overfitting during the training process. And the network training and prediction time is long [20].

GRU is simplified on the basis of LSTM, and the forget gate and the input gate are combined into a single reset gate r_t to erase the memory information to a certain extent, and the output gate is changed to an update gate Z_t, which is used to update the current hidden layer state to a certain extent., and its unit structure is shown in Fig. 5.

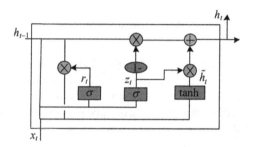

Fig. 5. GRU model structure diagram

The model input is the sample input at this moment x_t and the unit memory information at the previous moment, so that the h_{t-1} output result of the unit model.

$$\{z_t = \sigma\left(w_z \times [h_{t-1}, x_t] + b_z\right) r_t = \sigma\left(w_r \times [h_{t-1}, x_t] + b_r\right) h_t^{\sim} = tanh\left(w_h \times [r_t * h_{t-1}, x_t] + b_h\right) h_t = (1 - z_t) * h_{t-1} + z_t * h_t^{\sim}$$

$$(32)$$

The number of parameters of the GRU model is less than that of the LSTM model, so the GRU model is more computationally efficient, and it is easier to converge than the LSTM model during model training. However, with the reduction of model parameters, when faced with large-scale multivariate data sets, the ability of the GRU model to capture important information of time series will decrease, resulting in poor model prediction performance.

4   Online Transfer Learning

After completing the learning of all source tasks, the LSTM model can be trained and information transferred using the optimal information matrix and feature information of all source tasks. By entering the active and reactive power of all load nodes of the new task, the optimal knowledge matrix of the new task can be obtained instantly, and the optimized objective function can converge rapidly. to compare the TMSQ algorithm's optimization effect to that of other artificial intelligence algorithms. Six commonly used heuristic algorithms, including GA, CA, GWO, MSO, PSO, and TLBO, were introduced for testing and analysis. The optimization parameters of all algorithms were determined through simulation tests. See Table 1.

Table 1. Comparison algorithm parameter settings

Algorithm	Parameter	Settings
GA	Crossover Probability, Mutation Probability, Population Size	0.85, 0.15, 150
CA	Acceptance Rate, Population Size, Swing Factor, Convergence Factor	0.4, 150, [0,2], [−2,2]
GWO	Control Parameter, Population Size, Inertia Weight, Compression Factor	[0,2], 150, 0.98, 0.99
PSO	Acceleration Factor C1, Acceleration Factor C2, The Total Number Of Particle Swarms	1.5,2,150
TLBO	Population Size	150
MSO	Number Of Global Searchers, Number Of Local Searchers, Maximum Search Radius, Minimum Search Radius	5, 30, 1.414, 1×10^{-4}

For section 62, seven algorithms optimize the objective function respectively. TMSQ begins to converge after 30 iterations, and the optimization speed is second only to TLBO, but the obtained objective function value is much smaller than TLBO, and the convergence results are the best among the 7 algorithms. Each algorithm is run 30 times with 96 sections. Statistics are shown in Table 2.

Table 2. Result statistics of 96 sections of algorithm running 30 times

Algorithm	t /s	C_{gs}/kg	P_{loss}/MW	U_d /%	f	D	SD	RSD
GWO	7381.5	1994.1	8644.2	2062.5	4209.6	99.12	10.34	2.51×10^{-3}
TLBO	4314.3	2036.9	8646.3	2075.3	4229.6	59.68	8.11	1.86×10^{-3}
PSO	11333.8	2013.1	8675.5	2069.8	4228.5	39.63	6.89	1.38×10^{-3}
Q	Cannot be calculated							
GA	12441.6	2054.2	8671.6	2082.1	4247.2	37.59	6.59	1.51×10^{-3}
CA	15619.8	2004.2	8669.5	2059.4	4225.2	28.61	5.32	1.31×10^{-3}
MSO	5318.2	1965.6	8649.6	2087.4	4214.6	19.98	4.41	1.11×10^{-3}
TMSQ	986.1	1937.2	8629.7	2062.5	4187.0	12.66	3.22	8.64×10^{-4}

5 Conclusion

This study proposes and implements a transfer multi-searcher Q-learning method for carbon-energy composite flow reactive power optimization. Comparisons are made between intelligent algorithms such as the gray wolf evolutionary algorithm, the cultural algorithm, and the teaching and learning optimization algorithm in the IEEE 118 standard node system. The findings reveal that the suggested technique may demonstrably increase convergence speed and, consequently, get the best solution. to achieve inexpensive, low-carbon, and secure functioning of the electricity system. The following conclusions may be derived from the simulated example: 1) Using the information matrix of the Q-learning technology as a carrier, each searcher of the migratory multi-searcher Q-learning algorithm interacts with the environment in which it is situated and uses the information collected by each searcher. The timely reward is examined to update the searcher's information matrix and finally produce the searcher's optimal information matrix. 2) Binary coding is used to discretize continuous variables in the optimization and information storage of continuous variables, and the high-dimensional action space is partitioned into low-dimensional action spaces via the interconnected state-action chain, which effectively reduces the action space's dimensions. Avoid the dimensional plague of state-action space. 3) In the process of non-linear information transfer, long-term and short-term memory neural network technology is implemented to achieve network storage of multiple historical task information matrices and to then predict with high precision the optimal information matrices of new tasks by utilizing historical optimization information. Accelerate search times in order to quantify the carbon emission transfer process. In the carbon emission flow theory, carbon source, carbon loss, and carbon load are equivalent to power supply, network loss, and load in the power system. Carbon sources are carbon dioxide-emitting generators. Wind turbines and solar generators are examples of carbon-free, clean energy units that cannot be used as carbon sources. Carbon load refers to the active power demand of the power system as well as the user side's corresponding carbon emission responsibility. Carbon loss is the carbon emission liability connected with the transmission of electricity through the power system. In a real power system, energy flow refers to the movement of active power along the electrical network. Figure 1 displays the energy system's carbon recombination flow.

Acknowledgement. This research was made possible with funding from the National Natural Science Foundation of China (No.61862051), the Science and Technology Foundation of Guizhou Province (No.ZK[2022]549, No.[2019]1299), the Top-notch Talent Program of of Guizhou Province (No.KY[2018]080), the Natural Science Foundation of Education of Guizhou Province (No.[2019]203), and the Funds of Qiannan Normal University for Nationalities (No. Qnsy2018003, No. Qnsy2019rc09, No. Qnsy2018JS013, No. Qnsyrc201715).

References

1. Hai, T., Zhou, J., Muranaka, K.: Energy management and operational planning of renewable energy resources-based microgrid with energy saving. Electr. Power Syst. Res. **214**, 108792 (2023)
2. Hai, T., Abidi, A., Abed, A.M., Zhou, J., Malekshah, E.H., Aybar, H.Ş: Three-dimensional numerical study of the effect of an air-cooled system on thermal management of a cylindrical lithium-ion battery pack with two different arrangements of battery cells. J. Power Sour. **550**, 232117 (2022)
3. Hai, T., et al.: Thermal analysis of building benefits from PCM and heat recovery-installing PCM to boost energy consumption reduction. J. Build. Eng. **58**, 104982 (2022)

4. Hai, T., et al.: Design, modeling and multi-objective techno-economic optimization of an integrated supercritical Brayton cycle with solar power tower for efficient hydrogen production. Sustain. Energy Technol. Assessments **53**, 102599 (2022)
5. Hai, T., Delgarm, N., Wang, D., Karimi, M.H.: Energy, economic, and environmental (3 E) examinations of the indirect-expansion solar heat pump water heater system: a simulation-oriented performance optimization and multi-objective decision-making. J. Build. Eng. **60**, 105068 (2022)
6. Hai, T., et al.: Neural network-based optimization of hydrogen fuel production energy system with proton exchange electrolyzer supported nanomaterial. Fuel **332**, 125827 (2023)
7. Reddy, S., Panwar, L.K., Panigrahi, B.K., Kumar, R.: Modeling of carbon capture technology attributes for unit commitment in emission-constrained environment. IEEE Trans. Power Syst. **32**(1), 662–671 (2016)
8. Wang, J., et al.: Wind power forecasting uncertainty and unit commitment. Appl. Energy **88**(11), 4014–4023 (2011)
9. Hai, T., Wang, D., Muranaka, T.: An improved MPPT control-based ANFIS method to maximize power tracking of PEM fuel cell system. Sustain. Energy Technol. Assess. **54**, 102629 (2022)
10. He, L., Lu, Z., Zhang, J., Geng, L., Zhao, H., Li, X.: Low-carbon economic dispatch for electricity and natural gas systems considering carbon capture systems and power-to-gas. Appl. Energy **224**, 357–370 (2018)
11. Chen, S., Liu, P., Li, Z.: Low carbon transition pathway of power sector with high penetration of renewable energy. Renew. Sustain. Energy Rev. **130**, 109985 (2020)
12. Li, Y., et al.: Optimal stochastic operation of integrated low-carbon electric power, natural gas, and heat delivery system. IEEE Trans. Sustain. Energy **9**(1), 273–283 (2017)
13. Yixuan, C., Xiaoshun, Z., Lexin, G.: Optimal carbon-energy combined flow in power system based on multi-agent transfer reinforcement learning. High Voltage Eng. **45**(3), 863–872 (2019)
14. Khan, I.U., Javaid, N., Gamage, K.A., Taylor, C.J., Baig, S., Ma, X.: Heuristic algorithm based optimal power flow model incorporating stochastic renewable energy sources. IEEE Access **8**, 148622–148643 (2020)
15. Kang, C., Zhou, T., Chen, Q., Xu, Q., Xia, Q., Ji, Z.: Carbon emission flow in networks. Sci. Rep. **2**(1), 1–7 (2012)
16. Peng, M., Liu, L., Jiang, C.: A review on the economic dispatch and risk management of the large-scale plug-in electric vehicles (PHEVs)-penetrated power systems. Renew. Sustain. Energy Rev. **16**(3), 1508–1515 (2012)
17. Wang, D., Tan, D., Liu, L.: Particle swarm optimization algorithm: an overview. Soft. Comput. **22**(2), 387–408 (2017). https://doi.org/10.1007/s00500-016-2474-6
18. Han, C., Yang, B., Bao, T., Yu, T., Zhang, X.: Bacteria foraging reinforcement learning for risk-based economic dispatch via knowledge transfer. Energies **10**(5), 638 (2017)
19. Schmidlin, C.R., Jr., de Araújo Lima, F.K., Nogueira, F.G., Branco, C.G.C., Tofoli, F.L.: Reduced-order modeling approach for wind energy conversion systems based on the doubly-fed induction generator. Electr. Power Syst. Res. **192**, 106963 (2021)
20. Zhang, C., Li, J., Zhao, Y., Li, T., Chen, Q., Zhang, X.: A hybrid deep learning-based method for short-term building energy load prediction combined with an interpretation process. Energy Buildings **225**, 110301 (2020)

Multi-source Heterogeneous Data Fusion Algorithm Based on Federated Learning

Jincheng Zhou[1,3] and Yang Lei[1,2(✉)]

[1] School of Computer and Information, Qiannan Normal University for Nationalities,
Duyun 558000, Guizhou, China
`leiyang18791447441@163.com`

[2] School of Computer Sciences, Baoji University of Arts and Sciences, Baoji 721007, China

[3] Key Laboratory of Complex Systems and Intelligent Optimization of Guizhou,
Duyun 558000, Guizhou, China

Abstract. With the rapid advancement of science and technology, the number of edge devices with computing and storage capabilities, as well as the generated data traffic, continues to increase, making it difficult for the centralized processing mode centered on cloud computing to efficiently process the data generated by edge devices. Moreover, multimodal data is abundant due to the diversity of edge network devices and the ongoing improvement of data representation techniques. To make full use of heterogeneous data on edge devices and to tackle the "data communication barrier" problem caused by data privacy in edge computing, a multi-source heterogeneous data fusion technique based on Tucker decomposition is developed. The algorithm introduces tensor Tucker decomposition theory and realizes federated learning by constructing a high-order tensor with heterogeneous spatial dimension characteristics to capture the high-dimensional features of heterogeneous data and solve the fusion problem of heterogeneous data assuming no interaction. Combining and remembering. This method, unlike its predecessors, can efficiently integrate multi-source heterogeneous data without data transfer, therefore overcoming privacy and security-related data communication concerns. Finally, the effectiveness of the technique is confirmed using the MOSI data set, and the shortcomings of the original federated learning algorithm are solved by the updated federated weighted average algorithm. Subjective criteria are used to calculate the data quality for the improved federated average approach based on AHP. We present Influence, an improved federated weighted average method for dealing with multi-source data from a data quality perspective.

Keywords: Edge computing · Federated learning · Deep learning · Tensor theory · Heterogeneous data fusion

1 Introduction

Massive edge data will bring many challenges to a centralized data processing strategy based on cloud computing architecture in the information age. Moving all data to the cloud is inefficient and increases bandwidth use. Concurrently, network latency will

© The Author(s), under exclusive license to Springer Nature Singapore Pte Ltd. 2023
M. Yusoff et al. (Eds.): SCDS 2023, CCIS 1771, pp. 46–60, 2023.
https://doi.org/10.1007/978-981-99-0405-1_4

grow. When a link is shared, the data of the edge device is likely to be leaked, and user privacy cannot be guaranteed owing to an increase in privacy awareness. Distributed data processing technology is capable of overcoming the latencies and inefficiencies inherent to conventional cloud computing [1]. In response to the challenge of "data silos," Google introduced for the first time the notion of "federated learning" [2]. Different edge devices train the model with their own training samples, and by combining model parameters, it is possible to share data from many sources without compromising user privacy.

Moreover, the variety of edge devices leads to heterogeneous data categorization, semantics, and presence. Access to multimodal data is convenient. Multiple data modalities may describe the subject from a variety of perspectives. By reducing duplicate data and combining several data sources for correlation and supplemental analysis, it is possible to achieve the $1 + 1 > 2$ effect [3]. Frequently, multi-media data received via the Internet and on mobile devices is unstructured, as opposed to the typical organized, easily-storable data formats. In big data research, the processing of multi-source, heterogeneous data gathered by a huge number of edge devices has become a key obstacle that must be overcome. In the process of multimodal data fusion [4], scientists have focused on how to logically solve the heterogeneity issue and more successfully extract information across distinct modalities. Federated learning is a powerful machine learning approach that may be spread over a large number of parameters or computing nodes. It has been applied successfully in the finance sector and cross-industry collaboration. In machine learning, a single object will display several data types from various domains. This is referred to as "multimodal data." Typically, the business system analyzes several types of data to determine what clients are likely to want.

Data centralization has the potential to compromise data privacy in real-world implementations of the classic multi-source heterogeneous data fusion strategy.

Handling heterogeneous, multi-source data without compromising user privacy is difficult. First, business competitiveness and consumer knowledge of privacy protection have slowed data interoperability and information exchange, hindering the full exploitation of heterogeneous data's value. The data-driven model cannot be updated once the neural network evaluates it. Edge Computing's data structure and amount vary per device. Adapting neural networks to each network edge device's data would be difficult. The concept only applies to a single node or edge device with the same data properties. It can't maximize the value of IoT data.

This study presents a technique for achieving multi-source heterogeneous data fusion in edge computing without compromising user privacy that is based on an enhanced federated weighted average algorithm. Using the characteristics of the data structure collected by edge devices and the tensor Tucker decomposition theory, research can adaptively process multi-source heterogeneous data models on various edge devices, resolving the issue of inconsistent models for processing heterogeneous data in federated learning. Single-adaptability difficulty.

2 Related Work

The federated weighted average method and heterogeneous data fusion have both been improved in many ways.

2.1 Improved Federated Weighted Average Algorithm

Federated Machine Learning is a framework for machine learning that can help numerous agencies with data consumption and machine learning modeling while adhering to user privacy protection, data security, and government requirements. Federated learning as a remote machine learning paradigm may successfully address the issue of data silos by enabling collaborative modeling without data exchange. This technically removes data borders and enables AI collaboration. Moreover, privacy is safeguarded in certain ways, and data change is permitted.

Mobile and edge device popularity. [5] created "federated learning," an AI system in which a central server controls many clients without exchanging information. Federation offers several benefits. First, federated learning uses just up-to-date model parameters for aggregation, which reduces data transmission costs and increases network capacity. Second, the original data of the user is not transferred to the cloud, lowering the likelihood of a privacy violation when the link is supplied. On edge nodes or terminal devices, Federated Learning's model training may perform training and make decisions in real time, which is faster than in the cloud.

Integral to federated learning is the protection of data. Incorporating privacy protection into the aggregation technique, Ramage et al. devised a user-level differential privacy training strategy that successfully minimizes the likelihood of retrieving personally identifiable information from the transmission model. Korolova et al. and Hou et al. [8] combined gradient selection and secret sharing methodologies. This dramatically boosted the effectiveness of communication while preserving user privacy and data security.

In order to optimize time and energy for global federated learning, Zomaya et al. [9] explored federated learning over wireless networks. Tuor et al. [10] developed a control technique that combines global parameter aggregation and local model updates to minimize the loss function. Han et al. built In-Edge-AI for intelligent resource management [11].

Federated learning has disadvantages, such as inconsistent information sources. Due to the diverse origins of the training data, neither the problem of independent distribution nor the problem of having an equal number of training examples can be solved. If data sources are spread out in different ways, it is hard to combine sub-models from many different parties.

Federal Average (Federal Average, FedAvg) is the algorithm most often used inside the federated learning framework. The original FedAvg method is enhanced in terms of data quality. Due to the disparity in data quality across data sources, which results in an illogical distribution of weights, AHP is used to enhance the weights; individuals choose inaccurate criteria. Therefore, the pre-training mechanism is used to calculate the accuracy of each client, which is then used to determine each client's quality. The method of recalculating the weight update in the global model, when combined with the size of the client data, can produce a weight distribution scheme that is relatively reasonable. The test results show that the enhanced federated weighted average technique is more accurate than the standard federated weighted average technique.

2.2 Multi-source Heterogeneous Data Fusion

The expanding variety and volume of data in the data fusion system [12] motivates individuals to place a greater emphasis on system performance enhancement. Microsoft Research's Yu et al. [13] put different types of data fusion methods into three groups:

Data fusion techniques, features, and semantics "Stage-based data fusion" [14] refers to data mining in stages. Utilized GPS trajectory data and road network data to identify traffic anomalies [15], then gathered and analyzed social media data (such as Twitter) associated with anomaly locations. In this data fusion strategy, no data types interact. The advantages of combining diverse kinds of data are lost, and internal data fusion is difficult.

The approach of feature-based data fusion gathers and evaluates many data properties [16]. Therefore, both the quality of the recovered features and the fusion method will have a significant impact on the fusion result. Zhang [17] et al. achieved face recognition based on deep heterogeneity features by mixing deep learning feature vectors of varied dimensions. Wang [18] et al. non-linearly blended three distinct, significant human traits in order to more accurately predict body position. Zhang [19] et al. built a computational model for tensor deep learning by using tensors to describe the complexity of multi-source heterogeneous data, extending vector-space data to tensor space, and extracting features in tensor space. Chen et al. [20] created a tensor fusion network for multi-modal sentiment analysis and used a cartesian product to merge diverse modalities for sentiment categorization analysis.

[21] Methods based on semantic fusion comprehend the link between characteristics inside and across databases. It is believed that semantic-based fusion algorithms can comprehend the acquired qualities of heterogeneous data. Liu et al. [22] created a model for projecting the air quality of the whole city based on collaborative training. Two spatiotemporal data classifiers were designed using the geographical and temporal dependence of air quality. The spatio-temporal features are sent to multiple classifiers, which subsequently generate two sets of probabilities for potential labels, enhancing label selection.

Prior research was primarily concerned with the issue of combining heterogeneous data from several sources on a single node. There is no work report that talks about how hard it is to do federated learning, which means putting together information from different sources.

3 First Section Multi-source Heterogeneous Data Fusion Based on Federated Learning

This study focuses on the fusion of heterogeneous data from several sources when network edge devices cannot exchange data due to data confidentiality. Through the use of tensor decomposition theory, a high-order memory unit with characteristics of spatial dimension for heterogeneous data is created. Then, this memory unit is used to successfully combine many sources of heterogeneous data without compromising user privacy. Simultaneous adaptive learning of multi-source heterogeneous data is possible without increasing the size of the model [23].

3.1 Improved Federal Weighted Average Algorithm

This paper examines the implementation of federated learning and improved federated algorithms in edge computing to allow the learning of multi-user future characteristics without sacrificing user privacy. Figure 1 depicts the essential architectural structure. In this design, the system consists of edge nodes, IoT, training samples, and cloud servers. Edge nodes are connected to cloud servers through IoT (such as gateways and routers).

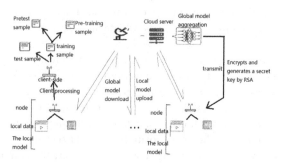

Fig. 1. Federated learning system model

Federated learning is a distributed learning system in which raw data is collected and stored on multiple edge nodes, model training occurs on the nodes, and the model is incrementally enhanced by the nodes and cloud server. Considering data quality differences across sources can provide an unfair weighting. Improved federated weighted average solves this issue. Federated learning may use local input from several separate edge nodes to train a common, generalized model. It could also use model transmission instead of data transfer to keep sensitive user information from getting out.

3.2 Overall Design of the Algorithm

Figure 2 shows that the multi-source heterogeneous data fusion strategy in this research consists of feature extraction, fusion, and selection modules. The module for extracting features uses data from multiple areas and a subnetwork. During initialization, the central control node delivers random network parameters to the model's edge nodes for extracting, merging, and figuring out features.

During model training, the edge node selects the appropriate feature extraction module depending on the structure of the local node's data set and assesses the feature extraction, feature fusion, and feature decision modules using the local data set. When the number of training rounds at the local node exceeds the threshold, the edge node's training cycle concludes. After training, the central control node is provided with the right training models. The feature fusion and feature determination modules employ average aggregation during model aggregation. To guarantee that derived features from the same modality are comparable, the feature extraction module performs the average aggregation of matching feature extraction sub-modules. The enhanced model is then sent to edge nodes for a fresh training cycle.

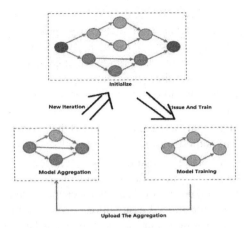

Fig. 2. Overall framework of the algorithm

3.3 Sub-module Design

Feature Extraction Module. This study considers audio, visual, and text data to be the heterogeneous data to be handled. Depending on how each modality works, this part of the module for feature extraction uses different sub-networks to pull out features from audio, visual, and textual input.

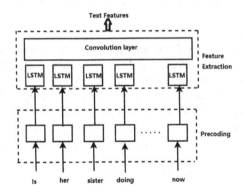

Fig. 3. Text feature sub-network

1) Feature audio and video subnetworks The COVAREP [24] framework for acoustic analysis and the FACET [25] framework for facial expression analysis are used to get audio and visual information from the MOSI dataset (sampling frequencies are 100 Hz and 30 Hz, respectively).
2) Text-exclusive subnetwork Written text and spoken text are grammatically and expressively separate, e.g., "I think it's fantastic, but I believe this approach is superior." Written dialects are rare. Dealing with a dynamic language like spoken language demands dynamic models and a focus on key words to capture distinctive

speech qualities. As depicted in Fig. 3, the text feature extraction network described in this study utilizes the global word vector to preprocess spoken words during the encoding stage and the long short-term memory (LSTM) network to learn time-related language and its representation prior to feeding it to the CNN network. Using a convolutional procedure to evaluate the input text in the convolutional layer permits the extraction of smaller and more localized features.

Feature Fusion Module. In this section, it is assumed that the heterogeneous data features to be processed are audio data features $z_a = (z_a^1, z_a^2, \cdots, z_a^q)$, visual data features $z_v = (z_v^1, z_v^2, \cdots, z_v^p)$, and text data features $z_t = (z_t^1, z_t^2, \cdots, z_t^m)$, respectively, and the feature output after the feature fusion module is Z. Next, the essential notion of the proposed Tucker decomposition-based heterogeneous data fusion approach will be described, with the aforementioned assumptions acting as prerequisites. Figure 4 depicts a high-order tensor whose feature space W contains heterogeneous data. Each tensor modality relates to a spatial mapping of disparate data attributes. When fusing heterogeneous data, the high-order tensor may utilize the characteristics of previous heterogeneous data modalities to correct it and can also remember the present heterogeneous data modal's attributes. Using Fig. 4 as an example, the z_t memory unit is a third-order tensor whose three dimensions correspond to the three heterogeneous data features z_a, z_v, and z_t, respectively. Space. By executing a modular multiplication between the feature space of heterogeneous data and the feature space corresponding to the memory unit, the memory unit with the feature of the heterogeneous data can be generated, and on this basis, further feature fusion operations may be done. Primarily, the fusion process consists of three phases:

Initially, the memory unit W_i was multiplied modularly with heterogeneous da-ta characteristics along the first order to produce a new memory unit with W characteristics, denoted by Z_a. Second, along the second order, the memory unit $W^{(1)}$ is multiplied modularly with the heterogeneous data characteristics, resulting in the memory unit W containing the Z_v sum and the Z_v characteristic Z_a. Memory unit $W^{(1)}$ then performs modular multiplication along the third-order and heterogeneous data features, resulting in a three-featured fusion tensor Z_t. The technique may be described in detail as follows:

$$Z = ((W \times_1 z_a) \times_2 z_v) \times_3 z_t, \tag{1}$$

Among them $W \in R^{R_1 \times R_2 \times R_3}$, $z_a \in R^{P \times R_1}$, $z_v \in R^{J \times R_2}$, $z_t \in R^{k \times R_3}$.

Feature Decision Module. This part makes judgments based on global features using the typical, fully connected layer. Among these judgments are the regression model's predictions and the probability prediction of the categorization model. These decisions are made based on the levels of the fused data. In this module, the error that exists between the target value and the anticipated value is assessed by using an L1 norm loss function, which is referred to as L1 Loss. Its specific expression is:

$$L1Loss(Y, Y^p) = L = (l_1, l_2, \cdots, l_n)^T = \begin{cases} sum(L), reduction = \text{'sum'} \\ mean(L), reduction = \text{'mean'} \end{cases} \tag{2}$$

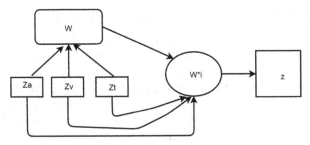

Fig. 4. Heterogeneous data fusion based on Tucker decomposition

where l_n the expression is:

$$l_n = \left| y_n - y_n^p \right| \tag{3}$$

y_n and are y_n^p the samples in the true value of the dataset Y and the predicted value of the model, respectively Y^p.

4 Experimental Results and Analysis

The current study studies the fusion of heterogeneous data from several nodes as well as single nodes in order to establish whether or not the suggested strategy is effective. The primary objective of the single-node heterogeneous data fusion experiment based on Tucker decomposition is to evaluate the performance of the algorithm described in this paper by implementing regression and classification tasks on multi-source heterogeneous data using a single node and integrating with several existing mainstream heterogeneous data sets. The experiment will be based on Tucker decomposition and a single-node heterogeneous data fusion experiment. This study assesses the efficacy of an approach using many nodes to conduct regression and classification on multi-source, heterogeneous data. This research is based on an experiment known as the Tucker decomposition-based multi-node heterogeneous data fusion experiment.

In this work, the pre-training method is used to identify the best weight for each client, while the federated average technique is used to find the suitable weight shift for each client.

4.1   Experimental Analysis of Single-Node Heterogeneous Data Fusion

Please do not indent the paragraph that begins a section or subsection. Also not indented are the introductory paragraphs that follow a table, figure, or equation.

However, subsequent paragraphs are indented. In this section, the emotion datasets with three modalities MOSI are respectively trained for regression task and classification task. Kit is the quantity of features created by the three modalities with the feature extraction sub-module, of which R_K is the first. The amount of feature extractions in R_K has a direct impact on training effectiveness and experimental performance. This experiment examines the effects of different feature extraction number combinations $(R_1, R_2,$ and $R_3)$ on the performance of regression and classification tasks. The feature extraction number for each modal in this experiment is set to (8, 16, 32) in order to evaluate the performance of the method presented in this research from the regression job and the classification task, as well as to compare the performance of the six techniques for a single node. The efficiency of heterogeneous data fusion from multiple sources.

Regression Task. Table 1 displays the quantitative experimental findings with the regression task for the number of modal feature extractions. Most of the work in this paper is about a technique for regression tasks between 0.95 and 1.05.

Table 1. MOSI dataset regression task MAE

R1	R2	R3		
		8	16	32
8	8	0.985688	0.963654	0.972488
	16	0.975782	1.008952	1.013652
	32	1.034458	0.989562	0.962625
	8	1.046685	0.985672	0.972362
16	16	1.042697	1.002648	1.008589
	32	1.012365	1.034829	1.005299
	8	1.009875	1.057514	1.022651
32	16	0.993598	1.004789	1.011268
	32	1.054587	0.996587	1.004126

The analysis of the observations shows that extracting eight, eight, and sixteen features from the three modalities improves the performance of the regression task, in that order.

In the experimental setup regression task, each mode extracts eight, eight, and sixteen features, respectively. The performance of the method presented in this study is compared to that of six other regression techniques in Table 2. The table demonstrates that the performance of this research's algorithm is comparable to that of the ideal regression algorithm. TFN, and much superior to that of the overwhelming majority of comparison algorithms. Existing algorithms for combining different kinds of data are only used on a single node, so they might not be good for federated learning.

Table 2. Performance comparison of regression tasks on MOSI dataset

Algorithm	MAE	Corr
SVM	1.858	0.055
DF	1.185	0.576
BC-LSTM	1.086	0.582
MV-LSTM	1.078	0.615
TFN	0.925	0.672
LMF	0.975	0.615
LMF	0.984	0.665

The efficiency of heterogeneous data fusion from several sources Regression tasks are more sensitive to the number of modal characteristics collected than classification tasks. In this test, the number of extractions for each modality is set at 8, 8, and 16, respectively. The performance of the method presented in this study is compared to that of six other classification techniques in Table 3. The evaluation index for the two-class task is Acc2 sum F1, while the evaluation index for the multi-class task is Acc7it. Table 3 demonstrates that the algorithm's classification performance is superior to TFN [27] and the overwhelming majority of comparative approaches. It is also comparable to the LMF [29] strategy.

Although the approach proposed in this paper performs poorly on a single point, it offers three merits in a federated learning system:

1) It accommodates a wider variety of data types. This technique, unlike prior algorithms [30], does not require the simultaneous input of all kinds of heterogeneous data during training, making it more appropriate for application in a diverse array of federated learning edge nodes.

2) Better data privacy protection. This algorithm [31] eliminates the potential for privacy leakage when various heterogeneous data are simultaneously transmitted to the same location for training [32].

3) The bandwidth of transmission is drastically lowered. This method is only needed to send and get the model parameters for the feature extraction sub-network that correspond to the heterogeneous data owned by the edge node. It is not needed to send and get the model parameters for getting all the features of the heterogeneous data.

Table 3. Performance comparison of classification tasks on MOSI dataset

Algorithm	Acc2	F1	Acc7
SVM	49.7	49.2	16.3
DF	69.3	68.7	25.2
BC-LSTM	72.8	73.2	27.6
MV-LSTM	76.7	74.2	32.6
TFN	74.1	74.1	31.8
LMF	77.5	76.8	32.4
This article	76.7	76.3	87.6

4.2 Experimental Analysis of Multi-node Heterogeneous Data Fusion

The tests in this section will analyze the algorithm's performance from two perspectives in order to validate the approach described in this article for the fusion of multi-source heterogeneous data within the modified federated weighted average algorithm.: (1) the performance of the algorithm in terms of the number of data sources, and (2) the performance of the algorithm in terms of the number of data sources. In this study [33], data deployment is used to assess the algorithm's adaptability to heterogeneous data. Table 4 categorizes the various techniques to place data sets on training sub-nodes into three groups:

1) Each training sub-data node's set comprises information gathered from a single architecture;
2) Highly skewed data, where each training sub-data node's set incorporates data from any two structures.
3) Each training child node in trimodal data has data from all structures.

The performance of a trained model with much the same inter-standardized data release strategy using heterogeneous data from different modulations demonstrates the universality and applicability of the method described in this work. This experiment selected characteristics (8, 8, and 16) from a mixture of numbers (R1, R2, and R3).

Table 4. Multi-node heterogeneous data deployment strategy

Data	Trimodal			Bimodal			Unimodal		
Type	Node			Node			Node		
Spoken language	√	√	√	√	√		√	√	√
Audio	√					√	√	√	√
Visual	√	√				√	√	√	√

Regression Task. When evaluating regression tasks, the MAE sum is the metric that is employed [34]. The results of the experiment are shown in Correlation Table 5. These modal data were used throughout the training process for the model that ended up having the greatest performance on these modal data for the regression challenge. The relationship that exists between the sample and the model's predicted value varies based on the training model that is being used. The multimodal training model provides backward compatibility for the acquisition of future intermodal connections as the number of states increases. In regressive tasks, increasing the number of modalities in the training data improves the performance of the model on the test set, which is independent of the number of modalities in the training data. This is the case not just as a result of learning each model but also owing to the multi-modal model that is used throughout the training process. Students not only look at the properties of the modal but also investigate the possible connections that may be made between different modals. In turn, the learned combinations of the possible intermodal connections are more diverse for the training model with a large number of modalities since there are more modalities to choose from. The sum increases in proportion to the degree of success achieved by the work on the regression.

Table 5. Regression task performance on MOSI dataset

Modal fusion model	Index	Unimodal	Bimodal	Trimodal
Unimodal	Mae	0.979	1.098	1.088
Data fusion	Corr	0.611	0.446	0.363
Bimodal	Mae	0.118	0.838	1.098
Data fusion	Corr	0.484	0.674	0.409
Trimodal	Mae	1.1327	1.0287	0.7942
Data fusion	Corr	0.487	0.641	0.758

Classification Task. The categorization job's indicators are Acc2, F1, Acc7, and the Acc2 sum. F1 is the evaluation index for binary classification, whereas Acc7 is the evaluation index for multiclassification.

The results of the experiments are shown in Table 6. It is required to establish which modal data works best with this modal data in order to train the model. This modal data must be used. The aggregation of data on the cloud makes it possible to blend many types of data with a single kind of training model. It is unable to learn the possible connections that exist between the modals, and all that it can do is find the best solution for the local training modal using the features of that modal. It is questionable if the potential connections that exist between the different modalities can be taught via multi-modal training. During the training of the model, it not only learns the characteristics of each modal but also the various connections that may be made between modals. The better understanding of data samples that results from the sharing of data is made possible by cloud aggregation.

Table 6. Classification task performance % on MOSI dataset

Modal fusion model	Index	Unimodal	Bimodal	Trimodal
Unimodal	Acc2	77.88	72.11	70.14
Data fusion	F1	78.03	69.98	64.91
	Acc7	39.66	33.87	31.99
Bimodal	Acc2	70.88	80.77	72.66
Data fusion	Corr	69.89	81.97	74.27
	Acc7	31.64	42.24	40.98
Trimodal	Acc2	75.12	81.01	87.23
Data fusion	F1	74.11	80.14	86.51
	Acc7	32.06	32.89	48.23

5   Conclusion

This study proposes a technique for combining heterogeneous data from various sources, and it does so by basing it on an enhanced version of the federated weighted average algorithm. This technique produces a high-order tensor with different data dimensions by using Tucker's theory of decomposition. Combining and reflecting on it. This method, in contrast to its predecessors, is able to integrate heterogeneous data from various sources in an effective manner without transferring any data at all. As a result, it is able to circumvent the obstacles to data transmission that are imposed by concerns over privacy and security. In addition, Based on the heterogeneous data structure provided by the training nodes, the method is able to adaptably manage diverse types of heterogeneous data. This is accomplished without increasing the train size of duplicate models, which contributes to an improvement in the effectiveness of distributed training. Utilize available communication capacity, eliminate transmissions that aren't essential, and reduce the demands placed on the computational and storage capabilities of network edge devices. In addition to this, the paradigm is more generalizable and has a wider application.

Acknowledgement. This research was made possible with funding from the National Natural Science Foundation of China (No.61862051), the Science and Technology Foundation of Guizhou Province (No. ZK[2022]549, No. [2019]1299), the Top-notch Talent Program of Guizhou Province (No. KY[2018]080), the Natural Science Foundation of Education of Guizhou Province (No. [2019]203), and the Funds of Qiannan Normal University for Nationalities (No. qnsy2018003, No. qnsy2019rc09, No. qnsy2018JS013, No. qnsyrc201715).

References

1. Zhou, J., Shen, H.J., Lin, Z.Y., Cao, Z.F., Dong, X.L.: Research advances on privacy preserving in edge computing. J. Comput. Res. Dev. **57**(10), 2027–2051 (2020)
2. Yang, Q., Liu, Y., Chen, T., Tong, Y.: Federated machine learning: concept and applications. ACM Trans. Intell. Syst. Technol. (TIST) **10**(2), 1–19 (2019)

3. Beyer, J., Heesche, K., Hauptmann, W., Otte, C., Kruse, R.: Ensemble learning for multi-source information fusion. In: Pratihar, D.K., Jain, L.C. (eds.) Intelligent Autonomous Systems, pp. 748–756. Springer, Heidelberg (2010). https://doi.org/10.1007/978-3-642-116 76-6_6

4. Hai, T., Zhou, J., Muranaka, K.: An efficient fuzzy-logic based MPPT controller for grid-connected PV systems by Farmland Fertility Optimization algorithm. Optik **267**, 169636 (2022)

5. Samuel, A., Sarfraz, M.I., Haseeb, H., Basalamah, S., Ghafoor, A.: A framework for composition and enforcement of privacy-aware and context-driven authorization mechanism for multimedia big data. IEEE Trans. Multimed. **17**(9), 1484–1494 (2015)

6. McMahan, H.B., Ramage, D., Talwar, K., Zhang, L.: Learning differentially private recurrent language models. arXiv preprint arXiv:1710.06963 (2017)

7. Beimel, A., Korolova, A., Nissim, K., Sheffet, O., Stemmer, U.: The power of synergy in differential privacy: combining a small curator with local randomizers. arXiv preprint arXiv: 1912.08951 (2019)

8. Xiaojun, C., Shuai, Z., Ye, D., Wei, H.: Efficient and secure federated learning based on secret sharing and gradients selection. J. Comput. Res. Dev. **57**(10), 2241 (2020)

9. Tran, N.H., Bao, W., Zomaya, A., Nguyen, M.N., Hong, C.S.: Federated learning over wireless networks: optimization model design and analysis. In: IEEE INFOCOM 2019-IEEE Conference on Computer Communications, pp. 1387–1395. IEEE (2019)

10. Wang, S., et al.: Adaptive federated learning in resource constrained edge computing systems. IEEE J. Sel. Areas Commun. **37**(6), 1205–1221 (2019)

11. Wang, X., Han, Y., Wang, C., Zhao, Q., Chen, X., Chen, M.: In-edge AI: intelligentizing mobile edge computing, caching and communication by federated learning. IEEE Netw. **33**(5), 156–165 (2019)

12. Zheng, Y.: Methodologies for cross-domain data fusion: an overview. IEEE Trans. Big Data **1**(1), 16–34 (2015)

13. Pan, B., Zheng, Y., Wilkie, D., Shahabi, C.: Crowd sensing of traffic anomalies based on human mobility and social media. In: Proceedings of the 21st ACM SIGSPATIAL International Conference on Advances in Geographic Information Systems, pp. 344–353 (2013)

14. Tao, H., et al.: SDN-assisted technique for traffic control and information execution in vehicular adhoc networks. Comput. Electr. Eng. **102**, 108108 (2022)

15. Liu, Z., Zhang, W., Quek, T.Q., Lin, S.: Deep fusion of heterogeneous sensor data. In: 2017 IEEE International Conference on Acoustics, Speech and Signal Processing (ICASSP), pp. 5965–5969. IEEE (2017)

16. Hai, T., Said, N.M., Zain, J.M., Sajadi, S.M., Mahmoud, M.Z., Aybar, H.Ş: ANN usefulness in building enhanced with PCM: efficacy of PCM installation location. J. Build. Eng. **57**, 104914 (2022)

17. Ouyang, W., Chu, X., Wang, X.: Multi-source deep learning for human pose estimation. In: Proceedings of the IEEE Conference on Computer Vision and Pattern Recognition, pp. 2329–2336 (2014)

18. Wang, W., Zhang, M.: Tensor deep learning model for heterogeneous data fusion in Internet of Things. IEEE Trans. Emerg. Top. Comput. Intell. **4**(1), 32–41 (2018)

19. Zadeh, A., Chen, M., Poria, S., Cambria, E., Morency, L.P.: Tensor fusion network for multimodal sentiment analysis. arXiv preprint arXiv:1707.07250 (2017)

20. Zheng, Y., Liu, F., Hsieh, H.P.: U-air: when urban air quality inference meets big data. In: Proceedings of the 19th ACM SIGKDD International Conference on Knowledge Discovery and Data Mining, pp. 1436–1444 (2013)

21. Hai, T., Abidi, A., Zain, J.M., Sajadi, S.M., Mahmoud, M.Z., Aybar, H.Ş: Assessment of using solar system enhanced with MWCNT in PCM-enhanced building to decrease thermal energy usage in ejector cooling system. J. Build. Eng. **55**, 104697 (2022)

22. Degottex, G., Kane, J., Drugman, T., Raitio, T., Scherer, S.: COVAREP—A collaborative voice analysis repository for speech technologies. In: 2014 IEEE International Conference on Acoustics, Speech and Signal Processing (ICASSP), pp. 960–964. IEEE (2014)

23. Hai, T., Zhou, J., Li, N., Jain, S.K., Agrawal, S., Dhaou, I.B.: Cloud-based bug tracking software defects analysis using deep learning. J. Cloud Comput. **11**(1), 1–14 (2022)

24. Ekman, P.: An argument for basic emotions. Cogn. Emot. **6**(3–4), 169–200 (1992)

25. Cortes, C., Vapnik, V.: Support-vector networks. Mach. Learn. **20**(3), 273–297 (1995)

26. Hai, T., Alsharif, S., Dhahad, H.A., Attia, E.A., Shamseldin, M.A., Ahmed, A.N.: The evolutionary artificial intelligence-based algorithm to find the minimum GHG emission via the integrated energy system using the MSW as fuel in a waste heat recovery plant. Sustain. Energy Technol. Assess. **53**, 102531 (2022)

27. Nojavanasghari, B., Gopinath, D., Koushik, J., Baltrušaitis, T., Morency, L.P.: Deep multimodal fusion for persuasiveness prediction. In: Proceedings of the 18th ACM International Conference on Multimodal Interaction, pp. 284–288 (2016)

28. Hai, T., et al.: Proposal 3E analysis and multi-objective optimization of a new biomass-based energy system based on the organic cycle and ejector for the generation of sustainable power, heat, and cold. Sustain. Energy Technol. Assess. **53**, 102551 (2022)

29. Fukui, A., Park, D.H., Yang, D., Rohrbach, A., Darrell, T., Rohrbach, M.: Multimodal compact bilinear pooling for visual question answering and visual grounding. arXiv preprint arXiv: 1606.01847 (2016)

30. Hai, T., et al.: Design, modeling and multi-objective techno-economic optimization of an integrated supercritical Brayton cycle with solar power tower for efficient hydrogen production. Sustain. Energy Technol. Assess. **53**, 102599 (2022)

31. Rajagopalan, S.S., Morency, L.-P., Baltrušaitis, T., Goecke, R.: Extending long short-term memory for multi-view structured learning. In: Leibe, B., Matas, J., Sebe, N., Welling, M. (eds.) ECCV 2016. LNCS, vol. 9911, pp. 338–353. Springer, Cham (2016). https://doi.org/10.1007/978-3-319-46478-7_21

32. Hai, T., Zhou, J., Mohamad Zain, J., Vafa, S.: Cost optimization and energy management of a microgrid including renewable energy resources and electric vehicles. J. Energy Resour. Technol. **145**, 1–16 (2022)

33. Liu, Z., Shen, Y., Lakshminarasimhan, V.B., Liang, P.P., Zadeh, A., Morency, L.P.: Efficient low-rank multimodal fusion with modality-specific factors. arXiv preprint arXiv:1806.00064 (2018)

34. Hai, T., et al.: Neural network-based optimization of hydrogen fuel production energy system with proton exchange electrolyzer supported nanomaterial. Fuel **332**, 125827 (2023)

Dynamic Micro-cluster-Based Streaming Data Clustering Method for Anomaly Detection

Xiaolan Wang[1,3], Md Manjur Ahmed[4], Mohd Nizam Husen[3(✉)], Hai Tao[2], and Qian Zhao[1]

[1] School of Computer, Baoji University of Arts and Sciences, Shaanxi, China
[2] School of Computer and Information, Qiannan Normal University for Nationalities, Duyun 558000, Guizhou, China
[3] Malaysian Institute of Information Technology (MIIT), Universiti Kuala Lumpur, Kuala Lumpur, Malaysia
mnizam@unikl.edu.my
[4] Department of Computer Science and Engineering, University of Barishal, 8254 Barishal, Bangladesh

Abstract. The identification of anomalies in a data stream is a difficulty for decision-making in real time. A memory-constrained online detection system that is able to quickly detect the concept drift of streaming data is required because the constant arrival of massive amounts of streaming data with changing characteristics makes real-time and efficient anomaly detection a difficult task. This is because of the nature of the data itself, which is constantly changing. In this study, a novel model for detecting anomalies using dynamic micro-clusters scheme is developed. The macro-clusters are generated from a network of connected micro-clusters. When new data items are added, the normal patterns that are formed in macro-clusters will update in tandem with the dynamic micro-clusters in an incremental fashion. An outlier may be understood from both a global and a local perspective by examining the global and local densities respectively. The effectiveness of the suggested approach was evaluated with the use of three different datasets. The findings of the experiment demonstrate that the suggested method is superior to earlier algorithms in terms of both the accuracy of detection and the level of computing complexity it requires.

Keywords: Micro-cluster · Data stream · Outlier detection · Macro-cluster

1 Introduction

With a large amount of data creating by the internet of things, the data stream's volume, variety, and velocity change with time [1]. Anomaly detection is used in more places. These include network intrusion detection, fraud detection in financial systems, and medical and industrial system monitoring [2]. Signature-based detection relies on anomalous signatures and can only identify known attacks, in contrast to anomaly detection. Anomaly detection may find new types of attack. Data stream anomalies are rare [3]. Most anomaly detection systems employ a static model [4]. Data steam patterns

M. Yusoff et al. (Eds.): SCDS 2023, CCIS 1771, pp. 61–75, 2023.
https://doi.org/10.1007/978-981-99-0405-1_5

in a practical setting usually vary over time [5], especially in the era of big data, when a massive of steaming data is being continually produced and changing. Applying an earlier static train-based classifies to the current streaming data will always provide erroneous result. For real-time anomaly detection, live detection on continually growing data streams is required.

Data stream clustering adapts clusters to shifting patterns. It can recognize unexpected events [6]. Using online clustering, which has limited storage capacity, incoming data may be temporarily stored. Adapting to the ever-changing pattern is usually required. The strategy may also be executed "bottom-up." Computing efficiency is a crucial criterion in online anomaly detection for real-time decision making. This criterion determines program execution. This measure answers "Can the app be utilized for real-time decision making?" This technique assumes [7] that anomalies occupied a relatively tiny portion of the entire data stream and could be differentiated from the regular patterns.

During this study, we developed the "Dynamic Micro-cluster-based Anomaly Detection on Streaming Data (DMADSD)" approach. An anomalous data item deviates from the norm or belongs to a tiny cluster. As fresh data is added, macro-clusters and dynamic micro-clusters update step-by-step. Instead of storing streaming data directly, the scheme only stores the statistical sampling information of the data items, which improves storage efficiency. Macro-clusters enhance storage efficiency. Local and global outliers could be identified by combining the local and global density thresholds. Three data sets were used to test the method's performance. The experiment shows that the new algorithm is more accurate and less complicated than previous ones.

2 Related Work

With the advancement of the internet of things in today's world, massive data streams are consistently produced and continue to expand over the course of time. Because it requires a labeled training dataset, supervised learning is not an option that can be used. It is common knowledge that labeling requires the manual assignment of experts, which requires a great deal of effort. Techniques that are supervised depend on the dataset that is used for training. Unsupervised approaches, on the other hand, may learn from datasets that have not been labeled and are thus independent of past datasets. Two of the most important methods of unsupervised machine learning are the clustering-based and auto encoder approaches.

Auto encoders may help identify cyber-attacks [8]. Using an error threshold, normal and abnormal samples may be differentiated. The NSL-KDD experiment proves the system's accuracy. Cyber-attacks are identified via clustering [10]. The data set is divided into micro-clusters, and each cluster's center is given a beginning value to boost classifier efficiency. Tested on KDD [9], CICIDS2017 [12], and Wormhole [10]. The results show that it outperforms other approaches. Offline model has two approaches. Because the offline model ignores network flow changes, its accuracy is affected when traffic patterns change.

Data stream clustering has been done in several ways [12–15]. As a CODAS [17] contribution, CEDAS [16] was recommended. Instead of saving data items directly, micro-clusters are used to construct a summary. New data are dynamically updating microclusters. "Energy" describes a microcluster's temporal property. BOCEDS [18] is an upgrade from CEDAS. The cluster's micro-radius may alter dynamically, unlike CEDAS. It uses a buffer to improve cluster quality. Online clustering techniques give adequate cluster quality, but they emphasize cluster accuracy above attack detection.

Online clustering has been used to identify cyber-attacks in recent years. [7] An incremental grid-based clustering approach was presented. Each feature subspace's outlier score was computed. Experiments reveal that the system has good detection performance but is slow. [19] A solution was developed for early cyber-attack detection on streaming data. A distance threshold determines whether a new cluster is forming or emerging into the targeting cluster. Once the targeting cluster receives the data item, it joins will be dynamically updated. Outliers are clusters with low density and a small size. It outperforms others. The huge number of clusters must be carefully examined to see whether they are normal or abnormal. Here, incremental cyberattack detection is mentioned [20]. GMMs summarize the data. While noises are filtered out, GMMs will be updated, or new ones produced. Many network datasets were tested with good results. The freshly created cluster must be analyzed for an attack. Model for identifying harmful events via data streaming clustering [6]. A new data item will instantly update the correct cluster. The dataset is never cached. Only cluster summaries are stored. Using distance, outliers were identified. This model's computing complexity is superior. The system's efficiency hinged on the initial clusters. [21] A sliding window methodology for identifying outliers was created. Outliers were evaluated by slope. Its detection and false alarm rates were high. Data items are directly stored in memory, which increases memory complexity.

3 Methodology

3.1 Cluster Structure

In proposed DMADSD, the newly arrived data items are not directly stored in storage. The scheme only stores the statistical sampling information of the data items in the form of the micro-cluster. The micro-clusters merge into macro-clusters which is represented as the generated data stream clusters.

3.1.1 Structure of the Micro-cluster

A micro-cluster $C_{micro}(u, n, label)$ is expressed by three information $u, n, label$. u is the center of the micro-cluster. n is defined as the density of the micro-cluster. It is the number of data items that are included in the micro-cluster, and its label is the label of the macro-cluster to which it belongs. In addition to these three pieces of information, the system parameter r_0 is a constant that represents the radius of the micro-cluster.

The density of the micro-cluster might be either above or below the Local density threshold, which is denoted by the symbol Lthreshold. This determines which of the two shapes the micro-cluster takes.

1. Core micro-cluster Mcore: The count of data items of micro-cluster is higher than the Lthreshold value.
2. Local outlier: The count of data items of micro-cluster is below the Lthreshold.

3.1.2 Structure of the Macro-cluster

A macro-cluster is generated from the joint micro-clusters. If both micro-clusters without question are core micro-clusters and at least one of the core micro-clusters is linked to the kernel region of the other core micro-cluster, then the two micro-clusters are considered to be joint.

According to our definition, the kernel area of the micro-cluster is the circle area with the same center as the microcluster when that circle's radius is set to $r_0/2$.

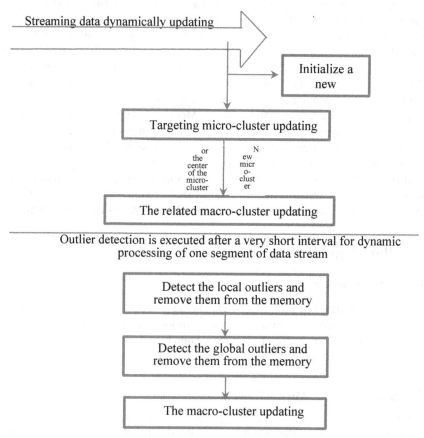

Fig. 1. The flow chart of the DMADSD

3.2 Algorithm of DMADSD

The dynamic updating phase and the outlier detection phase are the two stages that make up the execution of the DMADSD. Cluster represented as macro-cluster evolves along with the related micro-clusters dynamically updating as the new data item being received. Outlier detection is executed after a very short interval for dynamic processing of one segment of data stream. The flowchart is illustrated in Fig. 1. The algorithm executed in a two-phase process, Dynamic updating, and Outlier detection.

3.2.1 Dynamic Updating

In the process of the dynamic updating execution, data items are executed in one single-pass way. The scheme initiates from reading the first data item and the system parameter r_0, The algorithm of the dynamic updating phase is described as Algorithm 1. It contains follow three parts.

I.   Initialization
II. Micro-cluster updating
III. Macro-cluster updating

(1) Initialization
    The scheme initialization is to construct the synopsis information of the micro-clusters. It initiates when the program starts to read the first data item, or a new data item cannot find an existing micro-cluster which it falls within. A new micro-cluster $C_{micro}(u, n, label)$ is created by initializing its features. u is the data item. n is set to 1. $label$ is assigned to 0.

(2) Micro-cluster updating
    When a newly arrived data item is read by the system. The nearest existing micro-cluster $C_{micro}(u, n, label)$ is searched to judge whether it is the micro-cluster the newly arrived data item falls within. Calculating the distance between the newly arrived data item and the nearest micro-cluster, d. One of the following three cases will be happened:

1. $d > r_0$ means that the nearest micro-cluster is not the micro-cluster that the newly arrived data item falls within. Then a new micro-cluster is initialized.
2. $d \leq r_0/2$ means the newly arrived data item falls within the kernel area of the nearest micro-cluster. n, the count of the nearest micro-cluster increase by 1. u keep the same.
3. $\frac{r_0}{2} < d \leq r_0$ means the newly arrived data item does not fall within the kernel area of the nearest micro-cluster. n, the count of the nearest micro-cluster increase by 1. u updated to the mean of its data items.

(3) Macro-cluster updating
    Two cases for updating macro-cluster:

1. A new core micro-cluster has been created.
2. The center of the core macro-cluster has changed. If any of two cases happens, the macro-cluster updating will be activated. It first search for all the related macro-clusters, then update the joint list of every related macro-clusters. If the joint list has been changed, reset the labels of the macro-clusters.

3.2.2 Outlier Detection

The purpose of outlier identification is to locate and eliminate any and all outliers. Following a very brief pause, the dynamic processing of a single data segment will begin, and the outlier identification phase will then activate. Following the completion of the outlier identification procedure, the normal clusters, which are then represented in the memory as the normal patterns, are set aside. These clusters continue to develop and undergo incremental updates as the data stream idea drifts.

Algorithm 1: dynamic updating

Input: The data item s_i, r_0

1: Step 1: search the nearest micro-cluster C_{micro}
2:     if the distance d between the C_{micro} and the s_i, $s_i < r_0$
3:         update the n of C_{micro}, $n_{new} = n + 1$
4:         if s_i falls into outside of the kernel area of the C_{micro}
5:             update the center u of the C_{micro}, $u_{new} = \frac{n \times u + s_i}{n+1}$
6:             if $u_{new} > Lthreshold$
7:                 go step 2
8:                 exit
9:             [end if]
10:         else if $n_{new} = Lthreshold$
11:             go step 2
12:             exit
13:         else
14:             return
15:         [end if]
16:     else
17:         Initialize micro-cluster $O'(u, n, label)$
18:             $n = 1, u = O', label = 0$
19:         exit
20:     [end if]
21: Step 2: Find all the joint micro-clusters of the C_{micro}
22:     update the joint list for every joint micro-cluster
23:     if joint list has altered, then
24:         reset the label of the macro-clusters
25:     [end if]

The suggested DMADSD defines outliers by looking at them from both a global and a local viewpoint and basing their determinations on global and local density respectively. The value of LThreshold is used as a local threshold to determine whether or not a micro-cluster should be considered an outlier. A micro-cluster is considered a local outlier if its density, n, falls below a certain threshold called the LThreshold. As a result, a global threshold known as GThreshold has been established to determine whether or not a macro-cluster is an outlier. According to our definition, the density of a macro-cluster is equal to the total count of data items included inside it. It reflects the overall density of all of its joint microclusters. A macro-cluster is considered to be a global outlier if its density, N, falls below the GThreshold value. The method used during the period devoted to dynamic updating is referred to as Algorithm 2. It is composed of the following three sections:

I.   Detect and kill the local outlier
II. Detect and kill the global outlier
III. Macro-cluster updating

(1) Detect and kill the local outlier

After a very short interval for dynamic processing of one segment of data stream, all the local outliers are searched. We define the micro-cluster whose density *nsatisfied*, $n < LThreshold$ as a local outlier. After the searching processing, all the local outliers will be deleted from the memory and the serial number of the micro-clusters will be reset.

(2) Detect and kill the global outlier

We define that the total number of data items in a macro-cluster is its density. It represents the total density of its all the joint micro-clusters. The global outlier is defined as the macro-cluster whose density N is below the GThreshold. Find all the global outliers, then search and delete all the relevant joint micro-cluster. After reset the serial number of the micro-clusters, the label of the macro-clusters will be reset.

(3) Macro-cluster updating

As the global outliers being deleted from memory, the labels of the macro-clusters need to be reset.

Algorithm 2: Outlier detection

Input: the LThreshold and GThreshold
1.   search all the micro-clusters whose density $n\ satisfied,\ n < LThreshold$
2.   delete those micro-clusters from the memory.
3.   reset the serial number of the micro-clusters in the memory.
4.   search all the macro-clusters whose density $N\ satisfied, N < GThreshold$
5.   for every macro-cluster, $N < GThreshold$
6.   search all the relevant core-micro clusters in the macro-cluster.
7.   delete all the relevant core-micro clusters in the memory.
8.   reset the serial number of the micro-clusters in the memory.
9.   end for
10. reset the label of the macro-clusters.
     exit

---

4   Experiment Findings and Analysis

4.1   Dataset

In order to carry out the experiments, we make use of one synthetic dataset in addition to the two network datasets. The synthetic dataset has two dimensions and contains 4310 normal data items together with 743 anomalous data items resulting from three different types of assaults. Figure 2 (a) and (b) depict, respectively, a normal data stream that has not been subjected to any assaults and a data stream that has been subjected to attacks over time. The effectiveness of the system is analyzed with the use of not one but two different cyber data streams: the KDDCUP'99 dataset, which is a emulated data stream, and the CIDDS-001 data stream [11], generated from the real network environment accessing to the internet. One thousand meters is considered to be the length of one stream segment. In order to make the KDDCUP'99 dataset more representative of the actual world, the majority of the dataset will consist of standard data items. We use the whole normal dataset, but we choose just 4% of the assaults from each group. With regard to the CIDDS-001 dataset, all of the "regular" data items as well as the "attacker" data items have been chosen.

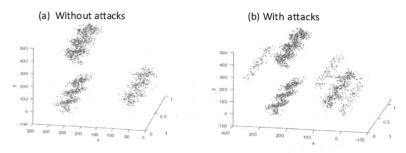

Fig. 2. Row synthetic dataset over time

4.2   Detection Performance Evaluation

(1)   The Synthetic Dataset

In order to demonstrate the effectiveness of the system's detection capabilities, we will be using a synthetic dataset with two dimensions. The typical dataset as well as three different sorts of assaults are simulated by this dataset. The typical pattern is continually evolving and changing as a result of the ongoing influx of data items. The synthetic data stream contains a total of 4310 normal data items in addition to 743 aberrant data items resulting from three different types of assaults. The at-tacks data items constitute around 15% of the total number of items. The detection rate and the false positive rate of the DMADSD are shown to have fluctuated over time in the manner shown in Fig. 3, which depicts the synthetic dataset. The detection rate (DR) is capable of reaching 100%, the detection accuracy increases with time, and the false positive rate (FPR) falls with time. After the processing of the first 2000 data items, the FPR tends to oscillate at around 4%.

Two other evolving data streams are created by using the same normal dataset and add outliers in proportions of 5% and 10% respectively. A comparison among three data streams with different proportion of outliers is made. The detection rate of three data streams with different proportion attacks are almost the same. The data stream which includes 5% attacks obtains the lowest FPR of 3.3% and the highest accuracy of 96.9%, while the data stream with 15% attacks has the highest FPR of 5.5% and the lowest accuracy of 95.1%. As the proportion of outliers increases, FPR decreases and the accuracy increase. Therefore, when outliers take up less proportion of whole data samples, the system will obtain the lower FPR and the higher accuracy.

(2) KDDCUP'99

The sensitivity of the LThreshold and GThreshold are shown in Table 1 under a variety of different settings with the radius r 0 equal to 0.413. As a result of the LThreshold being set between 7 and 9 and the GThreshold being set between 15 and 20, the system displays excellent performance. When LThreshold is set to 7 and GThreshold is set at 15 to 20, DR is able to obtain a success rate of 99.3%. The setting with the highest detection rate, 99.3%, also has the lowest false positive rate, 9.3%, and it is found to be (GThreshold = 16 or 17). Because LThreshold is less than 7, the true outlier micro-clusters have a chance of being identified as core micro-clusters, which then have a chance of forming into macro-clusters. Thereby, the outliers could be recognized as regular data flow if they aren't carefully examined. Due to the fact that the GThreshold was set lower than 15, some of the assault samples were incorrectly identified as regular traffic.

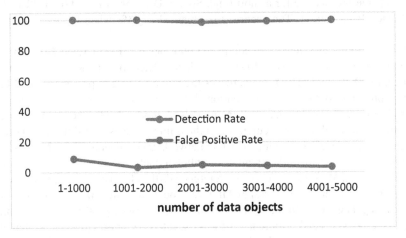

Fig. 3. The changing of the DR and the FPR on synthetic dataset

Table 1. The changing of DR and FPR under different setting for the LThreshold and GThreshold

DR		GThreshold						
FPR		14	15	16	17	18	19	20
LThreshold	6	83.2	83.2	86.5	86.5	86.5	87.4	87.4
		6.4	6.4	7.5	7.5	8.2	7.9	7.9

(*continued*)

Table 1. (*continued*)

DR		GThreshold						
FPR		14	15	16	17	18	19	20
	7	83.6	99.3	99.3	99.3	99.3	99.3	99.3
		6.4	10.7	9.3	9.3	12.1	13.0	13.0
	8	83.8	99.5	99.5	99.7	99.7	99.7	99.7
		6.1	12.4	12.4	13.1	13.1	13.8	13.8
	9	83.1	95.9	95.9	96.5	96.5	96.5	96.5
		6.5	14.3	14.3	14.5	14.5	14.8	14.8

Figure 4 illustrates the changing of the DR and the FPR of the DMADSD over time on KDDCUP'99 dataset. The parameters $r_0 = 0.413$, LThreshold = 7, GThreshold = 16. As the description of the variation trend on synthetic dataset, the FPR of the DMADSD on KDDCUP'99 dataset tends to be stable fluctuating slightly around 7.8% after the execution of the first 60000 data items. Therefore, FPR can be 7.8% as long as the scheme pre-operate for a short time. So, the DR is 99.3%, and the FPR is 7.8% on KDDCUP'99 dataset. The accuracy is obtained at 93% when the parameters are specified.

The preceding approaches are contrasted with one another in Table 2. When compared to other references, DMADSD has the highest detection rate, which is very nearly identical to 100%. DMADSD also achieves the highest levels of precision. The FPR is greater compared to those that are mentioned in the references [10, 20, 21]. The references [10], on the other hand, are offline models. A model that has been trained before to the traffic shift will not be accurate when the traffic changes over time since network traffics vary and develop over time in actual network environments. The DMADSD and Reference [6, 20, 21] are both examples of online models. Clusters are presented in the form of Gaussian Mixture Models in the reference [20]. When new data items are added, the system will update the Gaussian Mixture Models to reflect the new information. The system gets good performance for various cyber datasets. However, to differentiate attack, labeling is needed. Reference [6] was executed very fast, However, system efficiency was largely determined by the clusters the system generates from the beginning. Reference [21] obtains good detection performance. However, system has high memory complexity because the data items is stored directly not the statistical information.

(3) CIDDS_001

The value 0.04 has been assigned to the Radius variable in CIDDS 001. Both the LThreshold and the GThreahold are now set to the value of 12. We obtained a DR of 99.99%, which is quite near to 100%, an FPR of 1.31%, and an accuracy of 98.2% when these parameters were specified.

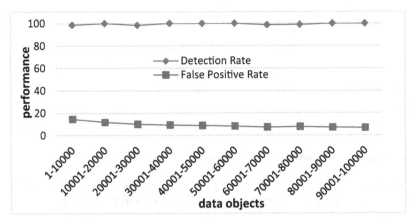

Fig. 4. The variation trend of the DR and the FPR of the DMADSD on synthetic dataset on KDDCUP'99 dataset

Table 3 presents the results of a comparison between the performance of DMADSD and that of earlier methods. To the best of my knowledge, there is no approach for system assessment that uses unsupervised online monitoring and makes use of the CIDDS-001 dataset. The DMADSD method is the first online approach, and it validates the algorithm by utilizing the CIDDS-001 dataset. Offline approaches include references [10] and references [22]. Training using the complete dataset is required in order to acquire the classifiers. Not only is the DMADSD better to the references [10, 22], but it is also more accurate. In addition to this, it is an online inference that does not call for classifier training to be completed in advance.

Table 2. Comparing results between previous unsupervised-based techniques on KDDCUP'99 data stream

Technique	Detectable attacks	Offline /online	DR	Accuracy	FPR
DMADSD	DoS, R2L, U2R, Probe	Online	99.2%	93%	7.8%
Yin et al. [6]	DoS	Online	73%–99%	–	9.17%-24.74%
Mahendra et al. 2020 [10]	DoS, R2L, U2R, Probe	Offline	84.70%	93.07%	2.73%
Bigdeli [20]	DoS, R2L, U2R, Probe	Online	98%	–	2%
Shou et al. [21]	Probe, U2R, R2L	Online	92.08%	–	6.26%

Table 3. Comparing results between previous unsupervised-based techniques on CIDDS-001

Method	DR	Accuracy	FPR
DMADSD	0.9999	0.982	0.0131
Prasad [22]	0.96379	0.97958	0.01422
Mahendra [10]	0.88	0.886	0.5371

4.3 Computational Complexity Evaluation

Computational complexity includes the space and time complexity. This section the space complexity and time complexity of the DMADSD will be evaluated.

4.3.1 Outlier Space Complexity Evaluation

The execution process of the DMADSD does not store all the arrived data items directly. The information of the micro-cluster as the statistical sampling data is stored. The space for the scheme of DMADSD includes the space for statistical information $C_{micro}(u, n, label)$ and the system parameters $(r_0, LThreshold, GThreshold)$. Therefore, the space complexity is $O(mN)$. N is the maximum count for the micro-clusters. m is the storage for $(u, n, label)$ and u is a v-dimension data, *nandlabel* are constant. Therefore, m is $(v + 2)$. Table 4 shows the memory consumption of three data streams.

Table 4. Memory consumption of three data stream

Data stream	Dimension	Maximum count	Space complexity
Synthetic Dataset	2	21	4*21
KDDCUP'99	38	110	40*110
CIDDS-001	7	62	9*62

As to offline anomaly detection methods, the entire dataset requires to train for the classifiers. The computational complexity is undoubtedly higher than that of the online applications which only store the statistical sampling information of the dataset. So here we only need to make comparisons with online techniques. Although reference [21] is the online technique, the statistical sampling data structure is not used but storing the data items directly. The space complexity is not analyzed in reference [20]. The space complexity in reference [20] depends on the count of GMMs. GMM is the three v-dimension data. Therefore, its space complexity is $O(3vN)$. For the same dataset, reference [20] has higher space complexity than the DMADSD. Table 5 shows the comparing results between the DMADSD and reference [18].

Table 5. The comparing results of the space complexity between the DMADSD and reference [18] on KDDCUP'99

Technique	Space consumption
The DMADSD	40*110
Bigdeli [18]	41*3*180

To the best of my knowledge, there is no unsupervised online anomaly detection approach that uses the CIDDS-001 dataset to test its algorithm. I say this because I have searched far and low for such a method. The CIDDS-001 dataset was used to test and assess the DMADSD algorithm, which makes it the first unsupervised online anomaly detection approach. Consequently, DMADSD has a more effective use of space compared to the strategies discussed in the references.

Table 6. Comparing result between the DMADSD and the previous techniques in terms of time consumption on KDDCUP'99

Technique	Data item size	Time consumption
DMADSD	100550	15 s
Yin [4]	1015061	—
Bigdeli [18]	82980	225 s
Shou [19]	50000	0.375 s

4.3.2 Time Complexity Evaluation

The time consumption in the DMADSD is the time consumption in the process of dynamic updating and the process of outlier detection. Dynamic updating contains nearest micro-cluster searching ($O(N)$), micro-cluster updating (O (1)), macro-cluster updating ($O(M)$), N and M are maximum count for the micro-clusters and macro-clusters respectively. N is larger than M. Outlier detection contains local outlier searching ($O(N)$) and global outlier searching ($O(M)$). Therefore, the time complexity of the DMADSD is $2*(O(N) + O(M))$ far less than $4* O(N)$. The result is superior to reference [6] with the time complexity of $O(n^2)$ where n is the total count of the entire data items. Table 6 illustrates the comparing results between the DMADSD and previous techniques in term of time consumption on KDDCUP'99. The DMADSD outperforms the technique in reference [20]. DMADSD process 100550 data items within 15 s, while the technique in reference [20] process 82980 within 225 s.

5 Conclusion

It is suggested to use a dynamic micro-cluster-based Streaming Data Clustering Method for Anomaly Detection (DMADSD). In the DMADSD method, clusters undergo dynamic updates and continue to develop throughout the course of time. The macro-cluster is formed by a network of connected micro-clusters. When new data items are added, the normal patterns that are formed in macro-clusters will update in tandem with the dynamic micro-clusters in an incremental fashion. From both a global and a local point of view, an outlier may be described using the global density and the local density. The micro-cluster that has a number of data items that is lower than the local density criterion is the one that is considered to be the local outlier. The macro-clusters that have a number of data items that is lower than the threshold for global density are the ones that are considered to be the global outlier. The experiment conducted on the fabricated dataset shows that the rate of false positives may be reduced once the system has been pre-operated for a brief period of time. The KDDCUP'99 dataset and the CIDDS-001 dataset are the actual network steaming data that are utilized in this study. The results of the experiments reveal that the suggested algorithm is superior to the referenced approaches in terms of both the detection performance and the computational complexity. The work that will be done in the future will focus on automatically adjusting the density threshold to correspond with various applications.

Funding. This work is supported by the Youth Science and Technology New Star Plan of Shaanxi Province (2021KJXX-50) and Technology New Star Plan of Shaanxi Province (No. 20JS09).

References

1. Zhai, Y., Ong, Y.-S., Tsang, I.W.: The emerging "big dimensionality." IEEE Comput. Intell. Mag. **9**(3), 14–26 (2014). https://doi.org/10.1109/mci.2014.2326099
2. Hai, T., Zhou, J., Li, N., Jain, S.K., Agrawal, S., Dhaou, I.B.: Cloud-based bug tracking software defects analysis using deep learning. J. Cloud Comput. **11**(1), 1–14 (2022)
3. Shi, Y., Peng, X., Li, R., Zhang, Y.: Unsupervised anomaly detection for network flow using immune network based k-means clustering (chap. 33). In: Data Science, (Communications in Computer and Information Science), pp. 386–399 (2017)
4. Sadik, S., Gruenwald, L.: Research issues in outlier detection for data streams. ACM SIGKDD Explor. Newslett. **15**(1), 33–40 (2014). https://doi.org/10.1145/2594473.2594479
5. Hai, T., Alsharif, S., Dhahad, H.A., Attia, E.A., Shamseldin, M.A., Ahmed, A.N.: The evolutionary artificial intelligence-based algorithm to find the minimum GHG emission via the integrated energy system using the MSW as fuel in a waste heat recovery plant. Sustain. Energy Technol. Assess. **53**, 102531 (2022)
6. Yin, C., Zhang, S., Yin, Z., Wang, J.: Anomaly detection model based on data stream clustering. Clust. Comput. **22**(1), 1729–1738 (2017). https://doi.org/10.1007/s10586-017-1066-2
7. Dromard, J., Roudiere, G., Owezarski, P.: Online and scalable unsupervised network anomaly detection method. IEEE Trans. Netw. Serv. Manag. **14**(1), 34–47 (2017). https://doi.org/10.1109/tnsm.2016.2627340
8. Choi, H., Kim, M., Lee, G., Kim, W.: Unsupervised learning approach for network intrusion detection system using autoencoders. J. Supercomput. **75**(9), 5597–5621 (2019). https://doi.org/10.1007/s11227-019-02805-w
9. Bay, S.D., Kibler, D., Pazzani, M.J., Smyth, P.: The UCI KDD archive of large data sets for data mining research and experimentation. ACM SIGKDD Explor. Newslett. **2**(2), 81–85 (2000). https://doi.org/10.1145/380995.381030

10. Prasad, M., Tripathi, S., Dahal, K.: Unsupervised feature selection and cluster center initialization based arbitrary shaped clusters for intrusion detection. Comput. Secur. **99**, 19 (2020). https://doi.org/10.1016/j.cose.2020.102062

11. Verma, A., Ranga, V.: Statistical analysis of CIDDS-001 dataset for network intrusion detection systems using distance-based machine learning. In: Procedia Computer Science, vol. 125, pp. 709–716 (2018). https://doi.org/10.1016/j.procs.2017.12.091. https://www.scopus.com/inward/record.uri?eid=2-s2.0-85040688913&doi=10.1016%2fj.procs.2017.12.091&partnerID=40&md5=b18bb5f2eb83d20d0a8654577709a0c9

12. Aggarwal, C.C., Han, J., Wang, J., Yu, P.S.: A framework for clustering evolving data streams. In: Proceedings - 29th International Conference on Very Large Data Bases, VLDB 2003, pp. 81–92 (2003). https://www.scopus.com/inward/record.uri?eid=2-s2.0-850122 36181&partnerID=40&md5=ba9b3babce1e0698d473b70d76f2062d. https://www.scopus.com/inward/record.uri?eid=2-s2.0-85012236181&partnerID=40&md5=ba9b3babce1e069 8d473b70d76f2062d

13. Cao, F., Ester, M., Qian, W.N., Zhou, A.Y.: Density-based clustering over an evolving data stream with noise. In: Proceedings of the Sixth Siam International Conference on Data Mining, p. 328 (2006)

14. Ruiz, C., Menasalvas, E., Spiliopoulou, M.: C-DenStream: using domain knowledge on a data stream. In: Gama, J., Costa, V.S., Jorge, A.M., Brazdil, P.B. (eds.) DS 2009. LNCS (LNAI), vol. 5808, pp. 287–301. Springer, Heidelberg (2009). https://doi.org/10.1007/978-3-642-04747-3_23

15. Ren, J., Ma, R.: Density-based data streams clustering over sliding windows. In: 6th International Conference on Fuzzy Systems and Knowledge Discovery, FSKD 2009, vol. 5, pp. 248–252 (2009). https://doi.org/10.1109/FSKD.2009.553. https://www.scopus.com/inward/record.uri?eid=2-s2.0-76549115319&doi=10.1109%2fFSKD.2009.553&partnerID=40&md5=f58d4f0a94fd24238b7ad6e84025bfc2

16. Hyde, R., Angelov, P., MacKenzie, A.R.: Fully online clustering of evolving data streams into arbitrarily shaped clusters. Inf. Sci. **382**, 96–114 (2017). https://doi.org/10.1016/j.ins.2016.12.004

17. Hyde, R., Angelov, P.: A new online clustering approach for data in arbitrary shaped clusters. In: Proceedings - 2015 IEEE 2nd International Conference on Cybernetics, CYBCONF 2015, pp. 228–233 (2015). https://doi.org/10.1109/CYBConf.2015.717 5937. https://www.scopus.com/inward/record.uri?eid=2-s2.0-84947967804&doi=10.1109%2fCYBConf.2015.7175937&partnerID=40&md5=4b211a62c8fe6bc814762baf234eea83

18. Islam, M.K., Ahmed, M.M., Zamli, K.Z.: A buffer-based online clustering for evolving data stream. Inf. Sci. **489**, 113–135 (2019). https://doi.org/10.1016/j.ins.2019.03.022

19. Škrjanc, I., Ozawa, S., Ban, T., Dovžan, D.: Large-scale cyber attacks monitoring using evolving Cauchy possibilistic clustering. Appl. Soft Comput. **62**, 592–601 (2018). https://doi.org/10.1016/j.asoc.2017.11.008

20. Bigdeli, E., Mohammadi, M., Raahemi, B., Matwin, S.: Incremental anomaly detection using two-layer cluster-based structure. Inf. Sci. **429**, 315–331 (2018). https://doi.org/10.1016/j.ins.2017.11.023

21. Shou, Z., Zou, F., Tian, H., Li, S.: Outlier detection based on local density of vector dot product in data stream. In: Yang, C.-N., Peng, S.-L., Jain, L.C. (eds.) SICBS 2018. AISC, vol. 895, pp. 170–184. Springer, Cham (2020). https://doi.org/10.1007/978-3-030-16946-6_14

22. Prasad, M., Tripathi, S., Dahal, K.: An efficient feature selection based Bayesian and rough set approach for intrusion detection. Appl. Soft Comput. **87**, 14 (2020). https://doi.org/10.1016/j.asoc.2019.105980

Federated Ensemble Algorithm Based on Deep Neural Network

Dan Wang[1,3] and Ting Wang[1,2(✉)]

[1] School of Mathematics and Statistics, Qiannan Normal University for Nationalities, Guizhou 558000, China
wangting32210@163.com
[2] School of Computer Sciences, Baoji University of Arts and Sciences, Baoji 721007, China
[3] Key Laboratory of Complex Systems and Intelligent Optimization of Guizhou, Guizhou 558000, China

Abstract. In the realm of multi-source privacy data protection, federated learning is now one of the most popular study topics. When the data being used is not local, its architecture has the ability to train a common model that can satisfy the needs of many parties. On the other hand, there are circumstances in which local model parameters are challenging to incorporate and cannot be used for security purposes. As a result, a federated ensemble algorithm that is based on deep learning has been presented, and both deep learning and ensemble learning have been used within the context of federated learning. Using the various integrated algorithms that integrate local model parameters, which improve the accuracy of the model and take into account the security of multi-source data, the accuracy of the local model can be improved by optimizing the parameters of the local model. This in turn improves the accuracy of the local model. The results of the experiments show that, in comparison to conventional multi-source data processing technology, the accuracy of the algorithm in the training model for the MNIST dataset, the digits dataset, the letter dataset, and the wine dataset is improved by 1%, 8%, 1%, and 1%, respectively, and the accuracy is guaranteed. Additionally, accuracy is guaranteed. It also improves the security of data and models that come from more than one source, which is a very useful feature.

Keywords: Federated learning · Federated ensemble algorithm · Deep neural network model · Ensemble algorithm · Deep learning

1 Introduction

The significance of data science in industrial engineering is growing as storage and computing power advance [1, 2]. Artificial intelligence, machine learning, smart manufacturing, and deep learning have all experienced rapid advancements in industrial engineering in recent years [3, 4]. Yet, as data science progresses, there remain two key obstacles [4]. At the outset, data governance is the most crucial part [5]. Second, data silos are a barrier to progress in contemporary industry [6–8], since more training

M. Yusoff et al. (Eds.): SCDS 2023, CCIS 1771, pp. 76–91, 2023.
https://doi.org/10.1007/978-981-99-0405-1_6

data would increase training performance. Since Google first presented the idea, professionals and academics have been worried about federated learning [9]. The essence of federated learning is that multiple data holders collaborate to train machine learning models without sharing their privacy-sensitive data, so as to meet the essential requirements of data security for "model-find data." The ability to keep personal information secret is a major selling point for this method many different areas [10].

Federated learning can be applied to smart city construction [11]. For example, literature [12] uses federated learning and urban computing to build a digital gateway, which can realize cross-domain modeling. Federated learning can also be applied to the medical field [13], to transfer the disease-oriented diagnosis model to the health status monitoring in the universal scenario, and then effectively solve the problem of combining medical care and health care [14].

It is not necessary to gather and store data in the cloud, much less integrate multiparty data, for federated learning since the training data is local to each data source [15]. As a result, the likelihood of a leak of secret information is drastically reduced using this strategy. Federated learning relies on data from multiple sources for training, but this diversity means that the training data isn't guaranteed to be independently distributed or of a consistent enough quantity to reliably train a unified model [16]. It is quite difficult to integrate multi-party sub-models if the training data distribution of the data sources is different [17]. Although the logistic regression model is used to train data from each data source in reference [18] and the neural network is used to integrate the multi-party sub-model in reference [19], the neural network model typically behaves as a non-convex function, and optimizing the model loss after averaging parameters is challenging. An examination of IID and non-IID distribution data (reference [20]) revealed that the non-IID distribution's final integration model fell short of expectations. Obtaining the model mean, gradient mean, or gradient update of the local model weights from the client is the focus of [21], where a federated averaging approach is devised and implemented for joint model training. In order to recover private information in accordance with the local model's gradient update, reference [22] presented a gradient depth leak mechanism for the federated average algorithm. This paper proposes a federated ensemble algorithm that uses the concept of ensemble learning to combine the individual models from multiple users, trains a global model that is satisfactory to all parties, and compares it with the traditional methods of integrating data training models [23]. The recent growth of machine learning services has raised concerns about data privacy. Homomorphic encryption permits inference on encrypted data at a 100- to 10,000-fold memory and runtime expense [39]. Frameworks require hundreds of gigabytes of DRAM to evaluate small models, restricting homomorphic encrypted DNN inference. This article explored the use of hybrid DRAM and persistent memory systems to circumvent these limits. Most computers nowadays use RSA to encrypt and decrypt their data. This work provided a revolutionary cryptanalysis approach for decrypting RSA using the public key. When the public key exponent is smaller than the RSA modulus, the new attack outperforms the Boneh-Durfee attack [40]. Experiments indicate the new method's effectiveness.

The experimental results show that the accuracy of the federated ensemble algorithm is improved compared with the traditional method of integrating data training models, and the security of multi-source data and models is also improved [24].

2 Basic Knowledge

2.1 Deep Learning

To create AI, we need to use machine learning, of which deep learning [25] is a subset. One kind of deep learning structure is the multilayer perceptron, which has many hidden layers and was popularized by work on artificial neural networks. To discover distributed feature representations of data, deep learning combines low-level features to form more abstract high-level representation attribute categories or features.

2.2 Federated Learning

To fulfill the goal of data security, the issue of data silos must be addressed, and federated learning [26, 27] is an algorithm optimization that does so while maintaining confidentiality. Federated learning allows the construction of federated models from data distributed across data owners and provides a blueprint for cross-enterprise data usage and model building so that enterprise private data is not localized, without violating data privacy protection regulations. Build and optimize machine learning models through parameter exchange under an encrypted mechanism.

2.3 Integrated Learning

The goal of ensemble learning [28] is to create a model with improved accuracy by combining numerous machine learning models, and a model that is combined is referred to as a weak classifier. It is necessary to train these weak classifier models sequentially with the training sample set since they are utilized simultaneously for prediction during the prediction phase. The stacking ensemble algorithm [29], the voting ensemble algorithm [30], and the blending ensemble algorithm [31] are often-used examples of such techniques.

2.4 Algorithm Description

At present, a common federated learning algorithm is the FedAvg algorithm (Federated Averaging) proposed by Google. Based on the FedAvg algorithm, the homomorphic encryption algorithm is introduced, and a privacy-preserving federated average learning algorithm is proposed, denoted as PP – FedAvg [32], as shown in Algorithm 1.

Algorithm 1: Federated Average Learning Algorithm PP- FedAvg.

Input: the department k's own database D_k, which b is the size of the local Batch, E represents the number of epochs, α represents the learning rate, and $\nabla L(\bullet, \bullet)$ represents the gradient optimization function;

Output: Updated local model parameters ω.

(1) Initialize the global model parameters ω^0
(2) Number of for rounds $t = 1, 2, \ldots do$
(3) $\{O_v\} \leftarrow O$ Select departments to participate in federated learning
(4) will ω^0 broadcast to O_v each department in $\{\}$
(5) for department $k \in \{O_v)$ in parallel do

(6) $\omega_{i+1}^k \leftarrow LocalUpdate(k, \omega_i)$
(7) end for
(8) end for

$$\text{Output } \omega_{i+1} \leftarrow \sum_{k=1}^{n} \frac{\beta_k \omega_{i+1}}{n} \tag{1}$$

Among them, the algorithm called by line 6 in Algorithm 1 is $LocalUpdate(k, \omega_i)$ shown in Algorithm 2.

Algorithm 2: LocalUpdate local model update

Input: the department k's own database D_k, b the size of the local batch (Batch), E the number of iteration cycles (epoch), the α learning rate, and the $\nabla L(\bullet, \bullet)$ gradient optimization function;

Output: Parameters of the local model ω_i.

(1) $LocalUpdate(k, \omega_i)$
(2) $\pi \leftarrow$ will be $D_k b$ split by size
(3) for $b \in \pi do$
(4) $\omega_i \leftarrow \omega_i - \alpha \nabla L(\omega_i, b)$
(5) end for
(6) end for
(7) Output the updated parameters ω_i

It should be noted that in Algorithm 1, after each round of parameter aggregation, the central server needs to determine whether it needs to continue to execute the federated average learning algorithm.

3 Implementation of Federated Integration Algorithm Based on Deep Neural Network

3.1 The Basic Idea of the Algorithm

In order to guarantee the safety of the model transmission process, the authors suggest encrypting the initial global model DNN using the RSA encryption technique before sending it to each data source in the federated integration algorithm based on deep neural networks. The safety of the data used to construct the model may be guaranteed by proper training. What follows is a breakdown of the algorithm's procedures:

The first step is for each data source and a trusted third party to construct a 256-byte key pair using the RSA encryption algorithm, send the public key to the trusted third party, and store the secret key locally. Emond, using the public key, encrypt the initial global model DNN network held by a trusted third party and send it to each data source; after receiving the encrypted network, each data source decrypts it using its own private key and trains the DNN to optimize the number of hidden layers and nodes. Make use of the local DNN model that best suits each data source;

The third step is for each data source to encrypt its local model parameters using the public key and send them to an impartial third party;

Fourth, the neutral party decrypts using the secret key, integrates the local models using either the stacking integration algorithm, the voting integration algorithm, or the averaging method, and chooses the best integration technique based on the integration results;

Finally, step 5 employs the ensemble mode chosen in step 4 to iteratively refine the local model until the precision of the revised global model satisfies the requirements.

3.2 Description of the Algorithm

The algorithm designed using the above algorithm flow is as follows:

Input: dataset $\{Di\}ni = 1$, i represents the number of data sources, DNN: f

Output: RSA generate key pair P_i, p_i, P_k, p_i, original global model f, local model h_i, updated global model h.

Generate secret key

for $i = 0$ to n

$P_i = RSA(x)$; $p_i = RSA(x)$; //this process is for each data sources,

x represents a random number, P_i represents the public key generated by RSA algorithm, p_i represents the private key generated by RSA algorithm

$$P_i = RSA(x); \quad p_i = RSA(x); \tag{2}$$

end for

Model training stage

$$y = P_i(f); \tag{3}$$

$$f = p_i(y); \tag{4}$$

for $i = 0$ to n

$$m_i = f\_train(D_i)$$
$$\{h_i\}_{i=1}^n f\{max\_score(\{m_{x,y}\}_{x=1,y=25}^{x=10,y=200})_i\}_{i=1}^n \tag{5}$$

end for

Integration model

for $i = 0$ to n

$$Y_i = Pk(hi); \quad h_i = pk(Yi); \tag{6}$$

$$h = stacking(\{h_i\}_{i=1}^n), h = voting(\{h_i\}_{i=1}^n), h = averag4(\{h_i\}_{i=1}^n) \tag{7}$$

end for

3.3 Performance Analysis

Compared with the traditional data fusion training model, the federated ensemble algorithm based on deep neural network proposed in this paper not only improves the accuracy but also improves the security of the model and data.

3.4 Complexity Analysis of Algorithms

The complexity of the algorithm in this paper is the sum of the complexity of the RSA encryption algorithm, the complexity of optimizing the local model, and the complexity of integrating multiple local models into an updated global model, that is, the time complexity is $O\left(\Sigma_l^D M_l^2 K_l^2 C_{l-1} C_l + n\right)$, where D is the network Depth, l represents l hidden layers, Cl represents the number of output channels of the lth layer, n is the complexity of the encryption algorithm; the space complexity is $O\left(\Sigma_{l=1}^D K_l^2 C_{l-1} C_l + \Sigma_{l=1}^D M^2 C_l\right)$ [33]. In fact, when the DNN model is used for initialization and the stacking integration algorithm is used for integration, the time complexity and space complexity of this algorithm are inevitably higher than those of the traditional data fusion algorithm [34].

3.5 Security Analysis of Algorithms

In this study, we use a federated learning architecture and ensemble learning to inform our algorithm. Due to the fact that the federated integration algorithm is trained using data from each data source, it meets the fundamental requirements that the data is not local and that the model locates the data, thereby providing some kind of security. At the level of the model, it may be roughly broken down into three sections: To ensure the security of the model during the model transmission process, the trusted third party uses a 256-byte key pair generated by the RSA encryption algorithm to encrypt the initial global model with the public key and transmit it to each data source; each data source then uses its private key to decrypt the initial global model and train it on its local data. To guarantee data privacy during model training, it is always stored locally; then, during model integration, each data source encrypts the local model using the public key and sends it to a trusted third party [35]. Different integration techniques are used to integrate the local model parameters after the third party decrypts them using the private key, guaranteeing the security of the model during the integration stage.

4 Experimental Analysis

4.1 Experimental Setup

The algorithms presented in this study are written in the Python programming language and implemented using the pycharm package. InterrCore i5-4200M CPU, 2.50 GHz processor, 8 GB of RAM, and Windows 10 are the operating systems for the lab's experiments. In terms of experimental data, we use the MNIST dataset, wine dataset, letter dataset, and digits dataset downloaded from UCI for experiments [36].

4.2 Experimental Analysis

When processing data from multiple sources, it is common practice to send all of the data to an impartial party for training [37]. After that, the Sigmoid activation function is applied, and the learning rate is reduced to 0.001 in the DNN network parameters so that the effect of the total number of hidden layers and nodes on the algorithm's accuracy can be investigated [38]. As can be seen in Fig. 1, the optimal number of nodes per layer

Table 1. DNN model changes in different layers under different data sets

Number of hidden layers	Mnist accuracy	Digits accuracy	Letter accuracy	Wine accuracy
1	0.935	0.840	0.977	0.492
2	0.955	0.864	0.979	0.501
3	0.963	0.875	0.978	0.501
4	0.964	0.870	0.978	0.504
5	0.965	0.850	0.978	0.505
6	0.968	0.827	0.978	0.509
7	0.969	0.802	0.977	0.507
8	0.967	0.776	0.976	0.510
9	0.968	0.735	0.975	0.513
10	0.969	0.701	0.975	0.515

Table 2. DNN model changes in different nodes under different data sets

Number of hidden layer nodes	Mnist accuracy	Digits accuracy	Letter accuracy	Wine accuracy
25	0.946	0.688	0.967	0.510
50	0.961	0.775	0.976	0.510
75	0.965	0.825	0.977	0.510
100	0.965	0.840	0.978	0.509
125	0.966	0.852	0.978	0.509
150	0.967	0.851	0.980	0.507
175	0.966	0.850	0.979	0.510
200	0.967	0.850	0.981	0.510

is 25 when the learning rate is 0.001. The effect of varying the number of hidden layers and nodes on the DNN model over the course of the same number of training iterations.

As can be observed in Table 1, the DNN model's performance varies among datasets. The DNN model's classification performance on the MIST data set improves with an increasing number of hidden layers, and ultimately it begins to converge. As a result, the DNN model for the digits dataset has five hidden layers, whereas the MNIST dataset has six. Performance in classification initially improves with more hidden layers, then worsens as the number of layers grows. When there are three hidden layers, the model's accuracy is at its best, and convergence is most likely to occur. In cases when there are more than three layers, a visible model is produced at The number of hidden layers is fixed at three for the digits dataset due to the over-fitting phenomenon's negative effect on accuracy; the DNN model's classification performance improves rapidly at low hidden-layer counts for the letters dataset. It's been going downhill recently. When there are two hidden layers, the model's accuracy is at its best, and it has a tendency to converge. Over-fitting occurs when there are more than two layers, which leads to a less reliable model. For the wine data set, with the current configuration of 2 hidden layers, the DNN model's classification performance improves at first and then begins to converge when the number of hidden layers is increased. When there are nine hidden layers, the model's accuracy is at its highest. Setting the number of hidden layers in the wine dataset to 9 results in the maximum degree and the model's tendency to converge.

After training the DNN model with a given data set and finding the optimal number of hidden layers, we conduct further experiments to examine the effect of varying the number of nodes in the hidden layers on classification accuracy. The results of these experiments are summarized in Table 2.

Based on Table 2, we can infer that the DNN model's performance will change depending on the data used. For the MNIST data set, the classification performance of the DNN model initially improves when the number of hidden layers is set to 6, and then begins to converge when the number of hidden layer nodes is increased. Once the number of nodes in the hidden layer reaches 150, the model converges on an answer. In the case of the digits dataset, the classification performance of the DNN model initially improves when using a depth of 3 hidden layers and then begins to converge as the depth is increased. When there are 100 nodes in the hidden layer, For the letter data set, when the number of hidden layers is set to 2, the DNN model causes its classification performance to rise first and then tends to converge with the increase of the number of hidden layer nodes, and when the hidden layer nodes are 175, the model tends to converge; for the wine data set, when the number of hidden layers is set to 9, the DNN model causes its classification performance to increase first and then tends to converge with the increase of the number of hidden layer nodes. The model tends to converge when the value is 175. It is clear from the above experimental findings that the technique of integrating data into a training model has varied impacts on different data sets, as do the effects of different layers and node counts on the output of the neural network. The neural network's mean after 100 iterations in this experiment was Tables 3, 4, 5, 6 and 7 detail the results of testing the DNN model on the Mnist, digits, letters, and wine datasets while varying the number of layers and nodes.

Table 3. Result change table of the Mnist data set in different layers and different numbers of nodes %

Layers	Number of nodes							
	25	50	75	100	125	150	175	200
1	90.85	93.99	94.59	93.89	94.56	94.83	94.85	94.55
2	93.85	95.86	95.56	95.25	96.78	96.23	96.88	96.77
3	94.78	96.22	96.78	96.85	97.85	96.84	96.54	96.55

(continued)

Table 3. (*continued*)

Layers	Number of nodes							
	25	50	75	100	125	150	175	200
4	94.55	96.55	96.56	97.05	97.95	97.59	96.45	97.69
5	95.77	96.86	96.52	97.05	97.56	97.85	97.65	97.58
6	95.87	96.85	96.86	97.55	97.58	97.55	97.56	97.86
7	95.85	96.26	96.55	97.88	97.75	97.75	97.78	97.78
8	95.69	96.86	96.23	97.66	97.82	96.89	97.61	97.14
9	95.56	96.56	97.87	97.85	97.84	97.25	97.25	97.86
10	95.85	96.82	97.89	97.85	97.78	97.89	97.33	97.55

It As shown in Table 3, the DNN model achieves a maximum accuracy of 97.45% when the number of hidden layers is 6 and the number of nodes is 150.

Data from MNIST, digits, letters, and wine are randomly split in half, with each half representing a different data source. In this study, we partitioned each data set into three categories, one for each of the three data generators. Figure 1 shows the public key being used to send the DNN network's initialization parameters to each data source; Fig. 2 shows this same network being encrypted and trained on each data source using the private key; and Tables 4, 5 and 6 illustrate how the local model on each data source is optimized. The data in Tables 4, 5 and 6 represent the accuracy of the DNN model after being run 100 times, ensuring the reliability of the experimental results.

MIIBIjANBgkqhkiG9w0BAQEFAAOCAQ8AMIIBC gKCAQEAwPutWbsVwbCHRfYgQluxHPwYPobzW +ANSkv3nL26b3sXI98E3oeQgL6NvU5xWBORuPjb 8Zg4TW3bZAFGhe6+2kHHZ+odk6eA6Eei2bmeapk zulelXxFnt2Jaq9tlKG2psfiNFm4oPbQcg7bk+L8Bxn 2+0KVCNU5g0t5RHGcpDXoKbUVqQ1muXfLV5x q9BhWfc8vHucTC72c4S1gSPJIBpLMzuyd3Ol+AhD MlgktuSTlpT1tcdxyZq1obnFvVM79op3gSVl1Lzkex 2qagBz7lyqWAA5gV56eSYxnYETZ1tkAflHJgBbw A6gMtVGn3drkl57e1B9JEtUozXsykO1wIDAQAB | MIIBIjANBgkqhkiG9w0BAQEFAAOCAQ8AMIIBC gKCAQEAvOYYFo+li5mWaxgbTmEklrp6giiUSE42 NUk5Ycf8eHJVRtinhrDg4qJcs2pc+P+CkcF5uQUK5 zrdCdzRsSp5Vlmh90lIdkWTstu0sEaZHqkWwZOXR 2MI75F5RKY3q60JU5mwkE4v6RnbZPyE1BdRjJy Mwl2pRpunnZgRIDV1DAWeEFrd44bSmNqsISqaag Nw5JEqFo+jEMWoOrnl1P7cTKOHrETXualEaChN HlztrgJCYGMlqjA85Ful63EJkYsTk9Fg2SSMIKpgK 5KQBwo010bgBhnJM39s6ksX8sXgZOW6hMdHtvut 7hyxYbN5oL2tqlCnIg6jatYmZvpdiqwIDAQAB

Fig. 1. Change of public key generated by RSA encryption algorithm

MIIEvAIBADANBgkqhkiG9w0BAQEFAASCBKYwggSiAgEAAoIBAQDA+6IZuxXBsIdF9iBCW7EeBg+hvNt4A1KSecvbpvexcj3wTeh5CAvee29TnFYE5G4+NvxmDj9Nbdv9kAUaF7r7nQedn6h2Tp4DoR6LZuZ5qmTO4h6VfEWe3YIqr2bgobmnx+H0Wbig9t8yDtuT4vwl8iIb7QpUJ11TmDS3IIEeZykNeggtRWpDWa5d8tXnGr0GiFZ9zy8z5zML.vZzhl.WBI8kgGksz07f3e4jHCEMyWCS25JOWlPW1x3HJmrWhuzW9Uzv2inefdJWXUvOR7IJapqAHPuXKpYADmBXnp5Jj6idgRNnW2QB+1lcmAFvADqAy1UsfdZuSXnt7UH0kS1SjNezKQ7XAgMBAAECggEAL7oOlTJmdZfSPxmeWxeRS2qPla8NtbgJjqpABm7CFeImfWqmMQ0rdlwRTY8TzNRvWyVkaPvMZ+snhfnAdiZusCp4DkZN14fs0yEKfSOC876s5igfXKAhAnAqGoptb4MNuXiQSVTyIMlAe1.ebIDZyOSHWfFhA1qR1.xWsv+QUlLU8asi+UV4PqYvK8snQEkyoPmuw6M5XAtK8Ttk3ZeNfcptid0yDM8wREYUnp6sq8ml.SWBQbYNn2Bb49hTW8ucjIZtnJejhuYslGY3jFfhAh603DCYgWb6QbNsx6tA8qwkWyaYefRsMF48H1DEGdv5fmyuVv4tXZFbHSvHpqUAQKBgQDkWJ+PUZzEZge577hrBkC28uNEvWAiFZrvvkSPTSMrdqX0rlnxUq3fxwnzZwO+7erPFHg+Hs0Zz1H6pQEBa3l.fjhDo4tPacZoW27y+aloe0F1pYmVRQloRQpkQrkGstngJZKEyfKRhq7m6cFQaF9EI.VtfZoMsQ3I.C+d666ONwKBgQDYWrl.jrQO+pn3Vo0Fcsu39h3dRFQxt3Lh+vcKpBFrcMyAoF4bQnjfLJNh01NvyWYGWQWJsKTjtcxdm9p+bAsMkTy2wJrfBj5jkhqsJ9w38WKdh7gGP0nwSIAxxzTXyJifnnqYCVyzowx3fnsycHZ3IlrT6iw9alPPLnFu40YQKBgEJm+BOvnjRvrhSDC6Uf+BudFk4J7lPtAGN5kbQmbubb3VYmkBExJdSJ+NJYOj3iQ0fO38rfNNP9SfKZI.enMnE+s1.mGh39rkbhDKr0xTK+19qIN4RfNFaVV44N8r7rnpYgMb2MfEnatD8rCLmp5OSQK2XYSwbbY1emSrhnP5dXAoGAFSNP5ZQUtX34oYQgRROxuah3grfIv0GjKqbcdUyoeBD4tFYHtvGebel2mdN0JEwyziNFUWtZJKEiBe5Ykiz1GUAaiWM6eW9YJ226Nin2v99CYpaZrXW323M9sQqCB2HqnALVrEztelhuUtnMaOhP3XoBpT1jBEP0X4trGSECgYAJZ2WDfKiiaqnTRaAqof9X1Ibw17qm0Gmq72SlaSVyQH0AGQzWTpq4LJ9FCop3SJ7iPSYouRQPGIB3XIEEnIQCaVdJmLO3tWq8tST19JzMgijw9SZFT7PhxvOowXNHWyx5XTjLWSKFMkdYI4gEEDVzc7I9EN+3dxG42I3YUmsg==

MIIEvgIBADANBgkqhkiG9w0BAQEFAASCBKgwggSkAgEAAoIBAQC85hgWj6WLmZZrGBtOYSSWunqCKJRITjY1STlhxx4clVG2KeGoODiolyzaIz44KRwXm5BQrn0t0L93NGxKnlWWalI35Uh2RZOy27SwRpkeqRbBk5dIfYwjvkXlHpjemQlTmbCQTipGdkdTUIFIGMoLzCXaIGm6edmBGUNXUMIBZ4QWi3jbKY2qwkKppqADDkkSoWj6MQtag6ueXUtzMo4esRNeSogRoKE0eX02oAkJgYyWqMDzkW4jrcQmRixOT0WDZJIyUqmArkpAHCjTXRuAGGckzfLzqSxfyx.e8kr5bqEx0c2+63ulHLFhu3mgva2qUKciDqNq1iZm+I2Kr AgMBAAECggEADIeKK3yFs4PFeWcI8KL65VCLL3T5WO5viAuuVbEJKwgSZfm7REwaXfxhCkK760rAPXV+lgtxOrw8xvBgOubUIBIzf06KEuY8jMGL86FLKMH4dPCQOTj1bBzL.b91IzjI0BRF2CW6AEB4ciiUII8ybIzjgtr7byz9PGS4nohSuizrtl+EPQEZuvFuLzXTwhl IS3Y6L+QSLILz7R3Zrds9BFcEvBnuz1zpF2II40iP7gVm07BGRt+Gmyvmxfdz4dGiGNfeGq2jV22oVpCcdBJV0nXi4MNq4DN7L+nQ5Cg8Osw5nG6QtUkpcvexSkNIvXFoyag9UfQ2pdhc6VQjl+TAK4QKBgQD666bHpDflho9NpydIAi1qhgZmpMy5O0OS1Y726j6hSasi.0e8uXx7qVCAuVrHN7d2nSIHCSaFlpWupkjUUYQ9KIkzLV5tXyiDm0UMDhDYr6olCgsPn95dDqkT20wlzvNBYX48KEzNjTH2RvFPB1xmqai4DPx5QssDPfe7gIJocwKBgQDAuj74F7d0fI9nzz0SGN72iiCzovx0Uwz7MdiksIUKDdQ5Xm+iKi5ugHQ2d8UwavONpCivraTziRnZ.uanx3f5D2IxcULwA0hW3Lm0VIALNSRI7fxJcV38wfimlsqvzl.bpFI8YvKycuv5tZVRIUmfr-C4pLeVR2a34RVxQzIDaDmEPkQKBgQ00Epdf+DdwxS2FRHojHLmwC7PAQBjfStdZZrUa7EbQGz2we8rd6exsGk0SjSvQoEmp7qIqeP2ugxjF2BE2ISeC1NYOITfiuOaiYHizCHM7pL.Tb0RaIWveswcQKgrmx.1Xuez71BwuTjkgbJIdGDxJRfmi7Ybi9o5yBtz5XCTvdAc3QKBgQCX17V1MX35GRE5YdMi6wk7GQkjOoY4AjTiX+HlFTqVwgvKdhJ1fIv1qqFv5BD94M2W6lblpwXDiKLudhUtDTYH1eFsI8nK+2eE2PRClosUH99BQ1NgIcmatCkutP7KbZwxnMvhq0XgH8kukopX9NfL+kgip5PkXBkkIqxD+A26T42aQKBgFsqZsAL36PISHpxDQ6tZfIWLpvRhSsGigMVQc5m31VkWVgpfo8UOlLJ191u90KFJgEXwWuWQuQD1PISfvXSxQxioLzsIsZ.VkQEBpA3eWwHAhc03xxSOfj2BInvF4y+C5+rw8TxIfaw7DPIKniC+2kzof0RMPSXuOi6wGZVW

Fig. 2. Change of private key generated by RSA encryption algorithm

Table 4. Results of different layers and different node numbers of data source 1 in the MNIST data set %

Layers	Number of nodes							
	25	50	75	100	125	150	175	200
1	87.52	90.28	90.82	92.25	91.44	91.93	92.80	92.91
2	86.22	91.87	90.52	91.54	91.30	91.81	91.93	92.78
3	88.45	89.33	89.23	89.68	90.88	90.90	91.47	91.90
4	89.29	90.88	89.73	89.45	90.23	90.07	90.34	91.07
5	89.63	90.88	90.38	90.28	90.97	90.43	90.49	90.50
6	90.25	92.25	92.38	92.82	91.19	91.19	91.84	91.40
7	90.75	93.78	93.35	93.28	93.35	93.01	93.20	93.70
8	91.85	93.86	94.25	94.52	93.70	93.90	94.17	93.79
9	91.68	93.25	94.45	94.88	94.07	93.94	94.05	94.30
10	91.55	93.56	94.28	94.88	94.13	94.04	94.04	94.43

It can be seen from Table 4 that when the number of hidden layers is 10 and the number of nodes is 200, the accuracy of the DNN model on data source 1 is the highest, reaching 95.54%.

Table 5. Results of different layers and different node numbers of data source 2 in the MNIST data set %

Layers	Number of nodes							
	25	50	75	100	125	150	175	200
1	87.22	89.82	91.30	92.53	92.00	92.28	93.28	92.72

(continued)

Table 5. (*continued*)

Layers	Number of nodes							
	25	50	75	100	125	150	175	200
2	84.32	89.02	91.17	91.60	92.41	92.86	92.18	92.62
3	89.11	90.29	88.88	90.90	91.40	92.28	92.67	92.87
4	89.94	90.40	89.36	89.48	89.78	90.33	91.01	91.42
5	89.62	90.72	91.02	90.43	91.07	90.62	91.29	91.71
6	90.29	91.60	92.33	92.17	92.12	92.47	92.72	92.88
7	91.29	92.82	92.92	92.61	92.87	93.14	93.39	93.26
8	91.25	92.14	92.72	92.82	93.30	93.71	93.81	94.21
9	91.03	92.15	93.22	93.79	93.52	93.49	94.05	94.33
10	91.53	92.59	93.33	93.29	94.09	94.32	94.27	94.27

It can be seen from Table 5 that when the number of hidden layers is 6 and the number of nodes is 200, the accuracy of the DNN model on data source 2 is the highest, reaching 95.44%.

Table 6. Results of different layers and different node numbers of data source 3 in the MNIST data set %

Layers	Number of nodes							
	25	50	75	100	125	150	175	200
1	87.78	90.28	90.24	91.42	91.70	92.24	92.47	92.70
2	87.94	89.19	90.47	90.71	91.40	91.94	92.08	92.42
3	89.67	89.91	88.92	90.44	90.48	91.10	91.46	91.46
4	89.44	89.89	89.70	89.74	90.01	90.42	90.44	90.12
5	89.70	90.80	90.90	90.84	90.94	90.29	90.40	90.20
6	90.45	91.40	91.55	91.07	91.44	91.14	91.72	91.92
7	90.80	91.75	92.22	92.59	92.70	92.57	94.07	94.79
8	90.05	91.94	92.79	94.04	94.19	94.24	94.44	94.02
9	90.64	92.46	92.84	94.72	94.97	94.87	94.74	94.68
10	90.44	94.02	94.40	94.72	94.64	94.94	94.17	94.94

Table 6 shows that the DNN model's accuracy on data source 3 peaks at 95.27% when the number of hidden layers is 10 and the number of nodes is 175. The results of applying the DNN model to the digits dataset from three distinct data sources, with varying numbers of layers and nodes, are shown in Tables 7, 8 and 9. The data in each table is obtained using DNN models at a 100 percent confidence level to assure accuracy. The mean of the fractional precisions.

Tables 7, 8 and 9 reveal that the DNN model on data source 1 achieves a maximum accuracy of 97.81% with 10 hidden layers and 150 nodes; with 8 hidden layers and 100 nodes, the model achieves an accuracy of 97.09%. The DNN model achieves a maximum accuracy of 97.72 percent on data source 2 when the number of nodes is 200; it achieves a maximum accuracy of 97.72 percent on data source 3 when the number of hidden layers is 2 and the number of nodes is 200. 97.62% was the highest percentage.

Table 7. Changes in the results of different layers and different node numbers of data source 1 in the digits data set %

Layers	Number of nodes							
	25	50	75	100	125	150	175	200
1	93.48	95.19	95.95	95.95	95.95	95.38	97.04	95.95
2	94.23	95.85	95.38	97.32	95.57	95.57	97.23	95.77
3	94.05	95.57	97.23	97.13	97.13	97.04	97.32	97.51
4	94.42	96.00	96.77	96.48	96.67	96.96	96.00	97.32
5	94.27	96.00	96.77	97.42	96.82	97.18	97.01	97.01
6	93.00	94.33	97.04	96.38	94.81	97.32	97.32	97.32
7	92.43	94.33	96.10	96.86	97.04	97.13	97.04	97.61
8	91.30	94.81	96.19	96.86	96.00	96.96	97.61	97.42
9	92.91	93.39	95.38	95.48	95.95	97.04	95.77	97.32
10	90.72	93.39	94.33	97.04	97.32	97.80	95.85	95.45

Table 8. Changes in the results of different layers and different node numbers of data source 2 in the digits data set %

Layers	Number of nodes							
	25	50	75	100	125	150	175	200
1	94.33	94.81	96.29	96.10	96.10	97.04	96.67	96.10
2	93.96	96.10	94.06	94.81	96.77	96.77	97.61	96.67
3	95.00	95.19	95.00	95.57	97.04	97.51	97.04	95.77
4	94.14	94.52	95.19	95.85	95.29	97.42	95.29	97.04
5	93.58	94.90	95.29	95.38	95.77	97.04	95.57	95.77
6	93.48	94.04	95.10	95.00	97.04	97.04	95.95	95.85

(continued)

Table 8. (*continued*)

Layers	Number of nodes							
	25	50	75	100	125	150	175	200
7	93.39	94.04	95.19	95.57	95.77	95.00	97.04	97.32
8	92.91	94.04	94.90	96.86	96.77	97.23	96.38	97.71
9	91.97	94.06	96.29	94.71	97.42	97.04	96.38	97.04
10	90.82	93.68	94.71	96.10	96.77	96.29	96.86	96.77

Table 9. Changes in the results of different layers and different node numbers of data source 3 in the digits data set

Layers	Number of nodes							
	25	50	75	100	125	150	175	200
1	93.00	93.29	93.20	96.38	96.00	96.48	96.29	96.29
2	94.62	96.00	94.90	94.90	94.90	96.10	97.42	97.61
3	93.77	96.00	96.00	96.00	96.86	96.77	96.29	96.96
4	92.81	93.87	94.80	93.87	95.48	95.00	97.04	95.77
5	92.43	93.48	93.95	95.85	94.71	95.10	95.00	95.95
6	92.52	93.39	94.04	95.85	95.48	95.00	95.10	95.57
7	91.49	93.77	95.00	94.90	95.00	95.29	97.13	95.57
8	91.01	93.20	94.62	96.19	94.42	96.77	96.48	97.13
9	91.87	93.29	93.39	94.71	96.00	96.67	96.00	94.90
10	91.01	93.68	94.23	94.33	96.19	96.77	96.29	96.48

4.3   Experimental Summary

The traditional multi-source data processing technology is to collect multi-source data for training, optimize the number of hidden layers and nodes, and improve the accuracy of the model. For the MNIST, digits, letter, and wine datasets, using traditional multi-source data processing techniques, the optimized model accuracy reaches 97.45%, 90.49%, 98.25%, and 52.91%, respectively. The federated ensemble algorithm based on deep learning proposed in this paper is to transmit the DNN model of initialization parameters to each data source using a 256-byte public key, each data source is decrypted with a private key, and then the DNN model of initialization parameters is stored in different sizes. For training on the data set, optimize the number of layers and nodes of the DNN model. For the MNIST data set, the number of hidden layers after optimization is 10, 9, and 10 respectively, and the number of nodes is 200, 200, and 175. The accuracies of the post-local model are 95.44%, 95.44%, and 95.27% respectively; for the digits dataset, the optimized hidden layers are 10, 8, and 2, and the number of nodes is 150,

200, and 200. The accuracy of the optimized local model is 97.82%, 97.72%, 97.62%. For the letter dataset, when the number of hidden layers after optimization is 2, 6, and 5, and the number of nodes is 200, 175, and 175, the accuracy of the optimized local model is 91.86%, 91.27%, and 91.78%. For the wine data set, the number of hidden layers after optimization is 10, 8, and 8, and the number of nodes is 25, 50, and 50. The accuracy of the optimized local model is 52.59%, 52.67%, and 51.79%. Then, the stacking integration algorithm and voting integration algorithm are used to integrate the local model parameters on different data sets. For the MNIST digits, letter, and wine data sets, the accuracy obtained by using stacking integration is higher than that of voting integration and average method integration. And the model variance of stacking ensemble is smaller than the model variance of voting ensemble. Compared with the traditional multi-source data processing technology and the federated average algorithm, the accuracy of the model established by this algorithm is guaranteed, and the security of the model and data is improved.

5 Conclusion

In this work, we present a distributed deep learning ensemble method. From the point of view of the model type, the security of the model is improved by encrypting the DNN model with initial parameters and transmitting it to each data source. By fine-tuning the DNN model's hidden layer The accuracy of the local model is enhanced by increasing the number of layers and nodes and by integrating the optimized local model using the stacking integration algorithm and the voting integration method, both of which take into consideration the security of multi-source data. On the assumption of verifying the model's correctness, the subsequent study applies the standard privacy protection technology to local model protection, therefore bolstering multi-source data security.

Acknowledgement. This research was made possible with funding from the National Natural Science Foundation of China (No. 61862051), the Science and Technology Foundation of Guizhou Province (No. ZK[2022]549, No. [2019]1299), the Top-notch Talent Program of of Guizhou Province (No. KY[2018]080), the Natural Science Foundation of Education of Guizhou Province (No. [2019]203), and the Funds of Qiannan Normal University for Nationalities (No. qnsy2018003, No. qnsy2019rc09, No. qnsy2018JS013, No. qnsyrc201715).

References

1. Hai, T., Zhou, J., Muranaka, K.: An efficient fuzzy-logic based MPPT controller for grid-connected PV systems by farmland fertility optimization algorithm. Optik 169636 (2022)
2. Tao, H., et al.: SDN-assisted technique for traffic control and information execution in vehicular adhoc networks. Comput. Electr. Eng. 108108 (2022)
3. McMahan, B., Moore, E., Ramage, D., Hampson, S., Arcas, B.A.: Communication-efficient learning of deep networks from decentralized data. In: Artificial Intelligence and Statistics, pp. 1273–1282. PMLR, April 2017
4. Konečný, J., McMahan, H.B., Yu, F.X., Richtárik, P., Suresh, A.T., Bacon, D.: Federated learning: strategies for improving communication efficiency. arXiv preprint arXiv:1610.05492 (2016)

5. Hai, T., Said, N.M., Zain, J.M., Sajadi, S.M., Mahmoud, M.Z., Aybar, H.Ş.: ANN usefulness in building enhanced with PCM: efficacy of PCM installation location. J. Build. Eng. 104914 (2022)

6. Yang, Q.: Challenges of GDPR to AI and countermeasures based on federal transfer learning. Commun. Chin. Assoc. Artif. Intell. **8**, 1–8 (2018)

7. Yang, Q., Liu, Y., Chen, T., Tong, Y.: Federated machine learning: concept and applications. ACM Trans. Intell. Syst. Technol. (TIST) **10**(2), 1–19 (2019)

8. Hai, T., et al.: Thermal analysis of building benefits from PCM and heat recovery-installing PCM to boost energy consumption reduction. J. Build. Eng. 104982 (2022)

9. Wang, S., et al.: Adaptive federated learning in resource constrained edge computing systems. IEEE J. Sel. Areas Commun. **37**(6), 1205–1221 (2019)

10. Liu, Y., Liu, Y., Liu, Z., et al.: Federated Forest [J/OL], 23 June 2020. https://arxiv.org/pdf/1905.10053v1.pdf

11. Hai, T., Alsharif, S., Dhahad, H.A., Attia, E.A., Shamseldin, M.A., Ahmed, A.N.: The evolutionary artificial intelligence-based algorithm to find the minimum GHG emission via the integrated energy system using the MSW as fuel in a waste heat recovery plant. Sustain. Energy Technol. Assess. **53**, 102531 (2022)

12. Sharma, S., Chen, K.: Privacy-preserving boosting with random linear classifiers. In: Proceedings of the 2018 ACM SIGSAC Conference on Computer and Communications Security, pp. 2294–2296, October 2018

13. Sun, C., Shrivastava, A., Singh, S., Gupta, A.: Revisiting unreasonable effectiveness of data in deep learning era. In: Proceedings of the IEEE International Conference on Computer Vision, pp. 843–852 (2017)

14. Kim, H., Park, J., Bennis, M., Kim, S.L.: On-device federated learning via blockchain and its latency analysis. arXiv preprint arXiv:1808.03949 (2018)

15. Hai, T., Zhou, J., Srividhya, S.R., Jain, S.K., Young, P., Agrawal, S.: BVFLEMR: an integrated federated learning and blockchain technology for cloud-based medical records recommendation system. J. Cloud Comput. **11**(1), 1–11 (2022)

16. Li, S., Cheng, Y., Liu, Y., Wang, W., Chen, T.: Abnormal client behavior detection in federated learning. arXiv preprint arXiv:1910.09933 (2019)

17. Zhun, L.G., Liu, Z.J., Liu, Z.J., et al.: Deep leakage from gradients [DB/OL], 23 June 2020. https://arxiv.org/pdf/1906.08935

18. Liu, Z.Y., Zhang, S.F., Liu, Y., et al.: Data augmentation method based on image gradient. J. Appl. Sci. **39**(2), 302–311 (2021)

19. Hai, T., et al.: Design, modeling and multi-objective techno-economic optimization of an integrated supercritical Brayton cycle with solar power tower for efficient hydrogen production. Sustain. Energy Technol. Assess. **53**, 102599 (2022)

20. Gao, H., Huang, W., Yang, X.: Applying probabilistic model checking to path planning in an intelligent transportation system using mobility trajectories and their statistical data. Intell. Autom. Soft Comput. **25**(3), 547–559 (2019)

21. Gao, H., Huang, W., Duan, Y., Yang, X., Zou, Q.: Research on cost-driven services composition in an uncertain environment. J. Internet Technol. **20**(3), 755–769 (2019)

22. Hai, T., et al.: Innovative proposal of energy scheme based on biogas from digester for producing clean and sustainable electricity, cooling and heating: proposal and multi-criteria optimization. Sustain. Energy Technol. Assess. **53**, 102618 (2022)

23. Preuveneers, D., Rimmer, V., Tsingenopoulos, I., Spooren, J., Joosen, W., Ilie-Zudor, E.: Chained anomaly detection models for federated learning: an intrusion detection case study. Appl. Sci. **8**(12), 2663 (2018)

24. Brisimi, T.S., Chen, R., Mela, T., Olshevsky, A., Paschalidis, I.C., Shi, W.: Federated learning of predictive models from federated electronic health records. Int. J. Med. Inform. **112**, 59–67 (2018)

25. Hai, T., et al.: The novel integration of biomass gasification plant to generate efficient power, and the waste recovery to generate cooling and freshwater: a demonstration of 4E analysis and multi-criteria optimization. Sustain. Energy Technol. Assess. **53**, 102588 (2022)

26. Zhang, W., et al.: Multi-source data fusion using deep learning for smart refrigerators. Comput. Ind. **95**, 15–21 (2018)

27. Lee, J., Sun, J., Wang, F., Wang, S., Jun, C.H., Jiang, X.: Privacy-preserving patient similarity learning in a federated environment: development and analysis. JMIR Med. Inform. **6**(2), e7744 (2018)

28. Hai, T., Delgarm, N., Wang, D., Karimi, M.H.: Energy, economic, and environmental (3 E) examinations of the indirect-expansion solar heat pump water heater system: a simulation-oriented performance optimization and multi-objective decision-making. J. Build. Eng. **60**, 105068 (2022)

29. Shen, G., Han, X., Zhou, J., Ruan, Z., Pan, Q.: Research on intelligent analysis and depth fusion of multi-source traffic data. IEEE Access **6**, 59329–59335 (2018)

30. Liu, J., Li, T., Xie, P., Du, S., Teng, F., Yang, X.: Urban big data fusion based on deep learning: an overview. Inf. Fusion **53**, 123–133 (2020)

31. Rivest, R., Shamir, A., Adleman, L.: A method for obtaining digital signatures and public-key cryptosystems. Commun. ACM **21**(2), 120–126 (1978)

32. Hai, T., et al.: An archetypal determination of mobile cloud computing for emergency applications using decision tree algorithm. J. Cloud Comput. (2022)

33. Lou, Y., Shi, R.H., Cao, L.X.: Security authentic cation model of session initiation protocol based on strong authentication technology. J. Comput. Appl. **30**(10), 2332–2335 (2006)

34. Hai, T., et al.: Neural network-based optimization of hydrogen fuel production energy system with proton exchange electrolyzer supported nanomaterial. Fuel **332**, 125827 (2023)

35. Yang, D.N., Xie, X.R., Ji, Z.K., Ji, W.W.: A privacy-preserving federated learning framework. Appl. Electron. Technol. (05), 94–97+103 (2022). https://doi.org/10.16157/j.issn.0258-7998. 211828

36. Lu, Y., Zheng, S.Z.: A comparative study of stacking learning and general integration methods [J/OL]. Highlights Sci. Paper Online **11**(4), 372–379 (2018)

37. Shi, X.C., Xie, C.L., Wang, Y.H.: Nuclear power plant fault diagnosis based on genetic-RBF neural network. J. Mar. Sci. Appl. **5**(3), 57–62 (2006)

38. Tao, H., et al.: Ranked-based mechanism-assisted Biogeography optimization: application of global optimization problems. Adv. Eng. Softw. **174**, 103301 (2022)

39. Lloret-Talavera, G., et al.: Enabling homomorphically encrypted inference for large DNN models. IEEE Trans. Comput. **71**(5), 1145–1155 (2021)

40. Susilo, W., Tonien, J., Yang, G.: Divide and capture: an improved cryptanalysis of the encryption standard algorithm RSA. Comput. Stand. Interf. **74**, 103470 (2021)

Performance Comparison of Feature Selection Methods for Prediction in Medical Data

Nur Hidayah Mohd Khalid, Amelia Ritahani Ismail[(✉)], Normaziah Abdul Aziz, and Amir Aatieff Amir Hussin

Department of Computer Science, Kulliyyah of Information and Communication Technology, International Islamic University Malaysia, PO. Box 10, 50728 Kuala Lumpur, Malaysia
amelia@iium.edu.my

Abstract. Along with technological advancement, the application of machine learning algorithms in industry, notably in the medical field, has grown and progressed quickly. Medical databases commonly contain a lot of information about the medical histories of the patients and patient's conditions, in addition, it is challenging to identify and extract the information that will be relevant and meaningful for machine learning modelling. Not to mention, the efficacy of the predictive machine learning algorithm can be enhanced by using only useful and pertinent information. Hence, feature selection is proposed to determine the significant features. Thus, feature selection should be fully utilized and applied when building machine learning algorithm. This study analyzes filter, wrapper, and embedded feature selection methods for medical data with the predictive machine learning algorithm, Random Forest and CatBoost. The experiment is carried out by evaluating the performances of the machine learning with and without applying feature selection methods. According to the results, CatBoost with RFE shows the best performance, in comparison to Random Forest with other feature selection methods.

Keywords: CatBoost · Feature selection · RFE · Lasso

1 Introduction

Huge number of real-world features often challenging to be handled in machine learning's application and not all features are crucial and significant to be used for predictive machine learning algorithm. In addition, irrelevant features can decrease the accuracy and the reliability performance of the machine learning. Thus, the during the past few years feature selection has risen as one of the important tool to be utilized in machine learning's development. Moreover, Breast Cancer [1] and Parkinson [2] are most familiar and high-risk diseases towards potential individuals. Women are more susceptible to Breast Cancer than men are because of the anatomy of the human body [2], while Parkinson diseases often occur to men compared to women [3]. It is a serious challenge for medical expert to analyze every features and diagnosis the patients with the diseases in a short time [4]. Hence, with the help of feature selection will reduce the size of the

M. Yusoff et al. (Eds.): SCDS 2023, CCIS 1771, pp. 92–106, 2023.
https://doi.org/10.1007/978-981-99-0405-1_7

data for the machine learning algorithm to predict whether the patient is at risk or not. With selecting only, the relevant features will increase the accuracy and quality of the decision making. The aim of this paper is to evaluate several of feature selection methods to achieve best machine learning's performance. The structure of this paper is as follows: Sect. 2 discussed the related study of feature selection methods, then in Sect. 3 explained about the experiment setup and result and lastly the paper is concluded in Sect. 5.

2 Related Work

A feature is a column and characteristic of the data in the dataset. Features are important inputs to develop the machine learning's algorithm but not all features are useful to be utilized, thus feature selection needs to be applied [5]. Feature selection is starting to be widely used in machine learning algorithm in order to improvise the performance of the algorithm. The objective of feature selection to select the significant and most influential features and deselect the irrelevant features that may affect towards the machine learning algorithm's predictions [6], moreover it is reducing the size of input data and training duration of machine learning algorithm. Several of research proved the efficiency of implying the feature selection to the machine learning in obtaining better performances and accuracy [7]. Dissanayke and Johar studied to identify Cleveland heart disease and the result obtained highest classification of accuracy 88.5%, and precision 91.3%, by using decision tree classifier with backward feature selection method [8]. Moreover, another research [9], also used similar dataset and Random Forest with SelectKbest yield the highest result of 95% accuracy and 97.6% precision score. Another research study done by Krisnabayu [10] used Hepatitis diseases dataset with Random Forest using svm-rfe as feature selection and obtained 87.9% of accuracy and 90.2% precision score. [1] analyzed on IDC Breast Cancer dataset by using CatBoost machine learning algorithm with Pearson correlation coefficient, gained accuracy of 92.6% and precision of 93.4%. From the related work indicates every researcher select different type of feature selection methods, those research studies do not perform comparative on the various feature methods. Therefore, this study will review the three methods of feature selection, Filter, wrapper and embedded with Random Forest and CatBoost machine learning algorithm.

3 Material and Methodology

In the present section, the evaluation of the experiments is done based on proposed feature selection methods. The two popular datasets from UCI Machine Learning Repository were chosen in for the experiment. While, as for the machine learning algorithm were Random Forest and Catboost.

3.1 Data

This study focusses on Breast Cancer Wisconsin [11] and Parkinson [12] dataset from UCI Machine Learning Repository. Breast Cancer Wisconsin consists of features including the target feature, diagnosis, and 569 instances. While Parkinson dataset includes 23 features including the target feature, status and 195 instances.

3.2 Feature Selection Methods

Feature selection consists of three categories, those are Filter method, Wrapper method and Embedded method (Chen et al. 2020). The three methods will be explained below.

a) Filter Feature Selection Methods

Filter method is filtering features based on the correlation between the target features and dependent features [13]. Filter method usually perform in pre-processing step and does not require any predictive model. Filter methods performs better when there is a large amount of data, moreover it can computes faster compared to other feature selection methods [14]. Below are the proposed methods that used during the experiment study:

Pearson Correlation
Pearson correlation is a test statistics to summarize the linear relationship and strength of the two features in the same dataset and commonly used to determine the relationship between studied data [15]. The significant of the Pearson correlation can be determined by p-value indicator. P-value defines as the probability of gaining the result that are "as extreme" or "more extreme" if the null hypothesis is correct [16]. The level of statistical significance of p-value is between 0 until 1. If p-value is equal or lower than the conventional 5%, the correlation is statistically significant and indicates that the two variables likely to have strong relationship, while if p-value is larger than 5%, then p-value is not statistically significant, means that the two variables have low or no meaningful correlation [17].

Mutual Information
Mutual information measures the degree to which a feature is dependent on another over a set of target feature [18]. Implementation of mutual information can be found in several fields, such medical analysis [19] and atmospheric sciences [20]. Range mutual information score is from zero or above zero, and it can be negative or positive value [21]. The higher the mutual information gain of the feature the higher rank and more influential of the feature compared to the other feature. The lower or zero the mutual information gain of the features indicates the two features are independent from each other.

b) Wrapper Feature Selection Methods

Wrapper methods use an independent measurement for the subset evaluation compared to Filter methods. Wrapper methods begin with searching the various subset of the features then building a model based on the selected subset [22]. The advantage of wrapper methods is to include the ability to account for feature dependencies and the selection of predictors and the relationship between feature subset searches [13]. The chosen wrapper methods used in this paper are mentioned below:

Sequential Features Selection
Sequential features selection algorithms also known as forward and backward approaches that belong to a family of greedy search algorithms by selecting the best

and optimal option based on the current condition. Sequential feature selection successively adds and removes features that can be relevant and significant to the predictive machine learning algorithm. The process of selecting and removing features iterates until it reaches in optimal performance. The two common sequential feature selections are backward feature selection (SBFS) and sequential forward feature selection (SFFS) [25], these modified methods often used in face recognition [26] and medical diagnosis [27, 28], and [29]. Advantages of Sequential Feature selection are, easy to interacts with model classifier and low risk of overfitting [30].

Selectkbest
Selectkbest is one of feature selection method provided from Scikit-Learn, it selects the most important features best on the k highest score [23]. SelectKbest consist of two parameters, scoring function and number of k. The default number of k is 10, which means it will return 10 selected significant features and Selectkbest can be used in regression and classification by determining the scoring function. As for regression problems is f_regression that returns F-Statistics and P-value [24], while for classification are chi2, best when the feature values are 0's and 1's and f_classif known as Anova test that returns P-value and F-statistics [7]. Benefits of SelectKbest are, time training of the machine learning is reduced due to less selected features and reducing overfit by avoiding making decision on redundant data [23].

Recursive Feature Elimination (RFE)
Recursive Feature Elimination or known as RFE recursively remove the least influential features and build a model based on the selected features. The process of choosing the significant features is repeated until it reached the optimum number needed to obtain the best performance of the algorithm [5]. It uses greedy optimization algorithm intending to find the most significant features [31]. Moreover, RFE can be performed on regression or classification machine learning algorithm. It is an effective tool and easy to configure for choosing the most significant features in a training dataset to predict the target class [32].

c) Embedded Feature Selection Methods

Embedded methods or known as algorithm-based method extract features that have most contribution towards the training process of machine learning algorithm []. Embedded methods usually perform during model building step. Additionally, embedded methods are known as a hybrid methods and tend to have more advantages compared to Filter and Wrapper methods [33].

Random Forest Built-In Feature Importance
Random Forest is an ensemble machine learning that consisting of many decisions trees [34]. It uses bagging techniques by selecting the optimal split point for the purpose of producing high performance. With the help of bagging techniques, feature selection can be conducted. Random Forest classifier and regressor consists of Feature_importances attribute to determine the important features by using gini importance [35] or mean decrease in impurity (MDI). Gini importance measures each of the feature's importance by deducting the sum of the squared probabilities of each class from one [36], also

known as the total decrease in node impurity. The larger the measure of gini importance, the more influential the feature is.

CatBoost Built-In Feature Importance

CatBoost is a gradient boosting algorithm built by Yandex company in 2017, that is great at handling categorical features. CatBoost has advantages such as fast learning speed compared to other boosting algorithm and produce high accuracy value [37] due to implementation of greedy strategy [38]. Moreover, Catboost provides method to calculate feature importance after model training by selecting the best features and remove irrelevant features from the dataset [39]. Feature importance is available in the CatBoost's parameter, and it can be used with CatBoost classifier and regressor. Feature importance is based on prediction values change [40], loss function change [39]. Predict values change demonstrates the average of prediction change if the value of feature changes [41]. Loss function changes often used ranking metrics and it calculates the difference between value of feature's loss function to determine the rank of feature importance [42].

Lasso Regression

Least absolute shrinkage and selection operator (lasso) is introduced in 1996 by Robert Tibshirani [43], a method that implies feature selection and regularization simultaneously. In order to regularizes the model parameter, Lasso shrinks the regression coefficients to zero, then the important features are selected after the shrinkage process [44]. Any features that shrink to zero will be removed and indicates as unnecessary features. The magnitude of lambda is the controlling factor in shrinkage and also known as optimal parameter section [45]. The default value of lambda is equal to 0.001, If the lambda is increases, it denotes that the number of insignificant feature increased, thus only significant features can be selected for the training machine learning model. A research study mentioned that Lasso regression is widely used medical field to detect early diseases and predict result of the diseases [45].

The following table (Table 1) provided summary details of the advantages and disadvantages of the three feature selection methods.

Table 1. Advantages and disadvantages of feature selection methods.

Feature selection	Advantages	Disadvantages
Filter	• Dependent on the entire features in the datasets • Computationally very fast • Useful when large number of features	• Does not remove multicollinearity • May be unable to identify the ideal selection of features
Wrapper	• Give better performance • Consist of greedy and non-greedy approach towards the feature selections	• Prone to overfit • Slower computationally compared to filter and embedded wrapper

(continued)

Table 1. (*continued*)

Feature selection	Advantages	Disadvantages
Embedded	• Less computationally expensive compared to wrapper • Less chance to overfit	• Very limited and unadaptable when algorithm changed, the feature also needed to be changed • Required longer time to execute when handle a huge amount of data

3.3 Summary of Feature Selection Methods

Based on the Table 1, each of the feature selection methods has their benefits and weakness. It is complicated to define the most effective feature selection method just by reading from the table above, thus, in order to find the best method that can provide optimal results with various type of data, this paper will review the several methods of feature selection.

4 Result and Discussion

The machine learning algorithm built in Jupyter lab, modern interactive development environment (IDE). The machine learning algorithm used in this paper were Random Forest and CatBoost. The evaluation metrics that we used to evaluate the performance of each algorithms were accuracy, precision, recall, f1 measure and Roc Auc.

Accuracy: Measures of how many predictions in the test datasets were correct, as a proportion of all predictions.

$$\text{Accuracy} = \frac{Number\ of\ correct\ predictions}{Total\ number\ of\ predictions} \tag{1}$$

Precision: Metrics that indicate how accurately the algorithm predicted a positive outcome from a negative outcome.

$$\text{Precision} = \frac{True\ Positive}{True\ Positive + False\ Positive} \tag{2}$$

Recall: Determines the proportions of correctly predicted outcomes. The algorithm effectively found results that were relevant when the recall was closer to 1.

$$Recall = \frac{True\ Positive}{True\ Positive + False\ Negative} \tag{3}$$

F1 Score: The combined precision and recall rate as a percentage. Low false positive and low false negatives are good indicators of the F1 Score. If the F1 score is closer to 1, it indicates excellent accuracy and positive prediction.

$$\text{F1 Score} = 2 \times \frac{Precision \times Recall}{Precision + Recall}. \tag{4}$$

Roc Auc Score: Known as Area Under the Receiver Operating Characteristic Curve, calculates the rank correlation between target feature and algorithm predictions.

$$TPR = \frac{True\ Positive}{True\ Positive + False\ Negative}$$

$$FPR = \frac{False\ Positive}{True\ Negative + False\ Positive}$$

$$Roc\ Auc\ Score = \int TPR \cdot (FPR) \tag{5}$$

4.1 Feature Selection Comparison's Result

The selected features in Pearson correlation are based on the P-value is larger than 0.05 and as for Lasso based on coefficient not lower than zero, while other filter method, wrapper methods and embedded methods are selecting the default top 10 best features. In this experiment, CatBoost and Random Forest algorithm were used to train the Breast Cancer Wisconsin and Parkinson diseases datasets. The result of both datasets was recorded into the table above. Based on the table, the result of the Breast Cancer Wisconsin and Parkinson dataset using between all features and selected features have shown significant differences.

a) **Comparison of all selected features Breast Cancer Wisconsin with Random Forest and CatBoost algorithm (Table 2)**

Table 2. Comparison of all selected features Breast Cancer Wisconsin with Random Forest and CatBoost algorithm

	Machine learning algorithm	
	Random forest	CatBoost
Accuracy	96.048	96.92
Precision	95.19	98.11
Recall	92.32	93.53
F1 score	92.32	95.68
Roc Auc	98.43	99.01

From Breast Cancer Wisconsin, the experiment was done by **selecting all the features** available from the dataset with Random Forest and CatBoost algorithm. Between the two results, **CatBoost** obtained higher performances compared to Random Forest, with accuracy of **96.92**, precision of **98.11**, recall of **93.53**, f1-score of **95.68** and Roc Auc of **99.01**.

Table 3. Comparison of Breast Cancer Wisconsin with filter method as feature selection

	Machine learning algorithm			
	Random forest		CatBoost	
	Feature selection			
	Pearson correlation	Information gain	Pearson correlation	Information gain
Accuracy	93.83	93.84	94.49	94.28
Precision	93.36	94.45	94.11	93.51
Recall	88.82	90.59	91.18	91.14
F1 score	91.40	92.62	92.46	92.16
Roc Auc	97.64	97.46	98.62	98.33

b) Breast Cancer Wisconsin and Filter Method as Feature Selection (Table 3)

From filter method, CatBoost show higher result by using Pearson correlation compared to Random Forest, with accuracy of **94.49**, precision of **94.11**, recall of **91.18**, f1-score of **92.4** and Roc Auc of **98.62**.

c) Breast Cancer Wisconsin and Wrapper Method as Feature Selection (Table 4)

Table 4. Comparison of Breast Cancer Wisconsin with wrapper method as feature selection

	Machine learning algorithm					
	Random forest			CatBoost		
	Feature selection					
	SelectKBest	SFS	RFE	SelectKBest	SFS	RFE
Accuracy	92.96	96.26	94.29	94.50	96.71	97.36
Precision	95.57	96.46	94.11	94.61	96.46	98.20
Recall	87.06	92.94	91.18	90.59	94.71	94.71
F1 Score	90.12	93.51	92.46	92.35	95.52	96.32
Roc Auc	97.35	98.14	98.62	98.51	98.92	99.45

In wrapper method, CatBoost with RFE shows higher performance in Accuracy of **97.36**, Precision **98.20**, recall **94.71**, f1 score of **96.32** and Roc Auc of **99.45** among them.

d) Breast Cancer Wisconsin and Embedded Method as feature selection (Table 5)

Table 5. Comparison of Breast Cancer Wisconsin with embedded method as feature selection

	Machine learning algorithm			
	Random forest		CatBoost	
	Feature selection			
	Built in feature importance	Lasso	Built in Feature importance	Lasso
Accuracy	94.51	93.84	97.14	94.27
Precision	95.32	96.78	97.56	92.97
Recall	90.59	90.59	94.71	91.76
F1 score	92.31	91.76	96.02	92.18
Roc Auc	97.71	97.65	99.10	98.42

Then in Embedded method, **CatBoost** with **built in feature selection** also shown significant result compared to random forest with accuracy of **97.14**, precision of **97.56**, recall of **94.71,** f1-score of **96.02** and Roc Auc of **99.10**.

Overall result for Breast Cancer Wisconsin, from the three methods of feature selection, CatBoost with RFE has the best result from them all.

e) Comparison of all selected features Parkinson diseases with Random Forest and CatBoost algorithm (Table 6)

Table 6. Comparison of all selected features Parkinson diseases with Random Forest and CatBoost algorithm

	Machine learning algorithm	
	Random forest	CatBoost
Accuracy	87.17	91.63
Precision	91.99	93.29
Recall	91.29	96.52
F1 score	91.19	94.58
Roc auc	93.26	97.59
Auc	0.9688	0.9643

From Parkinson dataset, the experiment was done by selecting all the features available from the dataset with Random Forest and CatBoost algorithm. Between the two results,

CatBoost obtained higher performances compared to Random Forest, with accuracy of **91.63**, precision of **93.29**, recall of **96.52**, f1-score of **94.58** and Roc Auc of **97.59**.

f) Parkinson diseases and filter method as feature selection (Table 7)

Table 7. Comparison of Parkinson diseases with filter method as feature selection

	Machine learning algorithm			
	Random forest		CatBoost	
	Feature selection			
	Pearson correlation	Information gain	Pearson correlation	Information gain
Accuracy	80.66	89.83	79.33	92.92
Precision	85.39	93.62	85.08	95.42
Recall	89.47	93.18	87.65	95.61
F1 score	87.09	93.05	86.20	95.22
Roc Auc	83.91	95.06	85.88	98.28

While from the filter method, **CatBoost** produce the significant result with **information gain** compared to Random Forest, with accuracy of **92.92**, precision of 95.42, recall of **95.61**, f1-score of **95.22** and Roc Auc of **98.28**.

g) Parkinson diseases and Wrapper Method as Feature Selection (Table 8)

Table 8. Comparison of Parkinson diseases with wrapper method as feature selection

	Machine learning algorithm					
	Random forest			CatBoost		
	Feature selection					
	SelectKBest	SFS	RFE	SelectKBest	SFS	RFE
Accuracy	87.79	87.79	91.67	92.92	95.54	93.50
Precision	92.66	91.65	94.12	95.42	96.97	93.88
Recall	91.36	92.20	94.77	95.61	97.42	98.26
F1 score	91.40	91.70	94.29	95.22	97.01	95.82
Roc Auc	96.34	92.41	96.41	98.28	98.50	97.47

In wrapper method, **CatBoost** with **RFE** has better performance compared to Random Forest algorithm, with accuracy of **93.50,** precision of **93.88**, recall of **98.26**, f1-score of **95.82** and Roc Auc of **97.47**.

h) Parkinson diseases and Embedded Method as Feature Selection (Table 9)

Table 9. Comparison of Parkinson diseases with embedded method as feature selection

	Machine learning algorithm			
	Random forest		CatBoost	
	Feature selection			
	Built in feature importance	Lasso	Built in feature importance	Lasso
Accuracy	87.17	87.83	93.54	92.96
Precision	91.99	93.65	94.59	95.05
Recall	91.29	90.61	97.42	95.76
F1 score	91.19	91.55	95.79	95.76
Roc Auc	93.26	95.36	98.74	96.65

In embedded method, CatBoost has better performance compared to Random Forest and Lasso with accuracy of **92.96**, precision of **95.05**, recall of **95.76**, f1-score of **95.25** and Roc Auc of **96.65**.

The tables below show the calculated values of Wilcoxon test of the statistical significance with the difference methods of features selections. The significance value of Wilcoxon test must be below than significance level of 0.05. The evaluation of Wilcoxon test is done by comparing the accuracy of full dataset of Breast Cancer Wisconsin and Parkinson dataset with the accuracy that has obtained from the number of selected features by feature selection methods.

Table 10. Wilcoxon test for comparison of features selection with Random Forest algorithm

	Pearson correlation	Information gain	SelectKBest	SFS	RFE	Built in feature importance	Lasso
P-value	0.17971	0.6547	0.6547	0.1797	0.6547	0.31731	0.6547

Table 11. Wilcoxon test for comparison of features selection with CATBoost algorithms

	Pearson correlation	Information gain	SelectKBest	SFS	RFE	Built in feature importance	Lasso
P-value	0.179712	0.65472	0.65472	0.6547	0.6547	0.1797	0.6547

For Table 10, the accuracy of initial features from Breast Cancer and Parkinson dataset is grouped together and then compared with accuracy obtained from each of the feature selection methods. The accuracy was obtained by using Random Forest algorithm, while in Table 11, the accuracy was obtained by using CATBoost algorithm. Based on the Table 10 and 11, the above test values show there are no statistically significant different between the initial number of features and numbers selected features due to the p-values are more than 0.05 and the values not far apart because the number of selected features are not in large differences.

4.2 Discussion

Based on all the graphs from Breast Cancer Wisconsin with three different methods of feature selection results, it can be concluded that, CatBoost algorithm perform better compared to Random Forest. While based on all the Parkinson diseases with three different methods of feature selections, Catboost also show higher performance in comparison to Random Forest. When applying the feature selection to both algorithms, CatBoost consistently outperform the result, and Random Forest did not score higher performance even with filtering the features. Among the three method of feature selection, RFE from wrapper method with CatBoost algorithm obtained the highest performance in Breast Cancer Wisconsin and Parkinson dataset. Regarding the significant statistical test, there is no statistically significant difference between the accuracy values.

5   Conclusion

In this study, the filter, wrapper, and embedded method of feature selections are proposed to enhance the performance of Random Forest and CatBoost machine learning algorithm with Breast Cancer Wisconsin and Parkinson's disease prediction. The prediction machine learning algorithm evaluated with and without the feature selection. The implement of feature selection has improved and increased the performances of the machine learning algorithm with the reference to accuracy, precision, recall, f1 score and Roc Auc score. Future work will focus on more medical datasets in order to strengthen the evidence of CatBoost with RFE feature selection can provide greatest and optimal performance, also to obtain the statistically significant difference between the test accuracy.

References

1. Roy, S.D., Das, S., Kar, D., Schwenker, F., Sarkar, R.: Computer aided breast cancer detection using ensembling of texture and statistical image features. Sensors **21**(11), 1–17 (2021). https://doi.org/10.3390/s21113628
2. Mei, J., Desrosiers, C., Frasnelli, J.: Machine learning for the diagnosis of Parkinson's disease: a review of literature. Front. Aging Neurosci. **13**(May), 1–41 (2021). https://doi.org/10.3389/fnagi.2021.633752
3. Cerri, S., Mus, L., Blandini, F.: Parkinson's disease in women and men: what's the difference? J. Parkinsons Dis. **9**(3), 501–515 (2019). https://doi.org/10.3233/JPD-191683

4. Knapič, S., Malhi, A., Saluja, R., Främling, K.: Explainable artificial intelligence for human decision support system in the medical domain. Mach. Learn. Knowl. Extr. 3(3), 740–770 (2021). https://doi.org/10.3390/make3030037

5. Chourib, I., Guillard, G., Farah, I.R., Solaiman, B.: Stroke treatment prediction using features selection methods and machine learning classifiers. IRBM 1, 1–9 (2022). https://doi.org/10.1016/j.irbm.2022.02.002

6. Zhang, F., Fleyeh, H., Bales, C.: A hybrid model based on bidirectional long short-term memory neural network and Catboost for short-term electricity spot price forecasting. J. Oper. Res. Soc. 1–25 (2020). https://doi.org/10.1080/01605682.2020.1843976

7. Pathan, M.S., Nag, A., Pathan, M.M., Dev, S.: Analyzing the impact of feature selection on the accuracy of heart disease prediction. Healthc. Anal. 2(February), 100060 (2022). https://doi.org/10.1016/j.health.2022.100060

8. Dissanayake, K., Johar, M.G.M.: Comparative study on heart disease prediction using feature selection techniques on classification algorithms. Appl. Comput. Intell. Soft Comput. 2021 (2021). https://doi.org/10.1155/2021/5581806

9. Senan, E.M., Abunadi, I., Jadhav, M.E., Fati, S.M.: Score and correlation coefficient-based feature selection for predicting heart failure diagnosis by using machine learning algorithms. Comput. Math. Methods Med. 2021 (2021). https://doi.org/10.1155/2021/8500314

10. Krisnabayu, R.Y., Ridok, A., Budi, A.S.: Hepatitis detection using random forest based on SVM-RFE (recursive feature elimination) feature selection and SMOTE. In: ACM International Conference on Proceeding Series, pp. 151–156 (2021). https://doi.org/10.1145/3479645.3479668

11. Wolberg, W.H., Mangasarian, O.L.: Multisurface method of pattern separation for medical diagnosis applied to breast cytology. Proc. Natl. Acad. Sci. U. S. A. 87(23), 9193–9196 (1990). https://doi.org/10.1073/pnas.87.23.9193

12. Little, M.A., McSharry, P.E., Roberts, S.J., Costello, D.A.E., Moroz, I.M.: Exploiting non-linear recurrence and fractal scaling properties for voice disorder detection. Biomed. Eng. Online 6, 1–19 (2007). https://doi.org/10.1186/1475-925X-6-23

13. Chen, C.W., Tsai, Y.H., Chang, F.R., Lin, W.C.: Ensemble feature selection in medical datasets: combining filter, wrapper, and embedded feature selection results. Expert Syst. 37(5), 1–10 (2020). https://doi.org/10.1111/exsy.12553

14. Suto, J., Oniga, S., Sitar, P.P.: Comparison of wrapper and filter feature selection algorithms on human activity recognition. In: 2016 6th International Conference on Computers Communications and Control, ICCCC 2016, no. ICCCC, pp. 124–129 (2016). https://doi.org/10.1109/ICCCC.2016.7496749

15. Pavithra, V., Jayalakshmi, V.: Hybrid feature selection technique for prediction of cardiovascular diseases. Mater. Today Proc. (2021). https://doi.org/10.1016/j.matpr.2021.03.225

16. Verploegh, I.S.C., Lazar, N.A., Bartels, R.H.M.A., Volovici, V.: Evaluation of the use of P values in neurosurgical literature: from statistical significance to clinical irrelevance. World Neurosurg. 161, 280-283.e3 (2022). https://doi.org/10.1016/j.wneu.2022.02.018

17. Muñoz Montoya, J.E., Carreño Rodríguez, J.N., Ardila Duarte, G., Maldonado Moran, M.Á., Luque Suarez, J.C.: Correlation of carbon dioxide and systolic velocity of the middle cerebral artery in patients with spontaneous subarachnoid hemorrhage of aneurysmal origin. Interdiscip. Neurosurg. Adv. Tech. Case Manag. 27 (2022). https://doi.org/10.1016/j.inat.2021.101402

18. Chen, J., Song, L., Wainwright, M.J., Jordan, M.I.: Learning to explain: an information-theoretic perspective on model interpretation. In: 35th International Conference on Machine Learning, ICML 2018, vol. 2, pp. 1386–1418 (2018)

19. Tsalatsanis, A., Hozo, I., Djulbegovic, B.: Meta-Analysis of mutual information applied in EBM diagnostics, pp. 1–14 (2020)

20. Zaidan, M.A., et al.: Exploring non-linear associations between atmospheric new-particle formation and ambient variables: a mutual information approach. Atmos. Chem. Phys. **18**(17), 12699–12714 (2018). https://doi.org/10.5194/acp-18-12699-2018

21. Benish, W.A.: A review of the application of information theory to clinical diagnostic testing. Entropy **22**(1), 97 (2020). https://doi.org/10.3390/e22010097

22. Arun Kumar, C., Sooraj, M.P., Ramakrishnan, S.: A comparative performance evaluation of supervised feature selection algorithms on microarray datasets. Proc. Comput. Sci. **115**, 209–217 (2017). https://doi.org/10.1016/j.procs.2017.09.127

23. Nair, R., Bhagat, A.: Feature selection method to improve the accuracy of classification algorithm. Int. J. Innov. Technol. Explor. Eng. **8**(6), 124–127 (2019)

24. Pires, A.C., Mendes, G.R., Santos, G.F.M., Dias, A.P.C., Santos, A.A.: Indirect identification of wheel rail contact forces of an instrumented heavy haul railway vehicle using machine learning. Mech. Syst. Sig. Process. **160**, 107806 (2021). https://doi.org/10.1016/j.ymssp.2021.107806

25. Sharan, R.V., Moir, T.J.: Pseudo-color cochleagram image feature and sequential feature selection for robust acoustic event recognition. Appl. Acoust. **140**(May), 198–204 (2018). https://doi.org/10.1016/j.apacoust.2018.05.030

26. Gu, N., Fan, M., Du, L., Ren, D.: Efficient sequential feature selection based on adaptive eigenspace model. Neurocomputing **161**, 199–209 (2015). https://doi.org/10.1016/j.neucom.2015.02.043

27. Mostafiz, R., Uddin, M.S., Alam, N.A., Mahfuz Reza, M., Rahman, M.M.: Covid-19 detection in chest X-ray through random forest classifier using a hybridization of deep CNN and DWT optimized features. J. King Saud Univ. - Comput. Inf. Sci. **34**(6), 3226–3235 (2021). https://doi.org/10.1016/j.jksuci.2020.12.010

28. Ahmad, G.N., Ullah, S., Algethami, A., Fatima, H., Akhter, S.M.H.: Comparative study of optimum medical diagnosis of human heart disease using machine learning technique with and without sequential feature selection. IEEE Access **10**, 23808–23828 (2022). https://doi.org/10.1109/ACCESS.2022.3153047

29. Aggrawal, R., Pal, S.: Sequential feature selection and machine learning algorithm-based patient's death events prediction and diagnosis in heart disease. SN Comput. Sci. **1**(6), 1–16 (2020). https://doi.org/10.1007/s42979-020-00370-1

30. Aziz, R., Verma, C.K., Srivastava, N.: Dimension reduction methods for microarray data: a review. AIMS Bioeng. **4**(2), 179–197 (2017). https://doi.org/10.3934/bioeng.2017.2.179

31. Chen, Q., Meng, Z., Su, R.: WERFE: a gene selection algorithm based on recursive feature elimination and ensemble strategy. Front. Bioeng. Biotechnol. **8**(May), 1–9 (2020). https://doi.org/10.3389/fbioe.2020.00496

32. Arslan, Ö.: Automated detection of heart valve disorders with time-frequency and deep features on PCG signals. Biomed. Sig. Process. Control **78**(January) (2022). https://doi.org/10.1016/j.bspc.2022.103929

33. Jović, A., Brkić, K., Bogunović, N.: A review of feature selection methods with applications. In: Proceedings of the 2015 38th International Convention on Information and Communication Technology, Electronics and Microelectronics, MIPRO 2015, pp. 1200–1205 (2015). https://doi.org/10.1109/MIPRO.2015.7160458

34. Schonlau, M., Zou, R.Y.: The random forest algorithm for statistical learning. Stata J. **20**(1), 3–29 (2020). https://doi.org/10.1177/1536867X20909688

35. la Cava, W., Bauer, C., Moore, J.H., Pendergrass, S.A.: Interpretation of machine learning predictions for patient outcomes in electronic health records, pp. 572–581. arXiv (2019)

36. Menze, B.H., et al.: A comparison of random forest and its Gini importance with standard chemometric methods for the feature selection and classification of spectral data. BMC Bioinform. **10**, 1–16 (2009). https://doi.org/10.1186/1471-2105-10-213

37. Khalid, N.H.M., Ismail, A.R., Aziz, N.A.: Interpretation of machine learning model using medical record visual analytics. In: Alfred, R., Lim, Y. (eds.) Proceedings of the 8th International Conference on Computational Science and Technology. LNEE, vol. 835, pp. 633–645. Springer, Singapore (2022). https://doi.org/10.1007/978-981-16-8515-6_48

38. Gao, W., Zhou, L., Liu, S., Guan, Y., Gao, H., Hui, B.: Machine learning prediction of lignin content in poplar with Raman spectroscopy. Bioresour. Technol. **348**(February), 126812 (2022). https://doi.org/10.1016/j.biortech.2022.126812

39. Kang, Y., Jang, E., Im, J., Kwon, C., Kim, S.: Developing a new hourly forest fire risk index based on Catboost in South Korea. Appl. Sci. 4–6 (2020)

40. Ambe, K., Suzuki, M., Ashikaga, T., Tohkin, M.: Development of quantitative model of a local lymph node assay for evaluating skin sensitization potency applying machine learning CatBoost. Regul. Toxicol. Pharmacol. **125**, 105019 (2021). https://doi.org/10.1016/j.yrtph.2021.105019

41. Khan, P.W., Byun, Y.C., Lee, S.J., Park, N.: Machine learning based hybrid system for imputation and efficient energy demand forecasting. Energies **13**(11) (2020). https://doi.org/10.3390/en13112681

42. Jani, D., et al.: An efficient gait abnormality detection method based on classification, 1–22 (2022)

43. Tibshirani, R.: Regression shrinkage and selection via the lasso. J. R. Stat. Soc. Ser. B **58**(1), 267–288 (1996). https://doi.org/10.1111/j.2517-6161.1996.tb02080.x

44. Heiskanen, M.A., et al.: Different predictors of right and left ventricular metabolism in healthy middle-aged men. Front. Physiol. **6**(DEC) (2015). https://doi.org/10.3389/fphys.2015.00389

45. Chintalapudi, N., et al.: LASSO regression modeling on prediction of medical terms among seafarers' health documents using tidy text mining. Bioengineering **9**(3), 1–14 (2022). https://doi.org/10.3390/bioengineering9030124

An Improved Mask R-CNN Algorithm for High Object Detection Speed and Accuracy

Qingchuan Liu[1,3], Muhammad Azmi Ayub[1], Fazlina Ahmat Ruslan[1],
Mohd Nor Azmi Ab Patar[1], and Shuzlina Abdul-Rahman[2(✉)]

[1] College of Engineering, Universiti Teknologi MARA, 40450 Shah Alam, Malaysia
411533094@qq.com, {muhammadayub,fazlina419,
azmipatar}@uitm.edu.my
[2] School of Computing Sciences, College of Computing, Informatics and Media, Universiti
Teknologi MARA, 40450 Shah Alam, Selangor, Malaysia
shuzlina@uitm.edu.my
[3] Hebei Institute of Machinery and Electricity, XingTai, China

Abstract. This paper aims at the problems of low grasping accuracy, low detection speed and low grasping success rate for object detection of robot grasping tasks. This research is significant for the robot to grasp tasks in complex environments, such as the disorderly placement of multi-target objects and partial occlusion objects. This paper analyzes the structure and principle of the algorithm in depth based on the Mask-R-CNN target detection algorithm. An improved target recognition, grabbing, and positioning algorithm based on this algorithm is proposed to solve the problem of low operation speed. This method uses adjacent frames as comparison templates to find image differences, thus improving recognition accuracy and reducing repeated estimation of regions. The pre-experiment results of targeting gears in a complex background exhibit better accuracy than the other methods. The CPU utilization of the algorithm proposed is also better than the other methods, which balance the detection speed and accuracy and have high research and reference value. Additionally, reducing the amount of data processing in the operation process during the data processing time and improving the operation efficiency.

Keywords: Target grasping and positioning · Mask-R-CNN · Accuracy

1 Introduction

Although it is effortless for humans to grasp various objects, autonomous robot grasping is still an open and difficult challenge. Robot grasping mainly includes three aspects: grasping perception, trajectory planning and grasping control [1]. There are many problems to be solved in each aspect. To perceive the grasping scene environment, the robot first needs to have a vision sensor to provide grasping scene images; Only by accurately grasping the target object can the grasping task's overall performance be improved. However, in the multi-object sorting scene of disorderly placement, partial occlusion and stacking, each algorithm's accuracy, real-time and generalization still need to be improved.

© The Author(s), under exclusive license to Springer Nature Singapore Pte Ltd. 2023
M. Yusoff et al. (Eds.): SCDS 2023, CCIS 1771, pp. 107–118, 2023.
https://doi.org/10.1007/978-981-99-0405-1_8

Grab detection technology is mainly used to detect the grab point or grab position suitable for the target object for a given image. It then determines the space coordinate of the target grab position in the real world, namely the manipulator coordinate system, according to the coordinate system conversion, to tell the manipulator in what attitude to grab the target object. At present, the main research algorithms and specific classifications of the grab detection technology are shown in Fig. 1.

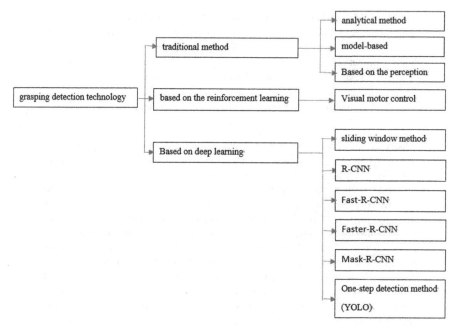

Fig. 1. Grasping technology algorithm

Among these algorithms, R-CNN, fast R-CNN, faster R-CNN, mask R-CNN, and Yolo are currently widely used [2]. Regarding detection speed, the recognition and boundary regression in the R-CNN model and SS algorithm lead to their most time-consuming. The SS algorithm still preprocesses fast R-CNN. Still, regional feature extraction is put into the network through ROI Pooling, and recognition and boundary regression are directly done through deep neural networks, so the algorithm's efficiency is improved. Fast R-CNN forms an efficient end-to-end model based on the application of RPN in the model and the identification and positioning of the detection network.

Mask R-CNN adds FCN branches to fast R-CNN to generate corresponding masks; that is, mask R-CNN is composed of fast R-CNN and FCN, of which fast R-CNN is composed of RPN, ROIAlign and fast R-CNN. Mask R-CNN is very efficient in the image's target detection process. Compared with a single detection method, its target detection task is more refined because the pixel-level annotation is fully provided in the model training. Thus, the classification of relevant backgrounds and targets can be further improved. However, due to the increase in decoupling steps, the operation cost of Mask R-CNN is more expensive; that is, many problems, such as long operation time and large consumption of operation resources. The YOLO algorithm divides the input into equal parts, directly sends it into the network, predicts the category and location of each part, and finally outputs the detection results. Compared with the previous algorithm, it does not need to extract the candidate region of the target and is faster. Still, it is less accurate than the algorithm based on region recommendation in detection and recognition. Therefore, this paper proposes an improved Mask R-CNN algorithm to balance detection accuracy and speed in complex scenes such as cluttered placement, partial occlusion and stacking.

2   Research on MASK-R-CNN Algorithm

2.1   MASK-R-CNN Principle

Mask R-CNN is an instance segmentation algorithm, which is mainly used for segmentation based on target detection. The former completes the target detection task, and the latter can accurately complete the semantic segmentation task. FCN is added to the Faster R-CNN algorithm to generate corresponding MASK branches [3]. Mask R-CNN algorithm is mainly Fast R-CNN + FCN, more specifically RESNext + RPN + ROI align + Fast R-CNN + FCN [4] (Fig. 2).

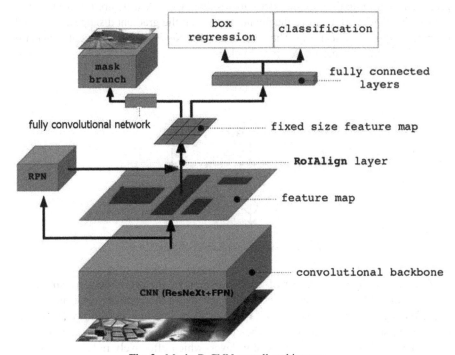

Fig. 2. Mask- R-CNN overall architecture

The target image is input into the network after image specific preprocessing. The process generates three tasks: classification, regression and segmentation. First, the features are extracted through the pre-trained feature extraction network RESNET + FPN to obtain the corresponding feature map; Secondly, the feature map is input into the area suggestion network RPN to generate a plurality of target candidate area ROIs. Then, the feature map and the generated multiple ROIs are input into the RoIAlign layer together so that each target candidate region's ROIs are normalized to the same scale feature map. This process ensures the pixels in the feature map are aligned with the original image's pixels. Finally, the corresponding target features are extracted from the feature map and then output to the FClayers and FCN for target classification and instance segmentation. That is, the accuracy of target recognition in complex backgrounds is improved by decoupling the relationship between multiple subtasks [5]. This makes Mask R-CNN significantly superior to template matching algorithms based on grey information [6] and single-stage deep learning target detection algorithm represented by SSD and YOLO [7] in target recognition accuracy.

Feature Extraction Network (ResNet + FPN). Mask R-CNN Feature Extraction Network is a standard CNN used to extract high-level visual features from the entire image. Because of the different positions of the objects in the picture, it is impossible to extract all the potential features of the objects in the image only by using convolutional neural networks. Therefore, this paper adopts the backbone structure of resnet101 and the FPN feature pyramid network [8]. RESNET (residual networks) is a network proposed by Kaiming's team in 2015. The residual network structure is introduced into the RESNET network to solve the phenomenon that the gradient disappears due to the deep network in deep learning. The core idea of ResNet is identity shortcut connection, which makes training easier. See Fig. 3 below.

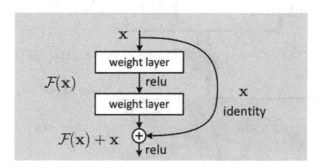

Fig. 3. Residual learning: a building block

Because the optimal number of layers required by the neural network structure is unknown in the training process, its depth depends on the complexity of the data set. Therefore, by adding skip connections to the network structure, it is allowed to skip the training of useless layer parameters when training the network structure and ignore the parameters of the network structure skip layer, which effectively reduces the number of parameters and improves the effectiveness of the model [9]. Therefore, the RESNET network structure is dynamic in training, and the number of layers is optimally adjusted in the training process.

FPN (feature pyramid network) mainly solves the problem of multi-scale target detection, as shown in Fig. 4 below. FPN adopts a top-down hierarchical structure with horizontal connections, from single scale input to building a network feature pyramid, and fuses different feature maps, so that each layer of the fused network has deep and shallow features.

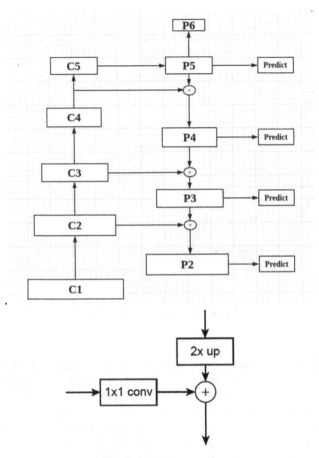

Fig. 4. FPN feature map

It can be seen from the figure that the bottom feature layer on the left obtains the same number of channels as the previous feature layer through 1 * 1 convolution; The upper feature layer gets the same length and width as the lower feature layer by upsampling, and then adds them together to get a new fused feature layer.

Regional Proposal Network (RPN). The region proposal network RPN is used to generate possible target candidate regions in the mask R-CNN. An image (of any size) is taken as the input region proposal network RPN. Its output is a set of target candidate regions ROI and each target candidate region has a score indicating whether or not it contains a detection target. This solves the problem that it takes too long to generate a detection region. It is recommended that the network RPN adopt the sliding window mechanism, which generates multiple anchors on the scale of the original image [10]. Through classification and regression of anchors, the regional location information of ROI and whether it contains the category information of the target can be obtained, as shown in Fig. 5 below.

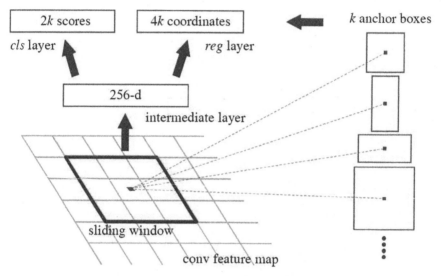

Fig. 5. Region proposal network

ROIAlign. To eliminate the negative impact of the quantization operation in ropool in fast R-CNN on the pixel accuracy of the mask prediction branch, the pixel mask is predicted more accurately. Mask R-CNN uses RoIAlign to cancel the quantization operation in RoIPool, calculates the accurate value of the input feature of the four sampling positions in each ROIALign through the bilinear interpolation algorithm [11], and uses maximum or average pooling for the feature, so that the pixels in the original image are completely aligned with the pixels in the feature map feature map. The final target candidate area ROI is normalized to the same scale, solving the problem of pixel area mismatch of image objects.

2.2 Improved MASK R-CNN Algorithm

Aiming at the problems of Mask R-CNN, this paper proposes to improve the loss function of Mask R-CNN by indirect frame subtraction. The specific method is that the detection cycle is divided into four times [12]. Each time, the recognition result of the previous time is taken as the background of the next time, and the change part is taken as the target. This method can reduce the computational difficulty and overcome the difficulty of small target recognition in a complex background by omitting the same part and detecting different parts.

The ROIAlign of the standard Mask R-CNN selects the most suitable feature map based on the following formula:

$$k = k_0 + \left(\sqrt{wh/224}\right) \tag{1}$$

where: K0, W and H are the area, width and height of the feature map, respectively. Different from Fast R-CNN and ROIAlign of Mask R-CNN quantizes the region of interest by bilinear interpolation. As shown in Fig. 6, on the premise that A11, A12, A21 and A22 are known, Mask R-CNN obtains B1 and B2 through linear interpolation, and then interpolates the obtained B1 and B2 to obtain the final interpolation point P, that is:

$$f(P) \approx \frac{y_2 - y}{y_2 - y_1} \cdot f(B_1) + \frac{y - y_1}{y_2 - y_1} \cdot f(B_2) \tag{2}$$

$$f(B_1) \approx \frac{x_2 - x}{x_2 - x_1} \cdot f(A_{11}) + \frac{x - x_1}{x_2 - x_1} \cdot f(A_{21}) \tag{3}$$

$$f(B_2) \approx \frac{x_2 - x}{x_2 - x_1} \cdot f(A_{12}) + \frac{x - x_1}{x_2 - x_1} \cdot f(A_{22}) \tag{4}$$

$$f(x, y) = \frac{f(A_{11})}{(x_2 - x_1)(y_2 - y_1)} \cdot (x_2 - x)(y_2 - y) + \frac{f(A_{21})}{(x_2 - x_1)(y_2 - y_1)} \cdot (x - x_1)(y_2 - y)$$
$$+ \frac{f(A_{12})}{(x_2 - x_1)(y_2 - y_1)} \cdot (x_2 - x)(y - y_1) + \frac{f(A_{22})}{(x_2 - x_1)(y_2 - y_1)} \cdot (x - x_1)(y - y_1) \tag{5}$$

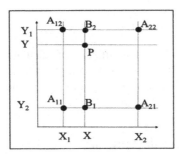

Fig. 6. Schematic diagram of ROI align bilinear interpolation of mask R-CNN

During training, to fit the ROIAlign feature distribution of the object in the picture, it is necessary to detect the target and its position through the loss function. $L_{mask-rcnn}$ can be described as:

$$L_{mask-rcnn} = L_{cls} + L_{box} + L_{mask} \tag{6}$$

$$L_{mask} = -\frac{1}{m^2} \sum_{k=1}^{k} \sum_{i=1}^{m^2} log\left[p_{ki}^* P_{ki} + \left(1 - p_{ki}^*\right)(1 - P_{ki})\right] \tag{7}$$

where: L_{cls}, L_{box} and L_{mask} are classification error, detection error and segmentation error respectively m. K, K, PKI * and PKI are respectively the length and width of the

ROI after the matching layer processing, the total number of model detection targets, the ith pixel value in the kth target real mask and the ith pixel value in the kth target prediction mask According to formula (4) and formula (5), since the L_{mask} function completes the targeted learning of image features by comparing the detection result with the labeled image pixel by pixel, although the detection accuracy of Mask R-CNN is improved, the operation amount is increased, and the detection speed is difficult to effectively guarantee Therefore, this paper uses the idea of indirect frame subtraction to improve, that is, after one recognition, the previous recognition result is taken as the background, and the change at the next time is taken as the target, to reduce the amount of calculation The specific method is to divide a detection cycle into four times t_0, t_1, t_2 and t_3. The time t0 is the target prediction mask of Mask R-CNN, while the time t_1, t_2 and t_3 take the real mask P'_{ki} of the previous acquisition time t_0 as the background. The formula (7) at this time is modified as follows:

$$L'_{mask} = -\frac{1}{m^2} \sum_{k=1}^{k} \sum_{i=1}^{m^2} log[p^*_{ki}P'_{ki} + (1 - p^*_{ki})(1 - P'_{ki})] \tag{8}$$

The modified loss function $L'_{mask-rcnn}$ is:

$$L'_{mask-rcnn} = L_{cls} + L_{box} + L'_{mask} \tag{9}$$

After improving Mask- R-CNN, the loss function of one complete cycle is:

$$L_{mask-rcnn} = L_{cls} + L_{box} + L_{mask}, t_0 \tag{10}$$

$$L_{mask-rcnn} = L_{cls} + L_{box} + L'_{mask}, t_1, t_2, t_3 \tag{11}$$

This method not only reduces the difficulty of calculation, but also overcomes the difficulty of identifying small equipment in a complex background by omitting the same part and detecting different parts. The recognition speed and accuracy are significantly improved.

3   Experiment and Result Analysis

The physical verification platform is built for grasping detection based on Intel's Realsense 3D camera. For different scenes, the experimental platform is used to complete the position detection and grasping of gears and verify the feasibility and generalization of the proposed target grasping positioning algorithm. The following Fig. 7 is the structure diagram of the robot visual grasping detection system.

To complete the verification of the algorithm, the industrial camera is calibrated to obtain the corresponding relationship between the target object in the camera coordinate system and the robot coordinate system, keep the position of the target object on the detection platform unchanged, adjust the pose of the manipulator to obtain different positions of the camera relative to the target object, and verify the accuracy and stability of the algorithm by recording the position data of the target object in the robot coordinate system, The target recognition time is used as an indicator of detection speed as seen in

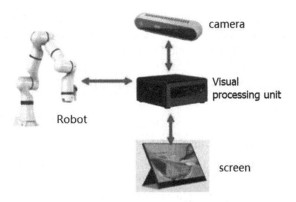

Fig. 7. System structure

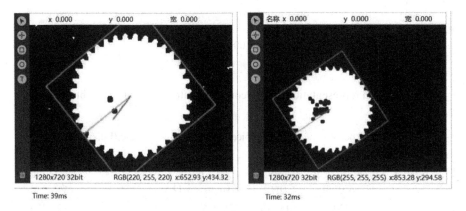

Fig. 8. Object detection

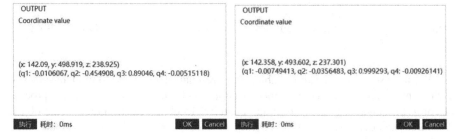

Fig. 9. Target object position detection

Fig. 8. (Figure 8 has three images, these three images were randomly selected during the object recognition process). From the images, we can see that the target recognition time is about 30 ms, which reflects the speed of target detection (Fig. 9).

By selecting 20 different camera points to detect and capture the target object, the capture success rate is 100%. The position data of the target object in the robot coordinate system is shown in the following Table 1.

Table 1. The position of the target object in the robot coordinate

Location Camera	Position object			Orientation object			
	X (mm)	Y (mm)	Z (mm)	Q1	Q2	Q3	Q4
P1	142.09	498.919	238.925	−0.010606	−0.454908	0.89046	−0.0051511
P2	142.397	496.755	238.429	−0.009061	−0.213474	0.976876	−0.0077621
P3	142.514	496.006	237.653	0.011079	0.964081	−0.26534	−0.0044452
……	……	……	……	……	……	……	……
P20	142.358	493.602	237.301	−0.007494	−0.0356483	0.999293	−0.0092614

The quaternion representation can be converted into Euler angles (Table 2).

Table 2. The position of the target object in the robot coordinate (Euler angles)

Location Camera	Position object			Orientation object		
	X (mm)	Y (mm)	Z (mm)	Ø	θ	ψ
P1	142.09	496.919	238.925	178.921	−0.814	125.870
P2	142.397	496.755	238.429	178.909	−0.825	155.338
P3	142.514	496.006	237.653	178.911	−0.828	30.7690
……	……	……	……	……	……	……
P20	142.358	493.602	237.301	178.909	−0.820	175.906

As can be seen from the above table, there are small errors in the coordinate values of each point, which are caused by camera accuracy and camera stability, or in the process of converting analog quantity to digital quantity. To obtain the accuracy of the object detection, the deviation rate of the coordinate value from the average coordinate value is taken as the standard.

$$X_a = \frac{\sum_{i=1}^{20} X_i}{20} \tag{12}$$

$$X_b = \frac{X_i}{X_a} \tag{13}$$

X_a is the average coordinate value of X, X_b is the deviation rate of the coordinate value from the average coordinate value, we can get the Y_b and Z_b with the same method, the minimum deviation rate of each coordinate value reaches 99.5%.

$$T_a = \frac{\sum_{i=1}^{20} T_i}{20} \tag{14}$$

And we can get the average object detection time is 34.8 ms from the formula (14). Compared with the original MASK R-CNN algorithm (detection accuracy is 99.6%, detection time is 38.8 ms), the detection accuracy of the algorithm remains unchanged. However, the target object detection speed is increased by about 10%, which proves the effectiveness of the improved algorithm.

4 Summary

This paper proposes an indirect frame subtraction method to improve the loss function of the Mask R-CNN algorithm. The proposed method was able to reduce the problem of high operation cost of the Mask R-CNN algorithm. Based on the depth image captured by the 3D camera, a physical object positioning and grasping platform is built. The accuracy and feasibility of the improved grabbing and positioning algorithm was verified. The experiment results show that the improved network has not reduced the detection accuracy compared with the original network, but has improved the detection speed, which provides a basis for the subsequent robot intelligent sorting and grasping applications.

Acknowledgements. The authors would like to express their gratitude to Research Management Center, Shah Alam, Selangor, Malaysia for the financial support from 600-IRMI/FRGS 5/3 (461/2019) through the Ministry of Higher Education grant (FRGS/1/2019/ICT02/UITM/02/10), and School of Computing Sciences, College of Computing, Informatics and Media, Universiti Teknologi MARA, Shah Alam, Selangor, Malaysia for the research support.

References

1. Li, J.Z.: Automatic building recognition method of UAV remote sensing image based on improved mask-RCNN algorithm. Bohai University (2021)
2. Shu, B.W.: Robot visual grasping method based on deep learning and application. Chongqing University of Technology (2022)
3. Huang, K., Li, Y.: Stereo vision and mask-RCNN segmentation based 3D points cloud matching for fish dimension measurement. In: 39th Chinese Control Conference (2020)
4. Bin, W.: Research on robot capture detection algorithms based on depth image and deep learning. Zhejiang University (2019)
5. Na, L., Tao, H.: Building extraction from mask-RCNN high-resolution remote sensing images. Remote Sens. Inf. **37**(03), 35–38 (2022)
6. Zeng, A., Song, S., Yu, K.: Robotic pick-and-place of novel objects in clutter with multi-affordance grasping and cross-domain image matching. In: 2018 EEE International Conference on Robotics and Automation (ICRA), pp. 3750–3757 (2018)

7. Tang, Y., Wang, H.: Feature extraction for side scan sonar image based on deep learning. In: 40th Chinese Control Conference, ShangHai (2021)

8. Jiang, C.Y.: Pavement crack detection based on improved mask-RCNN. Televis. Technol. **46**(06), 41–44 (2022)

9. Bo, S.F., Yun, B.Z.: Road information detection algorithm based on improved mask RCNN. J. Inf. Sci. Technol. Univ. Beijing (Nat. Sci. Ed.) **37**(03), 19–23 (2022)

10. Qi, C., Rui, C.L.: Power line identification method based on improved mask-RCNN. J. Shantou Univ. (Nat. Sci. Ed.) **37**(02), 65–68 (2022)

11. Yan, N.L., Dan, Y.D.: Design and research of bridge crack detection method based on mask-RCNN. Appl. Opt. **43**(01), 61–66 (2022)

12. Da, S.L.: Research on aluminum profile surface defect recognition technology based on deep convolutional neural network. University of Electronic Science and Technology (2022)

Computing and Optimization

Federated Learning with Class Balanced Loss Optimized by Implicit Stochastic Gradient Descent

Jincheng Zhou[1,3(✉)] and Maoxing Zheng[2]

[1] School of Computer and Information, Qiannan Normal University for Nationalities,
Duyun 558000, China
guideaaa@126.com
[2] School of Computer Sciences, Baoji University of Arts and Sciences, Baoji 721007, China
[3] Key Laboratory of Complex Systems and Intelligent Optimization of Guizhou Province,
Duyun 558000, China

Abstract. Federated learning is a paradigm for distributed machine learning in which a central server interacts with a large number of remote devices to create the optimal global model. System and data heterogeneity are now the two largest impediments to federated learning. This work suggests a federated learning strategy based on stochastic gradient descent optimization as a solution to the problem of heterogeneity-induced slow convergence, or even non-convergence, of the global model. This work estimates the average global gradient using locally uploaded model parameters without computing the first derivative or updating global model parameters through gradient descent. Allowing the global model to be used with fewer communication rounds. Obtain faster and more reliable convergence results. In experiments simulating varying degrees of heterogeneous settings, the strategy proposed in this work delivered faster and more stable convergence than FedProx and FedAvg. This work offers a strategy that decreases the number of communication cycles on highly heterogeneous synthetic datasets by around 50% compared to FedProx, therefore considerably enhancing the stability and durability of federated learning.

Keywords: Fast convergence · Optimization algorithm · System heterogeneity · Data heterogeneity · Implicit stochastic gradient descent · Global model · Central server · Distributed machine learning · Federated learning

1 Introduction

In recent years, as a result of the expansion of deep learning [1], many have recognized the great potential of artificial intelligence and feel that the technology may be applied to increasingly complex and cutting-edge industries [2]. Multiple users or industries get data, and user data is sensitive to privacy and security issues. It has grown more challenging to train machine learning models in a way that protects data privacy and improves the effectiveness of artificial intelligence technologies.

M. Yusoff et al. (Eds.): SCDS 2023, CCIS 1771, pp. 121–135, 2023.
https://doi.org/10.1007/978-981-99-0405-1_9

Under the assumption of protecting user data privacy, Google scientists McMahan et al. [3] proposed federated learning, which trains a network by coordinating a large number of geographically distributed devices. High-quality global models. The current algorithm for federated learning has significant problems. First, device heterogeneity is produced by differences in the CPU, GPU, ISP, battery, and network connection (3G, 4G, 5G, WIFI) of each device [4]. The traditional federated learning method FedAvg [3] discards devices that have not finished training within the given time, which is undesirable in real-world applications and wastes a substantial amount of computing resources. Second, the distribution and kind of data per device vary significantly [5], and the data across devices is not independently and identically distributed (non-IID), resulting in heterogeneous data. Model convergence effects in multiple situations are very heterogeneous or maybe nonexistent. These heterogeneities at the system level provide significant obstacles to federated learning.

The bulk of existing strategies for distributed optimization of heterogeneous problems are tailored to specific heterogeneous situations. For instance: Despite the fact that convergence is ensured in diverse data environments, references [6–8] advise enabling all devices to participate in each training cycle, which is impractical in federated environments [3]. This not only increases the communication overhead on the server, but devices participating in federated training should also be selected at random. There are more methods for addressing the problem of data heterogeneity by exchanging local data [9, 10]. Using a federated learning technique, the authors of [9] design an efficient and adaptable management system for mobile edge computing (MEC)-enabled industrial Internet of Things (IIoT). In the mentioned IIoT networks, each device must do certain computations with the aid of specific computational access points (CAPs). Although the performance of IIoT networks may be enhanced by adopting centralized resource allocation algorithms, this method is neither efficient nor adaptive. To solve this issue, they utilize a federated learning technique based on a deep reinforcement learning (DRL) algorithm to modify three parameters: the work offloading ratio, bandwidth allocation ratio, and transmit power. During the optimization phase, the optimization may decrease the normalized system cost while minimizing the communication cost. As shown in [10], federated learning may make it possible to enable distributed machine learning without disclosing the personal information or privacy settings of end devices. [Citation needed] On the other hand, when there is an excessive amount of concurrent access to cloud servers, the time required to provide model changes increases. It's possible that some local models are unnecessary because they have a gradient going in the opposite direction of the global model, which would result in countless additional communication costs. Existing research concentrates its efforts primarily on shortening the length of communication cycles and cleaning up local defect data; however, none of these methods takes into account the delay that is caused by operating a large number of concurrent servers. We are looking at a framework for edge-based communication optimization in order to reduce the number of end devices that are directly linked to the parameter server while also preventing the uploading of duplicate local updates. To be more specific, we cluster devices within the same network region and deploy mobile edge nodes in many network locations in order to act as hubs for cloud and end-device connections. This allows us to reduce the delay that is brought on by high server concurrency. In the meantime, we have devised a technique that makes use of cosine similarity in order to get rid of unnecessary models and cut down on wasted communication. On the other hand, this runs counter to the purpose of federated learning, which is to protect the confidentiality of user information. In the federated scenario, the literature [11] enhances the global model convergence speed in a heterogeneous data environment by implementing the momentum-based optimizer FEDYOGI on the server side, which boosts the model convergence speed but increases the server's computational load. It is unsuitable for situations with limited computing resources. In addition, some researchers use the quasi-Newton technique of the second order to optimize the model [12]. In the same heterogeneous environment as FedAvg, the number of communication rounds is reduced and the communication efficiency is improved while maintaining the same level of accuracy; nevertheless, the number of customers may grow as a result. The amount of local processing performed by the terminal.

In addition to data heterogeneity, the hardware of each client participating in federated training varies, resulting in substantial system heterogeneity between devices [13]. For instance, the current research progress on federated learning in a heterogeneous environment is given in the literature [14–18]. In the global model aggregation stage, the update technique is identical to that of FedAvg [3]. Within a certain timeframe, the server will destroy untrained devices instantly, and the model parameters for this training cycle cannot be supplied. Each device participating in the training lacks the ability to self-regulate and is incapable of doing a variable amount of local work dependent on its own hardware performance.

The update approach of nearest neighbor optimization is widely used in research to address the problem of federated learning heterogeneity, including efficient communication in distributed machine learning [19, 20] and the trade-off between fairness and robustness in federated learning [21, 22]. Conceptually, neighbor optimization and biased regularization are identical. In [23], the concept of biased regularization is investigated to re-parameterize FedAvg, and FedProx is proposed to use biased regularization to restrict the local model learned by each device to be closer. It is built on the global model and enables each participating device to do a customizable amount of work locally, thereby ensuring convergence in a variety of circumstances. Since FedProx optimizes global model parameters in the same way as FedAvg, it updates worldwide model parameters by averaging locally uploaded model data, resulting in slow global model convergence and a lack of direct global model parameter optimization.

This article provides a federated learning approach that is based on stochastic gradient descent optimization and the meta-learning mechanism of mini-batch approximation updating [24]. During the phase of the local model update, the optimization of the closest neighbor is used to ensure that the local model update is brought as close as possible to the global model. In order to bring the parameters of the global model up to date, the model aggregation process uses gradient descent to solve the predicted global gradient. Since the global model has fewer communication cycles, it may lead to faster and more consistent convergence.

The contributions of this work are mostly reflected in the three areas listed below:

1) Unlike existing methods, it does not simply average the global model parameters. During the phase of global model aggregation, model parameters uploaded locally are used to figure out the average global gradient, but the first derivative is not used.

2) To address the issue of delayed convergence or even non-convergence of the global model caused by heterogeneity, this work introduces a federated learning method based on implicit stochastic gradient descent optimization that updates the global model through implicit stochastic gradient descent. Model parameters might make it easier to update global model parameters, which would make it possible to speed up the convergence rate of the model with less computing power.

3) Capable of achieving the convergence effect of FedAvg in roughly 30 rounds and the convergence effect of FedProx in approximately 40 rounds on a diversified synthetic data set. Using the same convergence effect as FedProx, the strategy described in this paper cuts the number of communication rounds by about 50%.

4) A federated learning architecture based on class balance loss that accelerates model convergence by reweighting data classes is provided. In fashion-MNIST, only two communication rounds are required to achieve the target accuracy of 89%, a reduction of 114 communication rounds compared to the baseline technique. Upon convergence, the model's accuracy reaches 99.19%.

2   Client-Server Federated Learning Update Architecture

Federated learning update architectures consist mostly of client-server and decentralized peer-to-peer computing models. The client-server federated learning update architecture is the most prevalent. The training procedure consists mostly of two phases: the local model update phase and the global model aggregation phase. Figure 1 depicts the particular updating procedure.

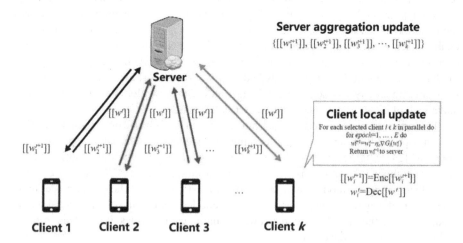

Fig. 1. Client-server federated learning architecture

Local Model Update. First randomly selects K clients, and then the server sends the global model parameters $[[w^t]]$ to the selected clients. Homomorphic encryption algorithm [25] encryption $[[w_i^{t+1}]] = Enc[w_i^{t+1}]$, and then upload to the server.

Global Model Aggregation. The server aggregates the encrypted model parameters from each client and $\{[[w_1^{t+1}]], [[w_2^{t+1}]], [[w_3^{t+1}]], \cdots, [[w_k^{t+1}]]\}$, performs a weighted average calculation on the model parameters. Finally, the server sends the updated global model parameters $[[w^t]]$ to the selected clients in the next round. The client receives the global model parameters and decrypts $w_i^t = Dec[[w^t]]$ them for the next round of model parameter updates. Repeat the above process until the loss converges.

3 Design of Federated Learning Algorithm for Implicit Stochastic Gradient Descent Optimization

In this section, the principal components of the federated closest neighbor optimization method and the implicit stochastic gradient descent optimization technique are outlined. Since the goal of federated learning is to train an ideal global model with the help of many devices and a central server, our ultimate goal is to:

$$\min \ wE_k\left[\left\{F_k(w_k) + \frac{\lambda}{2}\|w_k - w\|_2^2\right\}\right] \tag{1}$$

where: w_k is the approximate optimal solution obtained by device k in the local iterative process; w is the optimal solution that needs to solve the global model;, the $F_k(w_k) := E_{x_k \sim D_k}[L(f(w_k, x_i), y_i)]$ local data x_k of each device obeys different distributions D_k, and the loss function is the difference between the predicted value and the true value Difference. Equation (1) includes two optimization processes: 1) In the local model training stage, each device w learns a local approximate optimal through the global model parameters w_k; 2) In the global model aggregation stage, the server w_k uses implicit data uploaded by each device. Stochastic gradient descent to adjust the global model parameters w so that w the average distance from all is small. w_k The specific algorithm flow is:

    Enter: w^0 random initialization parameters, N total devices;

    Output: the final global model parameters w^{t+1}.

1) For global round number $t = 0, 1,..., T - 1$;
2) Server P_k randomly selects K devices with probability and specifies a fixed learning rate η_c;
3) Server sends the current global model w^t to the selected device;
4) Each device $k = 1, 2,..., K$ is calculated in parallel: $F \quad k(w_k) = \frac{1}{n_k}\sum_{i\in n_k} L(f(w_k, x_i), y_i)$;
5) $w_k^{t+1} = argarg[F_k(w_k) + \frac{\lambda}{2}\|w_k - w^t\|_2^2]$;

6) Repeat 4) to 5), end the parallel calculation, and each device transmits the calculation result to the w_k^{t+1} Server;

7) updates the global model parameters by gradient descent with a decaying learning rate η_g of a fixed number of rounds: $\lambda\left(w^t - w_k^*\right)$

$$w^{t+1} = w^t - \eta_g \lambda\left(w^t - \frac{1}{K}\sum\nolimits_{k\in S_t} w_k^{t+1}\right) \tag{2}$$

8) Server sends the updated model parameters w_k^{t+1} to Clients;

9) Repeat 2)–8) t times;

10) END

In Algorithm 1, steps 4)–6) are the local model training stage, 7)–9) are the server global model updating stage, and then the updated model parameters are sent to the equipment participating in the next round of training. Repeat the above process until the model loss converges.

3.1 Federation Nearest Neighbor Optimization

When the local model is being updated during the local model training stage, the nearest neighbor operator with parameters is first introduced in order to restrict the local model update and bring it closer to the global model. The Fedprox method [23] is the name given to this strategy for doing local optimization. The neighborhood goal for each apparatus k has been reformulated as

$$G_k(w_k) = F_k(w_k) + \frac{\lambda}{2}\|w_k - w^t\|_2^2 \tag{3}$$

where: λ is a hyperparameter that constrains the difference between the local model and the global model; w^t it represents the global model parameter after the t-th round of server aggregation updates.

3.2 Global Model Update Optimization Based on Implicit Stochastic Gradient Descent

After the local training is over, each device w_k^{t+1} uploads the updated model parameters to the server, The nearest neighbor operator with parameters is introduced largely during the local model training phase, when the local model is updated to restrict the local model update to be closer to the global model. The Fedprox algorithm [23] describes this technique to local optimization. Redefining the local purpose of each device k as.

Since the local objective function of the client is $G_k(w_k) = F_k(w_k) + \frac{\lambda}{2}\|w_k - w^t\|_2^2$, the assumption w_k^* is $G_k(w_k)$ the optimal solution of the objective function, and the function $Fk(w_k)$ is differentiable. From the first-order optimal conditions, we can get:

$$\nabla F\left(w_k^*\right) + \lambda\left(w_k^* - w^t\right) = 0 \tag{4}$$

From the chain rule, we can get:

$$\nabla G_k\left(w^t\right) = \left(\frac{\partial w_k^*}{\partial w^t}\right)^{\top} \nabla F_k\left(w_k^*\right) + \lambda\left(I - \left(\frac{\partial w_k^*}{\partial w^t}\right)^{\top}\right)\left(w^t - w_k^*\right)$$

$$= \lambda\left(w^t - w_k^*\right) + \left(\frac{\partial w_k^*}{\partial w^t}\right)^{\top} * \left(\nabla F_k\left(w_k^*\right) + \lambda\left(w_k^* - w^t\right)\right) = \lambda\left(w^t - w_k^*\right) \quad (5)$$

Therefore $\nabla G_k\left(w^t\right) = \lambda\left(w^t - w_k^*\right)$, Eq. (4) shows that the gradient estimate of the global model can be calculated by solving the approximate update of the current task. At round t, the selected device obtains an approximate optimal solution after updating round E using stochastic gradient descent on the local dataset w_k^{t+1}. The server can calculate the average global gradient by formula (4):

$$\nabla G\left(w^t\right) = \lambda\left(w^t - \frac{1}{K}\sum_{k \in S_t} w_k^*\right) \quad (6)$$

Since the exact local optimal solution w_k^* is difficult to estimate, this paper uses the suboptimal solution w_k^{t+1} instead w_k^*, so the global model parameters are updated as

$$w^{t+1} = w^t - \eta_g \lambda\left(w^t - \frac{1}{K}\sum_{k \in S_t} w_k^{t+1}\right) \quad (7)$$

In the formula: is S_t a subset $\eta_g = \frac{1}{t}\eta_{gi}$ of K devices; t is the current number of training rounds; is the learning rate decayed by a fixed number of rounds η_{g_i}; With the continuous increase of the number of communication rounds, the learning rate gradually decreases, which effectively ensures that the global model can gradually stabilize at a faster speed during the training process. The updated w^{t+1} global model parameters are used as the next round of training of Eqs. (3)–(6) that the federated learning algorithm based on implicit stochastic gradient descent optimization proposed in this paper directly optimizes the global model parameters, rather than simply averaging the local model parameters uploaded by all devices as Updated global model parameters. Because $\nabla G_k\left(w^t\right) = \lambda\left(w^t - w_k^*\right)$, on the server side, the $\lambda\left(w^t - \frac{1}{K}\sum_{k \in S_t} w_k^*\right)$ average global model gradient can be obtained with just a pass, thus avoiding solving the first derivative, and then using stochastic gradient descent to update the global model parameters. Compared with FedProx, this algorithm can use effective information more efficiently when the information is redundant. Secondly, in the process of iteration, it will quickly converge to the vicinity of the minimum value, which will speed up the convergence speed of the model.

3.3 Types of Balance Loss

Class balance loss adopted in this paper does not require prior knowledge of customer data distribution, Instead, when the local model is updated, it estimates the number of valid samples in the customer data and adds a class balance weight that is inversely proportional to the number of valid samples to the loss function, thereby accelerating the convergence of federated models [22].

Suppose a class S in the real world, the class capacity is $O = \{x \in N^*\}$, where each sample S_j is a subset of S and the capacity is 1. Therefore, the more data sampled, S_j the wider the coverage of S. The estimated total quantity of sampled data for comprehensive coverage of the classes rises with data and is limited by O. Consider that newly sampled data can only interact with previously sampled data in one of two ways: completely inside or completely outside a set of previously sampled data with probability p. The probability p will increase as the number of sampled data points increases. Due to the inherent similarity of real-world data, they may be compared. it is extremely probable that freshly added samples are near copies of old samples as the number of samples rises. Therefore, we apply weights to each selected sample to equalize their relative significance. The preceding model was constructed. The effective number of samples E l is the anticipated sample size, or the coverage capability of the sample for the class, where l is the original number of samples without image enhancement for the full sample class [22]. Valid samples E_l are:

$$E_l = \frac{1 - \beta^l}{1 - \beta} = \sum\nolimits_{j=1}^{l} \beta^{j-1} \tag{8}$$

where $\beta \in (0, 1]$. E_l It is an exponential function of l. With the increase of the sample size, it will E_l continue to increase. The larger the coverage area of this class, the closer to the real world situation. The sample S_j The contribution to the class is β^{j-1} that as the sampled data increases, S_j the contribution of the sample to the class is smaller. In order to balance the loss L_k, the loss is reweighted to establish a balanced loss BL_k. $BL_k = \frac{1}{E_l}L_k = \frac{1-\beta}{1-\beta^l}L_k$ Each client in client C, after receiving the federated model issued by the FL server, first calculates the weighting coefficient of each class of the local private data, and then updates the federated model.

4   Experiments and Results

To demonstrate the efficacy of the implicit stochastic gradient descent optimization technique described in this research, tests are conducted on 3 actual datasets and 3 synthetic datasets, classification and regression tasks are evaluated, and existing sample solutions are compared. FedProx [23] is compared to the traditional FedAvg [3] algorithm addressing the heterogeneity issue.

4.1   Experimental Setup

The simulation experiment was done on a Linux-powered server equipped with two GeForce GTX 1080 Ti and one GeForce GTX Titan X graphics cards. Tensorflow was used to create the code, and Python3 was used to implement the federated learning technique based on implicit stochastic gradient descent optimization [24]. Table 1 displays the hyperparameter settings, including the number of training rounds, number of iterations per round, number of selected devices, and learning rate.

Table 1. Setting of hyperparameters

Hyperparameters	Synthetic	Snet140	MNIST	EMNIST
N_{num_rounds}	200	800	200	200
N_{num_epochs}	20	20	20	20
B_{batch_size}	10	10	10	10
$N_{num\_clients}$	10	10	10	10
η_c	0.01	0.6	0.03	0.003
η_{gi}	0.75	1.1	0.75	0.95

The approach suggested in this research employs the same local solver as FedProx and FedAvg to assure the fairness of the evaluation process and outcomes. During simulation of the system's heterogeneous environment, the number of devices left behind is set to 0, 50%, and 90%, respectively. Creating artificial datasets This article generates local data via formula (9) in a manner similar to FedProx.

$$y = argmax(softmax(Wx + b)) \tag{9}$$

where: $W \in 10 \times 60$; $x \in 60$; $b \in 10$. A dataset of 30 devices is generated by formula a (7), and 10 devices are also randomly selected for training each round.

4.2 Real Datasets and Models

Sent140 [26] is a sentiment classification dataset for emoticon-containing textual content on Twitter. The task leverages a two-layer LSTM with 256 hidden layer units and each Twitter account corresponds to a device. The model accepts 25 characters as input, processes them via two LSTM layers and a fully connected layer, and generates one character per training sample as output.

MNIST [27] is an 09 handwritten digit recognition dataset used to research the issue of handwritten digit image classification using the logistic regression technique. In order to produce non-IID data, this study distributes data randomly over 1000 devices, each of which has just two types of numbers. The model's input is a 2828 dimensional picture, and its output is a 10-digit label ranging from 0 to 9.

EMNIST [28] is an extension of the MNIST dataset, which contains 09 digits and 26 English letters in upper and lower case, which constitutes a more difficult 62-class handwritten character image classification task, but only 10 lowercase letters are randomly selected in the experiment. The input to the model is a 2828-dimensional picture, while the output consists of labels for the 10 classes aj.

For each of the aforementioned datasets, the client's local data distribution follows a power-law distribution [29]. Locally, this article assigns 80% to the training set and 20% to the test set. Table 2 depicts the makeup of each device dataset.

Table 2. Datasets distribution on device

Data set	Equipment/unit	Total sample/piece	Average sample/piece
MNIST	1000	69028	72
EMNIST	221	18339	89
Sent140	769	40801	49

4.3   Analysis of Experimental Results on Synthetic Datasets

This research performs experiments on three mixed data sets: Synthetic 0 0, Synthetic 0.5 0.5, and Synthetic 1 1 in order to prove that the method in this paper has a quicker convergence time on heterogeneous data sets. The left-to-right data heterogeneity rises gradually, and the larger the heterogeneity, the greater its influence on model convergence. In this research, the convergence speed of the model is assessed by the loss reduction rate and the gradient variance change [30]. The findings are displayed in Table 3. To demonstrate the fairness and efficacy of the technique presented in this work, the restrictions are set to the same value throughout. The training loss and gradient variance in Table 3 demonstrate that the approach described in this study achieves the FedAvg convergence effect around the 30th round, the FedProx convergence effect around the 40th round, and continues to converge beyond the 40th round. The more steady and superior the convergence, the less the variation of the local gradient (VLG) [31]. VLG may be stated as

$$VLG = \frac{1}{K} \sum_{k=1}^{K} \| \nabla G(w^t) - \nabla G_k\left(w_k^{t+1}\right) \|^2 \tag{10}$$

In the experiment, the absence of system heterogeneity is mimicked by having all devices execute the same job. As the heterogeneity of the data grows, the global model convergence result will ultimately lean toward a certain interval; hence, this article represents the latter half of the communication cycle. The average test accuracy of the data is used as a measure for assessing the model's quality. Table 4 displays the average test accuracy on the synthetic data set. It can be shown that the method suggested in this study has a greater average test accuracy than FedProx and FedAvg.

Table 3. Analysis of experimental results of Synthetic_1_1 gradient variance

Algorithm Training epoch	FedAvg	FedProx	Ours
50	1.784	0.926	0.912
100	2.131	0.866	0.772

(*continued*)

Table 3. (*continued*)

Algorithm Training epoch	FedAvg	FedProx	Ours
150	1.994	0.812	0.714
200	1.592	0.672	0.551

Table 4. Average test accuracy on synthetic datasets

Data set	FedAvg	FedProx	This paper
Synthetic_0_0	79.8	83.8	85.3
Synthetic_0.5_0.5	79.5	81.6	84.6
Synthetic_1_1	69.9	75.3	76.5

4.4 Analysis of Experimental Results on Real Datasets

This section compares the stability and convergence effects of different algorithms on three commonly used real data sets for federation learning and one synthetic dataset whose Synthetic_1_1 client local category is set to 5, which simulates the federation settings of heterogeneity of different systems on the basis. This study replicates the heterogeneity of the system by confining the local workload of the device such that each device trains the given E, and for various heterogeneous settings, different E (E20) are randomly chosen to distribute 50% of the equipment presently engaging in training. When the fallout is zero percent, all devices execute the same amount of work (E = 20). In the specified global time period, when E20 occurs, FedAvg will lose these laggards, while this paper's algorithm and FedProx will merge these laggards, with the exception that this paper will effectively use the model parameters of merging laggards in the global model aggregation stage and use implicit random gradient descent to further optimize the global model. The training losses on the actual data set are shown in the table below, which depicts the experimental outcomes for individuals who have fallen behind by 50%. As the number of iteration rounds goes up, the average loss eventually stops changing. The table below shows that the proposed method converges much faster than FedAvg and FedProx (Tables 5, 6, 7 and 8).

Table 5. Analysis of experimental results of Synthetic_1_1 straggler 50% (training loss)

Algorithm Training epoch	FedAvg	FedProx	Ours
50	1.372	0.908	0.872

(*continued*)

Table 5. (*continued*)

Algorithm Training epoch	FedAvg	FedProx	Ours
100	1.177	0.847	0.731
150	1.362	0.872	0.683
200	1.069	0.658	0.554

Table 6. Analysis of experimental results of MNIST straggler 50% (training loss)

Algorithm Training epoch	FedAvg	FedProx	Ours
50	0.861	0.492	0.468
100	1.529	0.651	0.570
150	1.219	0.609	0.520
200	1.642	0.682	0.462

Table 7. Analysis of experimental results of EMNIST Dropper 50% (training loss)

Algorithm Training epoch	FedAvg	FedProx	Ours
100	12.342	12.181	12.097
200	15.651	20.477	20.572
300	13.473	12.432	11.368
400	17.736	4.842	6.447

Table 8. Analysis of experimental results of Sent140 stragglers 50% (training loss)

Algorithm Training epoch	FedAvg	FedProx	Ours
200	1.688	0.6665	0.741
400	0.921	0.711	0.669
600	0.897	0.589	0.571
800	0.839	0.587	0.542

The average test accuracy of the model in a highly heterogeneous environment is displayed in Table 9. The algorithm in this paper is 5% higher than FedProx on the MNIST dataset. In the experiment, the same hyperparameters are set on the Sent140 dataset to compare the operating times of different algorithms, and the running time of FedAvg, FedProx, and the proposed algorithms in this paper are 67 min, 108 min, and 108 min, respectively, at the number of communication rounds of 200.

Table 9. Average test accuracy of each algorithm in highly heterogeneous environment

Data set	FedAvg	FedProx	Algorithm
Synthetic_1_1	72.6	76.2	77.3
MNIST	76.8	81.5	86.3
EMNIST	50.3	68.2	68.2
Sent140	57.0	69.3	69.6

5 Conclusion

This paper presents a federated learning technique based on stochastic gradient descent optimization with implicit gradient descent. Instead of simply averaging the model parameters given by each device, the global model aggregation process now uses the locally uploaded model parameters to approximate the global gradient while avoiding the first derivative. Using stochastic gradient descent to update the parameters of the global model permits a more precise application of the effective information when duplicated information is available. As the number of communication cycles continues to increase, the global model will soon approach its minimum value. The experimental results on three synthetic datasets and three real datasets conclusively demonstrate that the algorithm can achieve faster and more robust convergence in heterogeneous environments, thereby significantly improving the performance of federated learning in practical application systems. Stability and toughness.

Acknowledgement. This research was made possible with funding from the National Natural Science Foundation of China (No. 61862051), the Science and Technology Foundation of Guizhou Province (No. ZK[2022]549, No. [2019]1299), the Top-notch Talent Program of of Guizhou Province (No. KY[2018]080), the Natural Science Foundation of Education of Guizhou Province (No. [2019]203, KY[2019]067), and the Funds of Qiannan Normal University for Nationalities (No. qnsy2018003, No. qnsy2019rc09, No. qnsy2018JS013, No. qnsyrc201715).

References

1. Hai, T., Zhou, J., Li, N., Jain, S.K., Agrawal, S., Dhaou, I.B.: Cloud-based bug tracking software defects analysis using deep learning. J. Cloud Comput. 11(1), 1–14 (2022)
2. Hai, T., Alsharif, S., Dhahad, H.A., Attia, E.A., Shamseldin, M.A., Ahmed, A.N.: The evolutionary artificial intelligence-based algorithm to find the minimum GHG emission via the integrated energy system using the MSW as fuel in a waste heat recovery plant. Sustain. Energy Technol. Assess. **53**, 102531 (2022)

3. Mcmahan, B., Moore, E., Ramage, D., et al.: Communication-efficient learning of deep networks from decentralized data. In: Proceedings of the 20th International Conference on Artificial Intelligence and Statistics, Fort Lauderdale, USA, pp. 1273–1282 (2017)
4. Wang, H., Yurochkin, M., Sun, Y., Papailiopoulos, D., Khazaeni, Y.: Federated learning with matched averaging. arXiv preprint arXiv:2002.06440 (2020)
5. Kopparapu, K., Lin, E., Zhao, J.: FedCD: improving performance in non-IID federated learning. arXiv preprint arXiv:2006.09637 (2020)
6. Yu, H., Yang, S., Zhu, S.: Parallel restarted SGD with faster convergence and less communication: demystifying why model averaging works for deep learning. In: Proceedings of the AAAI Conference on Artificial Intelligence, vol. 33, no. 01, pp. 5693–5700, July 2019
7. Liu, J., et al.: Adaptive asynchronous federated learning in resource-constrained edge computing. IEEE Trans. Mob. Comput. (2021)
8. Yu, H., Jin, R., Yang, S.: On the linear speedup analysis of communication efficient momentum SGD for distributed non-convex optimization. In: International Conference on Machine Learning, pp. 7184–7193. PMLR, May 2019
9. Guo, Y., Zhao, Z., He, K., Lai, S., Xia, J., Fan, L.: Efficient and flexible management for industrial internet of things: a federated learning approach. Comput. Netw. **192**, 108122 (2021)
10. Wang, T., Liu, Y., Zheng, X., Dai, H.N., Jia, W., Xie, M.: Edge-based communication optimization for distributed federated learning. IEEE Trans. Netw. Sci. Eng. (2021)
11. Reddi, S., et al.: Adaptive federated optimization. arXiv preprint arXiv:2003.00295 (2020)
12. Yang, K., Fan, T., Chen, T., Shi, Y., Yang, Q.: A quasi-newton method based vertical federated learning framework for logistic regression. arXiv preprint arXiv:1912.00513 (2019)
13. Dhakal, S., Prakash, S., Yona, Y., Talwar, S., Himayat, N.: Coded federated learning. In: 2019 IEEE Globecom Workshops (GC Wkshps), pp. 1–6. IEEE, December 2019
14. Wang, C., Yang, Y., Zhou, P.: Towards efficient scheduling of federated mobile devices under computational and statistical heterogeneity. IEEE Trans. Parallel Distrib. Syst. **32**(2), 394–410 (2020)
15. Malinovskiy, G., Kovalev, D., Gasanov, E., Condat, L., Richtarik, P.: From local SGD to local fixed-point methods for federated learning. In: International Conference on Machine Learning, pp. 6692–6701. PMLR, November 2020
16. Hanzely, F., Richtárik, P.: Federated learning of a mixture of global and local models. arXiv preprint arXiv:2002.05516 (2020)
17. Rothchild, D., et al.: FetchSGD: communication-efficient federated learning with sketching. In: International Conference on Machine Learning, pp. 8253–8265. PMLR, November 2020
18. Hai, T., Zhou, J., Muranaka, K.: An efficient fuzzy-logic based MPPT controller for grid-connected PV systems by farmland fertility optimization algorithm. Optik 169636 (2022)
19. Woodworth, B.E., Bullins, B., Shamir, O., Srebro, N.: The min-max complexity of distributed stochastic convex optimization with intermittent communication. In: Conference on Learning Theory, pp. 4386–4437. PMLR, July 2021
20. Tao, H., et al.: SDN-assisted technique for traffic control and information execution in vehicular adhoc networks. Comput. Electr. Eng. 108108 (2022)
21. Cui, Y., Jia, M., Lin, T.Y., Song, Y., Belongie, S.: Class-balanced loss based on effective number of samples. In: Proceedings of the IEEE/CVF Conference on Computer Vision and Pattern Recognition, pp. 9268–9277 (2019)
22. Hai, T., Said, N.M., Zain, J.M., Sajadi, S.M., Mahmoud, M.Z., Aybar, H.Ş.: ANN usefulness in building enhanced with PCM: Efficacy of PCM installation location. J. Build. Eng. 104914 (2022)
23. Li, T., Hu, S., Beirami, A., Smith, V.: DITTO: fair and robust federated learning through personalization. In: International Conference on Machine Learning, pp. 6357–6368. PMLR, July 2021

24. Li, T., Sahu, A.K., Zaheer, M., Sanjabi, M., Talwalkar, A., Smith, V.: Federated optimization in heterogeneous networks. Proc. Mach. Learn. Syst. **2**, 429–450 (2020)

25. Charles, Z., Konečný, J.: Convergence and accuracy trade-offs in federated learning and meta-learning. In: International Conference on Artificial Intelligence and Statistics, pp. 2575–2583. PMLR, March 2021

26. Aono, Y., Hayashi, T., Wang, L., Moriai, S.: Privacy-preserving deep learning via additively homomorphic encryption. IEEE Trans. Inf. Forensics Secur. **13**(5), 1333–1345 (2017)

27. Go, A., Bhayani, R., Huang, L.: Twitter sentiment classification using distant supervision. CS224N Project Rep. Stanford **1**(12) (2009)

28. LeCun, Y., Bottou, L., Bengio, Y., Haffner, P.: Gradient-based learning applied to document recognition. Proc. IEEE **86**(11), 2278–2324 (1998)

29. Cohen, G., Afshar, S., Tapson, J., Van Schaik, A.: EMNIST: extending MNIST to handwritten letters. In: 2017 International Joint Conference on Neural Networks (IJCNN), pp. 2921–2926. IEEE, May 2017

30. Tung, K.K., Tung, K.K.: Topics in Mathematical Modeling, vol. 10, p. 9781400884056. Princeton University Press, Princeton (2007)

31. Balles, L., Hennig, P.: Dissecting ADAM: the sign, magnitude and variance of stochastic gradients. In: International Conference on Machine Learning, pp. 404–413. PMLR, July 2018

Electricity Energy Monitoring System for Home Appliances Using Raspberry Pi and Node-Red

Nur Shazwany Zamani[1]([✉]), Muhammad Shafie Mohd Ramli[1], Khairul Huda Yusof[1], and Norazliani Md. Sapari[2]

[1] Faculty of Information Sciences and Engineering, Management and Science University, 40100 Shah Alam, Selangor, Malaysia
nur_shazwany@msu.edu.my

[2] School of Electrical Engineering, Faculty of Engineering, Universiti Teknologi Malaysia, 81300 Johor Bharu, Malaysia

Abstract. This paper research deals with the shortcoming of late electricity bills that are generated only after the electrician comes to the residential area and measures the reading of the electricity meter manually. Electricity bill is only submitted once a month in Malaysia. The main concern of the project is to design an Electricity Energy Monitoring System for Home Appliances using Raspberry Pi and Node-RED; consequently, to generate real-time bill. The architecture of the mechanism is designed on computer, using Node-RED-based coding and Circuito.Io-based simulation to achieve the goals of the project. The circuit design had been simulated before the real system was realized. Node-RED programming tool requires necessary coding to be keyed in into the Raspberry Pi. The microcontroller essentially provides the same function as NodeMCU, but is replaced with Arduino Uno as a more suitable choice, due to issues of the initial components having produced undesirable result. The outcome of this project is there are lots of information provided in dashboard form. The collected and generated data are stored in the SQLite database in Raspberry Pi. This project applies the Internet of Things (IoT) system to remotely monitor home appliances over the internet. In the proposed project, a current sensor senses the electricity energy, which then uploads the data via MQTT. The total consumption can be viewed using Node-RED.

Keywords: Raspberry Pi · Nodered · IoT system · Electricity consumption · Dashboard · NodeMCU · Over the Internet

1 Introduction

Electricity consumption has been a key concern in handling the rise of global electricity demand [1, 2]. The residential sector in Malaysia is one of the main contributors to the overall high demand for electricity. Traditionally, electricity bills are generated only after the electrician approaches and measures the reading of the electricity meter manually. Bill is only distributed once a month in Malaysia. As a result, consumers tend to forget or ignore their energy consumption over this span of time. This should be frequently monitored in order to achieve effective utilization of energy in a month. Many household

M. Yusoff et al. (Eds.): SCDS 2023, CCIS 1771, pp. 136–146, 2023.
https://doi.org/10.1007/978-981-99-0405-1_10

consumers use electrical energy inefficiently because they are unaware of how to use energy effectively in their daily lives.

The Internet of Things (IoT) has grown rapidly throughout the years. Many countries have adopted IoT into various sectors, such as automotive, healthcare, and industrial, and even household [3–5]. Year by year, electric energy consumption is growing at tremendous rate as all the technologies nowadays require electrical energy to operate. Lack of monitoring on efficient use and appliances will lead to wastage of energy [3].

Thus, smart monitoring system for the household sector is proposed through this study as it is able to automatically obtain data of electricity usage and cut the time of the billing process without the needing of staff to manually record electricity usage from the meter reading [6, 7].

2 Methodology

The methodology applied in this project is System Development Life Cycle (SDLC). This method is common for new students to develop new ideas of project. A successful System Development Life Cycle (SDLC) can result in a high-quality system that satisfies consumer standards, achieves completion within time and expense assessments, as well as ability to run successfully and efficiently in the existing Information of Technology infrastructure. Basically, this methodology breaks down a project into several phases to ease operation.

2.1 Planning, Analysis and Design

Planning phase is the first phase in the SDLC. It determines whether or not there is a need for a new system to meet the objective of the project. A preliminary plan (or a feasibility study) is required for students to acquire the resources to build a new infrastructure of the project whether modifying the previous project or enhancing new features. The project may also seek to meet or surpass the user's or consumer's expectations.

The second phase is where analysis of research is done to focus on the root of the user challenges or the need for improvement on previous project to ensure that the new system will fulfil the user requirements. At this phase, students are required to define the entire project in detail and check the project's feasibility.

The third phase describes, in detail, the necessary specifications, features and operations that will satisfy the functional requirements of the proposed system. Conceptual design is required to be done in this phase in order to meet the objective and scope of the project. The circuit diagram is usually designed using Circuit.io, followed by simulation conducted using Proteus software. Simulation visualizes the project's flow, while the circuit diagram reflects the construction of the project in the real world.

2.2 System Design

System conceptual design had been carried out to finalize the system design for both hardware and software development for the Electricity Energy Monitoring System for Home Appliances using Raspberry Pi and Node-RED as shown in Fig. 1. Hardware development focuses on identifying the perfect components and tools to suit the needs of the project. The architecture of the mechanism is based on the computational design and design from CIRCUITO.IO.

For software development, Node-RED-based coding and CIRCUITO.IO-based simulation had been utilized to achieve the goals of the project. The circuit was designed using CIRCUITO.IO, which was then simulated before the real model was constructed. Node-RED programming tool was used to program necessary coding needed for the project to be written on the Raspberry Pi.

Fig. 1. Flowchart of proposed project.

2.3 Block Diagram

The block diagram below (Fig. 2) shows the flow of Electricity Energy Monitoring System for Home Appliances using Raspberry Pi and Node-RED. The system has three segments which are input, processor, and output. The current sensor will start to measure the reading when there is a presence of load by the appliance. The Node MCU processor will create communication between the hardware and online services. The collected data will be processed by the algorithms inside the Raspberry Pi for current measurement. The Raspberry Pi will establish a connection between the SQLite database and the Node-RED, and the collected data will be displayed. Message Queuing Telemetry Transport

(MQTT) or known as an OASIS standard messaging protocol for the Internet of Things (IoT) allows the users to monitor the consumption in the form of dashboard on their desktop, laptop, or mobile phone.

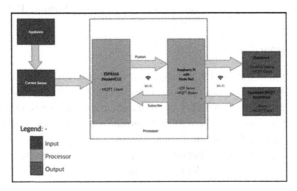

Fig. 2. Block diagram.

2.4 MQTT Connection

The connection process needs to be established to connect both IOT and hardware, which is MQTT connection between NodeMCU and Raspberry Pi are shown in Fig. 3. By this connection, the data from NodeMCU can be uploaded to Raspberry Pi which is represented as MQTT Broker, in order to display the data on Node Red Dashboard. The diagram below shows an established connection between the Node MCU and Raspberry Pi via MQTT Broker.

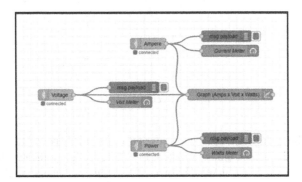

Fig. 3. MQTT connection.

3 Result and Discussion

Please This chapter discusses the results of the project. The prototype has gone through all the phases as described in the previous chapter. Discussion of results focus on the construction using the Node-RED and the coding from the Arduino IDE software.

3.1 Variant Comparison

During the execution of the coding program, two variants of the current sensor were used to compare their precision of data due to different sensitivity. Figure 4 shows the current reading for low variant, 5 A, which gave more accurate reading than the high variant current sensor, 30 A. The ACS712 with 5 A current sensor had more sensitivity, which was 185 mV/A to handle the current flow across the input Ip+ & Ip− when using home appliances to record the electric current reading. It is because most home appliances only consume a small amount of electric current.

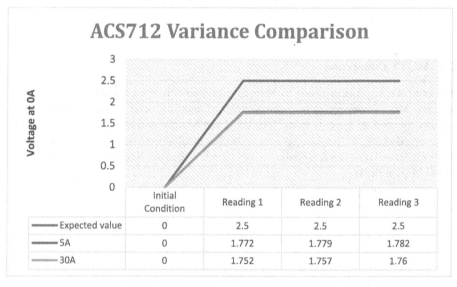

	Initial Condition	Reading 1	Reading 2	Reading 3
Expected value	0	2.5	2.5	2.5
5A	0	1.772	1.779	1.782
30A	0	1.752	1.757	1.76

Fig. 4. Zero current reading.

The result shown in Table 1 below was used to compare the percentage of error when there was no current across the input Ip+ & Ip−. The reading indicates the veracity of the electric current, as stated in the datasheet. This includes calculating the accuracy of the data to be compared with the theoretical part in the datasheet.

Table 1. Current sensor reading.

Aspect/Variants	5 A	30 A
Zero current reading	1.772 V–1.782 V	1.752 V–1.760 V
Voltage at 0 A (Datasheet)	VCC/2 = 2.5	VCC/2 = 2.5
Percentage of error	29.12%–28.72%	29.92%–29.6%

The formula to calculate the percentage of error for each ACS712 variant is stated below, for example, the reading for ACS712 5 A is 1.779 V. The Percentage of error is measured using Eq. (1):

$$Precision\ of\ ACS7125A = \frac{1.779}{2.5} \times 100\% = 71.16\%$$
$$Percent\ Error = 100\% - 71.16\%$$
$$= 28.84\%$$

(1)

3.2 Programming Result

The project was tested on a single home appliance, and several readings had been recorded to verify the accuracy of the reading based on value manipulation in coding syntax. Table 2 shows the coding syntax, where the value of 240 basically is the standard supply voltage in Malaysia, and required to be multiplied with the AmpsRMS that had been calculated in the previous coding line. The manipulation value is the offset value when no load is connected, therefore real consumption is obtained by subtracting the offset value.

Table 2. Program result.

Coding syntax	No load connected	100 W Home Appliance
(240*AmpsRMS) - 18 W	Ampere (A): 0.06 to 0.07 Voltage (mV): 0.01 Watts: −4.56 to −2.33	Ampere (A): 0.39 to 0.40 Voltage (mV): 0.07 Watts: 76.05 to 78.29
(240*AmpsRMS) - 20 W	Ampere (A): 0.06 to 0.07 Voltage (mV): 0.01 Watts: −6.56 to −4.33	Ampere (A): 0.39 Voltage (mV): 0.07 Watts: 74.05
(240*AmpsRMS) – 15 W	Ampere (A): 0.06 to 0.07 Voltage (mV): 0.01 Watts: −1.56 to 0.67	Ampere (A): 0.38 to 0.41 Voltage (mV): 0.07 to 0.08 Watts: 76.81 to 83.53

(continued)

Table 2. (*continued*)

Coding syntax	No load connected	100 W Home Appliance
(240*AmpsRMS) – 14 W	Ampere (A): 0.06 to 0.07 Voltage (mV): 0.01 Watts: −0.56 to 1.67	Ampere (A): 0.38 to 0.41 Voltage (mV): 0.07 to 0.08 Watts: 77.81 to 84.53
(240*AmpsRMS) - 13.5 W	Ampere (A): 0.06 to 0.07 Voltage (mV): 0.01 Watts: −0.06 to 2.17	Ampere (A): 0.38 to 0.41 Voltage (mV): 0.07 to 0.08 Watts: 78.31 to 85.03

3.3 Selected Offset Value

Throughout the results obtained using 100 W on a single home appliance, the assumption was then made: the accuracy of reading can be improved by changing the offset value that is required to subtracted with the calculated value to get the real consumption. Even though the objective of this observation could be achieved, an important thing that needs to be considered as one of the causes that might lead to unexpected value, which is the sensitivity of the ACS712 current sensor itself.

The sensitivity of ACS712 cannot be improved due to manufacturing circumstances, but the reading still can be tweaked to improve the precision of the reading to the nearest value of home appliance, based on processed data by using the coding syntax as shown in Table 3. From comparison, the best offset value to improve the real consumption reading is the 13.5-W, while the initial value when no load is connected should be nearest to 0, where the maximum value that can be achieved is 2.17 W.

Table 3. Selected offset value.

Coding syntax	100 W home appliance	Precision of reading
(240*AmpsRMS)-13.5 W	Ampere (A): 0.38 to 0.41 Voltage (mV): 0.07 to 0.08 Watts: 78.31 to 85.03	78.31% to 85.03% with Percentage of Error (21.69% to 14.97%)

The formula to calculate the percentage of error for offset value is shown below, for example the maximum reading value of 100 W home appliance is 85.03 W. The Percentage of error is measured using Eq. (2):

$$Precision\ of\ Reading = \frac{85.03}{100} \times 100\% = 85.03\%$$
$$Percentage\ of\ Error = 100\% - 85.03\%$$
$$= 14.97\%$$

$$(2)$$

3.4   Result Analysis

Observation was required to validate the feasibility of current sensor across the current consumption of home appliances. Several analyses were necessary to identify the capability of ACS712 current sensor in measuring current consumption accurately. The proposed project had been tested for four hours by using Home Appliances which consume 14 W a day. The results were then compared with saving analysis from Tenaga Nasional Berhad (TNB). Figure 5 below shows the dashboard of the proposed project as the result of electricity energy consumption.

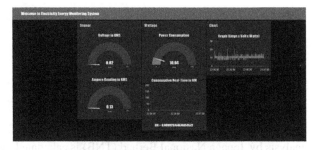

Fig. 5. Dashboard of proposed project.

The total consumption after four hours of using 14-W Home Appliance was RM 0.009930, and the average power consumption was 10.14 W based on current sensor reading. From the analysis result, the precision of reading and percentage of error can be calculated by using Eq. (3):

$$Precision\ of\ ACS712\ 5A = \frac{0.009930}{0.02} \times 100\% = 49.65\%$$
$$Percent\ Error = 100\% - 49.65\%$$
$$= 50.35\%$$

(3)

3.5   Saving Analysis (Tenaga Nasional Berhad)

Figure 6 below shows the estimation of saving analysis from Tenaga Nasional Berhad (TNB), which is RM0.02 for a single day with four hours of electricity usage. The calculation method used by TNB to measure single appliance is theoretical, whereby the estimation per day needs to be calculated first, and then multiplied with the average cost per kWh, which is RM0.3166 to get the real consumption.

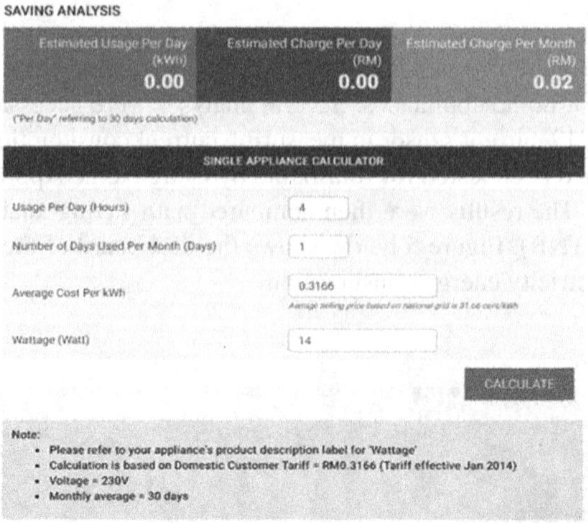

SAVING ANALYSIS

Estimated Usage Per Day (kWh)	Estimated Charge Per Day (RM)	Estimated Charge Per Month (RM)
0.00	0.00	0.02

("Per Day" referring to 30 days calculation)

SINGLE APPLIANCE CALCULATOR

Usage Per Day (Hours) — 4

Number of Days Used Per Month (Days) — 1

Average Cost Per kWh — 0.3166
Average selling price based on national grid is 31.66 cent/kWh

Wattage (Watt) — 14

CALCULATE

Note:
- Please refer to your appliance's product description label for 'Wattage'
- Calculation is based on Domestic Customer Tariff = RM0.3166 (Tariff effective Jan 2014)
- Voltage = 230V
- Monthly average = 30 days

Fig. 6. Saving analysis from tenaga nasional berhad (TNB).

The saving analysis by Tenaga Nasional Berhad (TNB) is calculated using Eq. (4):

$$Hours\ Per\ Day = 4\,\text{h}$$
$$Average\ Cost\ Per\ kWh = RM\,0.3166$$
$$Wattage\ (Watt) = 14$$
$$Estimate\ Per\ Day = 4\,\text{h} \times 14\,\text{W}$$
$$in\ kWh = \frac{56}{1000} = 0.056\ \text{kWh} \tag{4}$$
$$Estimate\ Per\ Day = 0.056\,\text{kWh} \times RM\,0.3166$$
$$Estimate\ Per\ Day = 0.0177296\ (Round\ off\ to\ 2DP)$$
$$Estimate\ Per\ Day = 0.02$$

3.6 Prototype Design

Figure 7 shows the final design of prototype for the Electricity Energy Monitoring System. The equipment had been tested during the assembly process, attached to a small home appliance, which was a 100 W Bulb. The Monitoring system was also tested during the assembly process to ensure the project not showing any sign of failure. As shown in Fig. 7, the 100 W Bulb was attached to the prototype as one of the demonstration parts.

Fig. 7. Prototype design with home appliance attached.

4   Conclusion

In conclusion, the Energy Monitoring System is a revolutionary implementation of the Internet of Things, developed to remotely manage home appliances over the internet from anywhere in the world. In the proposed project, the current sensor senses the current load generated by the appliances, and the current consumption is monitored by the NodeMCU. The system updates the data every second on the internet and displays it on Node-RED, and it sends the same information to the consumer's mobile phone thru MQTT.

The proposed system is capable of alleviating the burden of consumer, while making consumers be more aware and concerned about unwanted use of electricity at home. This IoT system has the features of monitoring electricity consumption and receiving sending notification to Telegram Application when the consumer exceeds the electricity usage. Also, by using the analytics function to detect electricity usage, consumers can set their budget on energy consumption for the upcoming month. The system can calculate the average daily usage based on the estimated budget.

Acknowledgment. The authors would like to thank the Ministry of Education (MoE) and Management and Science University (MSU) for sponsoring this work under Grant ID no. SG-017-012020-FISE.

References

1. Payne, J.E.: A survey of the electricity consumption-growth literature. Appl. Energy **87**(3), 723–731 (2010). https://doi.org/10.1016/j.apenergy.2009.06.034

2. Tang, C.F., Tan, E.C.: Exploring the nexus of electricity consumption, economic growth, energy prices and technology innovation in Malaysia. Appl. Energy **104**, 297–305 (2013). https://doi.org/10.1016/j.apenergy.2012.10.061
3. Shirsat, P.G.K., Bhangale, N.U., Gurav, U.Y., Jawale, S.A.: IoT Based Energy Monitoring System for Energy Conservation, pp. 758–763 (2020)
4. Al-Humairi, S.N.S., Kamal, A.A.A.: Design a smart infrastructure monitoring system: a response in the age of COVID-19 pandemic. Innov. Infrastruct. Solut. **6**, 144 (2021). https://doi.org/10.1007/s41062-021-00515-y
5. Al-Humairi, S.N.S., Zainol, M.H., Razalli, H., Raya, L., Irsyad, M., Abdullah, R., Daud, J.: Conceptual design: a novel Covid-19 smart AI helmet. Int. J. Emerg. Technol. **11**(5), 389–396 (2020)
6. Syafiq, S., Rosli, M.M., Daud, M., Rahman, A.F.A., Salleh, M.N.T., Mohamad, F.A.: Smart energy monitoring system for residential in Malaysia. In: ACM International Conference Proceedings Services, pp. 18–22 (2019). https://doi.org/10.1145/3361758.3361766
7. Wilson, C., Hargreaves, T., Hauxwell-Baldwin, R.: Benefits and risks of smart home technologies. Energ. dPolicy **103**, 72–83 (2017). https://doi.org/10.1016/j.enpol.2016.12.047

Short-Time Fourier Transform with Optimum Window Type and Length: An Application for Sag, Swell and Transient

Muhammad Sufyan Safwan Mohamad Basir[1](✉) [ID], Nur-Adibah Raihan Affendy[2],
Mohamad Azizan Mohamad Said[1], Rizalafande Che Ismail[3] [ID],
and Khairul Huda Yusof[4]

[1] Department of Electrical Engineering, Politeknik Mukah Sarawak, KM 7.5 Jalan Oya,
96400 Mukah Sarawak, Malaysia
muhammadsufyan91@gmail.com
[2] Department of Commerce, Politeknik Mukah Sarawak, KM 7.5 Jalan Oya,
96400 Mukah Sarawak, Malaysia
[3] Faculty of Electronic Engineering Technology, Universiti Malaysia Perlis, Perlis, Malaysia
[4] Faculty of Information Sciences and Engineering, Management and Science University,
U019(B) University Drive, Off Persiaran Olahraga, Section 13, 40100 Shah Alam, Selangor,
Malaysia

Abstract. The characteristics of power quality signals are non-stationary, where
the behaviour confirms the negative consequence in sensitive equipment. Modern
cross-term time-frequency distributions (TFDs) are able to characterize the power
quality accurately but suffer from a delay in measurement since the power quality
signals, in this case, sag, swell and transient, need to be analyzed in real-time.
It is shown that one window shift (OWS) properties of linear time-frequency
representation (TFR) results from short-time Fourier transform (STFT) satisfies
accuracy, complexity and memory. By optimally selecting the window length
of 512, the TFR is able to provide optimal time, and frequency localization, as
well as the spectral leakage, can be reduced by the Hanning window. The proposed
technique can accurately characterize the power quality signals averagely by 95%,
as well as the complexity and memory usage is low. Finally, the paper is concluded
by the recommendation of pre-setting for optimum window type and length for
real-time power quality measurement.

Keywords: Power quality · Short-time fourier transform · Window length ·
Hanning

1 Introduction

In a household, the electric power consumed depends on the load usage, and it varies over
time. High technology components nowadays have the capability to operate automatically depending on the surrounding, taking an example of air conditioning temperature

M. Yusoff et al. (Eds.): SCDS 2023, CCIS 1771, pp. 147–160, 2023.
https://doi.org/10.1007/978-981-99-0405-1_11

is varying over the room temperature. Thus, it is characterized by randomness and unpredictability [1]. Although these high technology components lead to the economically use of appliances, the disadvantage of high-frequency switching components introduces power quality. Obviously, the power quality from a load result from voltage and current imbalance levels cause the whole inter-network appliances to suffer as well as causes financial expenses not only to customers but also to electric power companies [2]. Practically, the power quality types are difficult to characterize, and other studies [3, 4] conclude the finding for electrical load data to be either normal or distorted.

It is a challenge to reduce the power quality since some power quality types, for example, transient and harmonic, are more sophisticated and costly than ordinary measurements. Characterizing the power quality is costly and time-consuming since it requires appropriate measurement tools [5–7], which are normally expensive. Furthermore, data taken is longer since it requires consideration of load usage for a certain period and measurement acquisition issues due to the oversampling or undersampling [8]. Therefore, in measuring the power quality signals, the pre-defined setting should be considered as follows:

- Sampling rate and size should be suitable with data acquisition equipment, and the component levels measured should follow the standards (i.e., IEEE Standard 519–1992);
- Window type and length should be optimized so different power quality (i.e., sag, swell, overvoltage, undervoltage, harmonic, inter-harmonic and transient) can easily be characterized;
- An appropriate classifier should be considered for the reliability of the measurement so a proper filtering circuit can be proposed.

This paper aims to determine the optimum window type and length for power quality signals, namely sag, swell and transient. The results obtained will further be used as a reference for the development of a real-time power quality monitoring system. The rest of this paper is organized as follows: Sect. 2 illustrates the model of power quality signals simulated using MATLAB. Section 3 describes the windowed short-time Fourier transform (STFT) concept for signal parameters represented using time-frequency representation (TFR) for various window types. Section 4 presents the proposed statistical method and equations for accuracy, computational complexity, and memory of STFT. Apart from that, Sect. 5 presents the comparative outcomes for various window types and lengths (128, 512, 1024, 2048, 4096 and 8192) in finding the optimum value. Finally, Sect. 6 provides a conclusion and recommendation in developing a real-time power quality monitoring system.

2 Power Quality Signal Modelling

In a simple manner, power quality disturbance is categorized into three, i.e., waveform distortion (harmonic and inter-harmonic), voltage variation (sag, swell, overvoltage and undervoltage) and transient signal. Fluctuations in signal amplitude, phase, and frequency in power system, taking an obvious example of solid-state devices, will cause sudden increase and decrease (usually associated with sag and swell events) in network signal as well as large amplitude at high-frequency components (transient) [9], are characteristically different, hence monitoring these kinds of signals are challenging. The test signal is modelled as tabulated in Table 1, using a complex exponential function equation standardized based on IEEE 1159–2009.

Table 1. Power quality signal characteristics.

Power Quality	Equation	Signal Component
Normal	$x_{norm}(t) = Ae^{j2\pi f_0 t}$	$A = 1$
Sag	$x_w(t) = e^{j2\pi f_0 t} \sum_{k=1}^{K} A_k \prod_k (t - t_{k-1})$	$A_1 = A_3 = 1, A_2 = 0.8, t_1 = 100\text{ms}, t_2 = 140\text{ms}$
Swell		$A_1 = A_3 = 1, A_2 = 1.2, t_1 = 100\text{ms}, t_2 = 140\text{ms}$
Transient	$x_{trans}(t) = e^{j2\pi f_0 t} \sum_{k=1}^{K} \prod_k (t - t_{k-1})$ $+ Ae^{-1.25(t-t_1)/(t_2-t_1)} e^{j2\pi f_1(t-t_1)} \prod_2 (t - t_1)$ $\prod_k(t) = 1 \qquad \text{for } 0 \le t \le t_k - t_{k-1}$ $\qquad\quad = 0 \qquad \text{elsewhere}$	$A = 0.5, f_1 = 1000\text{Hz}, t_1 = 100\text{ms}, t_2 = 115\text{ms}$

Following the equations derived, test signal parameters such as the starting time, t duration, $(t - t_{k-1})$ amplitude, A and frequency, f selected is not related to any applications; by means, the values are chosen just for the purpose of analysis. Fundamentally, A_1 and f_0 are set to 1 and 50 Hz respectively, taking 12000 Hz as sampling frequency, F_s with Nyquist theorem, in consequence, give the approximate 6000 Hz in maximum for the measurable frequency with 5000 number of samples, N_s.

The x_{norm}, as graphically shown in Fig. 1 (a), is modelled taking $A = 1$ with duration, $t_{duration}$ of $(1/F_s) \times N_s$, for the purpose of illustration and is not considered as power quality. Theoretically, analysis of a signal using short-time Fourier transform (STFT) may result in slipping either in time or frequency. Therefore, it is recommended to find the optimum window type and length to avoid inaccurate measurement. Based on the literature, analysis using linear time-frequency distributions (TFDs) is not only allocated to power quality. Still, it is extensively applied on the radar [10], high voltage [11] and recently towards electromyography [12]. Therefore, the optimum window type and length for different applications may be different; by means, it is necessary to use short window length for high-frequency applications and vice versa. In this case, the model of power quality signal, i.e., sag (Fig. 1 (b)) with $A_2 = 0.8$, swell (Fig. 1 (c)) with $A_2 = 1.2$ and transient (Fig. 1 (d)) are studied, in finding the optimum window length. This gives an advantage for pre-determined settings for the real-time monitoring system.

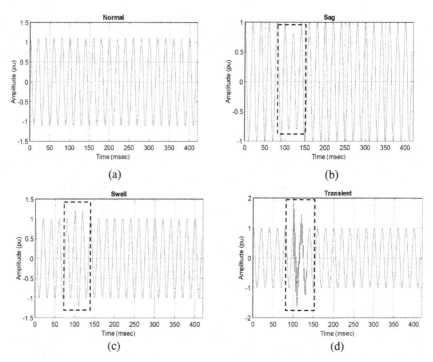

Fig. 1. Modelled power quality signal for (a) normal, (b) sag, (c) swell, and (d) transient.

3 Windowed Function for STFT

The Fourier transform, due to the weaknesses in time localization, is replaced with windowed based short-time Fourier transform (STFT). Window function, $w(t)$ as in Eq. (1), subjectively to the choices of types, i.e., derived with the root of the cosine function is plotted in Fig. 2 and length able to identify the nonstationarity aspects and pattern of signals resulting in three-dimensional spectrogram plot known as time-frequency representation (TFR). Since interference of power quality signal is involved with multiple frequency components, and some of them appear in a short duration of time, it is suggested to keep the time-frequency resolution, F_s/win_length, to a high value that could give a significance in avoiding artifacts [13].

$$S_x(t, f) = \left| \int_{-\infty}^{\infty} x(t) w(\tau - t) e^{-j2\pi f \tau} d\tau \right|^2 \tag{1}$$

Rectangular

$$w(n)_{rectangular} = 1, \ 0 \le n \le N-1$$

Hanning

$$w(n)_{hanning} = 0.5\left(1 - \cos\left(2\pi\frac{n}{N}\right)\right), \ 0 \le n \le N$$

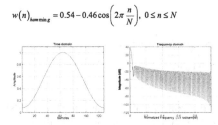

Leakage Factor: 9.15%

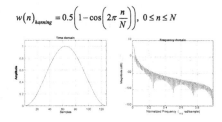

Leakage Factor: 0.05%

Hamming

$$w(n)_{hamming} = 0.54 - 0.46\cos\left(2\pi\frac{n}{N}\right), \ 0 \le n \le N$$

Flattop

$$w(n)_{flattop} = 0.21557895 - 0.41663158\cos\left(\frac{2\pi n}{L-1}\right) + 0.4277263158\cos\left(\frac{4\pi n}{L-1}\right)$$
$$- 0.083578947\cos\left(\frac{6\pi n}{L-1}\right) + 0.006947368\cos\left(\frac{8\pi n}{L-1}\right), \ 0 \le n \le L-1$$

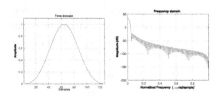

Leakage Factor: 0.03%

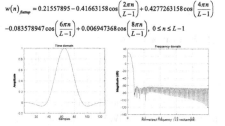

Leakage Factor: 0%

Blackman

$$w(n)_{tukey} = \begin{cases} \frac{1}{2}\left[1 + \cos\left(\pi\left(\frac{2n}{\alpha N}-1\right)\right)\right], & 0 \le n < \frac{\alpha N}{2} \\ 1, & \frac{\alpha N}{2} \le n \le N\left(1-\frac{\alpha}{2}\right) \\ \frac{1}{2}\left[1 + \cos\left(\pi\left(\frac{2n}{\alpha N}-1\right)\right)\right], & N\left(1-\frac{\alpha}{2}\right) < n \le N \end{cases}$$

Tukey

$$w(n)_{tukey} = \begin{cases} \frac{1}{2}\left[1 + \cos\left(\pi\left(\frac{2n}{\alpha N}-1\right)\right)\right], & 0 \le n < \frac{\alpha N}{2} \\ 1, & \frac{\alpha N}{2} \le n \le N\left(1-\frac{\alpha}{2}\right) \\ \frac{1}{2}\left[1 + \cos\left(\pi\left(\frac{2n}{\alpha N}-1\right)\right)\right], & N\left(1-\frac{\alpha}{2}\right) < n \le N \end{cases}$$

At $\alpha = 0$ it become rectangular, and at $\alpha = 1$ it become Hanning window

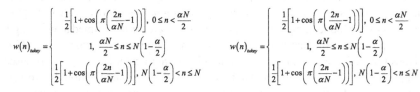

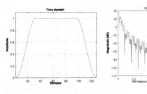

Leakage Factor: 0%

Leakage Factor: 3.56%

Fig. 2. Characteristics of various window types in time and frequency domain for win_length = 128.

Gaussian   **Kaiser**

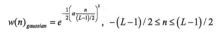

$$w(n)_{gaussian} = e^{-\frac{1}{2}\left(\alpha\frac{n}{(L-1)/2}\right)^2}, \quad -(L-1)/2 \le n \le (L-1)/2$$

$$w(n)_{kaiser} = \frac{I_o\left(\beta\sqrt{1-\left(\frac{n-N/2}{N/2}\right)^2}\right)}{I_o(\beta)}, \quad 0 \le n \le N$$

α is inversely proportional to the standard deviation,
σ, of a Gaussian random variable

$$\beta = \begin{cases} 0.1102(\alpha-8.7), & \alpha > 50 \\ 0.5842(\alpha-21)^{0.4}+0.07886(\alpha-21), & 50 \ge \alpha \ge 21 \\ 0, & \alpha < 21 \end{cases}$$

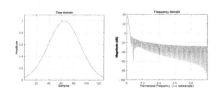

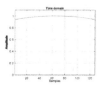

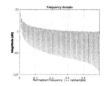

Leakage Factor: 0.01%   Leakage Factor: 8.38%

Fig. 2. (*continued*)

For the symmetric window, τ, we employ the concept of one sample shift (OSS), one window shift (OWS) or half window shift (HWS), which is identified as the centre position of the shifted window $w(\tau - t)$. It is varied to be better neither for accuracy nor computational speed. Cowell and Freear in [14] claimed that using Hanning window for linear frequency modulation (LFM) signal furnish with narrow effect between fundamental and frequency components cause the spectrogram to be mapped precisely [15]. Moreover, a study conducted by [16] for musculoskeletal disorder claimed a win_length of 1024 is appropriate for that application. This time same window type as in [14] is used. However, unfortunately, researchers in [17] did not agree. Hence [17] proposed win_length of 512 should be implemented throughout the same application. Interesting approaches in [18] develop a real-time power quality monitoring system, but the reliability of data itself can be debated since no standard window type or length are justified. This study is concerned about the aspect of choosing the right type and length of the window, which give a benefit in optimization of power quality signals to benefit in both time and frequency (See Fig. 3). Followed by pre-analysis for 128 window length in Fig. 2, the high leakage factor of 9.15% depicted by rectangular window contributes to inaccurate results, indicating the incapability in analyzing power quality signals. Based on the observation in Fig. 2, a cone shape window indicated by Hanning, Hamming, Flattop, Blackman and Gaussian with leakage factor correlate between 0% to 0.05%, promised a precise result if the algorithm complexity is ignored.

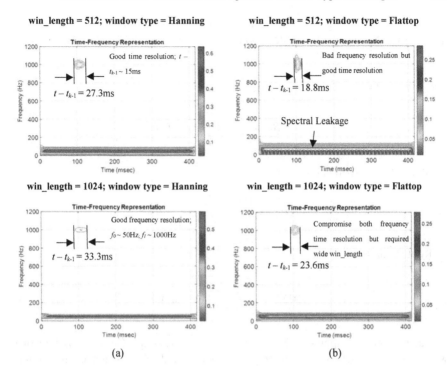

Fig. 3. Comparison of TFR for a transient signal using (a) Hanning with win_length 512 and 1024, (b) Flattop with win_length 512 and 1024.

4 Performance Measurements of Windowed STFT

In a theoretical manner, the performance of different window types is segregated based on the amount of leakage factor, following the hypothesis that the lower the value of leakage factor, the better the performance of the window. To ensure the reliability of this technique, measured parameters such as instantaneous root mean square (RMS) fundamental voltage, $V_{IRMS}(t)$, instantaneous RMS voltage, $V_{RMS}(t)$ and instantaneous total waveform distortion, $V_{TWD}(t)$ outcomes from time-frequency representation (TFR) are benchmarked with an actual value modelled using equations in Table 1. Rather than only focusing on the accuracy of the technique, other criteria that need to be highlighted are low in computational complexity and memory. The high complexity may affect the long term computational time, as well as the cost of the system will be expensive if the memory is high.

For the accuracy of analysis, the average error of the modelled signals based on statistical summaries using tendency to over or under forecast (BIAS), mean absolute percentage error (MAPE), and root means square error (RMSE) are implemented [19–21], aiming for lowest error for the reliability of the system. The results of the performance analysis are usually measured from the difference between actual value, A_t and measured value, F_t weighted by the number of data, n for every case as in Fig. 1. A graph of error versus win_length for various kinds is plotted to show the results, promising an optimum window for the future development of a real-time monitoring system.

a) *Accuracy of the Analysis*
   Tendency to over or under forecast

$$BIAS = \frac{1}{n} \sum_{t-1}^{n} (A_t - F_t) \tag{2}$$

Mean absolute percentage error

$$MAPE = \frac{100\%}{n} \sum_{t-1}^{n} \left| \frac{A_t - F_t}{A_t} \right| \tag{3}$$

Root mean square error

$$RMSE = \sqrt{\frac{1}{n} \sum_{t-1}^{n} \left| (A_t - F)^2 \right|} \tag{4}$$

Calculation of computational complexity is relatively simple (see Eq. (5)). It involves two variables, namely signal length, N and win_length, N_w, which is similar for a different window type. However, large complexity results in a delay in computational time. Therefore, the win_length selected is compromisable. In accordance, the same variable with additional Ns, either one sample shift (OSS), one window shift (OWS) or half window shift (HWS), are used to calculate the system memory, aiming for the smallest memory as possible throughout the optimum win_length selected.

b) *Computation Complexity of the Analysis*

$$Cr_{STFT} = N - N_w (N_w \log_2(N_w)) \tag{5}$$

c) *Memory Size of the Analysis*

$$Memory_{STFT} = \frac{N_w (N - N_w)}{N_s} \tag{6}$$

5   Optimization of Window for Reliability, Complexity and Memory

Having identified a power quality problem, the consideration is designing a measuring system that is cost-effective and reliable for different power quality nature. Normally, different types of loads may introduce different signal characteristics, which in our case, are normal, sag, swell and transient. Therefore, some detailed schemes will require some important decisions to be made [22], considering the need for windowed short-time Fourier transform (STFT) for optimum win_length and different window types to avoid spectral leakage.

As depicted in Fig. 4, the graph for mean absolute percentage error (MAPE) against win_length data is tabulated, ranging from 128 to 8192. Given that data in Fig. 4 (a)–(d) comprises the win_length of 128 measurements, it can be argued that the MAPE results show overestimated error. However, increasing the win_length does not guarantee the lowest possible error since MAPE indicated between 2048 to 8192 are dramatically increased. In the case of normal signal characteristics, the lowest MAPE recorded is at win_length of 512 with selected Gaussian, Hanning, Hamming and Blackman. The equation for the Flattop window did not correlate with the characteristics of the sinusoidal waveform at 512 with MAPE as high as 37% but shows a promising outcome when win_length is increased to 1024 indicated by 1.2% error at lowest for normal, sag and swell cases.

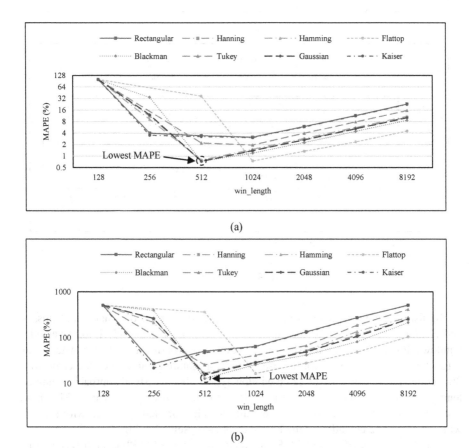

(a)

(b)

Fig. 4. MAPE signal using various window types and lengths for (a) normal, (b) sag, (c) swell and (d) transient.

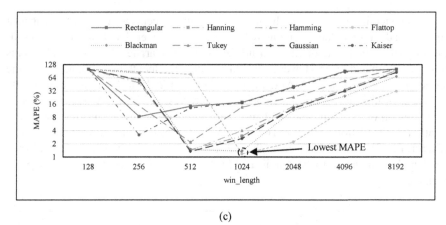

(c)

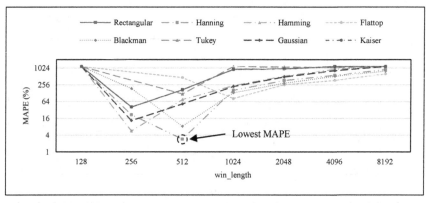

(d)

Fig. 4. (*continued*)

In distorted environments as plotted Fig. 4 (b)–(d), the use of Blackman, Gaussian and Hanning are considered since the possible error is considerably lower over other windows. It is obvious that the Hanning window is overperformed when transient characteristics occur. In Fig. 4 (d), the use of 512 for Hanning can reduce the error up to 86% compared to 256 with the same window type. Other statistical approaches, namely tendency to over or under forecast (BIAS) and root means square error (RMSE), are compared (see Fig. 5), taking average value for all four characteristics with selected win_length of 512 considering the lowest error as presented in Fig. 4.

The outcome for BIAS and RMSE are equivalent, while MAPE is slightly higher for all different window types. It can be clearly seen that the Flattop window is the worst, followed by Rectangular, Kaiser, Tukey, Hamming and Gaussian. For Hanning and Blackman, there are dramatic differences between both BIAS and RMSE with MAPE. The Hanning window is selected under the circumstance that it has the lowest error compared to Blackman.

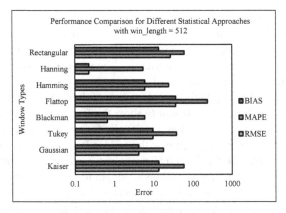

Fig. 5. Accuracy of power quality signal for win_length = 512.

The complexity of the measurement should be kept to the lowest value possible to ensure computational time can be reduced. Based on Eq. (5), different types of windows are not considered. By means, only signal length and win_length can affect the calculation. For the aforementioned above, the equation for memory is similar. The line graph in Fig. 6 shows the complexity and memory linearly increased with the increment of win_length. Thus, it is recommended to use the lowest win_length possible, but considering the changing of MAPE may cause wrong calculation, the optimum size of 512 is chosen.

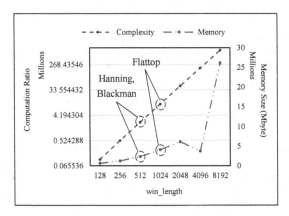

Fig. 6. Computational complexity and memory for different window lengths.

In comparison with win_length of 1024, the complexity and memory for 512 can be saved up to 78% and 44%, respectively. While for 128, although the complexity and memory can be reduced up to 95% and 73% respectively compared to 512, the absurd error as indicated in Fig. 4 (a)–(d) for all cases will affect measurement reliability.

There are few linear time-frequency distributions (TFDs), such as S-transform, which enhances the multi-scale window function to localize the time and frequency. However,

[23] concluded that the uniform resolution feature of Gaussian short-time Fourier transform (STFT) is not necessarily a disadvantage for time-frequency analysis. Moreover, based on the application studied related vibration signal, which is similar to this transient study, there is not much loss in time resolution. Therefore, the frequency for some of the cases can be more accurately localized.

The setting value of 512 with the representation of the STFT spectrogram is clearly indicated the time window was sufficient to show the frequency of the signal. Furthermore, the ability of the Hanning window specifically for normal, sag, swell and transient to be able to differentiate the components with a sudden frequency changing in the period from 0.1–50 ms interpret the STFT with Hanning can correctly characterize the signals. However, it is difficult to find the suitable win_length to resolve all the presented characteristics. Thus, the finding concluded that short win_length is good for highlighting the sudden changes, particularly a transient spike in the signal.

6   Conclusion

The analysis carried out confirms that the optimum window type and length that gives reasonable accuracy, which is averagely less than 5% error is by using Hanning with win_length of 512. However, the tradeoff for this technique is a high dependency on win_length. Thus, there may be temporal and spectral losses for different signal characteristics. A pre-determined win_length and window type can be used for future analysis within the scope of the study.

We, therefore, conclude a fact that the use of STFT benefited the low computational burden and size of the system used. Moreover, for different power quality characteristics modelled (frequency within 50–1000 Hz) as in Table 1, short win_length is adequate, thus benefiting for designing a low-cost real-time monitoring system.

In corresponding with the study in [24] for harmonic signal, the optimum win_length is seemly adequate to ours, but the Blackman window is considered more appropriate. Furthermore, the mean absolute percentage error (MAPE) indicated there are just slightly different compared to Hanning. Thus, we suggest using this setting to design a power quality system. Future studies will focus on signal characterization.

Acknowledgements. The research study was carried out successfully with contributions from all authors equally. The main research idea, simulation works, and manuscript preparation was contributed by Muhammad Sufyan Safwan Mohamad Basir. The challenge of power quality from an economic point of view and statistical approaches for STFT error calculation was prepared by Nur-Adibah Raihan Affendy. Mohamad Azizan Mohamad Said and Khairul Huda Yusof contributed to the modelling and simulating using MATLAB. Rizalafande Che Ismail for his support with study administration. The authors' responsibilities were as follows: design the research and write the manuscript; analyze data and validate; edited and conducted the research manuscript with final content. All authors have read and agreed to the published version of the manuscript. The authors would like to thank Politeknik Mukah Sarawak, Universiti Malaysia Perlis and Management and Science University for providing the support for this research.

References

1. Mageed, H., Nada, A.S., Abu-Zaid, S., Salah Eldeen, R.S.: Effects of waveforms distortion for household appliances on power quality. MAPAN **34**(4), 559–572 (2019)
2. Das, C.K., Bass, O., Kothapalli, G., Mahmoud, T.S., Habibi, D.: Overview of energy storage systems in distribution networks: placement, sizing, operation, and power quality. Renew. Sustain. Energ. Rev. **91**, 1205–1230 (2018)
3. Herraiz, S., Sainz, L., Clua, J.: Review of harmonic load flow formulations. IEEE Trans. Power Delivery **18**(3), 1079–1087 (2003)
4. Gursoy, E., Niebur, D.: Harmonic load identification using complex independent component analysis. IEEE Trans. Power Delivery **24**(1), 285–292 (2009)
5. Jopri, M.H., Ab Ghani, M.R., Abdullah, A.R., Manap, M., Sutikno, T., Too, J.: K-nearest neighbor and naïve Bayes based diagnostic analytic of harmonic source identification. Bull. Electr. Eng. Inform. **9**(6), 2650–2657 (2021)
6. Hussin, A.S., Abdullah, A.R., Jopri, M.H., Sutikno, T., Saad, N.M., Tee, Weihown: Harmonic load diagnostic techniques and methodologies: a review. Indonesian J. Electr. Eng. Comput. Sci. **9**(3), 690 (2018)
7. Jopri, M.H., Abdullah, A.R., Too, J., Sutikno, T., Nikolovski, S., Manap, M.: Support-vector machine and Naïve Bayes based diagnostic analytic of harmonic source identification. Indonesian J. Electr. Eng. Comput. Sci. **20**(1), 1–8 (2020)
8. Puce, A., Hämäläinen, M.: A review of issues related to data acquisition and analysis in EEG/MEG studies. Brain Sci. **7**(12), 58 (2017)
9. Lee, I.W.C., Dash, P.K.: S-transform-based intelligent system for classification of power quality disturbance signals. IEEE Trans. Ind. Electron. **50**(4), 800–805 (2003)
10. Wu, Q., Zhang, Y.D., Tao, W., Amin, M.G.: Radar-based fall detection based on Doppler time–frequency signatures for assisted living. IET Radar, Sonar Navigation **9**(2), 164–172 (2015)
11. Ghaderi, A., Mohammadpour, H.A., Ginn, H.L., Shin, Y.-J.: High-impedance fault detection in the distribution network using the time-frequency-based algorithm. IEEE Tran. Power Delivery **30**(3), 1260–1268 (2015)
12. Shair, E.F., Ahmad, S.A., Abdullah, A.R., Marhaban, M.H., Tamrin, S.M.: Selection of spectrogram's best window size in EMG signal during core lifting task. J. Telecommun., Electron. Comput. Eng. (JTEC) **10**(1–16), 81–85 (2018)
13. Shin, Y.-J., Powers, E.J., Mack Grady, W., Arapostathis, A.: Signal processing-based direction finder for transient capacitor switching disturbances. IEEE Trans. Power Deliv. **23**(4), 2555–2562 (2008)
14. Cowell, D.M.J., Freear, S.: Separation of overlapping linear frequency modulated (LFM) signals using the fractional Fourier transform. IEEE Trans. Ultrason., Ferroelect. Freq. Contr. **57**(10), 2324–2333 (2010)
15. Wen, H., Teng, Z., Guo, S.: Triangular self-convolution window with desirable sidelobe behaviors for harmonic analysis of power system. IEEE Trans. Instrum. Meas. **59**(3), 543–552 (2010)
16. Zawawi, T.N.S.T., Abdullah, T., Sudriman, R., Saad, N.M., Too, J., Shair, E.F.: Classification of EMG signal for health screening task for musculoskeletal disorder. Int. J. Eng. Technol. **8**(1.7), 219–226 (2019)
17. Too, J., Abdullah, A.R., Mohd Saad, N., Mohd Ali, N., Tengku Zawawi, T.N.S.: Application of gabor transform in the classification of myoelectric signal. TELKOMNIKA (Telecommun. Comput. Electron. Control) **17**(2), 873 (2019)

18. Abdullah, A.R., Saad, N.M., Sha'ameri, A.Z.: Power quality monitoring system utilizing periodogram and spectrogram analysis techniques. In: Proceedings of the 2007 IEEE International Conference on Control, Instrumentation and Mechatronics Engineering, pp. 770–774 (2007)
19. Angrisani, L., Daponte, P., D'Apuzzo, M., Testa, A.: A measurement method based on the wavelet transform for power quality analysis. IEEE Trans. Power Delivery 13(4), 990–998 (1998)
20. Willmott, C.J., Matsuura, K.: Advantages of the mean absolute error (MAE) over the root mean square error (RMSE) in assessing average model performance. Clim. Res. 30, 79–82 (2005)
21. Jopri, M.H., Abdullah, A.R., Sutikno, T., Manap, M., Ab Ghani, M.R., Yusoff, M.R.: A critical review of time-frequency distribution analysis for detection and classification of harmonic signal in power distribution system. Int. J. Electr. Comput. Eng. (IJECE) 8(6), 4603 (2018)
22. Stones, J., Collinson, A.: Power quality. Power Eng. J. 15(2), 58–64 (2001)
23. Jin, Y., Hao, Z.-Y., Zheng, X.: Comparison of different techniques for time-frequency analysis of internal combustion engine vibration signals. J. Zhejiang Univ.-Sci. A 12(7), 519–531 (2011)
24. Basir, M.S.S.M., Yusof, K.H., Faisal, B., Shahadan, N.H.: Optimised window selection for harmonic signal detection using Short Time Fourier Transform. In: AIP Conference Proceedings, vol. 2306, no. 1, p. 020020. AIP Publishing LLC (2020)

Data Analytics and Technologies

Cox Point Process with Ridge Regularization: A Better Approach for Statistical Modeling of Earthquake Occurrences

Alissa Chintyana[✉], Achmad Choiruddin, and Sutikno

Department of Statistics, Institut Teknologi Sepuluh Nopember, Surabaya 60111, Indonesia
alissachintya@gmail.com

Abstract. The inhomogeneous Cox point process is commonly used for modeling natural disasters, such as earthquake occurrences. The inhomogeneous Cox point process is one of the popular models for the analysis of earthquake occurrences involving geological variables. The standard two-step procedure does not however perform well when such variables exhibit high correlation. Since ridge regularization has a reputation in handling multicollinearity problems, in this study we adapt such a procedure to the spatial point process framework. In particular, we modify the two-step procedure by adding ridge regularization for parameter estimation of the Cox point process model. The estimation procedure reduces to either the Poisson-based regression or logistic-based regression. We apply our proposed method to model the earthquake distribution in Sumatra. The results show that considering ridge regularization in the model is advantageous to obtain a smaller value of the Akaike Information Criterion (AIC). Especially, Cox point process model with a logistic-based regression has the smallest AIC.

Keywords: Cluster point process · Earthquake modeling · Multicollinearity

1 Introduction

The spatial point process becomes one of the standard procedures for the statistical analysis of the distribution of earthquake occurrences in a region [1–3]. Recent studies consider inhomogeneous spatial point process models to study the spatial trend of the earthquake distribution due to geological variables using the Cox point process [4–6] or Gibbs point process [2, 7]. For example, the analysis of earthquake occurrences in Sumatra, Indonesia, using inhomogeneous Cox point processes [8, 9] has better properties when subduction zones, faults, and volcanoes are added to the model. The addition of such geological factors improves the model interpretability and earthquake risk prediction [4, 5]. The two-step estimation [10] is considered for the parameter estimation, where the parameters related to spatial trend are estimated in the first step and clustering parameters are estimated in the second step.

In employing point process models with geological covariates, one of the main challenges is handling the multicollinearity problem. It is quite natural that a high correlation

M. Yusoff et al. (Eds.): SCDS 2023, CCIS 1771, pp. 163–177, 2023.
https://doi.org/10.1007/978-981-99-0405-1_12

between geological variables appears since the locations of subduction, fault, and volcano can be close to each other, leading to a multicollinearity problem. One strategy is to apply a stepwise technique [5] to select only a fewer number of variables to include in the model. However, this can be problematic if all the variables are important.

To handle the multicollinearity issue when modeling the earthquake distribution, in this study, we involve ridge regularization in the inhomogeneous Cox point process estimation procedure. To consider ridge regularization, we adapt the two-step estimation [10] and modify the first step of the procedure by adding a ridge penalty. The second step for clustering parameter estimation follows the standard procedure [10]. The procedure is applied to model earthquake occurrences in the Sumatra region and compared to the ones which do not consider ridge regularization. Sumatra is located in western Indonesia. Earthquakes are a geological disaster that is prone to occur in Indonesia with more than 5,000 earthquakes occurring every year. The active fault "The Great Sumatran Fault" one of the fastest-moving faults in the world [11] makes Sumatra an earthquake-prone area located in a high seismic zone.

The rest of the paper is organized as follows. The study area and data description are detailed in Sect. 2 while the methodology is presented in Sect. 3. Section 4 discusses the results of the analysis and Sect. 5 provides a concluding remark.

2 Study Area and Data Description

The movement of the Indo-Australian plate which continues to actively sink under the Eurasian plate makes the Eurasian plate proceed to shift and causes a fault that extends from the northern tip to the southern tip of Sumatra. This movement produces an accretion zone and the Bukit Barisan Mountains with a volcanic strip in the middle, as well as an active fault "The Great Sumatran Fault" [12]. The result of the movement of the Indo-Australian and Eurasian plates is what causes Sumatra to have the potential to face earthquake threats from many sources. Sumatra is an island in the western part of Indonesia with $B = [92.5177; 109.1723] \times [-6.86350; 6.6476]$ (100 km^2).

The dataset that is used in this study is derived from the United States Geological Survey (USGS) major-shallow earthquakes (magnitude ≥ 5 M) in Sumatra during 2004–2018. There are 1192 earthquake coordinates (data points) that will be used for analysis. Based on records, from 2000 to 2018, there have been 9 to 19 destructive earthquakes (meaning that these earthquakes have resulted in fatalities, damage to buildings, environmental damage, and property losses) in Indonesia [13]. In [13] it also mentioned that the earthquake in Aceh (2004, 9.1M) was recorded as the largest earthquake in Indonesia with losses caused: a total of 227,900 people died and 1.7 million people were displaced in 14 countries from South Asia to East Africa. At that time the epicenter was 250 km southeast of Banda Aceh, at a depth of 30 km.

In general, the distribution of Sumatra's earthquake locations occurs in certain areas, namely in areas adjacent to subduction zones, faults, and volcanoes as shown in Fig. 1. Earthquakes are caused by the release of elastic energy stored in tectonic plates. When the fault is locked and continuous relative motion occurs between the plates causes an increase in stress. This movement continues until the pressure is sufficient to break through then suddenly slides and releases the stored energy causing an earthquake

[14]. The meeting (collision) of plates due to plates approaching each other is called subduction.

Table 1. Geological factor description.

Variable	Description	Unit
Fault	Distance to the nearest fault	100 km
Subduction zone	Distance to the nearest subduction	100 km
Volcano	Distance to the nearest volcano	100 km

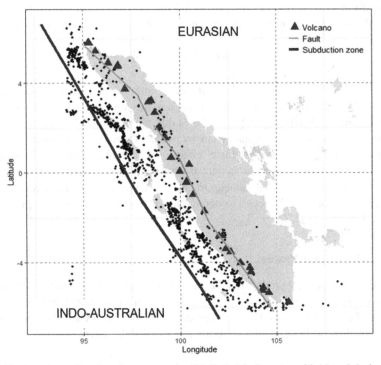

Fig. 1. The locations of earthquake occurrences (black dot) in Sumatra with $M \geq 5$ during 2004–2018 as well as locations of volcano (red triangle), fault (orange line), and subduction zone (blue line).

Subduction zones host major earthquakes, then the existence of a subduction zone can result in the formation of volcanic troughs and pathways [9]. Volcanic activity can also trigger earthquakes. Therefore, we considered three geological factors which are related to earthquake occurrences, i.e. the fault, subduction zone, and volcano, as has been proven in [5, 9, 14]. Geological factor data in the form of line segments (faults and subduction zones) and coordinates (volcanoes). Modeling with geological factors uses the value of the closest distance from the point of an earthquake (see Table 1). The distance used is the Euclidean distance. From Fig. 1, it can be seen that the location of the volcano in Sumatra is along the Sumatran Fault Line. This allows a high correlation between the closest distance to the volcano and the fault. It can also be seen from pixel correlation. To address the highly correlated covariates, in this study, we propose a modification of two-step estimation with ridge penalty.

3 Methodology

The inhomogeneous point process is a model with an intensity function that is not constant or varies spatially. Let inhomogeneous Poisson point process $\mathbf{X}$ consists of locations of the earthquake, then there is a spatial point pattern x, $x = \{x_1, x_2, ..., x_n\}$ in a certain observation window B, $B \subseteq \mathbb{R}^2$. In this model, varying intensities are influenced by spatial covariates. Then, the intensity can be modeled in a log-linear parametric model

$$\rho(x; \boldsymbol{\beta}) = \exp\left(\boldsymbol{\beta}^T \mathbf{z}(x)\right), \tag{1}$$

where $z(x) = (z_1(x), z_2(x), z_3(x))^T$ are the covariate (volcano, fault, subduction) distance to the nearest earthquake point and β is a regression parameter that corresponds to each covariate. According to [4], it shows that the best model for modeling earthquake cases in Sumatra is the Cauchy cluster model. Therefore, in this study, we apply the Cauchy cluster to model the cluster effect of earthquake activity. To estimate the parameter, we adopt a two-step procedure as described further in [4, 10]. The first step is the estimation of a first-order parameter to obtain $\hat{\boldsymbol{\beta}}$ with additional ridge regularization (Subsect. 3.3). The second step is to obtain cluster parameter $\hat{\boldsymbol{\psi}}$ which is presented in Subsect. 3.4.

3.1 Cauchy Cluster Process

The Cauchy cluster point process is a special form of the Neyman-Scott Cox Process that considers Bivariate Cauchy density [10] based on offspring and parent process activities. Let $\mathbf{C}$ be a Poisson process as the parent process with an intensity $\gamma > 0$. A new process will appear, $X_c, c \in C$, called the offspring process that has intensity [10]

$$\rho_c(x; \beta) = \exp\left(\varsigma + \beta^T \mathbf{z}(x)\right)h(x - c),$$

where h is a bivariate Cauchy density function. The bivariate Cauchy density function with scale parameter ω is the form of

$$h(x; \omega) = \frac{1}{2\pi\omega^2}\left(1 + \frac{\|x\|^2}{\omega^2}\right)^{-\frac{3}{2}}.$$

The parent points in this study are the location of the main earthquakes, while the location of the aftershocks is the offspring points.

Process $X = \cup_{c \in C} X_c$ is a Cox process with the intensity formulated in (2) [15]

$$\rho(x; \beta) = \gamma \, \exp\!\left(\varsigma + \beta^T \mathbf{z}(x)\right) = \exp\!\left(\beta_0 + \beta^T \mathbf{z}(x)\right), \tag{2}$$

where $\beta_0 = \varsigma + log\gamma$ represents the intercept and γ is the intensity of mainshock. Equation (2) is the intensity when there is a clustering effect. To find out the cluster parameter $\psi = (\gamma, \omega)^T$, the pair correlation function and K-function are used. Those two function, with $r = \|x_i - x_j\|$ and $x_i, x_j \in B$, as respectively follows

$$g(r; \omega) = 1 + \frac{1}{8\pi \gamma \omega^2}\left(1 + \frac{\|r\|^2}{4\omega^2}\right)^{-\frac{3}{2}}, \quad K(r; \omega) = \pi r^2 + \frac{1}{\gamma}\left(1 - \frac{1}{\sqrt{1 + \frac{r^2}{4\omega^2}}}\right).$$

3.2 Intensity Estimation

For the inhomogeneous Poisson point process, the non-constant intensity has an impact on the log-likelihood function depending on the location of the point in x [15] suwch that

$$\log L(\beta) = \sum_{x \in X \cap B} \log \rho(x; \beta) - \int_B \rho(x; \beta)dx, \tag{3}$$

where $\rho(x; \beta)$ is presented in (1). There are two standard strategies for estimating intensity function from (3), namely Poisson regression and logistic regression approach.

Poisson-Based Regression. In the Poisson regression approach, the integral function in (3) can be approximated by assigning quadrature weights

$$\int_B \rho(x; \beta)dx \approx \sum_{i=1}^{n+d} \rho(x_i; \beta)w_i,$$

with n being the number of data points, d being the number of dummy points, and w_i being positive quadrature weights. Berman and Turner [16] reconstructed (3) and then obtained

$$\log L(\beta) \approx \sum_{i=1}^{n+d} w_i(y_i \log \rho(x_i; \beta) - \rho(x_i; \beta)), \tag{4}$$

where $y_i = I_i/w_i$ with I_i is equal to 1 if x_i is a data point and equal to 0 if x_i is a dummy point. Term $\rho(x_i; \beta) = \rho(x; \beta)$ as shown in (1).

Logistic-Based Regression. The application of likelihood logistics is considered more efficient because it uses fewer dummy points than Poisson [17]. Although there is an increase in the variance of parameter estimates, this method avoids some of the bias and may have a better mean squared error overall [15]. This is also evidenced by the findings in [18]. The scenario in this approach is to generate dummy points according to the Poisson process **D** that has an intensity $\delta(x)$. The Poisson process **D** is independent of process **X** (consists of data points). Let **Y**, $Y = X \cup D$, then **Y** is also a Poisson point process with intensity $\rho(x) + \delta(x)$. For each point $y_j \in Y$, let I_j be the indicator function which is equal to 1 if the point y_j is a data point and equal to 0 when a dummy point.

Conditional on **Y**, if we treat y_j as a fixed location, the data will be consists only of the indicators $I_1, \ldots, I_{n+d}$, with n being the number of data points and d being the number of dummy points. The conditional probability of observing a point (first term) or a dummy point in the observation window is shown as [15]

$$P\{I_j = 1\} = p_j = \frac{\rho(y_j)}{\rho(y_j) + \delta(y_j)}, P\{I_j = 0\} = 1 - p_j. \tag{5}$$

The likelihood function of the logistic regression approach given the data **x** and the dummy **d** is formed by applying the Binomial distribution then the following equation is obtained [18]

$$\begin{aligned}
\log L(\beta) &\approx \sum_{j=1}^{n+d} I_j \log(p_j) + (1 - I_j) \log(1 - p_j) \\
&\approx \sum_{x \in \mathbf{x}} \log \frac{\rho(x; \beta)}{\rho(x; \beta) + \delta(x; \beta)} + \sum_{x \in \mathbf{d}} \log \frac{\delta(x; \beta)}{\rho(x; \beta) + \delta(x; \beta)}.
\end{aligned} \tag{6}$$

3.3 Ridge Regularization

In regression, ridge regularization is commonly used to overcome the case of multicollinearity. Ridge can be applied to all situations when the model used is linear [19]. In general, the regularization method tries to maximize Eq. (7) as the ridge penalized likelihood function [20]

$$Q(\beta) = \log L(\beta) - |B| \sum_{k=1}^{p} \frac{1}{2} \lambda \beta_k^2, \tag{7}$$

where $\log L(\beta)$ is log-likelihood Poisson regression (4) or logistic regression (6) with Taylor expansion, $|B|$ is the area of the observation domain, and $\lambda \geq 0$ is tuning parameter corresponding to β_k, $k = 1, 2, \ldots, p$ with p is the number of covariates.

Coordinate Descent Algorithm (CDA) method is applied to solve a ridge penalized problem with optimizes the target function iteratively until convergence. The CDA method is tried to solve a penalized problem so that the minimum function is obtained as follows

$$\min Q(\beta) = \min \left\{ -\log L(\beta) + |B| \sum_{k=1}^{p} \frac{1}{2} \lambda \beta_k^2 \right\}. \tag{8}$$

The key point in CDA is the optimization of each coordinate concerning the estimated parameter [20, 21]. Assume we have the estimate $\tilde{\beta}_l$ for $l \neq k, l, k = 1, 2, \ldots, p$. The coordinate descent method consists in partially optimizing (8) concerning β_k.

$$\min_{\beta_k \in R} Q\left(\tilde{\beta}_1, ..., \tilde{\beta}_{k-1}, \beta_k, \tilde{\beta}_{k+1}..., \tilde{\beta}_p\right). \tag{9}$$

The coordinate update for ridge regularization such as in [21] is presented in (10).

$$\tilde{\beta}_k \leftarrow \frac{S\left(\sum_{i=1}^{n+d} v_k z_{ik}\left(y_i - \tilde{y}_i^{(k)}\right), 0\right)}{\sum_{i=1}^{n+d} v_k z_{ik}^2 + n\lambda}, s \tag{10}$$

where $\tilde{y}_i^{(k)} = \tilde{\beta}_0 + \sum_{l \neq k} z_{il} \tilde{\beta}_l$ are the fitted values excluding the contribution from covariates, v_k are the weights, and $S(a, b)$ is the soft-thresholding operator such as

$$S(a, b) = \text{sign(a)}(|a| - b)_+ = \begin{cases} a - b & \text{if } a > 0 \text{ and } b < |a| \\ a + b & \text{if } a < 0 \text{ and } b < |a| \\ 0 & \text{if } b \geq |a|. \end{cases}$$

Term y_i and v_k in (10) adjust based on the intensity function approach used (Poisson-based regression or logistic-based regression). The update (9) and (10) is repeated for $k = 1, 2, ..., p$ until convergence.

3.4   Cluster Parameter Estimation

The second-order composite likelihood is a parameter estimation method to get the cluster parameter estimator $\psi = (\kappa, \omega)$. The second-order composite likelihood function is constructed from all pairs x_i, x_j of data points as represented in (11).

$$CL(\psi) = \sum_{i=1}^{n} \sum_{j=1, j \neq i}^{n} 1\{\|x_i - x_j\| < R\} \times$$

$$\left\{\log g(\psi) - \log \int_B \int_B 1\{\|x_i - x_j\| < R\} g(\psi) dx_i dx_j\right\}, \tag{11}$$

where $R > 0$ is the upper limit of the correlation distance from the model and $g(\psi)$ is the pair correlation function of the Cauchy cluster model (Subsect. 3.1). Parameter estimation of the Cauchy point process model using the kppm function in a spatstat R package [15]. Parameter estimation of the Cauchy point process model by considering ridge regularization is applied with the kppmenet function [6].

3.5   Model Interpretation and Selection

Interpretation is important to explain the values obtained from parameter estimation. In two-step estimation, we quantified the effect of geological factors at the first step by assessing parameter β. In the case where there is a covariate that is highly correlated with others, estimating β can be obtained by adding ridge regularization. Whereas, the spatial correlation parameter (pair correlation function and K-function) can determine the clustering effect.

To select the best model among the Cauchy model with Poisson regression approach, Cauchy with logistic regression approach, the Cauchy model based on the Poisson-based regression with ridge regularization, and Cauchy process with logistic-based regression with ridge regularization, we evaluated their AIC values and selected the best model with the minimum AIC. The AIC value [15] is defined by

$$AIC = -2\hat{L}_{max} + 2q,$$

where $\hat{L}_{max}$ is the maximum likelihood point process model and q is the number of overall estimated parameters.

We perform the envelope test to find out the goodness of the model. The envelope is the critical limit of the statistical test of the summary function [15]. In the envelope test, we first estimate the inhomogeneous K-function with the formula

$$\hat{K}_{inhom}(r) = \frac{1}{|B|} \sum_{i=1}^{n} \sum_{j=1, j\neq i}^{n} \frac{\mathbf{1}\{d_{ij} \leq r\}}{\hat{\rho}(x_i)\hat{\rho}(x_j)} e(x_i, x_j; r). \tag{12}$$

K-function is the cumulative average of the number of data points located at radius r from the data point. The value of r is the radius determined by the researcher. The concept of calculating the value of the K-function is to calculate the distance $d_{ij} = \|x_i - x_j\|$ of all pairs of distinct points. Term e_{ij} in (12) is edge correction weight [15] and term $\hat{\rho}(x_i)$, $\hat{\rho}(x_j)$ is intensity function. The K-function plot of the original data points will be compared with the results from the simulation of the point process model. A model is said to be good for modeling certain data if the K-function plot of the data point is in the K-function envelope interval.

The modeling steps are briefly described as follows. The first stage is the pre-processing data includes sorting the earthquake coordinate data according to the earthquake magnitude limit ($M \geq 5$) and the covariate coordinates based on the observation window limit. The next step is testing spatial trends and patterns of earthquake distribution, followed by modeling using the Cauchy cluster process. Parameter estimation for the model without regularization is obtained through the kppm function, while the model with regularization is obtained through the kppmenet function. Lastly, mapping earthquake risk predictions in Sumatra using the best model. The analysis steps are summarized in Fig. 2.

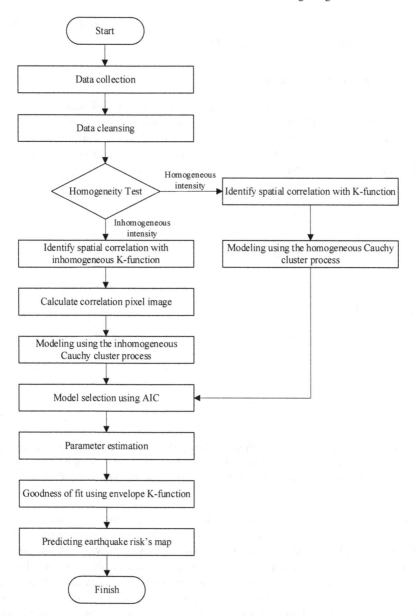

Fig. 2. Flowchart of modeling earthquake

4   Result

In this section, we will discuss the results of the analysis of earthquake data in Sumatra and their geological covariates. Starting with the exploration of the pattern of earthquake distribution, then followed by Sumatra earthquake modeling using the Cauchy cluster process. The Cauchy model is used by considering two approaches (Poisson-based and logistic-based regression) and the addition of the ridge penalty.

4.1 Exploratory Data Analysis

To find out the spatial trend of earthquake data in Sumatra, a Chi-Squared test was conducted with a null hypothesis of a stationary Poisson process. We use `quadrat.test` function of `spatstat` R package. The value of the chi-square statistic is 5622.5 and the p-value is equal to 2.2×10^{-16} with a significance level of 0.05. Hence, there is evidence of a spatial trend in Sumatra's earthquake data set.

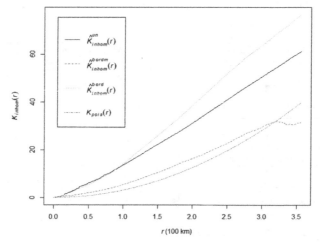

Fig. 3. Inhomogeneous K-function without correction (black line), inhomogeneous K-function with modified border correction (red line), Inhomogeneous K-function with border correction (green line), and Poisson process K-function (blue line) for the Sumatra earthquake data.

Next, cluster detection is employed by looking at the spatial correlation using the K-function (`Kinhom` function in R). Cluster detection uses `Kinhom` because the results of the Chi-Squared test concluded that the earthquakes in Sumatra were inhomogeneous. As shown in Fig. 3, all the inhomogeneous K-function lines are above the blue Poisson process line. It means that the distribution of earthquakes in Sumatra forms a cluster pattern. The inhomogeneous K-function with modified border correction showed clustering, so we apply the inhomogeneous Cox point process for modeling the earthquake in Sumatra.

Table 2. Pixel correlation matrix among the geological variables.

Covariate	Volcano	Fault	Subduction
Volcano	1.00000	0.99488 0.00000*	0.76309 0.00000*
Fault		1.00000	0.79073 0.00000*
Subduction			1.00000

* Correlation is significant at the 0.05 level (2-tailed)

Then, pixel correlation is used to analyze the distance correlation among geological factors. The method used is Pearson correlation. *The following* Table 2 *gives the correlation values across covariates.* A high correlation between covariates, especially in volcanoes with a fault can cause multicollinearity. Therefore, to avoid biased estimators, ridge regularization is applied. Modeling using ridge regularization is discussed further in the following section.

4.2 Inference and Model Selection

To model the earthquake occurrences in Sumatra involving geological variables, we consider a two-step estimation procedure, as described in [4, 10, 22]. The first step is intensity estimation considering ridge regularization (see Subsect. 3.3) and the second step is cluster parameter estimation (see Subsect. 3.4). We compare four models among the Cauchy model with the Poisson-based regression using kppm Poisson, Cauchy with logistic-based regression (kppm logistic), Cauchy model Poisson-based with ridge regularization (kppmenet Poisson), and Cauchy model logistic-based with ridge regularization (kppmenet logistic).

Table 3. The clustering estimator, the maximum composite likelihood, and the AIC values for each model to the earthquake data in Sumatra.

Method	$\hat{\gamma}$	$\hat{\omega}$	$\hat{L}_{max}$	AIC
kppm Poisson	0.5335	0.1307	946,896	$-1{,}893{,}787$
kppm logistic	0.5967	0.1245	915,517	$-1{,}831{,}024$
kppmenet Poisson	0.2896	0.1683	1,147,159	$-2{,}296{,}308$
kppmenet logistic	0.2877	0.1688	1,149,993	$-2{,}299{,}996$

The kppmenet is more prominent than the kppm with a higher maximum composite likelihood ($\hat{L}_{max}$) and smaller AIC, as represented in Table 3. The smallest AIC and the highest $\hat{L}_{max}$ belong to the kppmenet logistic-based. The difference between kppmenet Poisson and kppmenet logistic is not too far in either $\hat{\gamma}$, $\hat{\omega}$, $\hat{L}_{max}$, or AIC values. Based on the clustering estimator $\hat{\psi} = (\hat{\gamma}, \hat{\omega})$ of kppmenet logistic-based, there are 40 estimated mainshocks with the aftershocks distributed around each mainshock in a scale of approximately 17 km.

Table 4. The estimator regression of the geological variables based on the kppmenet logistic with ridge regularization.

Parameter	Estimate	exp ($\hat{\beta}$)	1/exp($\hat{\beta}$)
Intercept	−1.4111	0.2439	4.1001
Volcano	−0.1746	0.8398	1.1908
Fault	−0.2349	0.7907	1.2647
Subduction	−0.4226	0.6553	1.5261

All estimators β yielded negative values (Table 4). The estimation results are following the theory such as in [1, 14], which states that earthquakes are prone to occur at closer distances to the volcano, fault, and subduction zone. The subduction contributes the highest effect to the major earthquake occurrence in Sumatra. The risk of a major earthquake occurrence will increase by 1.53 times when the location is closer to 100 km from the subduction zone. This is following what has been stated in [23] that subduction zones host major earthquakes. The existence of a subduction zone can result in the formation of volcanic troughs and pathways [9] and also fault. It can trigger earthquakes.

Based on Fig. 4, the mean of the envelope K-function (dashed red line) is close to the empirical K-function (solid black line) that falls inside the envelope interval (grey area). In general, the Cauchy cluster model with logistic-based regression fits the earthquake distribution in Sumatra. It should be noted that at a radius above 250 km, there is a possibility of an underfit model due to the interval in the envelope K-function expanding downwards. The predicted intensity map shows that the risk of earthquakes in Sumatra tends to be high in areas located near the subduction zone, which is in the western part of Sumatra which borders the Indian Ocean and is predicted the highest risk in areas located in the north. The three main areas that have the highest risk of earthquake occurrences are Aceh, Simeule, and Bengkulu.

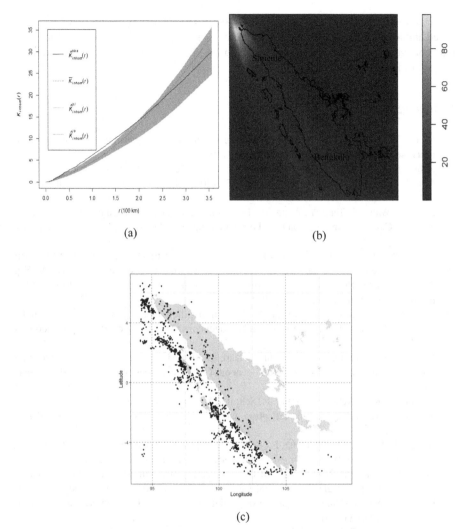

(a)   (b)

(c)

Fig. 4. (a) Envelope K-function for the Sumatra earthquake data based on the Cauchy cluster process using a logistic approach with ridge regularization, (b) Prediction map of the earthquake risk in Sumatra based on Cauchy Model using the logistic approach with ridge, and (c) Distribution of the locations of the Sumatra earthquake.

5   Concluding Remark

In this study, we modify of two-step estimation procedure for the inhomogeneous Cox point process to deal with correlated covariates. The Cauchy cluster point process was chosen for modeling the distribution of the earthquake in Sumatra with the addition of a ridge penalty to handle the multicollinearity case. In general, the Cauchy cluster model with ridge regularization obtains a higher maximum composite likelihood value. A Cauchy cluster model with a logistic-based approach produces the smallest AIC.

Nonetheless, the difference in $\hat{L}_{max}$ produced between the Cauchy cluster model Poisson-based and logistic-based was not very significant. To improve this issue, the future study may consider using other regularization methods [20, 24]. A more careful investigation is very useful for further study.

References

1. Ogata, Y.: Statistical models for earthquake occurrences and residual analysis for point processes. J. Am. Stat. Assoc. **83**(401), 9–27 (1988)
2. Zahra, A., et al.: Strauss point modeling for seismic activity: a case study of earthquakes. Model. Earth Syst. Environ. **8**(1), 1243–1251 (2021). https://doi.org/10.1007/s40808-021-01154-z
3. Shan, W., Wang, Z., Teng, Y., Wang, M.: Temporal and spatial evolution analysis of earthquake events in California and Nevada based on spatial statistics. ISPRS Int. J. Geo Inf. **10**(7), 465 (2021)
4. Choiruddin, A., Susanto, T.Y., Metrikasari, R.: Two-step estimation for modeling the earthquake occurrences in Sumatra by Neyman-Scott Cox point processes. In: Mohamed, A., Yap, B.W., Zain, J.M., Berry, M.W. (eds.) Soft Computing in Data Science 2021, CCIS, vol. 1489, pp. 146–159. Springer, Singapore (2021)
5. Choiruddin, A., Aisah, F.T., Iriawan, N.: Quantifying the effect of geological factors on distribution of earthquake occurrences by inhomogeneous Cox processes. Pure Appl. Geophys. **178**(5), 1579–1592 (2021)
6. Choiruddin, A., Susanto, T.Y., Husain, A., Kartikasari, Y.M.: kppmenet: Combining the kppm and elastic net regularization for inhomogeneous Cox point process with correlated covariates (2022)
7. Vasudevan, K., Eckel, S., Fleischer, F., Schmidt, V., Cook, F.A.: Statistical analysis of spatial point patterns on deep seismic reflection data: a preliminary test. Geophys. J. Int. **171**(2), 823–840 (2007)
8. Affan, M., Syukri, M., Wahyuna, L., Sofyan, H.: Spatial statistic analysis of earthquakes in Aceh Province year 1921–2014. Aceh Int. J. Sci. Technol. **5**(2), 54–62 (2016)
9. Lidyana, V., Darsono, Novita, S.S.: Distribution of earthquake in subduction zone and calculation of subduction angle in the Central Sumatra based on earthquake data period 1967–2016. In: 9th International Conference on Physics and Its Applications. IOP Conference Series 1153 (012021), Surakarta (2019)
10. Waagepetersen, R.P., Guan, Y.: Two-step estimation for inhomogeneous spatial point processes. J. Royal Stat. Soc. Series B (Stat Methodol.) **71**(3), 685–702 (2009)
11. Sahara, D.P., Widiyantoro, S.: The pattern of local stress heterogeneities along the central part of the Great Sumatran fault: a preliminary result. In: 7th Asian Physics Symposium. IOP Conference Series 1204 (012091), Bandung (2019)
12. Natawidjaja, D.H.: Updating active fault maps and sliprates along the Sumatran Fault Zone, Indonesia. In: Global Colloquium on GeoSciences and Engineering. IOP Conference Series 118 (012001), Bandung (2018)
13. BMKG: Katalog Gempa Bumi Signifikan dan Merusak Tahun, pp. 1821–2018. BMKG, Jakarta (2019)
14. Ohnaka, M.: Large earthquake generation cycles and accompanying seismic activity. In: The Physics of Rock Failure and Earthquakes, pp. 200–247. Cambridge University Press, Cambridge (2013)
15. Baddeley, A., Rubak, E., Turner, R.: Spatial Point Patterns: Methodology and Applications with R. CRC Press, New York (2015)

16. Berman, M., Turner, R.: Approximating point process likelihoods with GLIM. Appl. Stat. **41**(1), 31–38 (1992)
17. Husain, A., Choiruddin, A.: Poisson and logistic regressions for inhomogeneous multivariate point processes: a case study in the Barro Colorado Island plot. In: Mohamed, A., Yap, B.W., Zain, J.M., Berry, M.W. (eds.) Soft Computing in Data Science 2021, CCIS, vol. 1489, pp. 301–311. Springer, Singapore (2021)
18. Baddeley, A., Coeurjolly, J.F., Rubak, E., Waagepetersen, R.P.: Logistic regression for spatial Gibbs point processes. Biometrika **101**(2), 377–392 (2014)
19. Hastie, T.: Ridge regularizaton: an essential concept in Data Science. arXiv preprint arXiv: 2006.00371v1 (2020)
20. Choiruddin, A., Coeurjolly, J.F., Letué, F.: Convex and non-convex regularization methods for spatial point processes intensity estimation. Electron. J. Stat. **12**(1), 1210–1255 (2018)
21. Friedman, J., Hastie, T., Höfling, H., Tibshirani, R.: Pathwise coordinate optimization. The Ann. Appl. Stat. **1**(2), 302–332 (2007)
22. Jalilian, A., Guan, Y., Waagepetersen, R.P.: Decomposition of variance for spatial cox processes. Scand. J. Stat. **40**(1), 119–137 (2013)
23. Wirth, E.A., Sahakian, V.J., Wallace, L.M., Melnick, D.: The occurrence and hazards of great subduction zone earthquakes. Nat. Rev. Earth Environ. **3**(2), 125–140 (2022)
24. Choiruddin, A., Coeurjolly, J.F., Letue, F.: Adaptive lasso and Dantzig selector for spatial point processes intensity estimation. Bernoulli (2023)

Discovering Popular Topics of Sarawak Gazette (SaGa) from Twitter Using Deep Learning

Nur Ain Binti Nor Azizan, Suhaila Binti Saee[✉],
and Muhammad Abdullah Bin Yusof

Universiti Malaysia Sarawak, 94300 Kota Samarahan, Sarawak, Malaysia
{68283,21020459}@siswa.unimas.my, ssuhaila@unimas.my

Abstract. The emergence of social media as an information-sharing platform is progressively increasing. With the progress of artificial intelligence, it is now feasible to analyze historical document from social media. This study aims to understand more about how people use their social media to share the content of the Sarawak Gazette (SaGa), one of the valuable historical documents of Sarawak. In the study, a short text of Tweet corpus relating to SaGa was built (according to some keyword search criteria). The Tweet corpus will then be analyzed to extract the topic based on a topic modeling, specifically, Latent Dirichlet Allocation (LDA). Then, the topics will be further classified with Convolutional Neural Network (CNN) classifier.

Keywords: Topic modeling · Twitter analysis · Sarawak Gazette

1 Introduction

The introduction of new media such as Twitter, TikTok, Youtube, and Instagram impacted how society started sharing information. The Twitter platform, for instance, is widely used by people as it focuses on communication and virtual community-based network [5].

Some people shared historical context in their Tweets and comments with different aims, such as educating and reminiscing memories [10]. With so many user-generated posts, social media offers an extensive environment to learn about past and ongoing events significant to the flow of history. As there is seamless sharing, it is now possible to analyze historical content from social media with the advancement of artificial intelligence.

There are many considerable amounts of research that have been done to extract history-oriented content data from social media. [10] used machine learning to conduct an extensive comprehensive analysis of history-oriented content in microblogs to examine the peculiarities of tweets about history. Be that as it may, there is a low amount of studies done on Malaysian historical documents. This study will be using Sarawak Gazette as a medium for historical documents to understand historical document-oriented content in social media.

M. Yusoff et al. (Eds.): SCDS 2023, CCIS 1771, pp. 178–192, 2023.
https://doi.org/10.1007/978-981-99-0405-1_13

The study aims to build a short-text corpus of SaGa from Twitter and discover the pattern of popular topics from the corpus. It gathers information to preserve and immerse one's memories in society and participation in the historical subject in their social media; in this case, SaGa. As a result, researchers can examine how people refer to the past, why such connections emerge, and what functions they provide.

2 Related Works

2.1 Data Acquisition

In recent years, several types of research have been conducted that focus on discovering a certain topic from the Twitter corpus. However, from the collections of similar articles, only a few of them attempted to come across the historical topics [3, 10] or past events topics [9]; [13].

Several of the notable publications assessed use history-related and topic-modeling Twitter analysis, in which Tweets are examined using keywords or hashtags that have the historical context or a certain topic as features. A few relevant studies also jumped straight to the process and did not define the data acquisition procedure.

Most of the reviews of the literature focus on how academics used Twitter API as a data-collecting tool. The study from [3] analyzed Twitter profiles for the important historical events Tweet: – the 2nd Spanish Republic, The Spanish Civil War, and the Franco Regime. The research utilized Twitter API. Twitter provides a free Application Programming Interface (API), which is very useful to retrieve and analyze Twitter data programmatically and develop for the Twitter conversation. In addition to that, a technological aid, the tool t-hoarder kit_2, was employed. It is open-source software that allows developers to build and analyze Twitter data, making it easier to utilize in the analysis and data visualization.

In the study, [10] conduct an extensive comprehensive analysis of history-oriented content on Twitter to examine the peculiarities of Tweets about history. The research also utilized Twitter API. To collect the data from Tweets that imply history-oriented content and collective memories of previous events/entities, they apply hashtags-based crawling and a bootstrapping technique.

The first step involves defining seed hashtags selected by experts such as #history and hashtags that refer to past events such as #historical events. All of the selected hashtags were selected by historian choices and then queried to collect Tweets. All the tags linked to the seed hashtags were then collected and reviewed manually to ensure that the hashtags were indeed related to history. Finally, 147 collected hashtags were attained along with 2370252 Tweets.

2.2 Feature Extraction

Term Frequency times Inverse Document Frequency (TF-IDF) is a standard measure of how dense the frequency of a specific term is in several documents. It is commonly used to re-weight feature count in order to reduce the effect of more frequent but less valuable words while increasing the influence of rarer but more significant terms [15]. [7] use TF IDF to obtain the weight for terms in the Tweets document for the data structure.

The bag-of-words model was used in NLP processing and information retrieval in the past. The grammar and sentence structure will be ignored, and a phrase can be perceived or represented as bags of words.

Text-term Matrix will then be used to look for instances of specific words in the collection of words to comprehend the document based on its most important terms. Tokenization in [2] uses BoW for feature extraction in NMF model. [1] also utilized BoW in preprocessing by constructing the model on W (tokenized terms of each document) and V (a corpus of terms with frequency).

2.3 Different Approaches in Topic Modeling

Rule-based is usually used for text classification. [11] describe ruled-based to any categorization technique that uses IF-THEN features for class prediction. For example, [14] utilized rule-based classification on Tweets to identify the topic in Tweets regarding HPV vaccination.

One of the popular machine learning topic models used to extract topics from a text corpus is Latent Dirichlet Allocation (LDA). According to [8], The 'latent' term refers to something hidden or not fully formed. It creates probabilities of topics and words categorized into documents.

A study by [9] in 2016 applied the LDA model. The LDA setting was experimented on to create a more useful and cohesive topic and transpired. It is also worth noting that all retrieved topics were linked to the event described in the data.

According to the subjective analysis of the findings, LDA can derive extensive insights from the data. It retrieved all of the important event elements, such as the participants, geographic location, and how the event. For example, in the Gikomba dataset, topic 0: 'bomb' and 'blast' give initial insights into the bombing.

2.4 Recurrent Neural Network (RNN) and Convolutional Neural Network (CNN)

[12] present a supervised NTM (Topic Attention Model) with a Recurrent Neural Network (RNN). They demonstrate a unique approach to using document-specific (long text) topic modeling with a global topic vector obtained from NTM. In addition, they created a backpropagation inference that optimized combined models. TAM has improved learning tasks, such as regression and classification, and produced less ambiguity for document modeling.

RNN effectively retains the local patterns of a text string- both semantic and syntactic, but they struggle with long-range dependencies. [4] designed an RNN-based language model:- TopicRNN that uses latent topics to capture the semantic information of a text document.

There is two evaluation of performance for the methodology: word prediction and sentiment analysis. Penn TreeBank (PTB), a traditional benchmark for evaluating a new language model, was used for word prediction, while 1MDB 100k was used for sentiment analysis. They also utilized RNN (TopicRNN), LSTM (TopicLSTM), and GRU(TopicGRU).

In the same study by [4], TopicRNN was trained with various network sizes. [1] utilized data from the USA and offer a five layers adaptive approach to follow the trending topics of health on Twitter. The supervised approach is used as Convolutional Neural Network (CNN) to categorize and label the Tweets. Because the approach also used the word2vec model, it collects the correlation of words depending on the context, which improves the run time, prediction, and accuracy of Tweet tracking.

Tweepy, a python tool to collect Tweets, was used in the first layer. The cleaning and preparation procedures are detailed in the second layer, which changed Tweets into vectors. Word2vec was used in the third layer that turned the vector into a matrix used to initialize a neural network to predict the tagged Tweet. CNN classifier was then used in the fourth layer to label undetected Tweets from Word2Vec. Unlabeled data was then sent into the LDA model at the fifth layer, where new topics might be produced. The CNN model will be retrained for both the topics and Word2Vec.

2.5 Evaluation

There must be assessments of results for the study to be clear and logical. These tests were carried out to see how well the algorithms used in the research performed. The topic coherence analysis and the precision, recall, and F1 measurements evaluated the outcomes. It was also utilized to analyze the models to achieve accurate performance.

Train-test split is splitting the data into two parts, the first part is to sit or train the data using the algorithm, and the other part is to test and assess the accuracy of the data. Typical topic modeling such as LDA, LSA, and NMF did not rely on training data. But deep learning topic modeling approaches usually use train-test split for assessment reasons. For example, [4] also utilized a train-test split. The methodology, the TopicRNN, was initially tested on a word prediction task utilizing the Penn Treebank (PTB) component of the database. The Wall Street Journal is a newspaper published in the United States. The normal split is applied, with Sections. 0–20 (930K tokens) being used. Sections 21–22 (74K tokens) are for training, Sections. 23–24 (82K tokens) are for validation, and Sections. 23–24 (82K tokens) are for testing.

Calculating accuracy, precision, recall, and f-score are also vital. Precision was calculated to quantify the prediction of the class that belongs to the class, and recall quantifies the number of the class predictions made from all the datasets, fl-score was measured to provide a single score that stabilizes both the concerns precision and recall in one number. This type of evaluation will be useful if the algorithm used is the supervised algorithm.

In Nugruho et al. 2016, after the topic extraction and topic coherence evaluation, they evaluate the Tweet-topic accuracy by comparing the result of a manually labeled training dataset and measuring the precision (P) and recall (R) using F-score. The findings depicted that LDA outperforms NMF in terms of topic coherence.

[1] uses the confusion metrics of accuracy (1), recall (2), precision (3), and F1-score (4) to evaluate the results. In order to compare and contrast the suggested system, to predict and tag new Tweets, SVM and CNN algorithms were used. Unfortunately, both approaches have limitations due to the imbalanced datasets (Fig. 1).

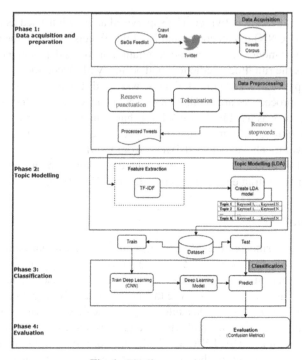

Fig. 1. Pipeline overview.

3 Methodology

This study will analyze the popular topics of the Sarawak Gazette from Twitter. It consists of 4 phases. Phase 1: Data acquisition and preparation, Phase 2: Topic Modelling, Phase 3: Classification, and finally, Phase 4: Evaluation.

The first phase is data acquisition and preparation. This phase is partitioned into two processes:- Data acquisition and data preprocessing. The study utilized a web crawler to extract the Tweets related to SaGa to create a short text corpus of Tweets, and then the acquired Tweets will be cleaned and normalized in the data preprocessing process. The Tweet acquired are dated from January 1, 2011, to December 31, 2021, and written in English.

Phase 2 is the deployment of the topic modeling to extort the relevant topic. Phase 2 is sectioned into two parts. The first part is feature extraction and the second part is, topic modeling with Latent Dirichlet Allocation (LDA). The study deployed TF-IDF as the feature extraction technique which merely entails running through the provided corpus once and computing document frequencies for all of its attributes. The LDA model was built with Gensim and the results were visualized by using pyLDAvis.

Phase 3 is the classification, where the Convolutional Neural Network (CNN) classifier will be used to predict the recurring topics from the Tweets. Finally, the fourth phase is where the confusion metric (accuracy, precision, recall, and f1-score) will be calculated and used as an evaluation method.

3.1 Data Acquisition and Data Pre-processing

An online free web crawler was utilized to extract the Tweets related to SaGa. Phantombuster is a cloud-based data extraction platform that scrapes important data from many social media websites to assist organizations in automating sales and advertising activities.

The Tweets will be collected by an online web crawler, Phantombuster, by feeding them with a list of relevant keywords from SaGa. The Tweets will be presented in a CSV file to ease the tasks after the tweet extraction.

The Tweets acquired are dated from January 1, 2011, to December 31, 2021. (10 years). Most of the Tweets obtained are in English because the study is gathering all Tweets from worldwide. This data collection activity generates unstructured Tweets that must be preprocessed. The first step is to crawl the selected keywords through Phantombuster. Tweets containing the queried keywords were fed into the crawler. [2] and [6] also utilized search using keywords in data collection method.

The study implemented keyword frequency analysis. The keywords are chosen from the e-Sarawak gazette websites, the Kuching in Pictures 1841–1946 by Ho Ah Chong and Sarawak Historical Event 1946–1960 by the same author. The three sources of keywords were named Document A, Document B, and Document C.

The study creates two types of search term sets: hashtags and strings. The search terms, which serve as the crawler's feed list, are provided in English and some Malay words. Table 1 displays the SaGa Feed list of keywords to crawl through Phantombuster. The hashtags were chosen as they depicted the most straightforward keywords; for example, #sarawakhistory is related closely to the historical context of Saga. In keyword frequency analysis, the keywords with a minor frequency were removed and replaced with new keywords with a better frequency. 51 keywords were finalized (Table 1).

Table 1. Keywords and frequencies

Keywords	Frequency in document A	Frequency in document B	Frequency in document C	Total
#sarawakhistory	0	0	0	0
#sejarahsarawak	0	0	0	0
Sarawak history	0	0	0	0
Sarawak gazette	9	12	3	24
Abang Haji Mustapha	0	2	2	4
Anthony Abell Sarawak	0	1	4	5
Anthony Brooke	2	2	2	6
anti cession Sarawak	0	4	13	17
Battle of North Borneo	0	0	0	0
Batu Lintang Camp	0	3	12	15

(continued)

Table 1. (*continued*)

Keywords	Frequency in document A	Frequency in document B	Frequency in document C	Total
British Borneo	3	0	2	5
Brooke's government	3	1	0	4
Brooketon colliery	6	0	0	6
Bujang Suntong	0	0	13	13
Charles Arden Clarke	0	1	7	8
Charles brooke	11	31	0	42
Charles Vyner Brooke	2	19	1	22
council negri Sarawak	18	43	33	94
Crown colony of Sarawak	0	0	6	6
Diocese of Labuan and Sarawak	0	0	0	0
Duncan Stewart sarawak	0	0	7	7
Dyaks	6	1	0	7
Fort Margherita	1	6	1	8
Ibans Sarawak	2	4	17	23
Japanese occupation Sarawak	0	8	5	13
Kuching Market Price List	126	0	0	126
liberation of kuching	0	0	0	0
Malay National Union	0	1	4	5
Malaya-Borneo	0	0	0	0
Parti Komunis Malaya	0	0	0	0
pergerakan pemuda melayu	0	0	3	3
Perjanjian Malaysia 1963	1	0	0	1
Perjanjian Persekutuan	0	0	0	0
pieces from the brooke past	1	0	0	1
Rajah of Sarawak	49	357	73	479
Ranee of Sarawak	4	28	2	34

(*continued*)

Table 1. (*continued*)

Keywords	Frequency in document A	Frequency in document B	Frequency in document C	Total
rosli dhoby	0	0	41	41
sarawak headhunter	0	0	0	0
Sarawak library	39	0	0	39
Sarawak Museum	14	10	0	24
Sarawak north borneo	8	9	1	18
Sarawak Ranger	1	11	4	16
Sarawak regatta	11	0	2	13
Sarawak Supreme Council	4	15	18	37
Sarawak Volunteer Force	4	5	1	10
Sumpitan	1	0	0	1
suruhanjaya cobbold	0	0	0	0
the cobbold comission	0	0	0	0
Tun Sir Henry H.S. Lee	0	0	0	0
white rajah	2	14	1	17
Prince Philip	2	15	0	17
upper Rejang	4	1	0	5
Cession Sarawak	38	125	101	264
Malaya Patriotic Fund	63	3	0	66
Rajah muda Sarawak	1	20	1	22
Charles Brooke Memorial	11	2	0	13
Sarawak turf club	63	3	0	66
Brooke Rule	0	11	5	16
Betram Brooke	0	12	1	13
Sarawak Union	7	0	1	8
Astana	7	51	22	80
Kayan	2	11	8	21
Rajah muda Sarawak	1	20	2	23

For the Phantombuster's setup, the first step is connecting to Twitter. Then the SaGa feedlist saved in the spreadsheet in google drive was used to scrape the Tweets. Phantombuster is non-case sensitive; thus, the inconsistency of each capital or lower letter would not affect the crawling process. The behavior is the limit of Tweets that the study aimed to scrape. Meanwhile, the setting was set so that the process was done automatically and repeated eight times per day.

The Data Acquisition process has yielded 11435 Tweets saved in a CSV file named SaGaTweets. Taking the precedent research of [1], the study randomly checked the acquired Tweets and removed the unrelated and insignificant Tweets to get more meaningful data. Data preprocessing involves three processes which are removing punctuation, tokenizing, and removing stopwords.

3.2 Topic Modeling with Latent Dirichlet Allocation

The study utilized the feature extraction technique Term Frequency-Inverse Document Frequency (TF-IDF). In TF-IDF, feature extraction merely entails running through the provided corpus once and computing document frequencies for all of its attributes.

After TF-IDF, Latent Dirichlet Allocation (LDA) topic modeling was applied. Models.TfidfModel function was used to create a model with six topics, one of which is a collection of terms, each of which provides a particular amount of weight to the topic. In LDA, the study initiated six topics, each with ten generated terms.

After developing the LDA model, the study needs to analyze the generated topics and related keywords. There is no better tool than the interactive chart in the pyLDAvis package, designed to function effectively with Google Colaboratory. The output of the LDA model is displayed in pyLDAvis.

To discover the ideal number of topics, the study creates numerous LDA models with varying numbers of topics (k) and selects the one with the highest coherence value. Choosing a 'k' that represents the end of a fast increase in topic coherence typically yields meaningful and interpretable topics. The optimal number of topics with the highest coherence value is six. Six topics were chosen considering that the dataset the study used is small. This can be regarded as the optimal number of topics to summarise the corpus. [1, 7, 9] also find the optimal topic number with topic coherence score.

3.3 Classification

One utilization of topic modeling is determining the topic of a given text. To do so, the study looks for that document's subject number with the largest topic percentage contribution. To identify the main topic in each Tweet, the study defined a new function and compared the dominant topic and its percentage contribution.

Before the classification procedure began, the dataset was divided into 80% for training and 20% for testing. The study has an 80:20 data splitting ratio on 4301 data, the train size would be 3440, and the test size would be 861. The first step in CNN to search for specific characteristics or patterns in the Tweets is to employ a pre-defined word embedding from the library. There are several open-source embeddings available; the study has utilized Word2Vec.

Then using the Keras model, the study inserted the input layers linked to convolutional layers, which conduct several jobs such as padding, striding, kernel operation, etc. This layer is regarded as a building block of convolutional neural networks. The filter/kernel is then slid over these embeddings to discover convolutions, which are then dimensionally lowered using the Max Pooling layer to reduce complexity and processing. Finally, there are entirely linked layers and an activation function on the outputs that will provide values for each class. The dense was set to 2 as the study has two topics.

3.4 Evaluation

The evaluation for the study utilized the sparse categorical cross-entropy (scce) function to generate a category index of the most probable matched category. There are three convolutional layers with kernel sizes 32, 64, and 128. The model is trained for 30 epochs or passes over 300 batch records of the training data. The study also employed the efficient Adam-Optimizer implementation to calculate the weights of stochastic gradient descent and measured accuracy and loss during training.

Then, the classification report is started with a confusion matrix, thus exploiting the function from sklearn.metrics and importing confusion_matrix and classification_report. The Confusion Matrix has two parameters: test and projected data values. The results display the precision, recall, f1-score, and support for all four topics.

4 Results

The results of the study can be divided into three analyses. The first one is the data analysis which involves the Tweets acquired during Phase 1. The study collected 11435 Tweets using 51 keywords and chose 4301 total Tweets for the study to be saved as the raw data. After going through a preprocessing phase, the Tweets are safely conserved in a CSV file and saved as a short text corpus.

Table 2. The topics and the keywords

Topic 0	Topic 1	Topic 2	Topic 3	Topic 4	Topic 5
rosli	british	record	charles	regatta	rosli
dhobi	makam	retrieve	white	library	dhoby
sarawak	masjid	kayan	kuching	fort	sarawak
duncan	pahlawan	sarawak	rajah	margherita	melayu
sibu	borneo	kilau	brooke	state	pergerakan
stewart	kayan	rentap	sarawak	colony	union
rukun	sarawak	trial	british	drama	malaya
gabenor	surat	cinta	rajahs	sarawak	borneo
gantung	sabah	kenyah	vyner	kuching	pemuda

The second analysis is the topic modeling results. After running the LDA model in implementation, the study verified that the LDA findings could determine the event and, in some cases, important figures and give some important information about the event

Fig. 2. The wordcloud visualization of the Topic and its keywords.

through manual examination of the obtained topics. The topics and the keywords were listed in Table 2 (Fig. 2).

The third analysis is the result analysis. The study used Convolutional Neural Network (CNN) as a model for classification. Four metrics of the confusion matrix are used to assess classification results: accuracy, recall, precision, and Fl-score. The study found that the accuracy of the model is considerably low at 68% because of the inconsistencies that happened when two languages were mixed.

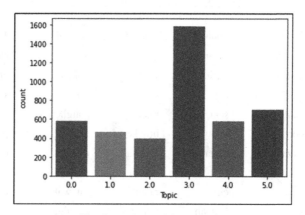

Fig. 3. Topics and frequencies.

Using the LDA model, the study also automates the model to label the dataset with its dominant topic Fig. 3. Displays the count plot for the distribution of the topic. Tweets labeled with Topic 3 have the highest distributed topic compared to other topics.

The model for classification used is Convolutional Neural Network (CNN). Four metrics are used to assess classification results: accuracy, recall, precision, and F1-score. Precision reflects the classifier's preciseness and refers to the number of linked predicted topics. Recall indicates how many accurate records are predicted, and F-scores define the harmonic average of precision and recall (Table 3).

Table 3. Four metrics to assess classification results

Topic	Precision	Recall	F1-score
0	0.71	0.53	0.61
1	0.38	0.41	0.40
2	0.51	0.39	0.44
3	0.78	0.90	0.84
4	0.64	0.49	0.55
5	0.67	0.74	0.70
Accuracy			0.68
Macro average	0.61	0.58	0.59
Weighted average	0.67	0.68	0.67

The dataset is imbalanced since 330 of the 861 instances are from Topic 3. (38% of the dataset). As a result, the predictor generally always classifies every given sample as belonging to Topic 3, achieving high precision and recall and F1-score for Topic 3 and lower scores for other topics.

5   Discussion

Overall, the study aims to understand more about how people use their social media to share the content of the Sarawak Gazette (SaGa), one of the valuable historical documents of Sarawak. By the completion of the study, three proposed objectives had been met, and the contributions of the study had also been addressed.

A list of tweets was crawled, varying from 2011 to 2021. Using 51 specific keywords, the study yielded considerably large Tweets amount from a variety of Twitter users worldwide. After going through a preprocessing phase, the Tweets are safely conserved in a CSV file and saved as a short text corpus. This corpus may be useful for future references. These Tweets offer public thoughts on Sarawak Gazette and assist us to discover how people perceive certain topics. After a manual observation, most of the Tweets related to SaGa were in picture format. Instead of writing in text, people chose to snip a part of the gazette and did not describe it more. Most Tweets also use a direct link to external websites on SaGa.

Latent Dirichlet Allocation (LDA) was used as a topic modeling approach. After running the model, the study specified six topics, each with ten generated terms. The study can infer that Topic 0 relates to the event of Duncan Stewart's assassination as the keywords contain terms such as 'duncan', 'stewart', 'sibu', 'rosli', and'dhobi'. Topic 1 and Topic 2 is quite unclear, but some keywords suggest that they might be on funeral and important historical figures. Topic 3 can be associated with Brooke's rule in Sarawak as it has terms such as 'sarawak', 'brooke', and 'rajah'. Additionally, the study deduced that Topic 4 mostly related to places in Sarawak.

The study demonstrated that the LDA findings could determine the event, and in some instances, significant figures mentioned in SaGa, and provide some relevant information about the event by manually analyzing the retrieved topics. Furthermore, Convolutional Neural Network (CNN) was used as the classifier to evaluate the model.

The classification method was further evaluated with a confusion matrix. The confusion matrix is utilized to calculate the accuracy of the deep learning algorithm in categorizing the data into its corresponding topics. The result shows that the model has a low accuracy result due to the mix of English and Malay languages.

One of the limitations is inadequate language resources. Because the study involves a mix of English and Malay Tweets, which include both official and informal word usage, it is difficult to find relevant work and appropriate dictionaries to utilize in the study. For example, adequate Malay stopword libraries and Malay embedding. Another limitation involves the insufficiency of SaGa resources online. The text version of SaGa cannot be found online, and the official websites only show the scanned version, with a few missing issue numbers.

6   Conclusion

This study has used Sarawak Gazette as a medium for historical documents to understand more about historical document-oriented content on Twitter. On the final note, three objectives were met by the end of the study. The first one is building a short-text corpus of Sarawak Gazette from Twitter. Next, predicting the topic used in Twitter related to Sarawak Gazette using deep learning goals has also been met. Third, the study evaluated the predicted topic's accuracy using standard measure metrics. Although all of the study's recommended methodologies produced considerable results, the experiment has its limitations, including the restricted capabilities of the model as there were inadequate Malay language library resources and SaGa resources.

The objective of enhanced text conceptualization can be reached in the future by improving automation. Topic modeling can increase the likelihood of uncovering latent topical patterns across the collection. In the future, the study may also use another topic modeling, such as Latent Semantic Analysis and Non-Negative Matrix Factorisation (NNMF), and compare the results to LDAs'. This would assist in enhancing the quality of topic modeling since they allow us to assess alternative models from both an overall and subject-specific perspective. Furthermore, instead of only using topic coherence to find the optimal topic number, it is feasible for the study to utilize NMI and topic coherence combined as done by [7]. Another thing that can be considered is the new search method using image searching, as most of the Tweets related to SaGa were in picture format.

Acknowledgements. The authors would like to express their heartiest thanks to Universiti Malaysia Sarawak (UNIMAS) and the Faculty of Computer Science and Information Technology (FCSIT), UNIMAS for the research opportunity and financial assistance.

The authors also extend heartfelt thanks to the family of Nur Ain. The authors were extremely grateful to the parents, Mr. Nor Azizan Bin Abdul Rashid, and Mrs. Che Wan Binti Che Man, for their love, prayers, caring, sacrifices, and understanding during the preparation of the study. Last but not least, special thanks to the author's friends for their continuous motivation and companionship throughout this research.

References

1. Asghari, M., Sierra-Sosa, D., Elmaghraby, A.: Trends on health in social media: analysis using twitter topic modeling. In: 2018 IEEE International Symposium on Signal Processing and Information Technology (ISSPIT), pp. 558–563. Louisville, KY, USA (2018). https://doi.org/10.1109/ISSPIT.2018.8642679
2. Casalino, G., Castiello, C., Del Buono, N., Mencar, C.: Intelligent twitter data analysis based on nonnegative matrix factorizations. In: Gervasi, O., et al. (eds.) ICCSA 2017. LNCS, vol. 10404, pp. 188–202. Springer, Cham (2017). https://doi.org/10.1007/978-3-319-62392-4_14
3. Congosto, M.: Digital sources: a case study of the analysis of the Recovery of Historical Memory in Spain on the social network Twitter. Cult. Hist. Dig. J. **7**, 015 (2019). https://doi.org/10.3989/chdj.2018.015
4. Dieng, A.B., Wang, C., Gao, J., Paisley, J.: TopicRNN: A recurrent neural network with long-range semantic dependency. In: Proceedings of ICLR (2017)
5. Komorowski, M., Huu, T., Deligiannis, N.: Twitter data analysis for studying communities of practice in the media industry. Telematics Inform. **35**, 195–212 (2018). https://doi.org/10.1016/j.tele.2017.11.001
6. Rasidi, N.M., Bakar, S.A., Razak, F.A.: Tweets clustering using latent semantic analysis. In: AIP (American Institute of Physics) Conference Proceedings, vol. 1830, no. 1, p. 020060. AIP Publishing LLC (2017)
7. Qomariyah, S., Iriawan, N., Fithriasari, K.: Topic modeling twitter data using latent dirichlet allocation and latent semantic analysis. In: AIP Conference Proceedings, vol. 2194, no. 1, p. 020093. AIP Publishing LLC (2019)
8. Seth, N.: Topic Modeling and Latent Dirichlet Allocation (LDA) using Gensim. Analytics Vidhya (2021)
9. Sokolova, M., et al.: Topic Modelling and Event Identification from Twitter Textual Data (2016)
10. Sumikawa, Y., Jatowt, A.: Analyzing history-related posts in twitter. Int. J. Digit. Libr. **22**(1), 105–134 (2020). https://doi.org/10.1007/s00799-020-00296-2
11. Tung, A.K.H.: Rule-based classification. In: Liu, L., Tamer Özsu, M. (eds.) Encyclopedia of Database Systems, pp. 2459–2462. Springer US, Boston, MA (2009). https://doi.org/10.1007/978-0-387-39940-9_559
12. Wang, X., Yang, Y.: Neural topic model with attention for supervised learning. In: International Conference on Artificial Intelligence and Statistics, pp. 1147–1156. PMLR (2020)
13. Yu, M., Huang, Q., Qin, H., Scheele, C., Yang, C.: Deep learning for real-time social media text classification for situation awareness – using Hurricanes Sandy, Harvey, and Irma as case studies. Int. J. Dig. Earth **12**, 1–18 (2019). https://doi.org/10.1080/17538947.2019.1574316

14. Zhang, H., et al.: Mining Twitter to assess the determinants of health behavior toward human papillomavirus vaccination in the United States. J. Am. Med. Inform. Assoc. **27**(2), 225–235 (2020)
15. Zhao, G., Liu, Y., Zhang, W., Wang, Y.: TFIDF based Feature Words Extraction and Topic Modeling for Short Text, pp. 188–191 (2018). https://doi.org/10.1145/3180374.3181354

Comparison Analysis of LSTM and CNN Variants with Embedding Word Methods for Sentiment Analysis on Food Consumption Behavior

Nurul Izleen Ramzi[1], Marina Yusoff[1,2], and Norzaidah Md Noh[1(✉)]

[1] School of Computing Sciences, College of Computing, Informatics and Media, Universiti Teknologi MARA, Shah Alam, Malaysia
norzaidah@uitm.edu.my

[2] Institute of Big Data Analytics and Artificial Intelligence (IBDAAI), Universiti Teknologi MARA, Shah Alam, Malaysia

Abstract. Lockdowns, working from home, staying at home, and physical distance are expected to significantly impact consumer attitudes and behaviors during the COVID-19 pandemic. During the implementation of the Movement Control Order, Malaysians' food preferences are already shifting away, influencing new consumption behavior. Since it has played a significant role in many areas of natural language, mainly using social media data from Twitter, there has been increased interest in sentiment analysis in recent years. However, research on the performance of various sentiment analysis methodologies such as n-gram ranges, lexicon techniques, deep learning, word embedding, and hybrid methods within this domain-specific sentiment is limited. This study evaluates several approaches to determine the best approach for tweets on food consumption behavior in Malaysia during the COVID-19 pandemic. This study combined unigram and bigram ranges with two lexicon-based techniques, TextBlob and VADER, and three deep learning classi-fiers, Long Short-Term Memory Network (LSTM), Convolutional Neural Networks (CNN), and their hybridization. Word2Vector and GloVe are two-word embedding approaches used by LSTM-CNN. The embedding GloVe on TextBlob approach with a combination of Unigram + Bigram [1,2] range produced the best results, with 85.79% accuracy and 85.30% F1-score. According to these findings, LSTM outperforms other classifiers because it achieves the highest scores for both performance metrics. The classification performance can be improved in future studies if the dataset is more evenly distributed across each positive and negative label.

Keywords: Deep learning · Lexicon-based technique · Long Short-Term Memory Network · Sentiment analysis

1 Introduction

COVID-19 is causing governments worldwide to put their citizens on lockdown as it spreads (Atalan 2020; Allain-Dupré et al. 2020). Malaysia is one of many countries

M. Yusoff et al. (Eds.): SCDS 2023, CCIS 1771, pp. 193–207, 2023.
https://doi.org/10.1007/978-981-99-0405-1_14

dealing with an increase in COVID-19 cases daily, prompting the Federal Government of Malaysia to implement a series of lockdowns (Tan 2022), beginning with the first Movement Control Order (MCO 1.0) on March 18, 2020, to break the transmission chain (Hashim et al. 2021).

This has resulted in researchers, scientists, and policymakers gathering data and experience to respond to current and future pandemic emergencies in the shortest time possible (Galanakis 2020). As a result, one of the most recent studies worldwide looks at how people consumed food during the COVID-19 pandemic. The emergence of the COVID-19 pandemic has had a significant impact on human health, causing lifestyle changes due to social isolation at home, physical inactivity, weight gain, behavioral changes, insufficient sun exposure, and food purchasing changes (Di Renzo et al. 2020). COVID-19 and related measures such as lockdowns, work-from-home, staying at home, and physical distance are also expected to have resulted in significant changes in food-related behaviors such as food consumption, food accessibility, food purchase, home cooking, and food delivery (Di Renzo et al. 2020; AlTarrah et al. 2021).

Even before the COVID-19 outbreak, it was widely acknowledged that food safety was a primary global concern. To achieve food security, everyone must constantly access sufficient, safe, and nutritious foods that meet their dietary preferences and needs (Tan et al. 2022a). Food security is a target of the Millennium Development Goals (MDGs), which were established in 2000, and it was later included in the 2030 Sustainable Development Goals (SDGs) (Galanakis 2020). This demonstrates how food systems are critical to achieving the SDGs' goal of universal access to safe and nutritious food to end hunger, achieve food security, improve nutrition, and promote a healthy lifestyle.

Social media platforms can provide valuable information for forecasting and explaining disease outbreak issues, characteristics, and status (Boon-Itt and Skunkan 2020). Furthermore, the most influential microblogging service Twitter has grown to be one of the most critical platforms for information exchange and self-documentation, allowing millions of people to express their opinions on various topics (Dubey 2020). As a result, Twitter is experiencing and conveying a wide range of perspectives, opinions, and emotions throughout numerous outbreak-related occurrences (Alamoodi et al. 2021).

Bennett et al. (2021) comprehensive research on the effect of lockdown during the COVID-19 outbreak on consumption practices in various population groups revealed that the impact of lockdown had both negative and positive effects on consumption practices worldwide. That negative consumption habits were associated with other undesirable lifestyle outcomes such as weight gain, mental health issues, and limited physical activity. If these changes continue, they may significantly impact the population's health in both the short and long term.

González-Monroy et al. (2021) compiled data from 826 studies and included 23 longitudinal studies in a systematic review to compare consumption behaviors before and after the COVID-19 pandemic to investigate changes in consumption behavior. It is thus possible to confirm the existence of consumption changes during the COVID-19 pandemic. Still, none of these findings suggest a shift toward a healthier diet, emphasizing the importance of protecting vulnerable populations from risk situations that may affect their health, in this case, their consumption behavior.

In fact, a Malaysian study found that the pandemic lockdown caused changes in consumption behavior, particularly regarding cereals and grains, as well as oils and fats, resulting in an increase in the prevalence of overweight and obesity among young Malaysians. In addition to the previously mentioned unhealthy consumption habits, emotional eating, and a lack of physical activity during pandemic isolation may exacerbate Malaysia's overweight and obesity crisis during the pandemic (Tan et al. 2022b). According to the National Health and Morbidity Survey 2019 (NHMS 2019), 50.1% of Malaysian adults are either overweight (30.4%) or obese (19.7%), making Malaysia the Southeast Asian country with the highest prevalence of obesity among adults (Institute of Public Health 2020).

Although some studies found changes in food consumption and healthier dietary practices during the lockdown, most saw either an increase in snacking and meal frequency or an increase in poor food choices and consumption practices. As a result, the COVID-19 lockdown resulted in positive and negative changes in eating habits, which may have short-and long-term health consequences. Even though many studies have focused on European populations, evidence shows that global intervention is required to help people adopt a healthy lifestyle during and after the lockdown, particularly in Malaysia.

This study aims to shed light on COVID-19-induced changes in food consumption behavior that significantly increased during the COVID-19 pandemic, affecting Malaysians' daily lives, and resulting in new consumption habits using social media data. As a result, during the pandemic phase of COVID-19, data was gathered and analyzed via Twitter to better understand how Malaysians interacted and expressed their concern about their food consumption behavior during that specific period.

2 Related Work

With the increasing influence of electronic word of mouth (eWOM) on people's ideas and decisions, sentiment analysis has emerged as a popular technique for processing subjective data in the field of text analysis studies (Li et al. 2022). SA is a computational-based study that extracts the emotive characteristics of text data, such as opinions, sentiments, attitudes, and perceptions toward various entities, such as topics, products, and services (Birjali et al. 2021). Twitter SA is being used by researchers as part of their literature review. SA papers on Twitter have been developed to assist us in detecting user behavior and situations in a variety of scenarios using a variety of techniques. Studies from previous research using DL approaches was compared and analyzed in order to detect patterns in SA.

Haque et al. (2019) performed sentiment analysis on IMDb movie reviews by comparing CNN, and LSTM and merging an ensemble of LSTM-CNN architectures to find the best architecture for the dataset. The authors proposed that all three architectures be trained. The CNN architecture was trained for 8 epochs with a batch size of 128, the LSTM network for 5 epochs with a batch size of 128, and the LSTM-CNN network for 6 epochs with the same batch size as the LSTM and CNN. They used a dataset of 50,000 movie reviews, divided into positive and negative ratings, and split the dataset 70:30 into training and testing data. Validation data were obtained from 20% of the training samples. CNN outperformed LSTM and LSTM-CNN in the experimental results, with an F-Score of 91%.

Ali and Yusoff (2021) proposed an online learning-based sentiment analysis of tweets using CNN-LSTM, LSTM-CNN, Bidirectional LSTM, and CNN-Bidirectional LSTM models that were built and tested on 23,168 tweets from 2020 to 2021 using random hyperparameter tuning. Even though using random oversampling increased the computational time, the LSTM-CNN model with random oversampling outperformed the other six models with an accuracy of 87.4 % and a loss value of 0.3432.

Yenter and Verma (2017) proposed a CNN-LSTM model for analyzing IMDb ratings. Unlike previous research, they concatenated findings after the LSTM layer was applied. The resulting model has the highest reported accuracy of 89 % when CNN and LSTM algorithms are used together. Other datasets, such as those for sentiment analysis or text categorization, may benefit from the combined power of the CNN-based LSTM architecture's numerous branches.

Shen et al. (2017) developed a novel architecture for analyzing sentiment orientation in the text by combining CNN and bidirectional Long Short-Term Memory (BiLSTM) models. They discovered that this combination provided an accuracy of 89.7 %, which was higher than the accuracy of either model alone.

Barry (2017) uses LSTM techniques to develop sentiment classification, evaluating pre-trained Word2vec and Glove embeddings and discovering that domain-specific corpora produce the best results. GloVe-DCNN method, which obtained unsupervised learning from a massive Twitter dataset for training and predicting sentiment labels with 95.84 % accuracy on the original dataset and 95.03 % accuracy on the balanced dataset for training and predicting sentiment labels. As features, they discovered that pre-trained GloVe embeddings outperformed pre-trained Word2vec embeddings.

Ra et al. (2020) used machine learning techniques to conduct a comprehensive review of tweets collected from the social media site Twitter. A variety of ML classifiers, including Naive Bayes, SVM, Max Entropy, Decision Tree, Boosting, and Random Forest, were used to assess the sentiment of tweets. When only three classes are used, the LogitBoost ensemble classifier outperforms all other classifiers in the experiment with 74 % accuracy.

A study on sentiment analysis algorithms for Twitter data was conducted (Alsaeedi and Khan 2019). This research looks into the various Twitter data sentiment analyses and their outcomes. When n-gram and bigram models were used, the accuracy of most ML algorithms, such as NB, Maximum Entropy, and SVM, was around 80%. Ensemble and hybrid-based Twitter sentiment analysis algorithms outperformed supervised ML approaches, achieving approximately 85% classification accuracy.

3   Material and Methods

This section describes the framework and the steps for implementing the solution. Figure 1 depicts the framework, which includes data collection, pre-processing, sentiment extraction, model design, and evaluation. Twint was used to scrape text data from Twitter for the dataset. Following that, the data was pre-processed to remove noise from the text. The dataset then was divided into three sections: training, testing, and validation. Using a labeled training dataset, deep learning models Long Short Term Memory

(LSTM), Convolutional Neural Networks (CNN), and a hybrid of LSTM and CNN are used to train the model. The following sections of this chapter go into greater detail about each stage. The framework is adopted from the previous work on sentiment analysis (Ali et al. 2021).

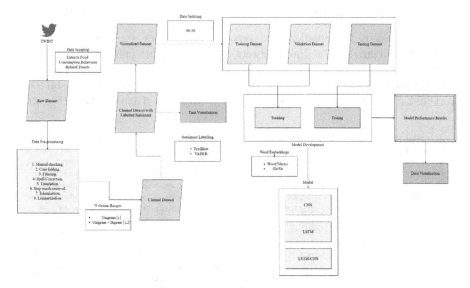

Fig. 1. Methodology framework

3.1 Data Collection

Data collection refers to the process of gathering relevant data from various sources in order to achieve the study's objectives. Web scraping techniques are used to extract information from webpages automatically by parsing hypertext elements and obtaining plain text information contained within them. TWINT was used to scrape approximately 30,000 data points between March 11, 2020, and March 31, 2022, which corresponds to the pandemic phase in Malaysia, using the indicated keywords.

Data Preparation. Data preparation is the process of transforming raw data scraped from Twitter tweets into more reliable data that can be used to analyze people's sentiments. The data is preprocessed and labeled during data preparation. Data pre-processing includes manual checks, case folding, filtering, spelling correction, translation, stop words removal, tokenization, normalization, and the use of n-grams. The accuracy of the model can be determined by examining how well the data has been labeled.

Data Pre-processing. The process of cleansing raw data before it is used for analysis is known as data preprocessing. Common data difficulties include insufficient data, noisy data, insufficient data size, missing values, erroneous or inexact values, and contradictory or redundant data. The data is 'cleaned' using the pre-processing approach, which includes removing outliers, filling gaps, deleting redundant data, and standardizing the data format. Cleaning the data can help to avoid issues like having the same repetitive tweet, which can have a negative impact on the accuracy of the result if ignored because the accuracy of the data can be improved with the use of cleansed data. To pre-process the collected data, several approaches are used, including manual checking of the data before tokenization, filtering, and normalization can be performed using Python.

Manual Checking. Grammatical and typographical errors are manually checked. Unwanted attributes such as links, retweet counts, and other unrelated data, such as tweets that are irrelevant and add no value to the research, are removed as part of the human checking process. The built-in 'Remove Duplicates' function in Microsoft Excel Workbook is also used to remove any tweets that are identical and unrelated (Fig. 2).

4	1.3E+18	1.3E+18	1.6E+12	8/18/2020 16:28	This pandemic is driving me to drink - This pandemic is driving me to
5	1.29E+18	1.29E+18	1.6E+12	7/29/2020 10:23	Reading an equities report and noted the phrase 'unusual consumpti
6	1.29E+18	1.29E+18	1.6E+12	7/27/2020 23:28	The #COVID19 pandemic has shifted Australian dietary habits. Lockdo
7	1.28E+18	1.28E+18	1.6E+12	7/19/2020 6:03	During the pandemic a myriad of factors, including reduced access to
8	1.28E+18	1.28E+18	1.59E+12	7/16/2020 13:33	The pandemic has had an immense impact on people's dietary habits
9	1.28E+18	1.28E+18	1.59E+12	7/16/2020 10:03	During the pandemic a myriad of factors, including reduced access to
10	1.28E+18	1.28E+18	1.59E+12	7/16/2020 1:02	During the pandemic a myriad of factors, including reduced access to
11	1.28E+18	1.28E+18	1.59E+12	7/15/2020 17:01	During the pandemic a myriad of factors, including reduced access to
12	1.28E+18	1.28E+18	1.59E+12	7/10/2020 13:08	NIGERIA – As a response to price fluctuations caused by the Covid-19
13	1.28E+18	1.28E+18	1.59E+12	6/30/2020 15:58	@Alex_Verbeek If concern & respect for the wellbeing of anima
14	1.25E+18	1.25E+18	1.59E+12	4/18/2020 15:39	According to the Dietary Guidelines for Americans, moderate alcohol
15	1.25E+18	1.25E+18	1.59E+12	4/9/2020 14:30	In Africa, the #COVID19 pandemic is affecting food consumption and
16	1.25E+18	1.25E+18	1.59E+12	4/4/2020 13:07	The #pandemic may trigger a change in #dietary_habits and in consur

Fig. 2. Redundant and unrelated data that must be removed

3.2 Case Folding

Case folding occurs when all uppercase characters in a tweet are converted to lowercase. Lowering the text to lowercase ensures that words like "COVID-19" and "covid-19," which are spelled similarly, are not confused because they are the same words. In this study, a Python script is used to lowercase the case.

3.3 Feature Extraction

N-grams are document-specific words, symbols, or token sequences. N-gram range sets of attributes used to characterize texts include Unigrams (n-gram size = 1), Bigrams (n-gram size = 2), and Trigrams (n-gram size = 3), as shown in Table 3.5 below. These three ranges can also be combined. For improved sentiment analysis results, N-grams are applied to the dataset. Setting n-gram ranges that use bigrams or trigrams can greatly improve the classification accuracy for tasks like SA because they can capture more complex expressions created by the combination of many words. SA is determined not only by the frequency of words but also by their combination (Garreta 2020). Instead of using single N-grams, the range of n-grams used for research in this project consist of Uni-gram and bigram combinations [1,2].

3.4 Data Labelling

After the data has been cleaned, it must be labelled in order to extract the sentiment of the data. The data was labelled using Python packages that employ a variety of sentiment analysis techniques. The algorithm used by these Python packages categorises tweets into three categories based on their polarity scores: positive, negative, and neutral. The cleaned tweet was included in the dataset file, from which the sentiment was extracted. Python code was then used to implement the VADER and TextBlob techniques. Each technique can be used to determine a text's polarity. Positive words received a score of $+1$, while negative words received a score of -1. In the meantime, neutral terms received a polarity score of 0. Following the retrieval of the sentiment, the polarity score was normalized to fall within the range $[-1.0, 1.0]$.

TextBlob. For each input text, the Textblob sentiment analyzer returns a polarity score and a subjectivity score. The polarity score range is a float between $[-1,1]$, with 1 denoting extremely positive sentiment and a score close to 0 denoting neutral sentiment. Subjectivity score ranges are also floated that fall within the range $[0,1]$, with 0 representing extreme objectivity and 1 representing extreme subjectivity.

VADER. To calculate text sentiment, VADER employs a set of lexical features or words that are classified as positive or negative based on their semantic orientation. VADER returns a Python dictionary with four keys and their values "neg," "neu," "pos," and "compound," which stand for Negative, Neutral, and Positive, respectively. The Compound score is computed by normalizing the other three scores, which are negative, neutral, and positive ranging from -1 to $+1$. The decision criteria are -1 for the most negative and $+1$ for the most positive, as in TextBlob. In contrast to TextBlob, VADER indicates not only whether a lexicon is positive, negative, or neutral but also how positive, negative, or neutral a given sentence is (Bonta and Janardhan 2019).

3.5 Model Development

This study involves performing the construction and implementation of the DL model. The best method for developing and executing this analysis is the hybrid method, as several previous studies have demonstrated a significant improvement in results using this method. In this study, the ML model was derived from a DL model, specifically CNN and LSTM. Based on prior research, these models are among the most popular, and they provide results that are both good and accurate in relation to their own investigation. To achieve the objective of this research, the dataset was trained and predicted using these models. Multiple studies have demonstrated a significant improvement in their conclusions when employing the hybrid technique; therefore, this is the optimal method for developing and executing the analysis.

Model Evaluation. In this section, the precision of the model was evaluated using the evaluation parameters. The dataset used for both training and testing with an 80:20 split. Once the data has been trained, the accuracy of the learning process is determined using testing data. The performance of DL models has been measured using four evaluation metrics: sensitivity score, precision score, F1 score, and accuracy score. The maximum and minimum accuracy scores are 1 and 0, respectively. These performance indicators are evaluated using TP (True Positive), TN (True Negative), FP (False Positive), and FN (False Negative) (False Negative). A prediction is TP if the model accurately predicts the positive class, while a result is TN if the model accurately predicts the negative class. Alternatively, FP is the prediction when the model incorrectly predicts the negative sample to be positive, and FN is the positive sample that was incorrectly predicted to be negative.

4   Classification Performance Results and Analysis

4.1   Parameter Setting

The parameters listed in Table 1 are used to compare the performance of CNN, LSTM, and LSTM-CNN hybrid models with various experiment types. For each of the three models, the employed parameters are largely identical and unaltered. Each experiment includes a limited number of additional variables.

Table 1. Parameter setting

Parameter	Value
Maximum number of words	10,000
Maximum length sentences	300
Validation split	80:20
Optimizer	Adam
Number of epoch	30
Activation function	ReLu, Sigmoid
Embedding dimensions	100
Sequence length	300
GloVe Dimension	100
Word2Vec Size	300
Batch Size	128

4.2   Computational Result for CNN

In this section, as depicted in Fig. 3, the results of comparing two distinct lexicons using two n-gram ranges based on word embeddings for the CNN model will be presented. The best performing lexicon for Word2Vec is VADER using [1,2] n-gram ranges with an accuracy of 75.44% and an F1-score of 74.45%, while the worst performing lexicon is TextBlob using unigram with an accuracy of 72.85% and an F1-score of 71.88%. The best-performing lexicon for GloVe is VADER, which uses [1,2] n-gram ranges with an accuracy of 82.91% and an F1-score of 82.55%. The worst-performing lexicon is TextBlob, which uses [1,2] n-gram ranges with an accuracy of 81.14% and an F1-score of 80.42%. VADER using [1,2] n-gram ranges, achieves the highest accuracy and F1 score among the two different word embedding techniques for classifying tweets about food consumption. Each of the lexicons that achieved accuracy between the highest and lowest on Word2Vec and GloVe on CNN models did not significantly deviate from one another. This concludes the consistency of each dataset for evaluating the effectiveness of sentiment analysis approaches in classifying tweets about food consumption.

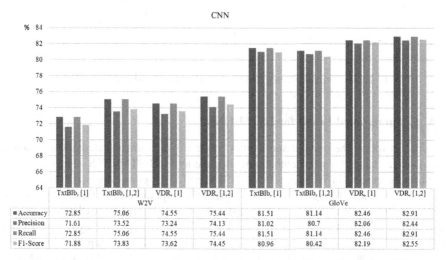

Fig. 3. The performance of the lexicons with word embeddings for CNN model

4.3 Computational Result for LSTM

In this section, Fig. 4 depicts the results of a comparison between two distinct lexicons using two n-gram ranges based on word embeddings for the LSTM model. The best performing lexicon for Word2Vec is VADER using [1,2] n-gram ranges with an accuracy of 79.47% and an F1-score of 78.27%, while the worst performing lexicon is TextBlob using unigrams with an accuracy of 77.33% and an F1-score of 76.03%. The highest performing lexicon for GloVe is TextBlob using [1,2] n-gram ranges with an accuracy of 85.79% and an F1-score of 85.30%, whereas the lowest performing lexicon is VADER using unigram with an accuracy of 83.62% and an F1-score of 82.20%. In addition, the accuracy achieved by each lexicon between the highest and lowest scores on Word2Vec and GloVe on LSTM models did not diverge significantly. This concludes the consistency of each dataset for evaluating the performance of sentiment analysis techniques in classifying tweets about food consumption.

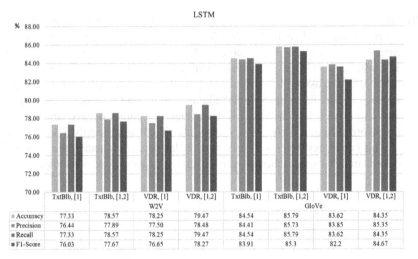

Fig. 4. The performance of the lexicons with word embeddings for LSTM model

4.4 Computational Result for LSTM-CNN

Figure 5 displays the comparison results between two distinct lexicons using two n-gram ranges based on word embeddings for the hybrid LSTM-CNN model. The top-performing lexicon for Word2Vec is VADER using [1,2] n-gram ranges with an accuracy of 76.10% and an F1-score of 75.77%. TextBlob's unigram lexicon has the lowest performance, with an accuracy of 74.27% and an F1-score of 72.14%. TextBlob using [1,2] n-gram ranges has the highest performance for GloVe, with an accuracy of 82.95% and F1-score of 82.14%, while Text-Blob using unigram has the lowest performance, with an accuracy of 80.60% and F1-score of 78.75%. The accuracy and F1 score achieved by each of the lexicons on Word2Vec and GloVe on hybrid LSTM-CNN models indicate that the use of [1,2] n-gram ranges yields the highest accuracy in classifying food consumption datasets, whereas unigram yields the lowest accuracy.

4.5 Summary of Results

In Table 2's summary of classification performance results, the orange highlighted boxes represent the highest F1-score performance results for CNN classifiers, the green highlighted boxes represent the highest F1-score performance results for LSTM classifiers, and the blue highlighted boxes represent the highest F1-score performance results for hybrid LSTM-CNN classifiers. CNN performs better on the VADER technique with [1,2] N-grams range using GloVe embeddings, achieving an accuracy of 82.91% and an F1-score of 82.50%, respectively. LSTM achieved the highest accuracy with 85.79 % and the highest F1-score with 85.30 % using the embedding GloVe on TextBlob method with [1,2] N-gram range. With an accuracy of 82.95 % and an F1-score of 82.1 %, hybrid LSTM-CNN performs best with the TextBlob technique [1,2] N-grams range and embedding GloVe.

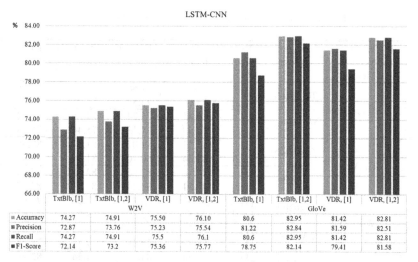

Fig. 5. The performance of the lexicons with word embeddings for hybrid LSTM-CNN model

TextBlob had the highest accuracy and F1 score among the three classifiers with the highest performance, with the exception of the CNN method, which achieved the highest performance using VADER. It can be demonstrated that the TextBlob lexicon works well with LSTM and hybrid LSTM-CNN. In addition, it can be seen that the combination of unigram and bigram [1,2] ranges on lexicons proves that it can improve the accuracy of classification performance, as the majority of classifiers with the highest performance use it. In addition, it can be observed that GloVe dominated most classifiers with the highest performance results. Consequently, LSTM that employs word embed-ding GloVe on TextBlob approach with [1,2] N-grams range outperformed the performance of all other classifiers because it utilized all lexicon techniques, word em-beddings, and n-grams that contributed to the high performance. In conclusion, GloVe and the combination of [1,2] n-grams range enhanced the performance of all approaches.

5   Discussion

The data collection and preprocessing phase have been the most time-consuming and difficult aspect of the entire project, as it requires extreme precision and care. According to the studies conducted, the preprocessing phase is crucial and must be executed properly. First, the obtained data was based on the geolocation of all Malaysian states in an effort to collect information regarding food consumption concerns in each state. Due to the fact that many Twitter users choose to conceal their location, the amount of data discovered is quite limited. As this is the only term being used by Malaysians to express their concern during the COVID-19 pandemic, a conclusion can be drawn regarding the collection of data pertaining to concern on food consumption-related behavior using "MCO" or "PKP"-related keywords.

In addition, the difficulty is exacerbated by certain keywords. The data collection was based on the hypothesis that during the lockdown, people will express feelings or

Table 2. Summary of classification performance results for all classifiers

Classifier	Word Vector Method	Lexicon Approach	N-Grams Range	Accuracy (%)	Precision (%)	Recall (%)	F1-Score (%)
CNN	Word2Vec	TextBlob	[1]	72.85	71.60	72.85	71.88
			[1,2]	75.06	73.52	75.06	73.83
		VADER	[1]	74.55	73.24	74.55	73.62
			[1,2]	75.44	74.13	75.44	74.45
	GloVe	TextBlob	[1]	81.51	81.02	81.51	80.96
			[1,2]	81.14	80.70	81.14	80.42
		VADER	[1]	82.46	82.06	82.46	82.19
			[1,2]	82.91	82.44	82.91	82.55
LSTM	Word2Vec	TextBlob	[1]	77.33	76.44	77.33	76.03
			[1,2]	78.57	77.89	78.57	77.67
		VADER	[1]	78.25	77.50	78.25	76.65
			[1,2]	79.47	78.48	79.47	78.27
	GloVe	TextBlob	[1]	84.54	84.41	84.54	83.91
			[1,2]	85.79	85.73	85.79	85.30
		VADER	[1]	83.62	83.85	83.62	82.20
			[1,2]	84.35	85.35	84.35	84.67
Hybrid LSTM-CNN	Word2Vec	TextBlob	[1]	74.27	72.87	74.27	72.14
			[1,2]	74.91	73.76	74.91	73.20
		VADER	[1]	75.50	75.23	75.50	75.36
			[1,2]	76.10	75.54	76.10	75.77
	GloVe	TextBlob	[1]	80.60	81.22	80.60	78.75
			[1,2]	82.95	82.84	82.95	82.14
		VADER	[1]	81.42	81.59	81.42	79.41
			[1,2]	82.81	82.51	82.81	81.58

opinions about food and discuss changes in their food consumption. It would be inappropriate to conduct a search using the phrases 'makan', 'makanan' and 'pengambilan makanan' alone, which in English means eat, food, and food intake. Numerous advertisements and articles have been generated using these keywords. This form of ambiguity was inevitable and could not be avoided due to the vast quantity of data collected. Due to the inability of the data to be automatically filtered from irrelevant texts that could lead to misinterpretation, the initial step of preparation consisted of extensive manual observations.

In addition, because Malaysia is a country with numerous languages, slangs, dialects, and abbreviations, the tweets could only reach a small portion of the complaints and opinions. For example, "x", "tk", and "tak" are the most common Malay abbreviations for "tidak", which means "no" in English. MALAYA's spelling corrector for Malay tweets led to the identification of a solution. However, there are still slang and Malay phrases that cannot be identified by the tool, and it took the tool between one and two hours to review one hundred pieces of data. Consequently, one of the reasons why preprocessing took so long is that data preprocessing typically involves manual observation.

This study employs a lexicon-based approach to data labeling, specifically VADER and TextBlob. This study employs a combination of N-grams to increase the effectiveness of SA. However, both methods produce imbalanced datasets for each sentiment label. All datasets are unbalanced if there are more positives than negatives. CNN, LSTM, and hybrid LSTM-CNN classifiers are used. The difficulty during this phase is that it typically takes at least two hours to run these classifiers, but the issue is likely due to RAM utilization of the hardware, as LSTM runs the least. Google Colab frequently crashes, necessitating numerous restarts and code executions. However, it is also evident that the data is unbalanced, which causes the data to run slowly. Consequently, confusion matrices are useful for analyzing the dataset because they provide an efficient performance measurement for the models. In consideration of the data's precision and recall value, this study employs F-measure as a replacement metric for determining the optimal outcome for an imbalanced dataset.

CNN performs better on VADER with [1,2] N-grams range using embeddings GloVe, achieving an accuracy of 82.91% and an F1-score of 82.51%, respectively. LSTM achieved the highest accuracy with 85.79 % and the highest F1-score with 85.30 % using the embedding GloVe on TextBlob method with [1,2] N-gram range. With an accuracy of 82.95% and an F1-score of 82.15%, hybrid LSTM-CNN performs best with the TextBlob technique [1,2] N-grams range and embedding GloVe. The percentages of each model's accuracy and F1 score did not differ significantly. The range of accuracy for all models is between 72.85% and 85.79%, which is not very large, whereas the range for the F1 score is between 71.88% and 85.79%. LSTM outperformed the hybrid of LSTM and CNN in terms of accuracy and F1-score in this study, despite requiring more training time than other classifiers. Despite being the slowest to train, LSTM has the advantage of being able to examine long sequences of inputs without increasing the size of the network, making it a much better choice for text classification (Rehman et al. 2019).

6   Conclusion

This paper focuses on Twitter data to build and analyze CNN, LSTM, and hybrid LSTM-CNN models for classifying sentiments toward food consumption behavior during the COVID-19 pandemic in Malaysia. Most hybrid LSTM-CNN models outperform LSTM and CNN models in text classification. Using the collected Twitter Data, LSTM outperformed the LSTM-CNN hybrid in terms of accuracy and F1-score. The comparison includes Lexicon approaches as well. More datasets in the same or different domains are expected to be used in the evaluation of CNN, LSTM, hybrid LSTM-CNN, and other deep learning models in the future.

Acknowledgements. The authors would like to thank Institute for Big Data Analytics and Artificial Intelligence (IBDAAI) and Universiti Teknologi MARA. The registration fees is funded by Pembiayaan Yuran Procding Berindeks (PYPB), Tabung Dana Kecemerlangan Pendidikan (DKP), Universiti Teknologi MARA (UiTM), Malaysia.

References

Atalan, A.: Is the lockdown important to prevent the COVID-19 pandemic? Effects on psychology, environment and economy-perspective. Annals of medicine and surgery **56**, 38–42 (2020)

Allain-Dupré, D., Chatry, I., Michalun, V., Moisio, A.: The territorial impact of COVID-19: managing the crisis across levels of government. OECD Policy Responses to Coronavirus(COVID-19) **10**, 1620846020–909698535 (2020)

Hashim, J.H., Adman, M.A., Hashim, Z., Radi, M.F.M., Kwan, S.C.: COVID-19 epidemic in Malaysia: epidemic progression, challenges, and response. Frontiers in public health **9** (2021)

Galanakis, C.M.: The food systems in the era of the coronavirus (Covid-19) pandemic crisis. Foods **9**(4), 523 (2020)

Di Renzo, L., et al.: Eating habits and lifestyle changes during COVID-19 lockdown: an Italian survey. Journal of translational medicine **18**(1), 1–15 (2020)

AlTarrah, D., AlShami, E., AlHamad, N., AlBesher, F., Devarajan, S.: The impact of coronavirus covid-19 pandemic on food purchasing, eating behavior, and perception of food safety in Kuwait. Sustainability **13**(16), 8987 (2021)

Tan, S.T., Tan, C.X., Tan, S.S.: Food security during the COVID-19 home confinement: A cross-sectional study focusing on adults in Malaysia. Human Nutrition & Metabolism 200142 (2022a)

Tan, S.T., Tan, C.X., Tan, S.S.: Changes in dietary intake patterns and weight status during the COVID-19 lockdown: A cross-sectional study focusing on young adults in Malaysia. Nutrients **14**(2), 280 (2022)

Boon-Itt, S., Skunkan, Y.: Public perception of the COVID-19 pandemic on Twitter: Sentiment analysis and topic modeling study. JMIR Public Health and Surveillance **6**(4), e21978 (2020)

Dubey, A.D.: Twitter Sentiment Analysis during COVID-19 Outbreak. Available at SSRN 3572023 (2020)

Alamoodi, A.H., et al.: Sentiment analysis and its applications in fighting COVID-19 and infectious diseases: a systematic review. Expert systems with applications **167**, 114155 (2021)

Bennett, G., Young, E., Butler, I., Coe, S.: The impact of lockdown during the COVID-19 outbreak on dietary habits in various population groups: a scoping review. Frontiers in nutrition **8**, 626432 (2021)

González-Monroy, C., Gómez-Gómez, I., Olarte-Sánchez, C.M., Motrico, E.: Eating behaviour changes during the COVID-19 pandemic: a systematic review of longitudinal studies. Int. J. Environ. Res. Public Health **18**(21), 11130 (2021)

Li, H., Chen, Q., Zhong, Z., Gong, R., Han, G.: E-word of mouth sentiment analysis for user behavior studies. Information Processing & Management **59**(1), 102784 (2022)

Birjali, M., Kasri, M., Beni-Hssane, A.: A comprehensive survey on sentiment analysis: Approaches, challenges and trends. Knowledge-Based Systems **226**, 107134 (2021)

Haque, M.R., Lima, S.A., Mishu, S.Z.: Performance Analysis of Different Neural Networks for Sentiment Analysis on IMDb Movie Reviews. In: 2019 3rd International Conference on Electrical, Computer & Telecommunication Engineering (ICECTE), pp. 161–164. IEEE (2019 December)

Ali, M.S., Yusoff, M.: Comparison Performance of Long Short-Term Memory and Convolution Neural Network Variants on Online Learning Tweet Sentiment Analysis. In: International Conference on Soft Computing in Data Science, pp. 3–17. Springer, Singapore (2021 November)

Yenter, A., Verma, A.: Deep CNN-LSTM with combined kernels from multiple branches for IMDb review sentiment analysis. In: 2017 IEEE 8th Annual Ubiquitous Computing, Electronics and Mobile Communication Conference (UEMCON), pp. 540–546. IEEE (2017 October)

Shen, Q., Wang, Z., Sun, Y.: Sentiment analysis of movie reviews based on cnnblstm. In: International Conference on Intelligence Science, pp. 164–171. Springer, Cham (2017 October)

Barry, J.: Sentiment Analysis of Online Reviews Using Bag-of-Words and LSTM Approaches. In: AICS, pp. 272–274 (2017)

Ra, M., Ab, B., Kc, S.: Covid-19 outbreak: Tweet based analysis and visualization towards the influence of coronavirus in the world (2020)

Alsaeedi, A., Khan, M.Z.: A study on sentiment analysis techniques of Twitter data. International Journal of Advanced Computer Science and Applications **10**(2) (2019)

Garreta, R.: N-gram range. MonkeyLearn (2020). Retrieved 15 July 2022, from https://help.mon keylearn.com/en/articles/2174105-n-gram-range

Bonta, V., Janardhan, N.K.N.: A comprehensive study on lexicon based approaches for sentiment analysis. Asian J. Comp. Sci. Technol. **8**(S2), 1–6 (2019)

Institute for Public Health: National Health and Morbidity Survey (NHMS) 2019: Noncommunicable diseases, healthcare demand, and health literacy—Key Findings (2020)

Data Mining and Image Processing

Towards Robust Underwater Image Enhancement

Jahroo Nabila Marvi$^{(\boxtimes)}$ ⓘ and Laksmita Rahadianti ⓘ

Faculty of Computer Science, Universitas Indonesia, Depok 16424, Indonesia
jahroo.nabila01@ui.ac.id

Abstract. Underwater images often suffer from blurring and color distortion due to absorption and scattering in the water. Such effects are undesirable since they may hinder computer vision tasks. Many underwater image enhancement techniques have been explored to address this issue, each to varying degrees of success. The large variety of distortions in underwater images is difficult to handle by any singular method. This study observes four underwater image enhancement methods, i.e., Underwater Light Attenuation Prior (ULAP), statistical Background Light and Transmission Map estimation (BLTM), and Natural-based Underwater Image Color Enhancement (NUCE), and Global–Local Networks (GL-Net). These methods are evaluated on the Underwater Image Enhancement Benchmark (UIEB) dataset using quantitative metrics, e.g., SSIM, PSNR, and CIEDE2000 as the metrics. Additionally, a qualitative analysis of image quality attributes is also performed. The results show that GL-Net achieves the best enhancement result, but based on the qualitative assessment, this method still has room for improvement. A proper combination between the non-learning-based component and learning-based component should be investigated to further improve the robustness of the method.

Keywords: Image enhancement · Image restoration · Deep learning · Underwater images

1 Introduction

Underwater images tend to suffer from degradations due to absorption and scattering. Light absorption by the water particles creates dim and blurry images. Scattering, which occurs when the light collides with particles in water, causes a hazy appearance [1]. Color distortion is also a common occurrence in underwater environments since different wavelengths are attenuated to different degrees [2]. Longer wavelengths, such as red light, attenuated quickly in water, which is why underwater images often appear in green-bluish tone [3]. These degradations pose challenges to underwater vision-related tasks. To overcome these problems, the development of underwater image enhancement methods becomes necessary.

Due to the lack of reliable ground truth, human perception plays a great role in underwater image enhancement. The curation of reference images of underwater image enhancement benchmark (UIEB) dataset [4], for example, was done with the aid of

M. Yusoff et al. (Eds.): SCDS 2023, CCIS 1771, pp. 211–221, 2023.
https://doi.org/10.1007/978-981-99-0405-1_15

human volunteers. The research shows that the volunteers favor the enhanced image with the following characteristics: improved contrast and genuine color. As such, underwater image enhancement methods are mostly developed with these two characteristics in mind.

Underwater image enhancement methods can be divided into three categories: non-physical-based, physical-based, and learning-based methods. Nonphysical-based methods directly modify the pixel values [5], while physical-based takes the image formation process into account. Learning-based methods, specifically deep learning, takes the advantage of training data by learning its feature representation and using it to produce an enhanced image. Each of these methods have their limitations. Due to the complex nature of underwater scenes, formulating a non-physical or physical-based method might become too complicated. In certain cases, these two types of methods might also be unable to adapt to the wide variety of degradations present in the underwater image. Conversely, deep learning-based methods often require a large training dataset to achieve satisfactory results, which can be difficult due to the currently limited availability of real-world underwater image dataset. The deep learning-based methods also lack flexibility and robustness since the parameters will be fixed after the training [6].

The wide variety of underwater image enhancements methods produce different results. These methods affect the image quality attributes, such as color, texture, and contrast, differently to various degrees. For example, there may be a method that is able to reduce the color cast but fail to improve the contrast or preserve the details of the image. To get a holistic good quality of enhanced image, in this paper, we observe the performance of existing enhancement methods and try to pinpoint the needs for attribute improvement.

2   Underwater Image Enhancement

2.1   Non-Physical-Based Methods

Sometimes referred to as model-free or enhancement-based, these methods directly modify the pixel value without directly considering the physical properties of water. Histogram equalization, white balance, and retinex are some of the examples of this method. Generally, approaches that fall under the non-physical category often combine several enhancement techniques.

The methods proposed by Abdul Ghani et al. [7], Natural-based underwater color enhancement (NUCE), is an example of this category. NUCE [7] consists of 4 enhancement processes: color cast neutralization, dual-intensity image fusion, mean equalization using particle swarm optimization (PSO), and unsharp masking. The first enhancement process, color cast neutralization, computes the pixel intensity for each RGB color channel to determine the superior color channel and inferior color channel. The color channel with the highest intensity will be regarded as the former while the other two channels will be regarded as the latter. The superior color channel is then used as a reference to compensate for the inferior color channel. The compensation is done based on the calculated gain factors. The second enhancement process, dual-intensity image fusion, first computes the minimum, maximum, mean, and median value of each image histogram. The mean and median value are used to determine the average point. This point is used as the reference to separate the image histogram into two regions: lower stretched-region and upper stretched-region. The stretching process is done based on the method proposed by Iqbal et al. [8]. The expected output of this process is an image with enhanced contrast. The third enhancement process, mean equalization, adopts the gamma correction-based method. Since the enhancement result is determined by a constant value, gamma, Abdul Ghani et al. [7] used PSO to obtain the appropriate value of this coefficient. The fourth enhancement process, unsharp masking, is employed to increase the sharpness of the image.

Similarly, the model designed by Li et al. [9] also employs 4 enhancement processes: red channel compensation, white balance, modified McCann Retinex [10], and adaptive histogram transformation. The red channel compensation is performed based on the color filter array (CFA) to produce a color-corrected image. The color of the image is further improved by performing white balance. In this method, the RGB values of the white-balanced image are obtained by dividing each color channel with its maximal value within the original image. Then, to improve the illuminance of the image, the modified McCann Retinex with dense pixels is adopted. To further improve the image visual appearance, a piecewise linear function is proposed for the adaptive histogram transform [9].

2.2 Physical-Based Methods

Also known as model-based or restoration-based, this method considers the degradation process of underwater to restore the image. The most well-known image formation model used for this method is Jaffe-McGlamery model, which can be expressed as follows [11]:

$$I_\lambda(x) = J_\lambda(x)t_\lambda(x) + B_\lambda(1 - t_\lambda(x)) \qquad (1)$$

where λ refers to the RGB channel and x refers to the pixel position. $I_\lambda(x)$ represents the captured image, $J_\lambda(x)$ represents the original scene, $T_\lambda(x)$ represents the transmission map, and B_λ represents background or atmospheric light. Therefore, physical-based methods often rely on background light and transmission map estimation [5]. Underwater light attenuation prior (ULAP) [11] and background light-transmission map estimation (BL-TM) [3] are two examples of physical-based methods that adopt this image formation model. The main feature of ULAP is the proposed linear model for the depth map estimation. Song et al. [11] defined the model based on their finding that there is a strong relation between the maximum value of G-B intensity and value of R intensity and the scene depth change. BL-TM estimates the transmission map of the red channel based on the new underwater dark channel prior (NUDCP). The scene depth map is estimated using ULAP and an adjusted reverse saturation map (ARSM) to compensate and modify the coarse transmission map of the R channel. As for the transmission map of the G-B channel, the estimation is made based on the difference of attenuation ratios between R channel and G-B channels [3]. A variation of white balance is used as the post-processing.

2.3 Deep Learning-Based Methods

In recent years, deep learning has been widely adopted to enhance underwater images. Some models are based on Convolutional Neural Networks (CNN), e.g., Global–Local

Network with Compressed Histogram Equalization (GL-Net) [6], Global Structure-guided Recovery (GSR) [12], and Underwater CNN based on Structure Decomposition (UWCNN-SD) [5]. These three methods share one thing in common: they used branched networks. GL-Net designed two branches, Network-G and Network-L, to compensate for the global distorted color and local reduced contrast, respectively. The compressed histogram equalization is used to further improve the visual quality of the image [6]. Similarly, GSR implements two branches to estimate the local feature and global feature of the image separately. A soft attention weight map is also implemented to better integrate the estimated local and global features. UWCNN-SD involves two stages to enhance the image: preliminary enhancement network and refinement network. In the preliminary enhancement network, the input image is first decomposed into low-frequency (LF) and high-frequency (HF) using discrete cosine transform (DCT). The LF and HF components are processed separately in its respective network branch. The refinement network further processes the LF and HF that have been combined to achieve the final enhanced image.

There are also models that employ Generative Adversarial Networks (GAN) e.g., Underwater Conditional GAN (U-cGAN) [13] and Fast Underwater Image Enhancement GAN (FUnIE-GAN) [14]. The key feature of U-cGAN is the implementation of dual discriminators. It comprises two sub-discriminators that share the same structure but different weights. Each discriminator processes different sizes: the original size and the half of the original size. The dual discriminators are expected to guide the generator to generate high-quality images. FUnIE-GAN generator is based on U-Net with fewer parameters to reduce the computational burden, thus allowing the network to achieve fast inference time. The discriminator of this model is based on Markovian Patch-GAN.

3 Methodology

In this paper, four methods are observed, i.e., ULAP [7], BL-TM [3], NUCE [5], and GL-Net [14]. The source code for ULAP,[1] BL-TM,[2] and GL-Net[3] are provided by the author in their Github repository. The code for NUCE in this experiment is adopted from an unofficial Github repository[4] with a slight modification in the color channels stacking function to avoid distorted pixels from occurring. GL-Net in this experiment is reimplemented in Tensorflow-Keras 2.8 framework. For the hyperparameter settings of GL-Net, the learning rate is set to 0.0001 using Adam optimizer. The number of batches and epochs are set to 1 and 60 respectively.

---

[1] https://github.com/wangyanckxx/Single-Underwater-Image-Enhancement-and-Color-Restoration/tree/master/Underwater%20Image%20Color%20Restoration/ULAP

[2] https://github.com/wangyanckxx/Enhancement-of-Underwater-Images-with-Statistical-Model-of-BL-and-Optimization-of-TM

[3] https://xueyangfu.github.io/projects/spic2020.html

[4] https://github.com/prashamsatalla/Underwater-image-color-enhancement-with-PSO-python-implementation

3.1 Dataset

Underwater Image Enhancement Benchmark (UIEB) [4] is selected as the dataset in this experiment. The dataset was constructed with three objectives in mind, which are content diversity, large number of data, and the availability of reference images. This dataset comprises 890 paired images and 60 unpaired images serves as a challenging set. Only paired images are used in this research. Since the published dataset is presented as is, the data splitting then must be performed first. As various experiments conducted by various studies may have different data shuffles or proportions, a fair benchmarking of existing models is only possible by re-training and re-testing them. This is to ensure that there is no overlap between the seen (train) data and the unseen (test) data. For this reason, this experiment only compares the models that are locally trained and tested. In this experiment, 700 and 78 images are randomly selected as the training set and the validation set respectively to train GL-Net. The remaining 112 images are then used as the test set. All of the images are resized to 256×256 prior to the data split.

3.2 Evaluation Metrics

Three full-reference metrics are used to evaluate the enhancement result quantitatively, i.e., peak-signal-to-noise-ratio (PSNR), structural similarity (SSIM), and CIEDE2000 (ΔE_{00}).

3.2.1 PSNR

Given two images x and y, with size $M \times N$, PSNR is defined as follows:

$$PSNR = 10 \log_{10} \left(\frac{MAX^2}{MSE} \right) \tag{2}$$

where mean squared error (MSE) is defined as:

$$MSE = \frac{1}{MN} \sum_{i=1}^{M} \sum_{j=1}^{N} (x_{ij} - y_{ij})^2 \tag{3}$$

where MAX is the maximum possible value of the pixel. If the image is represented in 8-bit, for example, this value becomes 255. As lower MSE increases the PSNR value, a high PSNR therefore indicates a high-quality image. The unit of this measurement is decibel (dB).

3.2.2 SSIM

SSIM is a perceptual metric that measures the similarity between two images based on these three visual perception attributes, i.e., luminance (l), contrast (c), and structure (s). Given two images x and y, SSIM can be defined as follows [15]:

$$SSIM(x, y) = [l(x, y)]^{\alpha} [c(x, y)]^{\beta} [s(x, y)]^{\gamma} \tag{4}$$

where α, β, and γ are the parameters that weigh their corresponding components. A high SSIM value will indicate a higher-quality image.

3.2.3 CIEDE2000 (ΔE_{00})

ΔE_{00} measures the difference between two colors based on CIELAB color space. It is defined as follows [16]:

$$\Delta E_{00} = \sqrt{\left(\frac{\Delta L'}{k_L S_L}\right)^2 + \left(\frac{\Delta C'}{k_C S_C}\right)^2 + \left(\frac{\Delta H'}{k_H S_H}\right)^2 + R_T \left(\frac{\Delta C'}{k_C S_C}\right)^2 \left(\frac{\Delta H'}{k_H S_H}\right)^2} \quad (5)$$

where ΔL, ΔC, and ΔH, are the CIELAB metric lightness, chroma, and hue differences, respectively. S_L, S_C, and S_H are the weighting functions for the lightness, chroma, and hue components, respectively. k_L, k_C, and k_H, are the parametric factors for lightness, chroma, and hue components, respectively. R_T is an interactive term between the hue and chroma differences [16]. A small ΔE_{00} indicates a small color difference between the enhanced image and the reference image and consequently, a higher-quality image.

4 Result

Table 1. Average value of SSIM, PSNR, and ΔE_{00} of various enhancement methods

Method	SSIM↑[0,1]	PSNR↑[0,∞]	ΔE_{00}↓[0,100]
NUCE [7]	0.8293	17.9867	13.8115
ULAP [11]	0.7512	16.7700	17.4573
BL-TM [3]	0.7738	16.4093	15.0810
GL-Net [6]	**0.9053**	**22.2232**	**8.8400**

Table 1. shows the quantitative evaluation results of NUCE, ULAP, BL-TM, and GL-Net. Based on the experiment results, it is evident that GL-Net achieves the best SSIM, PSNR, and ΔE_{00} score followed by NUCE. BL-TM outperforms ULAP in SSIM and ΔE_{00} but slightly underperforms in PSNR. To further understand the performance of each method, we inspect the qualitative result and present the sample of the images in Fig. 1.

4.1 Enhancement Result Analysis

Figure 1 shows the qualitative result of NUCE, ULAP, BL-TM, and GL-Net. Visually, we can see how the image enhanced by GL-Net produces the best result, which goes in accordance with its quantitative result. This method is able to handle images with various types of color cast and low contrast.

In terms of color correction, the other three methods perform differently. The color correction method of NUCE produces various results depending on the image scene. As mentioned in Sect. 2, NUCE uses a superior color channel (color channel with the highest pixel intensity) as the reference to compensate for the inferior color channel

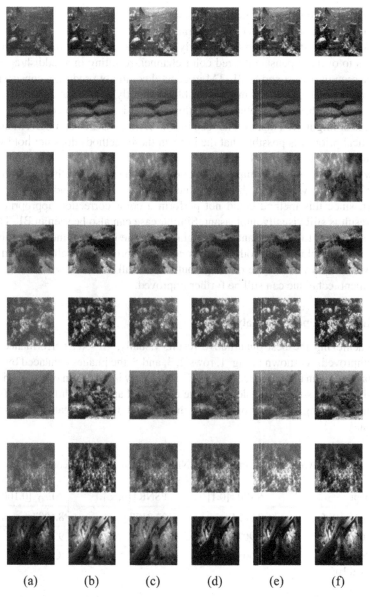

(a)	(b)	(c)	(d)	(e)	(f)

Fig. 1 Qualitative result of various enhancement methods. (a) raw image (b) reference image (c) NUCE (d) ULAP (e) BL-TM (f) GL-Net (Color figure online)

(color channel with the mid and lowest pixel intensity). The mean value of each channel is also equalized. This works well when the dominant color of the image is the cause of the color cast, as can be seen in rows 3 to 6. However, in underwater images, there are scenes where the dominant color is part of the background color. Rows 1 and 2 are examples of this type of scene. Since the color correction in this method is purely based on the pixel intensity, the background color will be affected during this process as well, which may result in unnatural color appearance.

ULAP, in this dataset, could not properly reduce the color cast. In certain images, it also tends to overcompensate the red color channel, resulting in a reddish appearance as can be seen in rows 7 and 8. BL-TM in general could not produce a consistent color correction. In some cases, this method is able to slightly reduce the color cast, as seen in rows 1, 5, and 6. In some other cases, this method is unable to correct the color of the images or might even distort it as seen in row 4. Since ULAP and BL-TM are based on statistical prior, it is possible that the prior in these methods does not hold with the dataset used in this experiment.

How these three methods improve the contrast of the images in this experiment also varies. For ULAP, we can see how the objects in rows 1, 5, 6, and 7 appear clearer. However, since this method could not perform a color correction appropriately, the overall result is still visually unpleasant. Similar case can also be seen in BL-TM. This method also tends to over-enhance the brightness of the image. In the case of low light images, for example row 8, both methods could not produce a well-enhanced image. NUCE works well in this type of image but the overall result shows that the contrast enhancement technique can still be further improved.

4.2 GL-Net Component Analysis

Despite achieving the best quantitative result, visually, GL-Net performance can be further improved. As shown in Fig. 1. rows 2, 3, and 5, the images enhanced by GL-Net appear brighter than the reference images. This possibly indicates an over-enhancement. Row 6 shows how some of the details in the image still appear slightly foggy. To gain a better understanding of the performance of this method, we investigate each component individually.

Table 2 Average value of SSIM, PSNR, and ΔE_{00} of GL-Net components

Component	SSIM↑[0,1]	PSNR↑[0,∞]	ΔE_{00}↓[0,100]
Compressed HE Only	0.8824	22.3177	**8.6987**
GL-Net Only	**0.9073**	**22.4736**	9.5372
GL-Net with compressed HE	0.9053	22.2232	8.8400

Table 2. shows the qualitative evaluation result of each GL-Net component. Based on the experiment result, it is found that adding compressed HE to the intermediate image produced by GL-Net deters the average SSIM and PSNR score. This addition, however, improves the average ΔE_{00} score. The lowest average ΔE_{00} is achieved by the component compressed HE.

Figure 2. shows the samples of qualitative results of each GL-Net component. From this figure, we can see how each component behaves differently in various conditions. We present images where one component outperforms the others.

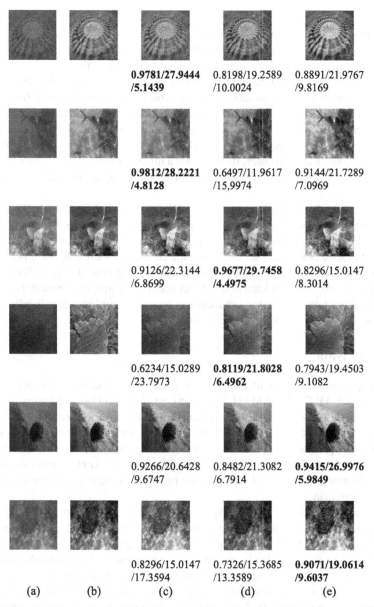

Fig. 2 Qualitative result of each GL-Net component accompanied with metric score. The score below the picture denotes SSIM, PSNR, and ΔE_{00}, respectively. (a) raw image (b) reference image (c) GL-Net only (d) Compressed HE only (e) GL-Net with compressed HE

Rows 1 and 2 of Fig. 2 are examples where the enhancement result from GL-Net achieves the best result. In row 1, the addition of compressed HE distorts the image while row 2 shows an over-enhanced result. Directly applying compressed HE does not remove the color cast and produces a visually unpleasing result. Rows 3 and 4 show that compressed HE outperforms GL-Net with and without compressed HE. Unlike the images in rows 1–2, the images in rows 3–4 mainly suffer from low contrast. Despite not achieving the best result, we can see how GL-Net with compressed HE produces a better color and contrast improvement compared to GL-Net only.

Rows 5 and 6 demonstrate that the addition of compressed HE to GL-Net improves the overall result. Visually, we can see a noticeable contrast improvement from column (c) to column (e), which in turn also improves all the three metric scores. Similar to what happened in rows 1 and 2, direct enhancement by compressed HE results in a color distortion. The image enhanced by GL-Net alone removes the severity of the color degradation, but in certain cases, it still shows a hint of color cast as seen in row 5. Row 6 shows the case where GL-Net is able to remove the color cast but fails to improve the contrast.

In summary, the addition of compressed HE to GL-Net, depending on the situation, can either improve the color or produce an over-enhanced image. Compressed HE alone works well with low contrast images but performs poorly when a strong color distortion is present despite achieving the lowest average ΔE_{00} in this experiment. It is likely that our test dataset contains many images with a degradation type similar to 3(a) and 4(a). However, it is important to keep in mind that underwater images generally have a wide variety of degradations. An ideal enhancement method should be able to handle any type of degradations along with its degree of severity.

5   Conclusion

In this paper, we have presented the performance of four underwater image enhancements, i.e., ULAP [7], BL-TM [3], NUCE [5], and GL-Net [14]. Additionally, we perform both quantitative and qualitative evaluation on the enhancement results. Based on our experiment result and analysis, GL-Net generates the best enhancement result quantitatively and qualitatively. NUCE, depending on the image scene, may either reduce the color cast or produce an unnatural color appearance. The contrast enhancement also needs further improvement. ULAP could not provide a sufficient color correction while BL-TM result is inconsistent.

GL-Net is a method that combines 2 components, so we also have analyzed the performance of each component separately; the learning-based and non-learning-based components. The addition of non-learning-based components, compressed HE, to GL-Net can improve the color, but in certain cases, it may result in an over-enhancement or distort the image. Therefore, to further improve the robustness of this method, a proper combination between learning and non-learning-based components must be investigated. Furthermore, a larger amount of data may be required to allow the learning-based component to learn more varieties of underwater scenes. We will incorporate this in our future work.

References

1. Han, M., Lyu, Z., Qiu, T., Xu, M.: A review on intelligence dehazing and color restoration for underwater images. IEEE Trans. Syst. Man Cybern, Syst. **50**, 1820–1832 (2020). https://doi.org/10.1109/TSMC.2017.2788902

2. Lu, H., Li, Y., Serikawa, S.: Single underwater image descattering and color correction. In: 2015 IEEE International Conference on Acoustics, Speech and Signal Processing (ICASSP), pp. 1623–1627. IEEE, South Brisbane, Queensland, Australia (2015). https://doi.org/10.1109/ICASSP.2015.7178245

3. Song, W., Wang, Y., Huang, D., Liotta, A., Perra, C.: Enhancement of underwater images with statistical model of background light and optimization of transmission map. IEEE Trans. on Broadcast. **66**, 153–169 (2020). https://doi.org/10.1109/TBC.2019.2960942

4. Li, C., Guo, C., Ren, W., Cong, R., Hou, J., Kwong, S., Tao, D.: An underwater image enhancement benchmark dataset and beyond. IEEE Trans. on Image Process. **29**, 4376–4389 (2020). https://doi.org/10.1109/TIP.2019.2955241

5. Wu, S., Luo, T., Jiang, G., Yu, M., Xu, H., Zhu, Z., Song, Y.: A two-stage underwater enhancement network based on structure decomposition and characteristics of underwater imaging. IEEE J. Oceanic Eng. **46**, 1213–1227 (2021). https://doi.org/10.1109/JOE.2021.3064093

6. Fu, X., Cao, X.: Underwater image enhancement with global–local networks and compressed-histogram equalization. Signal Processing: Image Communication. **86**, 115892 (2020). https://doi.org/10.1016/j.image.2020.115892

7. Mohd Azmi, K.Z., Abdul Ghani, A.S., Md Yusof, Z., Ibrahim, Z.: Natural-based underwater image color enhancement through fusion of swarm-intelligence algorithm. Applied Soft Computing. **85**, 105810 (2019). https://doi.org/10.1016/j.asoc.2019.105810

8. Iqbal, K., Odetayo, M., James, A., Salam, R.A., Hj Talib, A.Z.: Enhancing the low quality images using Unsupervised Colour Correction Method. In: 2010 IEEE International Conference on Systems, Man and Cybernetics, pp. 1703–1709. IEEE, Istanbul, Turkey (2010). https://doi.org/10.1109/ICSMC.2010.5642311

9. Li, C., Tang, S., Kwan, H.K., Yan, J., Zhou, T.: Color correction based on CFA and enhancement based on retinex with dense pixels for underwater images. IEEE Access. **8**, 155732–155741 (2020). https://doi.org/10.1109/ACCESS.2020.3019354

10. McCann, J.J., Frankle, J.A.: Method and apparatus for lightness imaging. U.S. Patent 4384336A. 53 (1983)

11. Song, W., Wang, Y., Huang, D., Tjondronegoro, D.: A rapid scene depth estimation model based on underwater light attenuation prior for underwater image restoration. In: Hong, R., Cheng, W.-H., Yamasaki, T., Wang, M., Ngo, C.W. (eds.) Advances in Multimedia Information Processing – PCM 2018, pp. 678–688. Springer International Publishing, Cham (2018). https://doi.org/10.1007/978-3-030-00776-8_62

12. Lin, R., Liu, J., Liu, R., Fan, X.: Global structure-guided learning framework for underwater image enhancement. Vis Comput. (2021). https://doi.org/10.1007/s00371-021-02305-0

13. Yang, M., Hu, K., Du, Y., Wei, Z., Sheng, Z., Hu, J.: Underwater image enhancement based on conditional generative adversarial network. Signal Processing: Image Communication. **81**, 115723 (2020). https://doi.org/10.1016/j.image.2019.115723

14. Islam, M.J., Xia, Y., Sattar, J.: Fast underwater image enhancement for improved visual perception. IEEE Robot. Autom. Lett. **5**, 3227–3234 (2020). https://doi.org/10.1109/LRA.2020.2974710

15. Wang, Z., Bovik, A.C., Sheikh, H.R., Simoncelli, E.P.: Image quality assessment: from error visibility to structural similarity. IEEE Trans. on Image Process. **13**, 600–612 (2004). https://doi.org/10.1109/TIP.2003.819861

16. Luo, M.R., Cui, G., Rigg, B.: The development of the CIE 2000 colour-difference formula: CIEDE2000. Color Res. Appl. **26**, 340–350 (2001). https://doi.org/10.1002/col.1049

A Comparative Study of Machine Learning Classification Models on Customer Behavior Data

Nur Ida Aniza Rusli[✉] [iD], Farizuwana Akma Zulkifle, and Intan Syaherra Ramli

Computing Sciences Studies, College of Computing, Informatics and Media, Universiti Teknologi MARA, Cawangan Negeri Sembilan, Kampus Kuala Pilah, 72000 Kuala Pilah, Negeri Sembilan, Malaysia
{idaaniza,farizuwana,intan3885}@uitm.edu.my

Abstract. Competent marketers aim to accurately predict consumer desires and needs. With the advancement of machine learning, different machine learning models could be applied to solve various challenges, including precisely determining consumer behavior. Meanwhile, discount coupons are a frequent marketing approach to boost sales and encourage recurring business from existing customers. Accordingly, the current study seeks to analyze customer behavior by assessing an in-vehicle coupon recommendation system dataset as the case study. The dataset, which was obtained from the University of California-Irvine (UCI) machine learning repository, could predict consumer decisions as to whether accept the discount coupon influenced by demographic and environmental factors, such as driving destinations, age, current time, and weather. This study also compared six machine learning classification models, including Bayesian Network (BayesNet), Naïve Bayes, Instance-Bases Learning with Parameter-K (Lazy-IBK), Tree J48, Random Forest, and RandomTree, on the dataset to identify a suitable model for predicting customer behavior through two test modes, namely cross-validation and percentage split. The model performance was evaluated by analyzing factors, such as accuracy, precision, processing time, recall, and F-measure, for the model development. The findings discovered that Naïve Bayes and Lazy-IBK consumed the least amount of prediction time, although with the lowest accuracy. RandomTree was the highest processing time, whereas Random Forest provided the highest accuracy, precision, recall and F-measure values.

Keywords: Data mining · Machine learning · Classification · Customer behavior

1 Introduction

The emergence of market economies necessitates the increased competitiveness of different companies by prompting the enterprises to invest significant financial resources in strategizing and marketing their products efficiently. As such, customer behavior analysis is essential to corporations in forecasting customer behavior, increasing sales, improving services, optimizing markets, managing inventory, and detecting fraudulent activities

© The Author(s), under exclusive license to Springer Nature Singapore Pte Ltd. 2023
M. Yusoff et al. (Eds.): SCDS 2023, CCIS 1771, pp. 222–231, 2023.
https://doi.org/10.1007/978-981-99-0405-1_16

[1, 2]. Recently, machine learning has attracted researchers as an application to analyze customer behavior [3–5]. Machine learning extracts insights and discovers patterns in the available data to draw meaningful and useful conclusions [6, 7]. The process could be performed via supervised or unsupervised approaches with relevant algorithms, such as neural networks, decision trees, logistic regression, and support vector machines.

Classification is a supervised method which maps the data into specific groups and precisely organizes all items in a dataset into respective target categories. Although several studies proposed classification algorithms to manage customer behavior, more research efforts are required on specialized solutions for business challenges, including customer behavior issues. Nevertheless, a viable machine learning model is unavailable for business-related data, such as customer behavior datasets [8]. Therefore, this study aims to identify the most optimal classification algorithm to predict customer behavior by conducting a comparative study of supervised classification models.

The study employed an in-vehicle coupon recommendation dataset as a case study to determine the most appropriate algorithm, which could associate customer attitudes upon receiving a coupon with the coupon usage probability. The dataset was tested on six classification models, namely Bayesian Network (BayesNet), Naïve Bayes, Instance-Bases Learning with Parameter-K (Lazy-IBK), Tree J48, Random Forest, and RandomTree by using Waikato Environment for Knowledge Analysis (WEKA) data mining tool and through four evaluation measures, which were accuracy, precision, recall and F-measure. Section 2 illustrates the research methodology, Sect. 3 delineates the study results with a discussion, and Sect. 4 concludes the study findings.

2 Research Methodology

The current elucidates the study methodology which commences with data descriptions, data preprocessing, model development, and model evaluation, as depicted in Fig. 1. The study findings or research knowledge could be further applied in future studies.

2.1 Dataset Description

The in-vehicle coupon recommendation dataset was collected from an Amazon Mechanical Turk survey and published in the University of California-Irvine (UCI) machine learning repository in 2017 before being updated in 2020. The publicly available dataset was composed of significant customer behavior data to forecast the probability of an individual utilizing a received coupon based on demographic and environmental parameters. Meanwhile, the survey focused on analyzing driver behaviors through multiple factors, such as driving destinations, age, marital status, current time, and weather. A driver would be classified as "Y = 1" if the driver accepted the coupon, otherwise, the driver would be rated as "Y = 0". Table 1 outlines 26 attributes and 12,684 instances in the in-vehicle recommendation dataset [9, 10].

2.2 Data Preprocessing

Data preprocessing, which involves compressing data, identifying correlations between variables, normalizing data, and removing outliers, is critical to producing high-quality

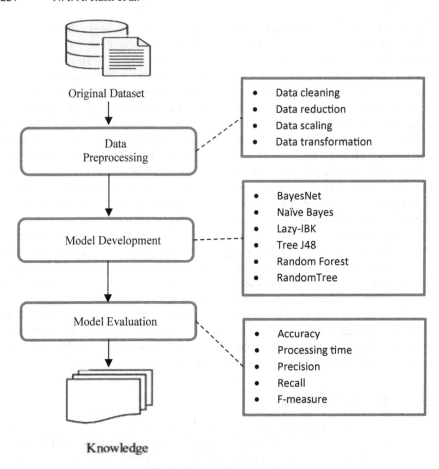

Fig. 1. Research methodology.

Table 1. In-vehicle recommendation system dataset attributes

Attribute type	Attribute
Nominal	Destination, passenger, weather, time, coupon, gender, marital status, education, occupation, income, car, bar, CoffeeHouse, CarryAway, RestaurantLessThan20, Restaurant20To50
Numeric	Temperature, hasChildren, toCoupon_GEQ5min, toCoupon_GEQ15min, toCoupon_GEQ25min, direction_same, direction_opp, Y
String	Expiration, age

data for machine learning models. Data mining researchers are highly concerned with data preprocessing since the process would significantly impact the machine learning model functioning. As such, the process should be ensured to achieve the research objectives by establishing an accurate and representative model. The data preprocessing procedures are described as follows:

- Data cleaning. Data preprocessing begins with cleaning the dataset by locating the missing data, amending contradicting values, removing noisy data, and detecting outliers. Data cleaning is crucial as any inconsistency would consequentially impact the mining process, thus resulting in inaccurate and unsatisfactory output [11, 12]. In the present dataset, six attributes (cars, bar, CoffeeHouse, CarryAway, Restaurant-LessThan20, and Restaurant20To50) possessed missing values, which were filled by implementing the ReplaceMissingValue filter in Weka. The filter replaced all null data with the mean value of an attribute to prevent the loss of potentially useful information during the mining process. The InterQuartileRange filter was subsequently applied to the dataset to uncover and exclude outliers, which were data anomalies or abnormalities.
- Data reduction. This study eliminated two string attributes, namely expiration and age attributes, from the dataset due to incompatibilities to be processed in the Weka.
- Data scaling. Data scaling, also known as data normalization, is the process of minimizing attribute range values to a common range. Examples of large scales include values ranging from 0.01 to 1000. Importing data normalization could lower the value magnitudes to a low-range scale, which allowed the current study to remove all redundant data and speed up the mining process [13]. Hence, the present study applied min-max normalization scaling into the temporary attribute by converting the range value to spanning from 0.0 to 1.0.
- Data transformation. This study applied a discretization filter to numerical attributes by setting the numerical attributes to a 3-bin unsupervised discretization, which was crucial as processing continuous attributes was more challenging on Weka. Correspondingly, numerical data was translated into an alternative format to facilitate the knowledge base creation [14]. For instance, numeric attributes, including has_children, toCoupon_GEQ5min, toCoupon_GEQ15min, toCoupon_GEQ25min, direction_same, and direction_opp, were transformed into more meaningful nominal data.

2.3 Model Development

Classification models have been extensively applied in most customer behavior studies. In this study, six classifiers, namely BayesNet, Naïve Bayes, Lazy-IBK, Tree J48, Random Forest, and RandomTree, were implemented on Weka via two test modes, which were cross-validation and percentage Split.

- BayesNet is a widely applied classifier based on Bayes' theorem, which presumes the subset of attributes are independent of one another and forms a BayesNet model based on conditional probability. The BayesNet model comprises nodes and edges, with nodes representing random attributes and edges reflecting the associations between random attributes [15, 16].
- A Naïve Bayes classifier is a simple model based on a probabilistic approach, which assumes attributes are independent of each other. The classifier allows predicting the

class of additional instances based on the probabilities appearing in existing instances [17, 18].

- Lazy-IBK, also recognized as K-Nearest Neighbour (KNN), is a non-parametric classification method to determine which group each instance belongs to by measuring the probability of which group the instance is most similar to. The model is called a "lazy learner" as a training set and assumptions are not required for the underlying data distribution [19].
- Tree J48 is a supervised machine learning classification model, which categorizes numerical and categorical data based on the C4.5 decision tree algorithm by applying the divide-and-conquer principle. The model could accurately predict outcomes from incomplete data [3].
- RandomTree is a supervised categorization model which applies the bagging concept to produce random data collection efficiently from a large set of trees known as the Random Forest [20].
- Random Forest is a supervised machine learning algorithm which produces results by referring to forecasts of the decision trees to overcome regression and categorization issues [20]. Moreover, the algorithm encompasses multiple classification models to generate pertinent resolutions to intricate issues and predicts outcomes by garnering the mean output from different decision trees, wherein more trees would improve outcome prediction precision degrees.

2.4 Model Evaluation

Table 2 portrays the evaluation of classification models via the confusion matrix.

Table 2. The confusion matrix.

		Actual class	
		Positive (P)	Negative (N)
Predicted class	Positive (P)	True Positive (TP)	False Positive (FP)
	Negative (N)	False Negative (FN)	True Negative (TN)

- True Positive (TP): An accurate identification of a ground-truth bounding box
- False Positive (FP): An erroneous discernment of an imaginary entity of negligence of an actual item
- False Negative (FN): An undiscovered ground-truth bounding box
- True Negative (TN): A correct classification of negative instance

The most commonly employed performance metric to evaluate classification models is accuracy (1), which is the simplest measure to calculate the proportion of correctly classified instances. Nonetheless, the general accuracy measurement is inadequate in highly non-normal data distribution, as a naive classifier could not effectively detect positive samples although possessing high accuracy levels in predicting negative objects. To resolve imbalanced classification, three additional metrics were introduced to acquire an optimal categorization equilibrium, namely precision (2), recall (3), and F-measure (4), to appraise the performance of the six classification models. Precision, or positive predictive value, measures the exactness or percentage of tuples that the classifier labels as positive precisely belong to the positive class. Recall or sensitivity examines the completeness or percentage of positive tuples labelled by the classifier as positive, whereas the F-measure provides the harmonic mean between precision and recall with 1.0 as the overall perfect score.

$$Accuracy = \frac{TP + TN}{P + N} \tag{1}$$

$$Precision = \frac{TP}{TP + FP} \tag{2}$$

$$Recall = \frac{TP}{TP + FN} \tag{3}$$

$$F-score = \frac{2 \times precision \times recall}{precision \times recall} \tag{4}$$

To validate the data, this study executed the k-fold cross-validation and percentage split approaches on the training set to predict variability. The results are compared to determine the performance of the classifiers. The k-fold cross-validation functions by dividing the data repository into k components and trains the model based on multiple train-test splits to accurately demonstrate the model performance on concealed data. In the applied machine learning discipline, k = 10 is the most prominent option to avoid bias while producing optimal results [21]. Therefore, the cross-validation procedure with k = 10 folds was applied for model evaluation. In addition, the holdout technique was implemented to randomly partition the data into two independent training and test sets, which was highly feasible and suitable for a huge dataset. Generally, two-thirds of the data were apportioned as the training set to establish the model, with another one-third as the test set to appraise model accuracy. In this study, the holdout method involved a percentage split between 70% of the training set and 30% of the test set.

3   Results and Discussion

Comparative analysis of six classification models, namely BayesNet, Naïve Bayes, Lazy-IBK, Tree J48, Random Forest, and RandomTree, was conducted. During the model evaluation, the data were partitioned into training and test sets via cross-validation and holdout.

Table 3 illustrates the accuracy and processing time of each classifier through the cross-validation and percentage split techniques. The results demonstrated that Random Forest produced the highest accuracy with 76.1% through cross-validation with k = 10 folds and 76.72% via a percentage split of 70:30. Conversely, Lazy-IBK exhibited the lowest accuracy with 63.9% through cross-validation with k = 10 folds and 62.0% via the percentage split of 70:30.

The findings also revealed that tree-based algorithms, including Tree J48, Random Forest, and RandomTree, possessed higher accuracy on the employed dataset than the other three models, with RandomTree manifesting the highest processing time of 0.56 s via cross-validation and 0.06 s through the holdout approach. Overall, the cross-validation technique produced a higher accuracy degree in five classifiers (except for Random Forest) compared with the holdout procedure, despite the difference being minimal.

Table 3. The classification accuracy and processing time

	Cross-validation with k = 10 folds	Processing time (s)	Percentage split (70:30)	Processing time (s)
BayesNet	67.72	0.05	66.87	0.01
Naïve Bayes	67.70	0.00	66.80	0.00
Lazy-IBK	63.90	0.00	62.00	0.00
Tree J48	74.64	0.03	73.27	0.01
Random forest	76.10	0.56	76.27	0.06
Random tree	67.00	0.03	65.13	0.01

The analysis proceeded with subsequent evaluation measures, which were precision, recall, and F-measure. The findings uncovered that Random Forest generated the highest degrees with the Lazy-IBK as the lowest in precision, recall, and F-measure through both procedures of cross-validation with k = 10 folds and holdout with a percentage split of 70:30, as portrayed in Fig. 2 and Fig. 3. The results propounded that Random Forest

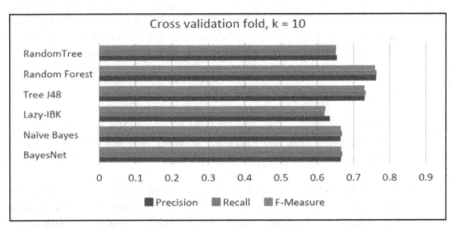

Fig. 2. Weighted average precision, recall, and F-measure values via cross-validation with k = 10 folds

was a more accurate classification model in terms of the present dataset exactness and completeness, as the F-measure values discovered in both techniques were the highest, which were 0.758 and 0.759 respectively. Hence, the overall findings demonstrated that cross-validation with k = 10 folds produced higher levels of precision, recall, and F-measure compared to the holdout method with a percentage split of 70:30, as outlined in Table 4.

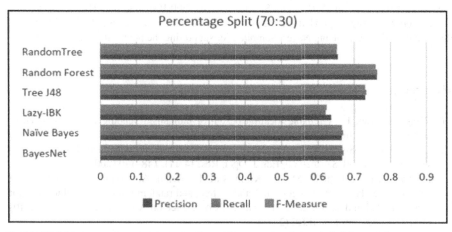

Fig. 3. Weighted average precision, recall, and F-measure values via holdout with a percentage split of 70:30

Table 4. The weighted average precision, recall and F-measure values

Classifier	Cross-validation with k = 10 folds			Percentage Split of 70:30		
	Precision	Recall	F-measure	Precision	Recall	F-measure
BayesNet	0.674	0.677	0.675	0.665	0.669	0.666
Naïve Bayes	0.673	0.677	0.674	0.664	0.668	0.665
Lazy-IBK	0.657	0.639	0.642	0.635	0.620	0.623
Tree J48	0.744	0.746	0.742	0.730	0.733	0.730
Random Forest	0.759	0.761	0.758	0.762	0.763	0.759
Random Tree	0.674	0.670	0.672	0.654	0.651	0.652

4   Conclusion

This study classified in-vehicle coupon recommendation data through six classification algorithms, namely BayesNet, Naïve Bayes, Lazy-IBK, Tree J48, Random Forest, and RandomTree, by performing k = 10 fold cross-validation and holdout (percentage split)

methods. The results revealed that RandomTree demonstrated the highest processing time of 0.56 s via cross-validation and 0.06 s through holdout, albeit with the highest accuracy. In terms of precision, recall, and F-measure, the findings discovered that Lazy-IBK produced the lowest precision, recall, and F-measure values through both techniques of cross-validation with k = 10 folds and holdout with a percentage split of 70:30.

Acknowledgment. The authors would like to thank the Universiti Teknologi MARA for funding the research project under MyRa Grant Scheme File No.: 600-RMC/GPM LPHD 5/3 (180/2021). The authors gratefully acknowledge the College of Computing, Informatics and Media, Universiti Teknologi MARA, Cawangan Negeri Sembilan for supporting the publication of this paper.

References

1. Wang, M., Yao, J.: A reliable location design of unmanned vending machines based on customer satisfaction. Electron. Comm. Res. 1–35 (2021)
2. Grigoroudis, E., Siskos, Y.: Preference disaggregation for measuring and analysing customer satisfaction: the MUSA method. Eur. J. Oper. Res. **143**(1), 148–170 (2002)
3. Hermawan, D.R., Fatihah, M.F.G., Kurniawati, L., Helen, A.: Comparative study of J48 decision tree classification algorithm, random tree, and random forest on in-vehicle coupon recommendation data. In: 2021 International Conference on Artificial Intelligence and Big Data Analytics, pp. 1–6. IEEE (2021)
4. Raju, S.S., Dhandayudam, P.: Prediction of customer behaviour analysis using classification algorithms. In: AIP Conference proceeding, vol. 1952, no. 1, pp. 020098-1–020098-7. AIP Publishing LLC, New York, USA (2018)
5. Kanavos, A., Iakovou, S.A., Sioutas, S., Tampakas, V.: Large scale product recommendation of supermarket ware based on customer behaviour analysis. Big Data Cogn. Comput. **2**(2), 11–29 (2018)
6. Khoa, B.T., Oanh, N.T.T., Uyen, V.T.T., Dung, D.C.H.: Customer loyalty in the Covid-19 pandemic: the application of machine learning in survey data. In: Somani, A.K., Mundra, A., Doss, R., Bhattacharya, S. (eds.) Smart Systems: Innovations in Computing. SIST, vol. 235, pp. 419–429. Springer, Singapore (2022). https://doi.org/10.1007/978-981-16-2877-1_38
7. Sanjay, M., Shruthi, G.: Customer attrition prediction using machine learning algorithms (2022)
8. Quynh, T. D., Dung, H. T. T.: Prediction of customer behavior using machine learning: A case study. In: Proceedings of the 2nd International Conference on Human-centered Artificial Intelligence (Computing4Human 2021), pp. 168–175. CEUR Workshop Proceedings, Da Nang, Vietnam (2021)
9. Wang, T., Rudin, C., Doshi-Velez, F., Liu, Y., Klampfl, E., MacNeille, P.: A Bayesian framework for learning rule sets for interpretable classification. The J. Mach. Learn. Res. **18**(1), 2357–2393 (2017)
10. UCI Machine Learning Repository: https://archive.ics.uci.edu/ml/datasets/in-vehicle+coupon+recommendation. Last accessed 22 Aug 2022
11. Ilyas, I.F., Rekatsinas, T.: Machine learning and data cleaning: which serves the other? J. Data Inform. Qual. (JDIQ) **14**(3), 1–11 (2022)
12. Ranjan, M., Bansiya, A.: Data cleaning rules based on conditional functional dependency. Res. J. Eng. Technol. Med. Sci. **4**(2), 6–9 (2021)
13. Beniwal, S., Arora, J.: Classification and feature selection techniques in data mining. Int. J. Eng. Res. Technol. (IJERT) **1**(6), 1–6 (2012)

14. Erkal, B., Ayyıldız, T.E.: Using machine learning methods in early diagnosis of breast cancer. In: 2021 Medical Technologies Congress (TIPTEKNO), pp 1–3. IEEE (2021)
15. Choudhury, S., Bhowal, A.: Comparative analysis of machine learning algorithms along with classifiers for network intrusion detection. In: 2015 International Conference on Smart Technologies and Management for Computing, Communication, Controls, Energy and Materials (ICSTM), pp 89–95. IEEE (2015)
16. Wang, K.: Network data management model based on Naïve Bayes classifier and deep neural networks in heterogeneous wireless networks. Comput. Electr. Eng. **75**, 135–145 (2019)
17. Ye, Z., Song, P., Zheng, D., Zhang, X., Wu, J.: A Naive Bayes model on lung adenocarcinoma projection based on tumor microenvironment and weighted gene co-expression network analysis. Infect. Dis. Model. **7**(3), 498–509 (2022)
18. Chellam, A., Ramanathan, L., Ramani, S.: Intrusion detection in computer networks using lazy learning algorithm. Procedia Comput. Sci. **132**, 928–936 (2018)
19. Panigrahi, R., Borah, S.: Rank allocation to J48 group of decision tree classifiers using binary and multiclass intrusion detection datasets. Procedia Comput. Sci. **132**, 323–332 (2018)
20. Mohan, L., Jain, S., Suyal, P.,Kumar, A.: Data mining classification techniques for intrusion detection system. In: 2020 12th International Conference on Computational Intelligence and Communication Networks (CICN), pp. 351–355. IEEE (2020)
21. Van Nguyen, T., Zhou, L., Chong, A.Y.L., Li, B., Pu, X.: Predicting customer demand for remanufactured products: a data-mining approach. Eur. J. Oper. Res. **281**(3), 543–558 (2020)

Performance Evaluation of Deep Learning Algorithms for Young and Mature Oil Palm Tree Detection

Soh Hong Say[1], Nur Intan Raihana Ruhaiyem[1]([✉]) [ID], and Yusri Yusup[2] [ID]

[1] School of Computer Sciences, Universiti Sains Malaysia, USM 11800, Penang, Malaysia
intanraihana@usm.my

[2] School of Industrial Technology, Universiti Sains Malaysia, USM 11800, Penang, Malaysia

Abstract. Oil palm trees one of the most essential economic crops in Malaysia have an economic lifespan of 20–30 years. Estimating oil palm tree age automatically through computer vision would be beneficial for plantation management. In this work, the object detection technique is proposed by applying high-resolution satellite imagery, tested with four different deep learning architectures, namely SSD, Faster R-CNN, CenterNet, and EfficientDet. The models are trained using TensorFlow Object Detection API and assessed with performance metrics and visual inspection. It is possible to produce automated oil palm trees detection model on age range estimation, either young or mature based on the crown size. Faster R-CNN is identified as the best model with total loss of 0.0047, mAP of 0.391 and mAR of 0.492, all with IoU threshold from 0.5 to 0.95 with a step size of 0.05. Parameter tuning was done on the best model and further improvement is possible with the increasing batch size.

Keywords: Image annotation · Young oil palm tree · Mature oil palm tree · Tree crown size

1 Introduction

Nowadays with the aid of computer vision techniques, most objects can be detected by computers instantly through the implementation of deep learning architectures, and they can be deployed in various fields, including agriculture. It is understood that the economic lifespan for oil palm trees is around 20–30 years, hence the age of the oil palm tree would be a vital factor in oil palm plantation. As one of Malaysia's most essential economic crops, it would be beneficial if computer vision could automate the oil palm trees' age range detection. Three main objectives were identified in this work; to build an automated oil palm trees detection model on age range estimation, either young or mature, to compare the performance of the oil palm trees age range detection model under different object detection model, and to evaluate the performance of the best-performed model under different parameter tuning. It is aimed to produce an automated detection model to estimate the age range of oil palm trees through satellite images. This approach gives data on plant development, which is particularly valuable for tracking the plant's

M. Yusoff et al. (Eds.): SCDS 2023, CCIS 1771, pp. 232–245, 2023.
https://doi.org/10.1007/978-981-99-0405-1_17

growth that will eventually contribute to oil palm tree output. Once the model is created, it can be further researched or developed by the client to infuse different functions such as disease detection, anomaly detection, and many more.

2 Background Studies

2.1 Domain Background

Precision agriculture is a management strategy that collects, processes, and analyses various data and information to support decisions based on estimated variability for improved resource use efficiency, productivity, quality, profitability, and sustainability of agricultural production. The farmers now can obtain information such as crop health, soil humidity, and temperature instantaneously and control the resources precisely with the aid of various technologies, including remote sensing. Unique cameras are used to capture the physical conditions of the Earth remotely and the captured images are applied for further analysis. Among three major types of remote sensing platforms, satellite-based platforms produced high-resolution large area covered images without noise (Shafi et al. 2019).

The oil palm industry started implementing remote sensing in oil palm cultivation. Research and developments on various application, such as tree detection and age estimation, has been done to monitor the use change effectively and continuously (Chong et al. 2017). Machine learning and deep learning have been utilized in the process to achieve the objective. A review study shows that the presence of remote sensing and machine learning solved the scarcity of consistent cultivation information in various research. However, no model has been presented to distinguish oil palm trees from other species that seem similar, such as date palm and coconut palm. This might cause classification errors while analyzing large scale, varied cultivation (Khan et al. 2021).

Yarak et al. (2021) had proposed an automatic tree detection with health classification using high-resolution aerial imagery. The collected image of 2000 × 2000 pixels is separated into 25 images with 200 × 200 pixels each before proceeding for labelling. By feeding 90% of the data into various convolutional neural network (CNN) architectures, it is possible to get a decent oil palm tree detection model with high-performance metrics scoring using Resnet-50. It is suggested to increase dataset size and variation, besides increasing overlapping between images for model performance improvement and error reduction in oil palm tree detection at the edge of the image respectively.

Besides that, a study suggested a separated young and mature oil palm tree detection model through satellite imagery. Two different CNN models were built on young and mature oil palm tree detection respectively by using LeNet architecture. The oil palm tree dataset only contains trees in the center while there are no oil palm tree features in the background dataset. By feeding 80% of the dataset for training, this approach overcome the overlapping crown problem and separated the oil palm tree from the background (shadows and other plants), hence highly improving the overall accuracy of the detection to more than 90% (Mubin et al. 2019).

Moreover, it is possible to further elevate the age estimation of oil palm trees by relating tree height with tree age through LiDAR. The integration of tree's crown with height model and multiregression levitate the overall accuracy of 84.91% over all five blocks of plantation points (Rizeei et al. 2018). There are some remarkable studies on the oil palm tree detection and age estimation to be mentioned as shown in the table below (Table 1).

Table 1. Research on oil palm tree detection and age estimation.

Author	Dataset	Algorithm	Objective
Li et al. 2017	Quickbird satellite imagery	CNN, artificial neural network	Oil palm tree detection and counting
Li et al. 2019	Quickbird satellite imagery	Two-stage CNN	Oil palm tree detection
Daliman et al. 2016	WorldView-2 satellite imagery	Haar-based rectangular windows	Young oil palm tree recognition
Augustin et al. 2016	IKONOS satellite imagery	Segmentation-based fractal texture analysis	Oil palm tree age detection

2.2   Image Annotation Techniques

Image annotation is a data labelling process by assigning labels to the objects in images before it is ready for model training, usually in a manual way. It is an important step for a supervised learning task as the model depends on the labels fed during the training session. The annotation guides the model during the training hence the model produced could predict and recognize the objects from unannotated images. Some of the common types of image annotation would be the bounding box, polygon, line and spline, landmark, and 3D cuboid. The bounding box is a rectangular box that involves object localization within an image. It is the most common used image annotation in computer vision. A 3D cuboid would be the 3D version of the bounding box. Polygon, as it sounds, annotates an irregular shape, which precisely defines the object's shape and location. Line and spline usually are used for lane detection and recognition. Landmark, a method of identifying key points of interest in a photograph, is commonly used for minute object detection and shape variation.

2.3   Object Detection Techniques

Object detection is a computer vision task that recognizes the object class and its location within an image or video. It is a combination of image classification and object localization, with the image as input and class label bounding box as output. With the popularity of deep learning, a new deep learning architecture named Convolutional Neural Network (CNN) has been widely used for object detection. CNN, a type of feedforward neural network, uses the concept of local receptive fields, pooling, and shared weights to improve training speed and local properties signal capturing at the same time. Some of the most popular object detection models include Single-Shot Detector (SSD), Faster

Region-Based CNN (Faster R-CNN), EfficientDet and CenterNet. A study has been done on some of these algorithms to check on their object detection performances. By using PASCAL VOC 2007 dataset, SSD and Faster R-CNN produced models with 78.8% to 81.6% mean average precision (mAP). It is mentioned that CNN reduces computation cost through parameter sharing, besides only smaller training sets required due to parameter sharing (Hakim and Fadhil 2021).

Another feature that could be applied to the object detection model is transfer learning. As a high-performance starting point, models are pre-trained on large datasets with similar properties before applying them to the new dataset. This approach reduces time consumption on model training by avoiding the full training process, besides solving low training data availability problems (Bonet et al. 2020).

Single Shot Detector (SSD) is the extension of the You Only Look Once (YOLO) method, where it extends the bounding box and classification predictions in a single feed-forward network by combining multiple feature maps to detect objects of multiple sizes (Hakim and Fadhil 2021). The model works by extracting features from training images in the backbone model such as VGG-16 network. The decreasing size of feature map layers is added on VGG-16 where fine-grained large feature maps capture small objects and coarse-grained small feature maps for large object detection. By applying SSD for single tree detection, it is possible to achieve 97.6% accuracy for palm plantation (Zheng and Wu 2021).

Faster R-CNN improvised the detection method of its predecessors by introducing Region Proposal Networks (RPN) in the Fast R-CNN model. RPN plays its role in detecting regions from the image that might be containing objects. It is worth noting that RPN shares convolutional layers with the object detection network. This feature helps the model become computational efficient compared to R-CNN and Fast R-CNN uses old generation region proposal techniques such as selective search (Hakim and Fadhil 2021).

EfficientDet is introduced to solve two major challenges in object detection, namely efficient multi-scale feature fusion and model scaling. By applying EfficientNet as network backbone and novel Feature Pyramid Network structure – Bi-Directional Feature Pyramid Network (BiFPN) as multi-scale feature representation, it is possible to accomplish better accuracy with fewer parameters and the number of floating-point operations (FLOPs) compared to previous object detection models on MS-COCO dataset. BiFPN can learn the importance of different input features, and further promotes the model adapting to various resolution inputs (Tan et al. 2020).

CenterNet is the extension of the keypoint-based object detection pipeline Corner-Net by introducing centre pooling and cascade corner pooling into the model. Center pooling aids the centre key points in obtaining more recognised visual patterns inside objects, making the centre element of a proposal easier to comprehend. Cascade corner pooling provides the ability to perceive internal information to the original corner pooling module. The model is more robust to feature-level noises and produced better results of at least 4.9% more average precision compared to existing one-stage detectors on MS-COCO dataset (Duan et al. 2019).

Besides the mentioned CNN architecture, other common architectures are suitable for image processing such as YOLO, LeNet, AlexNet, VGG Net and GoogleNet. Each architecture has its pros and cons; hence a user should understand the extension of these models before applying them to their tasks.

2.4 Data Splitting Techniques

Data splitting is a common technique used for model validation. The dataset is split into training, and testing set. The model learns the features from training set and get validation from testing set. This step ensures the model performance without worrying overfitting problem (Joseph 2022). Aside from training and testing set, sometimes a set of data named validation set is separated from training set to use for model validation during training stage. One of the commonly used ratios is 80:20, which indicates 80% data for training and 20% data for testing; or 80:10:10, 80% for training data, 10% each for validation and testing respectively. This split is expressed from Pareto principle, a thumb rule used by practitioners. In practice, other ratios such as 70:30, 60:40 and 50:50 are being applied too (Joseph 2022). There is no standard solution for the data splitting ratio. It should be adapted according to the project needs.

3 Research Methodology

3.1 Data Collection and Extraction

The data were collected from an open-source satellite imagery site. Many sources provide satellite imagery and are free to download. Spatial resolution is used as the measurement unit for satellite imagery clarity. It is defined as the size of one pixel on the ground. For example, 10 m spatial resolution represented 10 m $\times$ 10 m area on the ground for each pixel. The lower the value of spatial resolution, the more detailed a satellite image would be. As the focus of this work is on tree detection, high-resolution imagery is important for the model to be able to detect the details of the trees. Hence, Google Earth Pro is selected as the platform for satellite imagery data collection. Besides high spatial resolution, the image format used is friendly for model training and the AOI can be customized based on the usage purpose.

Image collection is done on various locations in Google Earth Pro, including Pulau Carey, Selangor, Kampung Kelanang, Selangor, Kampung Endah, Selangor, and Tanjung Dua Belas, Selangor. The young and mature plantations are confirmed, and the images of the plantation are downloaded from the software. To ensure the consistency of image data, the image timestamp is set at 15/10/2021 with 500 m eye elevation, 0° heading and tilt. Five different images from the mentioned locations are collected for each category (young, mature) with a resolution of 3840 $\times$ 2160 pixels per image. These images are ready to be pre-processed before transferring to the model training stage.

3.2 Data Pre-processing

After data collection, data pre-processing was carried out to convert data into a format that is suitable for model training. Object detection is the combination of classification and localization. Hence, it is important to process the data so that it contains the location information of the object in the image before proceeding to model training. In data pre-processing, there are two sub-methods: (1) **image splitting** using Pine Tools (splitting images to smaller size to increase the sample size) and (2) **image annotation** using *LabelImg* (to point the location of the trees). Then model training was done on several object detection models such as SSD, faster R-CNN, CenterNet and EfficientDet.

3.3 Model Training

TensorFlow Object Detection API (TFOD API) was selected as the platform for developing object detection solutions. There were four basic steps done before model training: (1) **data partitioning** (80% for training and 20% for testing), (2) **create label map** for 'young' and 'mature', (3) **create TensorFlow records** for train and test data, and (4) **configure training pipeline**. Once the training pipeline is configured, it is ready to proceed with model training. TensorBoard will be pulled out through coding to inspect the live training process of the model. It is a platform that provides the measurements and visualizations required for machine learning. Besides tracking experiment parameters such as loss and accuracy, it has some superb abilities such as visualizing the model graph, project embeddings into a lower-dimensional environment. Figure 1 shows the sample of TensorBoard that tracks the model training. The trained model was saved and ready for inference to test out the model's ability to carry out the requested task, which is detecting oil palm tree age in this context.

The trained model shall be loaded into an inference model to test out its ability to detect oil palm tree ages in novel image data. Figure 2 shows the result of the model detecting young oil palm trees in the new image through the inference model with the confidence of more than 50%. Model training was repeated on different pre-trained models that are available on TensorFlow 2 Detection Model Zoo, including SSD, Faster R-CNN, CenterNet, and EfficientDet. The selection of the model will be based on the better detecting speed and COCO mAP for each model category.

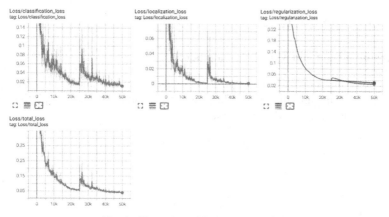

Fig. 1. TensorBoard for model training.

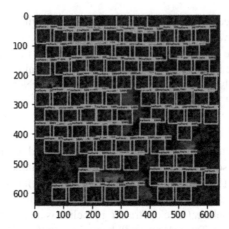

Fig. 2. Oil palm tree age estimation in inference model.

3.4 Performance Evaluation

To evaluate the performance of the model, three metrics were used in this process; loss, mean average precision (mAP) and mean average recall (mAR). Loss indicates the difference in prediction towards the actual result. The lower the loss, the better the prediction ability. Precision is the ratio of true positive (TP) versus the total number of predicted positives. It measures the percentage of the correct model's prediction. While the recall is the ratio of true positives versus the actual number of positives. Average precision (AP) summarizes the precision-recall curve into a single value, representing the weighted sum of precisions at each threshold. The mAP is then gained by dividing the summation of AP by the number of classes. It calculates the score by comparing the ground-truth bounding box to the detected box. The higher the score, the better the model's detection accuracy.

4 Results and Analysis

4.1 Training Data and Model Development

The dataset contains images and the positions of each tree, or bounding box. The dataset comprised 1171 mature trees and 1176 young trees, and the dataset is split into 80:20 ratios as shown in the table below (Table 2).

Table 2. Number of bounding boxes in the training dataset.

Dataset	Number of bounding boxes	
	Mature	Young
Training	895	899
Testing	276	277
Total	**1171**	**1176**

The model is selected with the moderate detection speed and COCO mAP as shown in the table below. These models had been trained beforehand by the provider with COCO 2017 dataset. Besides having a similar network backbone, the outputs of these models are in the form of boxes which fit the purpose of the training (Table 3).

Table 3. Selected models from repository.

Model	Speed (ms)	COCO mAP (%)
CenterNet ResNet101 V1 FPN 512×512	34	34.2
EfficientDet D1 640×640	54	38.4
SSD ResNet101 V1 FPN 640×640	57	35.6
Faster R-CNN ResNet101 V1 640×640	55	31.8

In terms of detection speed, CenterNet does provide a faster speed at 34 ms with a decent mean average precision of 34.2%. It has the fastest detection speed among all the selected models. While in terms of mAP, EfficientDet could detect the objects in COCO dataset with up to 38.4% mAP which is the highest among all the selected models. These pre-trained models have been used in the model training with the parameters shown in the table below (Table 4).

Table 4. Setting for model training.

Parameter	CenterNet	EfficientDet	SSD	Faster R-CNN
Class number	2			
Batch size	1			
Steps	250,000	300,000	25,000	25,000
Fine tune checkpoint type	Detection			
Evaluation metrics set	coco_detection_metrics			

4.2 Model Performance Evaluation

Loss, mean average precision (mAP) and mean average recall (mAR) were used to compare the performance of trained models. The performance of the models is recorded as shown in the table below. The performance is evaluated based on the maximum detection of 100 bounding boxes.

Since COCO detection metrics was applied in this work, the definition of AP and AR is the same as the mAP and mAR respectively mentioned in the methodology. Table 5 shows all metrics were calculated for 10 Intersection over Union (IoU) threshold from 0.5 to 0.95 with a step size of 0.05. This procedure ensures the better localization of the detectors. For area = small, it indicates the detection for small objects within pixel area of 322, while pixel area within 322 and 962 for medium area object.

Table 5. Performance evaluation on trained models with IoU = 0.50:0.95.

No	Performance metrics	SSD	Faster R-CNN	CenterNet	EfficientDet
1	Total loss	0.0515	0.0047	0.0946	0.0657
2	**AP** [area = all]	0.184	0.391	0.283	0.235
3	**AP** [area = small]	0.036	0.165	0	0
4	**AP** [medium]	0.185	0.391	0.284	0.236
5	**AR** [area = all]	0.247	0.492	0.409	0.332
6	**AR** [area = small]	0.4	0.7	0	0
7	**AR** [area = medium]	0.247	0.492	0.41	0.333

By comparing the total loss across all models in the table above, it seems that Faster R-CNN has a very low total loss in the training stage compared to the other three models. The loss difference is at 10 times. There is room for improvements in terms of model training for SSD, CenterNet and EfficientDet so that the loss can be reduced further near to the best-performed model. Faster R-CNN outperforms by having the highest overall mAP (Metric No. 2) and mAR (Metric No. 5), followed by CenterNet, EfficientDet and SSD models respectively. With the higher value of mAP and mAR in the Faster R-CNN model, the model is less susceptible to false positive detection and false negative detection respectively. A detection is categorized as a false positive if the prediction has a lower IoU than the threshold value or detected the object with false labels. False negative when there is no detection for the object or no correct box detection. With checking on the mAP and mAR for small object detection (Metric No. 3 and Metric No. 6), it is found that CenterNet and EfficientDet have zero value. CenterNet and EfficientDet not able to detect objects lower than a pixel area of 32^2. Surprisingly, Faster R-CNN and SSD models can detect objects smaller than the tree size in the image. In terms of medium object detection (Metric No. 4 and Metric No. 7), the value for all models is similar to their respective overall mAP and mAR. The size of the trees falls under the medium object category; hence it is reasonable to produce such results.

Visual Inspection. This section discusses the model performance by evaluating the detection result of the models in the model inference stage and comparing it with the actual count of the trees in the image. Table 6 below presents the detection result of each model on different images. The green box indicates mature trees while the blue box indicates young trees. All bounding boxes are generated with a 50% confidence level and above (IoU $\geq$ 0.5). The amounts of correctly detected trees for each model are recorded in Table 7.

Table 6. Model detection on the unseen images.

Image	SSD	Faster R-CNN	CenterNet	EfficientDet
Mature				
Young				
Mix				

By inspecting the detection ability of each model visually, the Faster R-CNN model outperforms with the highest number of correct detections and near to the actual count. No false detection is observed in the model. However, the model has weak detection in the image with a mixture of young and mature trees, especially the low number of young trees detected. The EfficientDet and SSD models are underperformed with very little detection across all images, besides a low volume of false detection in mature tree image as listed in Table 8. The low value of mAR explains the high volume of the undetected object in the images. An abnormal detection is synthesized by the SSD model where it categorizes a large area in the mix tree image as "Mature". CenterNet as the second well-performed model, produced a high volume of false positive results, especially in young tree image and mixed tree image as shown in Table 6.

From the results, Faster R-CNN generalizes well with an outstanding ability to learn the characteristics of the young and mature trees and detect them in the unseen image.

Table 7. Count for correctly detected trees.

Image		Actual	SSD	Faster R-CNN	CenterNet	EfficientDet
Mature		88	18	72	20	12
Young		160	1	100	70	5
Mix	Mature	34	0	17	0	1
	Young	64	16	5	9	2
Total		**346**	**35**	**194**	**99**	**20**

Table 8. Error in tree detection

Image		Error	SSD	Faster R-CNN	CenterNet	EfficientDet
Mature		"Young"	1	0	4	2
Young		"Mature"	0	0	17	0
Mix	Mature	"Young"	0	0	1	0
	Young	"Mature"	0	0	22	0

Not to mention it can be trained in a shorter time frame compared to the other three models.

4.3 Parameter Tuning on Best Performed Model

The best-performed model in this project, Faster R-CNN ResNet101 is tuned with two major training parameters, batch size and training steps. Model A has an increased batch size of 5 while the training steps are doubled for Model B. In terms of model training time, the duration is tripled for Model A while the duration is doubled for Model B. The time taken for model training are recorded as shown in Table 9. The visual inspection and performance metrics of the newly trained models are compared with the previous settings. The training results are shown in the Table 10.

Table 9. Time taken for model training under parameter tuning

Model	Initial model	Model A	Model B
Time taken	1:08:04.78	3:33:15.80	2:12:36.16

In terms of training loss, there is not much difference between the models. Model A and Model B have slightly decreased total loss compared to the initial model. However, significant improvement is observed in Model A in terms of mAP and mAR. A 27% increase in overall mAP and a 17% increase in overall mAR compared to the initial model.

Table 10. Faster R-CNN model detection on unseen images

Image	Initial Model	Model A	Model B
Mature			
Young			
Mix			

In terms of small object detection, Model A has a one-fold increase in small object mAP. Now the model has a better ability in detecting trees of smaller sizes (Table 11).

Table 11. Performance evaluation on Faster R-CNN models with IoU = 0.50:0.95.

No	Performance metrics	Initial model	Model A	Model B
1	Total loss	0.0047	0.0050	0.0049
2	**AP** [area = all]	0.391	0.498	0.388
3	**AP** [area = small]	0.165	0.35	0.16
4	**AP** [area = medium]	0.391	0.498	0.388
5	**AR** [area = all]	0.492	0.577	0.495
6	**AR** [area = small]	0.7	0.7	0.8
7	**AR** [area = medium]	0.492	0.577	0.494

By checking the model detection visually, Model A has significant improvement with the increasing number of detections in mature tree image, and young trees detection in mixed tree image. The model's ability in detecting smaller trees as in the mixed tree image is convinced with the higher value in a small object. Usually increasing batch size decrease the model's ability to generalization. With the decaying learning rate, it is possible to improve the model's validation loss. Model B has a similar performance as the initial model. The same number of detection numbers across all models in the young tree image is due to the limitation of maximum detection at 100 bounding boxes.

Overall, it is possible to further improve the model's performance with parameter tuning, accompanied by lengthened training time (Table 12).

Table 12. Count for correctly detected trees for Faster R-CNN models

Image		Actual	Initial model	Model A	Model B
Mature		88	72	80	72
Young		160	100	100	100
Mix	Mature	34	17	17	17
	Young	64	5	30	4
Total		346	194	227	193

5 Conclusion

In a nutshell, four different models have been created to determine the age range of the oil palm trees automatically through satellite images. The performance of the models has been compared with metrics such as loss, mAP and mAR and it is obvious that the Faster R-CNN ResNet101 model outperforms all models available in this project. Parameter tuning is done on the best model to check if there is further improvement. The model with increased batch size boosted the model's ability in recognizing oil palm tree age range, especially in detecting the smaller size of trees. To achieve the stated purpose, the object detection technique is applied in this project. Starting from data collection, high-resolution satellite imagery for oil palm plantation is collected to ensure the characteristics of the tree canopy is reserved as much as possible. The image data is then pre-processed and included with bounding boxes. The data is fed into TensorFlow Object Detection API for model training. With the application of TensorFlow Object Detection API, it is possible to train object detection models with different architectures. Four different models have been selected from the API repository and trained for the oil palm tree age estimation. Loss, mAP and mAR are utilized as the performance metrics to find out the most effective object detection model for oil palm trees age range estimation. It turns out that Faster R-CNN ResNet101 outperformed with promising performance metrics among all trained models. By further tuning the best-performed model, Faster R-CNN ResNet101 with batch size and training steps, it is possible to yield a better result by increasing the batch size. Significant improvement is observed in Model A in terms of mAP and mAR. Now the model has a better ability in detecting trees of smaller sizes. Although the training time is lengthened, it is possible to further improve the model's performance with parameter tuning.

References

Shafi, U., Mumtaz, R., García-Nieto, J., Hassan, S.A., Zaidi, S.A.R., Iqbal, N.: Precision agriculture techniques and practices: from considerations to applications. Sensors (Switzerland) **19**(17), 1–25 (2019)

Chong, K.L., Kanniah, K.D., Pohl, C., Tan, K.P.: A review of remote sensing applications for oil palm studies. Geo-Spatial Inf. Sci. **20**(2), 184–200 (2017)

Khan, N., Kamaruddin, M.A., Sheikh, U.U., Yusup, Y., Bakht, M.P.: Oil palm and machine learning: reviewing one decade of ideas, innovations, applications, and gaps. Agriculture (Switzerland) **11**(9), 1–26 (2021)

Yarak, K., Witayangkurn, A., Kritiyutanont, K., Arunplod, C., Shibasaki, R.: Oil palm tree detection and health classification on high-resolution imagery using deep learning. Agriculture (Switzerland) **11**(2), 1–17 (2021)

Mubin, N.A., Nadarajoo, E., Shafri, H.Z.M., Hamedianfar, A.: Young and mature oil palm tree detection and counting using convolutional neural network deep learning method. Int. J. Remote Sens. **40**(19), 7500–7515 (2019)

Hakim, H., Fadhil, A.: Survey: convolution neural networks in object detection. J. Phys. Conf. Ser. **1804**(1) (2021)

Bonet, I., Caraffini, F., Pena, A., Puerta, A., Gongora, M.: Oil palm detection via deep transfer learning. In: 2020 IEEE Congress on Evolutionary Computation (CEC), pp. 1–8. IEEE, Glasgow, UK (2020)

Tan, M., Pang, R., Le, Q.V.: EfficientDet: scalable and efficient object detection. In: Proceedings of the IEEE Computer Society Conference on Computer Vision and Pattern Recognition (CVPR), pp. 10778–10787. IEEE, Seattle, WA, USA (2020)

Duan, K., Bai, S., Xie, L., Qi, H., Huang, Q., Tian, Q.: CenterNet: keypoint triplets for object detection. In: Proceedings of the IEEE International Conference on Computer Vision, pp. 6568–6577. IEEE, Seoul, Korea (South) (2019)

Joseph, V.R.: Optimal ratio for data splitting. Stat. Anal. Data Mining ASA Data Sci. J. **4**(15), 531–538 (2022)

Rizeei, H.M., Shafri, H.Z.M., Mohamoud, M.A., Pradhan, B., Kalantar, B.: Oil palm counting and age estimation from WorldView-3 imagery and LiDAR data using an integrated OBIA height model and regression analysis. J. Sens. (2018)

Zheng, Y., Wu, G.: Single shot MultiBox detector for urban plantation single tree detection and location with high-resolution remote sensing imagery. Front. Environ. Sci. **9** (2021)

Object Detection Based Automated Optical Inspection of Printed Circuit Board Assembly Using Deep Learning

Ong Yee Chiun and Nur Intan Raihana Ruhaiyem$^{(\boxtimes)}$

School of Computer Sciences, Universiti Sains Malaysia, USM 11800, Penang, Malaysia
intanraihana@usm.my

Abstract. Advancement of technologies in the electronics industry has render decrease in electronic components sizes and increase in number of components on Printed Circuit Board (PCB). Industries specialize in manufacturing Printed Circuit Board Assembly (PCBA), also implementing manual visual inspection in In Process Quality Control (IPQC) verification process to ensure quality of products. Such technology advancement has increased workload of operators and time taken to perform inspection. This study is aimed to reduce time consumption and cognitive load of operators, while ensuring consistency of visual inspection during component verification process by utilizing deep learning models to perform object detection based automated optical inspection of images consisting electronic components. Three deep learning algorithms were used in the study, which are Faster R-CNN, YOLO v3 and SSD FPN. Both Faster R-CNN and SSD FPN utilized ResNet-50 backbone, whereas YOLO v3 was built with Darknet-53 backbone. Various input image dimension and image resizing options were explored to determine the best model for object detection. At the end of the study, SSD FPN with input image dimension resized to 640 × 640 by keeping image aspect ratio and with padding is concluded as the best localization and classification model to perform object detection for various types of components present in digital image.

Keywords: Object detection · Printed circuit board · Printed circuit board assembly · Deep learning

1 Introduction

Over the years, advancement of machine learning approaches has aid in development of automated optical inspection (AOI) system to carry out optical inspection of electronic components (Abd Al Rahman and Mousavi 2020). AOI inspection incorporated with machine learning has been widely used to replace human visual inspection system given its enhanced performance in terms of speed, consistency, and accuracy. AOI inspection can be distributed into three fundamental steps: machine vision, processing software, and control system (Wang et al. 2016). Machine vision will aid in capturing image of DUT. The image will be passed to the processing software, which will process the image

© The Author(s), under exclusive license to Springer Nature Singapore Pte Ltd. 2023
M. Yusoff et al. (Eds.): SCDS 2023, CCIS 1771, pp. 246–258, 2023.
https://doi.org/10.1007/978-981-99-0405-1_18

and determine the condition of the device under testing (DUT). Control system will then act accordingly based on the inspection result from processing software.

There are numerous options and concerns needed to be considered before setting up imaging systems, including number of cameras, types of cameras, capability of cameras and etc. (Li and Yang 2011). A single camera is sufficient to serve as part of the imaging system, while more cameras allow the possibility of 3D capability and contribute to better imaging. Streaming video system is beneficial when speed is vital as compared to accuracy, whereas still image system is commonly known to be more accurate. Light source is one of the key elements to build a satisfactory imaging system. Appropriate lighting enhances image detection and ameliorates prediction performance (Yilong et al. 2018). Light emitting diode (LED) lighting is commonly used due to its stable quality light properties, whereas infrared (IR) or ultraviolet (UV) lighting is occasionally used to carry out specific defect detection. Positioning of lighting plays an important role to ensure that areas to be inspected are well lit. Presence of shadows casted by components due to poor lighting position might lead to reduction of detection performance.

Various methods can be utilized in processing software, which include image matching and algorithm-based programming. Image matching involves comparison of DUT with an accurately manufactured board, also known as "golden board" (Chen et al. 2016). Algorithm-based programming is commonly referred as machine learning, which can be divided into two main approaches: supervised machine learning and unsupervised machine learning (Lehr et al. 2021). Continuous advancement of computer vision facilitates development of automated optical inspection using various approaches such as XGBoost, CNN, and YOLO (Jabbar et al. 2018; Schmidt et al. 2021; Yang et al. 2020; Lin et al. 2018).

The main scope of this research work is to develop a deep learning model to localize and classify object in image. The goal of this work is to reduce time consumption and cognitive load of operators, and to ensure consistency of visual inspection during component verification process by utilizing deep learning models to perform object detection based automated optical inspection. Thus, the objectives of the work are (1) to develop a deep learning localization model for objects present in digital image, (2) to establish a deep learning classification model for various types of components present in digital image, and (3) to achieve highest accuracy possible for the developed localization and classification model while ensuring efficiency of the model.

2 Background Studies

2.1 Object Detection

Computer vision is a popular field in artificial intelligence (AI) that enables systems to extract information from visual inputs and carry out actions based on the information obtained. One of the important computer vision tasks is to perform object detection by localizing and classifying instances of objects present in digital images. Different objects in a scene will be localized and labels will be assigned to bounding boxes of objects.

Traditional Detectors. Traditional object detectors were built based on designed features. Viola-Jones (VJ) detector applied sliding windows approach to detect window that contains human faces by integrating techniques of integral image, feature selection and detection cascades to achieve real-time human faces detection (Jones and Viola 2003). Integral image speeds up convolution process by allowing computation-al complexity of each window independent of its window size. Adaboost algorithm was utilized in feature selection, whereas a multi-stage detection paradigm was brought in as detection cascades to minimize computational overhead. Histogram of Oriented Gradients (HOG) detector was proposed to improve feature transformation and shape contexts (Wang et al. 2009). Overlapping local contrast normalization was utilized to increase accuracy. Input images were rescaled for multiple times to detect instances of varying sizes without altering the size of detection window. De-formable Part-Based Model (DPM) was known to be an extension of HOG detector (Felzenszwalb et al. 2008). DPM involved usage of various techniques such as hard negative mining, bounding box regression, and context priming to improve accuracy. Cascade architecture was implemented to compile the detection models with the aim of achieving higher detection speed.

Two-stage Detectors. Introduction of deep convolutional network into object detection task had emerged as a major breakthrough due to the saturated performance obtained from handcrafted features using traditional detectors. Region Based Convolutional Neural Network (R-CNN) was proposed to perform object detection with greatly improved accuracy (Girshick et al. 2015). Selective search was used to extract region proposals, where the proposals were then rescaled and fed to CNN model to perform feature extraction. Linear SVM classifiers were used in predicting presence of object and classifying predicted objects. Despite the significant improvement of mean Average Precision (mAP) as compared to DPM, RCNN is known to be slow in detection due to redundant feature computations on overlapped proposals. Spatial Pyramid Pooling Network (SPP-Net) was introduced to overcome the drawback of R-CNN that requires fixed-size input (He et al. 2015). SPP layer enables generation of constant length representation without rescaling image with varying size. SPPNet is more efficient than R-CNN comparatively without compromising detection accuracy as the convolutional features in SPPNet are not repeatedly computed. Fast R-CNN was proposed as an improvement of R-CNN and SPPNet by providing significant advancement on detection speed and prediction accuracy (Girshick 2015). Instead of feeding constant region proposals to CNN each time, Fast R-CNN carries out convolution operation once and a feature map is generated from the operation. Faster R-CNN was then introduced to overcome the bottleneck of Fast R-CNN (Ren et al. 2015). Region Proposal Network (RPN) was used in Faster R-CNN to replace selective search that were used in R-CNN and Fast R-CNN. The efficiency of Faster R-CNN allows it to be deployed in real-time object detection tasks.

One-stage Detectors. You Only Look Once (YOLO) was introduced as the first one-stage detector that abandoned two-stage detectors paradigm of localizing objects using regions (Redmon et al. 2016). YOLO splits images into grid and predicts class probability of bounding boxes present in each grid. Built based on the philosophy of applying a single neural network to the input image, YOLO works extremely fast, and improvement of detection accuracy were observed in v2 and v3 editions. Single Shot MultiBox Detector (SSD) was proposed as the second one-stage detector (Liu et al. 2016). It involves usage of multi-reference and multi-resolution techniques which enhances detection of small objects, allowing it to overcome the drawback of YOLO. RetinaNet was introduced to overcome class imbalance problem by enhancing Cross-Entropy Loss (CE) and proposing a new loss function known as focal loss (FL) (Lin et al. 2017a). RetinaNet is effective in performing task to detect dense and small-scale objects.

2.2 Application of Object Detection Using Deep Learning

Object detection using deep learning has been applied to great benefit in all sorts of contexts, from medical image analysis to automation of SMT defects detection and classification, with new applications emerging all the time. Multi-scale CNN was utilised in classification of medical image, in particular classifying lesion based on lesion appearance and locating lesion location (Shen et al. 2015). Landmark classification and localisation of anatomical regions, such as heart, descending aorta and aortic arch, was performed using pre-trained CNN architectures (De Vos et al. 2016). CNN appears to be the most popular approach when it comes to identifying organs and regions in medical imaging systems as it yielded accurate outcome (Baumgartner et al. 2016).

One of the effective strategies to mitigate the spread of COVID-19 virus during pandemic is by wearing a face mask. YOLOv3 and Faster R-CNN were utilized to monitor the practice of wearing face masks by performing face mask detection (Singh et al. 2021). Temperature screening is vital in COVID-19 case detection as elevated body temperature is a frequently reported manifestation (Vetter et al. 2020). Thermal detection was performed using RetinaNet to capture and detect temperature of specific point within predicted bounding boxes (Farady et al. 2020).

Object detection using deep learning is widely applied in electronics manufacturing industry. CNN arises as one of the popular techniques to perform AOI (Yang et al. 2020; Metzner et al. 2019; Wei et al. 2018; Lim et al. 2019). Faster R-CNN were used in solder joint defect detection and PCB surface defects due to its improved efficiency (Zhang and Shen 2021; Hu and Wang 2020). YOLOv3 has gained some popularity in electronics components detection, wafer die defect detection, and SMD LED chips defect detection (Gao et al. 2021; Chen et al. 2020; Chen and Tsai 2021).

3 Research Methodology

3.1 Data Collection

Vitiny UM10 HDMI/USB Autofocus Digital Microscope was utilized to collect images of PCBA. The digital microscope is built with 4x objective lens and can perform magnification from 13x to 140x. Build-in LED lighting ensures that the environment is well-lit during data collection. PCBA of varying appearance with various components were subjected to image collection. Each image contains at least one type of component, with image dimension of 1920 × 1080.

3.2 Data Annotation

A total of 1635 images were obtained. The images collected were subjected to data annotation to classify 5 classes of components, namely capacitor, resistor, IC, diode, and fuse. Data annotation was performed by referring to the Bill of Material (BOM). BOM contains details of components used to assemble a product. Classes of components are indicated explicitly in the BOM, with information of designated location of components. Data annotation was carried out by comparing the location of components on schematic diagram to the designated location in BOM (Fig. 1).

Fig. 1. Data sample for each class, namely capacitor, resistor, IC, diode, and fuse (from left to right).

Components leads were included during data annotation as part of components characteristics other than component body. Each component has its distinctive traits that facilitate model development during feature extraction at backbone stage. For example, diode has two leads in the collected dataset, whereas IC has many leads (Fig. 2).

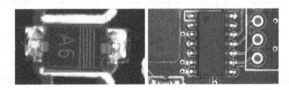

Fig. 2. Data annotation sample of diode (left) and IC (right), blue box indicating annotation.

A total of 2854 instances were obtained from the annotated data. Table 1 depicts number of count and percentage of class distribution. The number of instances from each class ranged between 468 and 656. Each class contributed to around 20% of total number of instances. The class distribution is almost equal, and no data imbalance was observed. After confirmation that balanced dataset was achieved, the data were further split into 70% training and 30% testing. The data were then converted into a single TF-Record format to ensure its compatibility with Tensorflow framework.

3.3 Modelling and Evaluation

The computing environment to perform modelling and evaluation are listed in Table 2. All training and testing were performed on AMD Ryzen 9 5900HX processor, with the aid of NVidia GTX3070 graphic card. Anaconda was set up as development environment, while CUDA and CuDNN were employed for CPU/GPU level. Tensorflow object detection

Table 1. Class distribution.

Class	Count	Percentage
Capacitor	656	23%
Diode	589	21%
Fuse	468	16%
IC	593	21%
Resistor	548	19%
Total	2854	100%

Table 2. Computing environment.

Device	Configuration
Operation system	Windows 10
Memory	16 GB RAM
Processor	AMD Ryzen 9 5900HX processor
GPU accelerator	CUDA Toolkit 11.2, cuDNN SDK 8.1.0
GPU	NVidia GTX3070 laptop GPU
Software library	Tensorflow

API which was built on top of Tensorflow was implemented. Detection models pre-trained on COCO 2017 dataset, which is also referred as Model Zoo, were used to initialise the models for component detection task.

Three different algorithms were explored to compare their performance. Table 3 depicts models developed for object detection. Both two stage detector and one stage detectors were included in the study, namely Faster R-CNN, YOLO v3 and SSD FPN.

Table 3. Algorithms developed in the study.

Algorithms	Detectors	Backbone
Faster R-CNN	Two-stage	ResNet-50
YOLO v3	One-stage	Darknet-53
SSD FPN	One-stage	ResNet-50

Two-stage detector is known to perform better in terms of accuracy, whereas one-stage detector is reported to excel in terms of speed. Faster R-CNN is one of the best performing algorithms among two-stage detectors, which makes it indubitable to be selected as one of the algorithms in this study (Ren et al. 2015). YOLO v3 is the pioneer of one-stage detector to perform object detection task using simpler architecture and sees the problem as single regression task (Redmon and Farhadi 2018). Therefore, it was chosen to compare the performance between two-stage detector and one-stage detector. However, the accuracy of YOLO v3 is less satisfactory as compared to Faster R-CNN (Ren et al. 2015; Redmon and Farhadi 2018: An incremental improvement, 2018). Ramification of one-stage detector has led to development of SSD, which is known to have fast detection speed without conforming accuracy (Liu et al. 2016). FPN arises as better feature extractor which generate multi-scale feature maps with better quality information than regular feature pyramid (Lin et al. 2017b). Thus, SSD using FPN as feature extractor was included in the study to compare its performance with other one-stage detector and two-stage detector. ResNet-50 was utilized as backbone to perform feature extraction in Faster R-CNN and SSD FPN; whereas Darknet-53 was utilized as backbone in YOLO v3. Image dimension was rescaled before being input into the model. Table 4 shows image rescaling options and image dimension that were defined in the study.

Table 4. Image resizing options and image dimension that were used in the study.

Algorithm	Image resizing options	Dimension
Faster R-CNN	Keep aspect ratio	640 × 640
	Fixed shape	640 × 640
	Fixed shape	1024 × 1024
YOLO v3	Fixed shape	416 × 416
	Fixed shape	608 × 608
SSD FPN	Keep aspect ratio	640 × 640
	Fixed shape	640 × 640
	Fixed shape	1024 × 1024

Keep aspect ratio resizer allows image to be compressed to satisfy the minimum and maximum size constraints. The aspect ratio of the image is being kept by addition of padding to fill up spaces in order to meet the size constraints. Fixed shape resizer stretches and compresses the image into the defined length and width, ignoring the aspect ratio of the original image. Various image dimension was explored to study the impact of input image dimension on performance of model. Quantification of object detection results were carried out using mAP. Comparison of mAP at .75 IOU between Faster R-CNN, YOLO v3 and SSD FPN was performed. The best performing model was selected by considering the mAP and computing resources trade off.

4   Results and Discussion

4.1   Comparison of Input Image Size

Table 5 depicts image resizing options that were used in the study. Images were resized before they were being fed into the model due to large original image size and limitations of computational resources. Two different types of images resizing options were explored, namely fixed shape resizer and keep aspect ratio resizer. In fixed shape resizer, the input image was stretched or compressed to a defined height and width. On the other hand, keep aspect ratio resizer resizes the input image by satisfying the minimum and maximum size constraints.

Table 5. Comparison of model performance with various image resizing options.

Algorithm	Image resizing options	Dimension	mAP	Train duration (min)
Faster R-CNN	Keep aspect ratio	640 × 640	0.9378	142.17
	Fixed shape	640 × 640	0.9481	145.67
	Fixed shape	1024 × 1024	0.9540	463.65
YOLO v3	Fixed shape	416 × 416	0.9456	149.90
	Fixed shape	608 × 608	0.9361	212.52
SSD FPN	Keep aspect ratio	640 × 640	0.9708	113.40
	Fixed shape	640 × 640	0.9683	161.82
	Fixed shape	1024 × 1024	0.9713	584.47

Faster R-CNN achieved highest mAP at 0.9540 while using fixed shape resizer with dimension 1024 × 1024. It was observed that fixed shape resizer will beget higher accuracy as compared to fixed aspect ratio resizer in Faster R-CNN. One of the plausible explanations is that the defined anchor boxes ratio is a good fit to detect instances when the input images were compressed into square. YOLO v3 network down sampled the images by 32, therefore the width and height must be set as multiple of 32. The standard input resolution for YOLO v3 is 416 × 416. Theoretically, input resolution 608 × 608 should yield better mAP as compared to input resolution 416 × 416 (Redmon and Farhadi 2018: An incremental improvement, 2018). In this study, YOLO v3 with fixed input image size of 416 × 416 achieved higher mAP at 0.9456 as compared to fixed input image size of 608 × 608. Limitations on GPU resources might have led to poor model learning, which can be observed from the fluctuations observed in graph of Generalized Intersection Over Union (GIOU) loss over training steps as shown in Fig. 3. Greater fluctuations were observed in GIOU loss over time of YOLO v3 training with image resolution 608 × 608, indicating that the model learning was not ideal.

FPN which acts as feature extractor was added to the backbone of SSD with ResNet-50. SSD FPN requires feature map to be of the same size, therefore the images were resized to squares. Padding was added in input image for SSD FPN with keep aspect ratio resizing option to generate squared images as input. SSD FPN achieved highest mAP at 0.9713 when image dimension is defined as 1024 × 1024 using fixed shape resizer. Comparison of mAP between different image resizing options of dimension 640 × 640 has indicated that addition of padding while keeping the original aspect ratio of image gave rise to better mAP than stretching and resizing the image into squares. However, limitation of computational resources has restricted experimentation on SSD FPN model training and testing using keep aspect ratio resizer with image dimension 1024 × 1024.

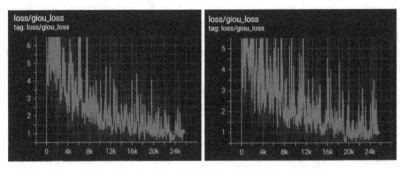

Fig. 3. GIOU loss of YOLO v3 training with image resolution 416 × 416 (left) and 608 × 608 (right).

4.2 Training Time

Table 6 describes number of steps set for each algorithm. Number of steps in Faster R-CNN and SSD FPN were set in configuration, whereas number of steps in YOLO v3 was generated by defining number of epochs while taking number of training data and batch size into consideration.

Table 6. Number of steps set in each algorithm.

Algorithms	Number of steps
Faster R-CNN	25000
YOLO v3	25430
SSD FPN	25000

The training time of algorithm was greatly influenced by number of steps and input image resolution. Table 5 shows train duration for each algorithm with varying input image resolution. It can be concluded that large input image resolution will lead to significant increase in model training duration. Greater number of steps will also give rise to longer train duration.

Other than input image resolution and number of steps, one of the most prominent factors that will affect train duration is limitation of GPU resources. GPUs are suitable to perform large matrix multiplications in neural network as they are optimized for highly-parallel processing. GPU used in this study enables train batch size of 2.

4.3 Accuracy and Resource Trade Off

High fluctuations of training loss over time commensurate with small batch size. The highly fluctuating training loss was observed in Faster R-CNN. However, all three algorithms – Faster R-CNN, YOLO v3 and SSD FPN showed descending trend in training loss. Convergences were observed in all algorithms with a minimum of 25,000 steps.

Figures 4 and 5 summarize comparison of mAP and comparison of train duration among Faster R-CNN, YOLO v3 and SSD FPN with different input image dimension and image resizing options.

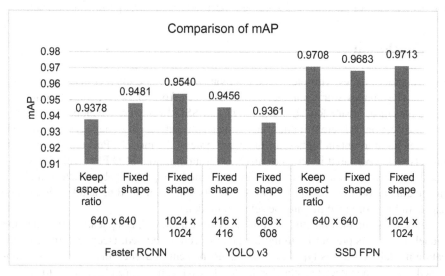

Fig. 4. Comparison of mAP among various algorithms.

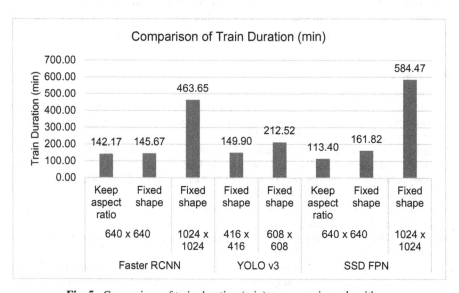

Fig. 5. Comparison of train duration (min) among various algorithms.

It can be observed that SSD FPN achieved highest mAP as compared to Faster R-CNN and YOLO v3. In terms of train duration, SSD FPN is enlisted in the leaderboard with shortest training time. Although there is a minute rise in mAP using SSD FPN when trained with input image dimension of 1024 × 1024, the corresponding train duration had increased significantly, which is not effective considering the accuracy and computing resource trade off. SSD FPN with input image dimension resized to 640 × 640 by addition of padding and keeping aspect ratio is the best performing model.

5 Conclusion

In this study, images with electronic components from five distinct classes were collected. The images were annotated with instances from class resistor, capacitor, IC, diode and fuse. Faster R-CNN, YOLO v3 and SSD FPN were developed to perform object detection. Different input image dimension and varying image resizing options were explored to obtain highest accuracy possible of the models. Performance of these models were compared in terms of mAP and train duration. SSD FPN with ResNet-50 backbone was concluded as the best performing model to perform object detection. Input image dimension were resized to 640 × 640 by addition of padding and keeping image aspect ratio before feeding into the selected model.

In conclusion, the objectives of this study were achieved. Deep learning localization model for objects present in digital image has been developed. Deep learning classification model for various types of components present in digital image has been established. Highest accuracy possible for the developed localization and classification model has been achieved while ensuring efficiency of the model. Despite this study has been successfully carried out, there are still errors in localizing and classifying components in digital image. Based on the limitations of this study, analysis can be extended by collecting more data and further distributing classes of components.

References

Rahman, Abd Al, Mousavi, A.: A review and analysis of automatic optical inspection and quality monitoring methods in electronics industry. IEEE Access **8**, 183192–183271 (2020). https://doi.org/10.1109/ACCESS.2020.3029127

Baumgartner, C.F., Kamnitsas, K., Matthew, J., Smith, S., Kainz, B., Rueckert, D.: Real-time standard scan plane detection and localisation in fetal ultrasound using fully convolutional neural networks. In: International Conference on Medical Image Computing and Computer-Assisted Intervention, pp. 203–211 (2016)

Chen, S.H., Tsai, C.C.: SMD LED chips defect detection using a YOLOv3-dense model. Adv. Eng. Inform. **47**, 101255 (2021)

Chen, S.-H., Kang, C.-H., Perng, D.-B.: Detecting and measuring defects in wafer die using GAN and YOLOV3. Appl. Sci. **23**, 8725 (2020)

Chen, Y.-J., Fan, C.-Y., Chang, K.-H.: Manufacturing intelligence for reducing false alarm of defect classification by integrating similarity matching approach in CMOS image sensor manufacturing. Comput. Ind. Eng. **99**, 465–473 (2016)

De Vos, B.D., Wolterink, J.M., Jong, P.A., Viergever, M.A., Išgum, I.: 2D image classification for 3D anatomy localization: employing deep convolutional neural networks. In: Medical Imaging 2016: Image Processing, pp. 517–523 (2016)

Farady, I., Lin, C.-Y., Rojanasarit, A., Prompol, K., Akhyar, F.: Mask classification and head temperature detection combined with deep learning networks. In: 2020 2nd International Conference on Broadband Communications, Wireless Sensors and Powering (BCWSP), pp. 74–78 (2020)

Felzenszwalb, P., McAllester, D., Ramanan, D.: A discriminatively trained, multiscale, deformable part model. In: 2008 IEEE Conference on Computer Vision and Pattern Recognition, pp. 1–8 (2008)

Gao, S., Qiu, T., Huang, A., Wang, G., Yu, J.: Electronic components detection for PCBA based on a tailored YOLOv3 network with image pre-processing. In: 2021 IEEE 17th International Conference on Automation Science and Engineering (CASE), pp. 1435–1440 (2021)

Girshick, R.: Fast R-CNN. In: Proceedings of the IEEE International Conference on Computer Vision, pp. 1440–1448 (2015)

Girshick, R., Donahue, J., Darrell, T., Malik, J.: Region-based convolutional networks for accurate object detection and segmentation. In: IEEE Transactions on Pattern Analysis and Machine Intelligence, pp. 142–158 (2015)

He, K., Zhang, X., Ren, S., Sun, J.: Spatial pyramid pooling in deep convolutional networks for visual recognition. IEEE Trans. Pattern Anal. Mach. Intell. **9**, 1904–1916 (2015)

Hu, B., Wang, J.: Detection of PCB surface defects with improved faster-RCNN and feature pyramid network. IEEE Access **8**, 108335–108345 (2020)

Jabbar, E., Besse, P., Loubes, J.-M., Roa, N. B., Merle, C., Dettai, R.: Supervised learning approach for surface-mount device production. In: International Conference on Machine Learning, Optimization, and Data Science, pp. 254–263 (2018)

Jones, M., Viola, P.: Fast multi-view face detection. Mitsubishi Electric Research Lab TR-20003-96, 2 (2003)

Lehr, J.J., Hoang, V.N., Wrangel, D.V., Krüger, J.: Supervised learning vs. unsupervised learning: a comparison for optical inspection applications in quality control. IOP Conference Series: Materials Science and Engineering, 012049 (2021)

Li, Z., Yang, Q.: System design for PCB defects detection based on AOI technology. In: 2011 4th International Congress on Image and Signal Processing, pp. 1988–1991 (2011)

Lim, D.-U., Kim, Y.-G., Park, T.-H.: SMD classification for automated optical inspection machine using convolution neural network. In: 2019 Third IEEE International Conference on Robotic Computing (IRC), pp. 395–398 (2019)

Lin, T.-Y., Dollár, P., Girshick, R., He, K., Hariharan, B., Belongie, S.: Feature pyramid networks for object detection. In: Proceedings of the IEEE Conference on Computer Vision and Pattern Recognition, pp. 2117–2125 (2017a)

Lin, T.-Y., Goyal, P., Girshick, R., He, K., Dollár, P.: Focal loss for dense object detection. In: Proceedings of the IEEE International Conference on Computer Vision, pp. 2980–2988 (2017b)

Lin, Y.-L., Chiang, Y.-M., Hsu, H.-C.: Capacitor detection in PCB using YOLO algorithm. In: 2018 International Conference on System Science and Engineering (ICSSE), pp. 1–4 (2018)

Liu, W., et al.: SSD: single shot multibox detector. In: European Conference on Computer Vision, pp. 21–37 (2016)

Metzner, M., Fiebag, D., Mayr, A., Franke, J.: Automated optical inspection of soldering connections in power electronics production using convolutional neural networks. In: Automated Optical Inspection of Soldering Connections in Power Electronics Production Using Convolutional Neural Networks, pp. 1–6 (2019)

Redmon, J., Farhadi, A.: YOLOV3: an incremental improvement. arXiv preprint arXiv:1804.02767 (2018)

Redmon, J., Divvala, S., Girshick, R., Farhadi, A.: You only look once: unified, real-time object detection. In: Proceedings of the IEEE Conference on Computer Vision and Pattern Recognition, pp. 779–788 (2016)

Ren, S., He, K., Girshick, R., Sun, J.: Faster R-CNN: towards real-time object detection with region proposal networks. In: Advances in Neural Information Processing Systems (2015)

Schmidt, K., Rauchensteiner, D., Voigt, N.T., Bönig, J., Beitinger, G., Franke, J.: An automated optical inspection system for PIP solder joint classification using convolutional neural networks. In: 2021 IEEE 71st Electronic Components and Technology Conference (ECTC), pp. 2205–2210 (2021)

Shen, W., Zhou, M., Yang, F., Yang, C., Tian, J.: Multi-scale convolutional neural networks for lung nodule classification. In: International Conference on Information Processing in Medical Imaging, pp. 588–599 (2015)

Singh, S., Ahuja, U., Kumar, M., Kumar, K., Sachdeva, M.: Face mask detection using YOLOv3 and faster R-CNN models: COVID-19 environment. Multimedia Tools Appl. **80**(13), 19753–19768 (2021). https://doi.org/10.1007/s11042-021-10711-8

Vetter, P., Vu, D.L., L'Huillier, A.G., Schibler, M., Kaiser, L., Jacquerioz, F.: Clinical features of covid-19. BMJ (2020)

Wang, W.C., Chen, S.L., Chen, L.B., Chang, W.J.: A machine vision based automatic optical inspection system for measuring drilling quality of printed circuit boards. IEEE Access **5**, 10817–10833 (2016)

Wang, X., Han, T.X., Yan, S.: An HOG-LBP human detector with partial occlusion handling. In: 2009 IEEE 12th International Conference on Computer Vision, pp. 32–39 (2009)

Wei, P., Liu, C., Liu, M., Gao, Y., Liu, H.: CNN-based reference comparison method for classifying bare PCB defects CNN-based reference comparison method for classifying bare PCB defects. J. Eng. **2018**(16), 1528–1533 (2018)

Yang, Y., et al.: A high-performance deep learning algorithm for the automated optical inspection of laser welding. Appl. Sci. **10**(3), 933 (2020)

Yilong, W.U., Junling, W.E., Zhang, P.: Application of AOI light source modes in multi-chip modules inspection. In: 2018 19th International Conference on Electronic Packaging Technology (ICEPT), pp. 141–143 (2018)

Zhang, K., Shen, H.: Solder joint defect detection in the connectors using improved faster-RCNN algorithm. Appl. Sci. **11**(2), 576 (2021)

Mathematical and Statistical Learning

The Characterization of Rainfall Data Set Using Persistence Diagram and Its Relation to Extreme Events: Case Study of Three Locations in Kemaman, Terengganu

Z. A. Hasan[1,2] 🆔 and R. U. Gobithaasan[2,3(✉)] 🆔

[1] Institute of Engineering Mathematics, University Malaysia Perlis, Arau, Perlis, Malaysia
[2] Faculty of Ocean Engineering Technology and Informatics, University Malaysia Terengganu, Kuala Nerus, Terengganu, Malaysia
gr@umt.edu.my
[3] Special Interest Group on Modelling and Data Analytics, Data and Digital Science Cluster, University Malaysia Terengganu, Kuala Nerus, Terengganu, Malaysia

Abstract. Floods are recurring phenomena at certain locations because of excessive rainfall, resulting in the overflow of lakes, drains, and rivers. In this work, we employ Persistence Homology (PH) to investigate the relationship between rainfall and flood that occurred from 1997 to 2018. Three stations in Kemaman, Terengganu, have been chosen to study this relationship. Persistence Diagram (PD) is one of the most powerful tools available under the umbrella of PH for detecting topological signatures in high dimension points cloud. In this paper, we use the rainfall time series dataset and express it in higher dimensions by selecting the embedded dimension, $M = 5$, , and manipulating the time delay τ to obtain the maximum persistence. Then, we compared with past flood events which are labelled based on water level and PD's max score to identify its suitability for flood identification. The area under the curve of receiver operation characteristics (ROC) have been used to measure the performance with three different thresholds for station 4131001, 4232002, and 4332001. The results clearly show PD's significance to characterize the rainfall dataset as normal and flood events. The employed maximum persistence is robust despite missing data values.

Keywords: Topological data analysis · Persistent homology · Rainfall · Flood events

1 Introduction

Understanding the Earth's water cycle can help us understand how global warming will exacerbate droughts and floods. Both floods and drought are natural disasters that occur unpredictably and sometimes become annual events. In Malaysia, flood events have been reported since 1886 where they occur at a state in Malaysia called Kelantan. This major flood is known as the "Storm Forest Flood," because it destroyed hundreds of square

© The Author(s), under exclusive license to Springer Nature Singapore Pte Ltd. 2023
M. Yusoff et al. (Eds.): SCDS 2023, CCIS 1771, pp. 261–274, 2023.
https://doi.org/10.1007/978-981-99-0405-1_19

kilometers of low-lying forest in Kelantan, in 1926. J. M Gullick calls it 'the mother and father' of floods [1]. In 1967, another major flood engulfed Malaysia which was reported by the Department of Irrigation and Drainage (DID) [2] and Noor et al. [3]. The next major flood occurred in 1971, in which the Malaysian government declared a National Flood Emergency on 5th January 1971 [3]. The most recent major flood appeared in 2014 which affected the east coast of Peninsular Malaysia, Kelantan, Terengganu, and Pahang. Kelantan was hit by the worst flood where flood level reached up to 5 to 10 m which equals to a 3rd to 4th-floor building [4]. The 2014 flood impacted more than 200,000 victims and caused economic loss over RM1 billion [5].

There are three types of floods in Malaysia which are monsoonal flood, flash flood, and tidal flood. These three floods are classified based on the location and geography of the area. In general, Malaysia is a country located near the equator and has an equatorial climate. As a result, Malaysia has a uniform temperature, high humidity, and has a large rainfall distribution. Rainfall distribution is strongly influenced by wind gust patterns and local topographic properties. That is the reason the rainfall distribution of area in Malaysia is not distributed uniformly as it depends on the sea faces which presents various characteristics [6]. East coast states in peninsular Malaysia receive maximum rainfall between November-January, while west coast peninsular states receive maximum rainfall between October- November, and April-May annually.

Floods have their own pattern that can be linked to recurring events. Periodicity refers to the occurrence of a recurring event. A time series with periodicity will display a cycle (n- dimensional holes) if it is embedded in higher dimension using Taken's embedding. This periodicity can be identified topologically using shape invariant methodology known as Topological Data Analysis (TDA). TDA is a data analysis framework proposed by Carlsson (2009) [7] based on the notion of algebraic topology [8]. Recently, TDA has been explored in time series analysis with real data such as stock market [9–13], environmental time series [14], hydrological [15, 16], video data [17], medical and biology [18–22]. TDA is a well-known method to extract topological features in the data. The strategy from the applications mentioned here is based on quantifying homology using persistent homology (PH), to extract shape invariants from high-dimensional, complex, and large data [23, 24].

Recently, [25] introduced sliding window 1-persistence (SW1Pers) to identify periodicity pattern in time series which is very practical as it can be used to rank and classify periodicity using the smooth and noise synthetic data. Their method only uses one persistence or best feature in persistent diagram (PD) of 1D holes to identify the periodicity. The approach has been applied to generate data and tested to discover periodicity in synthetic data with various noises [18]. However, SW1Pers has not yet been evaluated in terms of missing data values.

In this study, we investigate further the approach used by [25], which is the experiment aimed at describing the rainfall data from the hydrological dataset and testing the stability in the presence of missing value data. From the pattern and score of the data, we can analyze the variability of the rainfall pattern and relationship with the water level as well as the flood events. To demonstrate this result, we start with the explanation of the water level and rainfall stations in detail. This is segmented yearly starting from 1st June until 31st May the following year. Then, it is compared to the summary of the flood records extracted from the DID reports. It is then followed by the methodology of this work; TDA, sliding window for time series data, and pre-processing. The data is then embedded in a higher dimension and referred to as a point cloud. The persistence diagram is then generated with dimension 5 using the Ripser library [26]. Then, for each data segment, we extract maximum persistence score and verified with ROC for its suitability. Finally, we conclude that the maximum persistence can characterize rainfall data in three stations as shown with the threshold value to classify flood and normal events.

2 Station and Dataset

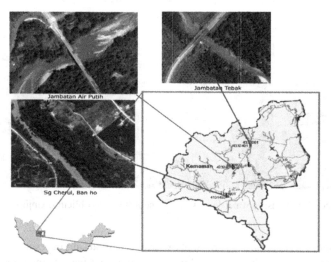

Fig. 1. Rainfall stations (4131001, 4232002, and 4332001) and water level (4131453, 4232401 and 4332401) at Kemaman, Terengganu.

Table 1. Summary of stations at 3 locations in Kemaman, Terengganu

Station number	Station type	Coordinate	Missing value (%)	Period
4131001	Rainfall	04°08′00″ N, 103°10′30″ E	3.37	1985–2019
4131453	Water level	04°08′00″ N, 103°10′30″ E	29.29	1975–2019
4232002	Rainfall	04°16′15″ N, 103°11′55″ E	11.46	1985–2019
4232401	Water level	04°16′15″ N, 103°11′55″ E	23.55	1992–2019

(continued)

Table 1. (*continued*)

Station number	Station type	Coordinate	Missing value (%)	Period
4332001	Rainfall	04°22′40″ N, 103°15′45″ E	14.6	1985–2019
4332401	Water level	04°22′40″ N, 103°15′45″ E	3.44	1997–2019

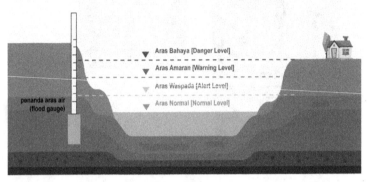

TAHAP NILAI AMBANG ARAS AIR
(WATER LEVEL THRESHOLD)

Fig. 2. Zone level by using water level measurement (https://publicinfobanjir.water.gov.my/)

Kemaman, Terengganu is an area that experiences floods almost every year. Flooding in the Kemaman area is due to a combination of physical factors, including high tides and high altitudes, as well as heavy rain. According to [27] the summary of flood events showed that Kemaman is one of the locations where flood cannot be avoided because of the rain intensity in a short period of time as well as the overflow of its river. The authority in Malaysia named as the Department of Irrigation and Drainage (DID) has been playing a pivotal role studying flood characteristics over the years. The flood variables that are recorded include rainfall quantity, water level, streamflow, suspended sediment, evaporation, and water quality. Regarding water level, the DID has issued three important levels of warning, alert, and danger as shown in Fig. 2. Zone level by using water level measurement (https://publicinfobanjir.water.gov.my/).

In this study, three locations were selected where each location has a water level station and a rainfall station. These three selected locations have slightly different rainfall characteristics and consist of three different rivers: the Cherul River, the Kemaman River, and the Tebak River. The main basin or river is the Kemaman River which is connected to the Cherul River and the Tebak River and ends at South China Sea as shown in Fig. 1. This basin covers 1984 km^2 of catchment area and 77 km long. All data provided by DID is in raw format. Then the cleaning process is carried out and the missing data for these 6 stations is reported in Table 1. We use the water level to label the threshold zone based on the level of measurement as illustrated in Fig. 2.

Figure 3 shows the rainfall plot for three locations. All the annual data is divided evenly with a total of 365 days except for the leap year that contains 366. As the high quantity of rain occurs during monsoon season from November to January, thus, the set of 365 days have been chosen from 1st June until 31st May.

3 Kemaman Flood History

Terengganu's terrain, which consists mostly of lowlands, makes the country vulnerable to flooding. Other factors such as exposure to monsoon winds that bring heavy rains from October to March also cause flooding every year. Sometimes floods can occur up to four times a year and cause a lot of casualties and damages. The summary of flood in this three-location is summarized in Table 2.

Table 2. Summary of flood history in Tebak, Air Putih, and Cherul.

Year Range	Location (no. of victims)	Flood period	Damages (RM)
2009–2010	Tebak (655)	3–4/12/2009	Not reported
	Air Putih		
	Cherul (0)		
2010–2011	Tebak (72)	7/1/2011	RM5M (Kemaman)
	Air Putih (63)	29–31/12/2010	
	Cherul (0)		
2011–2012	Tebak (92)	24/11/2011	Not reported
	Air Putih (2)	24/11/2011	
	Cherul (0)		
2012–2013	Tebak (321)	25–30/12/2012	RM7.15M (Terengganu)
	Air Putih (750)	25–30/12/2012	
	Cherul (0)		
2013–2014	Tebak (155)	12–13/1/2014	RM3.437M (Terengganu)
	Air Putih (not specific)	3/12/2013	
	Cherul (0)		
2014–2015	Tebak (699)	17–25/12/2014	RM1.1M (Kemaman)
	Air Putih (1792)	17–25/12/2014	
	Cherul (199)	17–25/12/2014	
2016–2017	Tebak (not specific)	26/12/2016–26/1/2017	RM2.272M (Terengganu)
	Air Putih (not specific)	26/12/2016–26/1/2017	
	Cherul (not specific)	26/12/2016–26/1/2017	

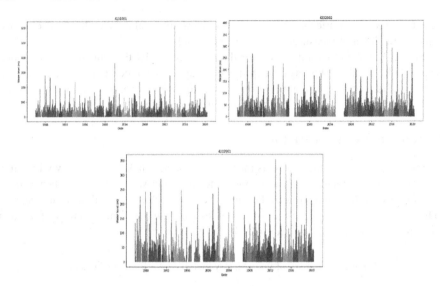

Fig. 3. Line plot of Rainfall data with evenly segmented from 1st June until 31st May

4 Topological Data Analysis

There are two main branches in TDA; Persistent Homology and Mapper [7, 28]. This paper used PH which is developed based on the homology group from Algebraic Topology. The main idea of PH is to encode the structure of higher dimensional data by means of simplicial complex.

4.1 Simplicial Complex

A simplicial complex is something that can be imagined as a generalization of graph of higher dimensions. Let a vertex set V, a simplex $\rho \subseteq V$ be considered as a collection of vertices. For example, 0-simplex contains a vertex, 1-simplex is a vector with an edge with two vertices and 2-simplex is a triangle with three edges and three vertices. A simplicial complex K is a collection of simplices $\rho \subseteq V$ so that if $\rho \in K$ and $\gamma \leq \rho$ then $\gamma \in K$ where γ is the face of ρ.

4.2 Homology

Let K be a simplicial complex consisting of finite set of simplices that closed under the face relation, where two simplices share the same face. We denote that d dimensional simplices in K are $\rho_1, \ldots, \rho_L$. A d-dimensional chain is a formal sum of the d-dimensional simplices $\alpha = \sum_{i=1}^{L} a_i \rho_i$. The collection of all d-dimensional chains form a vector space and denote as $C_d(K)$. Let S be a simplicial complex and $\sigma \in S, \sigma = [v_0, v_1, \ldots, v_k]$. The boundary homomorphism or the maps of $\partial_d : C_d(S) \to C_{d-1}(S)$ is,

$$\partial_d \sigma = \sum_{i}^{d} (-1)^i [v_0, v_1, \ldots, \hat{v}_i, \ldots, v_d] \tag{1}$$

where $\hat{v}_i$ indicates that the v_i is removed from the sequence. The k-chains that have boundary 0 are called k ycles that form group Z_k. Meanwhile, the k-chains that are the boundary of $(k + 1)$-chains that form k-boundaries group is denoted as B_k. The quotient group $H_k(K) = Z_k/B_k$ is the homology group of K.

4.3 Persistent Homology

Let V_k be the point cloud. To construct the V_k into simplicial complex, we need to use Vietoris-Rips [23, 29]. Lets define a set of points $W_j(r) \subset V_k$ so that any points $w_{j1}, w_{j2} \in W_j(r)$ satisfy $D(w_{j1}, w_{j2}) \leq 2r$ and we denote this as

$$VR(W_j(r)) = \left\{ X : D(w_{j1}, w_{j2}) \leq 2r, X \in \mathbb{R}^M \right\} \tag{2}$$

where r is the radius and $D(w_{j1}, w_{j2})$ is the Euclidian distance. In simple words, the increasing radius, r will change the structure of the simplicial complex. Thus, the information of topological features such as connected components and holes of the structure are recorded at various resolutions. A too-small radius gives no additional information of data and too large leaves only one big component with no structure provided. Starting with $r = 0$, we keep track of the feature changes when r increases continuously. The features such as hole appears at $r = b$ and disappears at $r = d$. Thus, this hole appears in the range of a multiset of tuples in the form of (b, d) and is illustrated in persistence diagram as points $(b, d) \in \mathbb{R}^2$.

For any topological space X (Rips-complex, $VR(V_k(r))$), the homology provides with a vector space $H_p(X)$ for each dimension $p = 0, 1, \ldots, n$. The homology $H_1(X)$ is an important topological feature in this research, where it represents the number of one-dimensional holes in the space.

5 Sliding window persistence for maximum persistence H_1.

Sliding window persistence is the methodology implemented from [18, 30]. Figure 4 shows the flow chart for this study.

5.1 Preprocessing

Moving Average
First, we smoothen the rainfall dataset using moving average (MA). MA is a simple technique that is helpful to reduce the randomness variation in the data. We select moving average of 14 days to smooth the rainfall data.

Standardization
Data standardization is the process of converting data to a common format so that we can process and analyze it uniformly. Standardization of data is important for several reasons. First, it helps set up clear and consistently defined elements and attributes and provides a comprehensive catalog of the data that we have. Having a good understanding

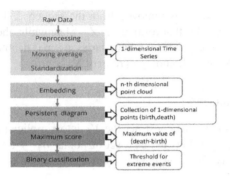

Fig. 4. Flow of data classification

of the data is an important starting point, namely whatever insight we are trying to get to and the problem we are trying to solve.

Let the raw data $\{O(d), d = 1, 2, \ldots, N\}$ be the observation data collected where d is day count. Then, the standardization is

$$O_{std}(d) = \frac{O(d) - \mu(O)}{\sigma(O)} \tag{3}$$

$$\mu(O) = \frac{\sum_{d=1}^{N} O(d)}{N} \tag{4}$$

$$\sigma(O) = \sqrt{\sum_{d=1}^{N} (O(d) - \mu(O))^2} \tag{5}$$

where $\mu(O)$ and $\sigma(O)$ be the mean and standard deviation of the $O(d)$ respectively.

5.2 Embedding Rainfall Dataset into Higher Dimension

Embedding is a reconstruction process to generate point cloud data from the time series. The combination of time-delay embeddings with a topological approach can provide the framework for periodic systems [31]. Taken's embedding [32] is an important step to transform the rainfall into a point cloud data for persistent homology (PH) processing.

Let the standardization of the rainfall and water level data $\{O_{std}(d), d = 1, \ldots, N\}$, be parameter τ and $M \in \mathbb{N}$. Then, the embedding is defined as

$$\phi(d) = (O_{std}(d), O_{std}(d + \tau), \ldots O_{std}(d + (M - 1)\tau \tag{6}$$

where the embedding point cloud in $\mathbb{R}^M$. The point cloud formed only contains the observation of the standardized time series and ignores the time domain. This ensures analysis of the topological feature or shape exists in simplified space known as the Euclidean space. There are several suggestions to choose the embedding dimension, M. Practically, dimension M is more than twice the original dimension and is sufficient to represent the topological invariant shape. The roundness shape is the most periodic pattern with the most well-defined topology shape where the window size, $M \times \tau$ must cover a complete oscillation in the series [30].

Figure 5 illustrates the rainfall data from station 4131001 (year 2013–2014) embedded to dimension $M = 5$ wit $\tau = 1$ and $\tau = 9$. The point cloud is visualized using principal component analysis (PCA) [33] projected into dimension 2.

5.3 Persistence Diagram

Persistence diagram (PD) is a very useful tool to illustrate the summaries of the topological information of a point cloud. It is proposed by Edelsbrunner et al. (2002) [34] which is similar to topology called persistence barcode proposed by Carlsson et al. (2005) [35]. This tool represents all the collection of the birth-death o in a persistence diagram denoted as $dgm(k)$. The lifetime is the collection of intervals of every k-homology class that appears at $r = b_i$ and disappears once $r = d_i$ represented as a tuple (b_i, d_i).

All points stored in $dgm(k)$ are above the diagonal line $\Delta = \{(x, x) : x \geq 0\}$. Note that the further a point is located from the diagonal line, the longer the lifetime of the hole is, which in return is subjected as a focus of this study. However, the closest point to the diagonal is the shorter lifetime that is usually treated as noise. The most periodic pattern that corresponds to a n-D hole appears in the point cloud. Hence, the maximum lifetime of the PD is,

$$maxlife = max(b_i - d_i) \tag{7}$$

5.4 Maximum Score

The maximum score is a value obtained from the persistent homology H_1. Perea (2015) [25] proposed 1-persistence score to quantify the periodic event in signal analysis. The maximum score is defined as,

$$PD_{max} = max(maxlife(M, \tau) \tag{8}$$

where τ is the corresponding optimal time delay.

5.5 Confusion Matrix

The confusion matrix for binary classification is matrix 2x2 generated to perform the classification with target 2 class. In this study, we used it to classify whether the rainfall, is a normal event or causes flood. In general, confusion matrix [36] with 2×2 must have the item, true positive, false positive, false negative, and true negative. To answer the performance for the maxscore that we obtained, the actual and predicted results were determined based on the confusion matrix. For binary values, we have the actual value as 0 (normal) and 1 (flood). However, the predicted value (maxscore) obtained is in real number. Thus, to ensure that our confusion matrix works, we must test for continuous threshold from 0 to 1 to classify normal and flood events by using receiver operating characteristics (ROC).

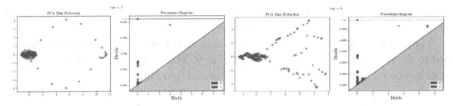

Fig. 5. The embedding rainfall data station 4131001 (year 2013–2014) to point cloud with PCA reduction ($M = 5$ and $\tau = 1, 9$) and the PD.

5.6 Area Under the Receiver Operating Characteristics

The area under the curve of receiver operation characteristics (AUC-ROC) is the performance measurement for the classification with the various settings of thresholds [37]. The AUC-ROC can help us give feedback on the extreme event detected. In short, the higher the AUC value, the better the performance to distinguish between flood and normal. When AUC $= 1$, we then classify perfectly between normal and flood. In contrast, when AUC $= 0$, the classifier can do nothing to distinguish between normal and flood. The calculation of the AUC-ROC is based on the confusion matrix, which is formulated to the sensitivity and specificity as

$$sensitivity = \frac{TP}{TP + FN} \tag{9}$$

$$specificity = \frac{TN}{TN + FP} \tag{10}$$

where sensitivity tells us what proportion of the flood class got correctly classified. Then, the ROC curve was plotted based on the true positive rate (sensitivity) against the false positive rate (1 - specificity).

6 Results and Discussions

6.1 Stability of Maximum Scores with Missing Value

Missing values are an inevitable part of working with real world data. The question here is whether to account for the missing value or not. Since TDA can still encode the topological information adequately even with some missing data, it was decided to disregard the missing data for this investigation. Stability was evaluated using actual data from stations 4131001 (2013–2014) in cases of missing values. The maximum score for this year is calculated, and then 5% of the data is removed at random with 30 repetition, yielding a maxscore average. This procedure is repeated for 10%, 15%, 20%, 25%, 30%, 35%, 40%, 45% and 50% missing data. The stability of an orbit of a dynamical system characterizes whether nearby orbits will remain in a neighborhood of that orbit or be repelled from it. Figure 6 demonstrates the plotted average maximum score of that station. According to the graph, 2013–2014 had seen greatest reduction of 35.80%, while 2014–2015 saw the least reduction of 0.81%. Results for the years 2000 to 2003 decreased by more than 20%, while in 2015 there was a decrease by only or around 9%.

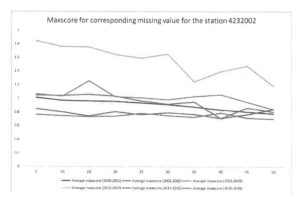

Fig. 6. Line plot of average maxscore for station 4232002 with missing value (5% to 50%) from 2000–2016

6.2 Maximum Scores of Rainfalls

When the dimension is constant, sliding window persistence is used to get the highest score with its corresponding τ. From June 1st to May 31st, the rainfall data sets were divided evenly. Then, $O(d)$ is denoised using moving average of 14 days. After that, the $O(d)$ is standardized and then embedded into a higher dimension by using a constant dimension, $M = 5$ and integer $1 \le \tau \le 73$, which is the window size, $M \times \tau$ which covers the entire segment. The segment's $dgm(k)$ is generated and the maximum persistence is stored. After assessing all the τ, we obtained the maximum score, and normalized it. The bar plot of the normalized result is shown in Fig. 7.

The maximum scores we obtained were used as a flood prediction score in normalized formed (from 0 to 1), and the water level zone is used as a label, with water levels above the danger zone labelled as flood (1) and below that level labelled as normal (0). To normalize, we use the minmax formula as follows:

$$\widehat{PD}_{max}(i) \frac{PD_{max}(i) - PD_{max}(i_{min})}{PD_{max}(i_{max}) - PD_{max}(i_{min})} \tag{11}$$

As shown in Table 3, each location has a river that can be used as a label. AUC-ROC was used for the three locations studied to provide a clearer picture of the performance. Rainfall score is used to classify this binary classification as normal or flood events. The ROC can be used to calculate the best threshold for determining flood and normal conditions. Each station obtained a different threshold value based on the findings, as shown in Table 4. The accuracy of classification using this approach is shown in the AUC findings. The greatest percentage of categorization is given by station 4131001 (Cherul), at 100%, followed by stations 4232002 (Air Putih) at 71.15% and 4332001 (Tebak) at 88.24%. Thus, maximum scores from PD obtained from rainfall demonstrate remarkable results, with an average classification percentage at 86.46%.

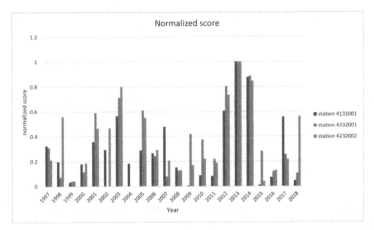

Fig. 7. Normalized maximum score for station 4131001, 4232002 and 4332001 from $a = 1997$ until $v = 2018$

Table 3. Flood label for station 4131001, 4232002 and 4332001 from $a = 1997$ until $v = 2018$

Year	a	b	c	d	e	f	g	h	i	j	k	l	m	n	o	p	q	r	s	t	u	v
4131001	0	0	0	0	0	0	0	0	0	0	0	0	0	0	0	0	1	1	0	0	0	0
4232002	1	0	0	0	0	0	1	1	-	0	0	1	1	0	0	1	1	1	0	0	0	0
4332001	1	1	0	1	1	0	1	1	-	1	0	1	1	1	1	1	1	1	1	1	0	1

Table 4. The AUC-ROC score and threshold for station 4131001, 4232002 and 4332001

Station	AUCROC	Threshold
4131001	1	0.8504
4232002	0.7115	0.7671
4332001	0.8824	0.3365

7   Conclusion

In this paper, we use the PH framework to describe the flooding that occurred in three different areas of Kemaman, Terengganu: Tebak, Air Putih, and Cherul. The Tebak region is most often affected by flood occurrences, followed by the Air Putih and the Cherul regions. By using Taken's embedding, the PH approach was used to locate the maximum score of PD for rainfall data. By setting dimension $M = 5$, we can search the maximum score with the corresponding τ by using the sliding window persistence algorithm.

This information might be classified as floods or regular occurrences depending on the water level. Additionally, we can also check whether the maximum score can be used to categorize the data into normal and flood classes based on the labels supplied. The AUC-ROC has shown that this method is effective in characterizing the flood with average at 86.46%. The noise was reduced using a moving average of 14 days and standardization of rainfall data. This allows for a more accurate characterization of flood occurrences. As can be shown in the experiment, the method used is stable up to a missing value of 50%.

In this analysis, we characterized using just the maximum score, which highlights one feature while disregarding the other 1D holes. Thus, in the future, research into the remaining features in the topological summary will be conducted to find a correlation to the flood events.

Acknowledgments. This work was supported by the Ministry of Education Malaysia grant FRGS/1/2019/STG06/UMT/02/2. The authors also acknowledge Department of Irrigation and Drainage Malaysia for providing the rainfall and water level data.

References

1. Gullick, J.M.: Old Kuala Lumpur. Oxford Univ Press, New York (1994)
2. Kelantan Flood Report. Drainage and Irrigation Department Kelantan (1967)
3. Syamimi, I.N., Azharudin, M.D., Rodzi, A.R.M.: Sejarah banjir besar di semenanjung malaysia, 1926–1971. J. Perspekt. **6**(3), 54–67 (2014)
4. Eliza, N., Mohamad, H., Yoke, W., Yusop, Z.: Rainfall analysis of the Kelantan big yellow flood 2014. J. Teknol. **4**, 83–90 (2016)
5. Akasah, Z.A., Doraisamy, S.V.: 2014 Malaysia flood: impacts & factors contributing towards the restoration of damages. J. Sci. Res. Dev. **2**(14), 53–59 (2015)
6. Muhammad, N.S., Abdullah, J., Julien, P.Y.: Characteristics of rainfall in peninsular Malaysia. J. Phys. Conf. Ser. **1529**(5) (2020)
7. Carlsson, G.: Topology and data **46**(2) (2009)
8. Munkres, J.R.: Elements of Algebraic Topology. Addison Wesley (1993)
9. Gidea, M., Katz, Y.: Topological data analysis of financial time series: landscapes of crashes. Phys. A Stat. Mech. its Appl. **491**, 820–834 (2018)
10. Gidea, M., Goldsmith, D., Katz, Y., Roldan, P., Shmalo, Y.: Topological recognition of critical transitions in time series of cryptocurrencies. Phys. A Stat. Mech. its Appl. 123843 (2020)
11. Yen, P.T.W., Cheong, S.A.: Using topological data analysis (TDA) and persistent homology to analyze the stock markets in Singapore and Taiwan. Front. Phys. **9**(March), 1–19 (2021)
12. Yen, P.T., Xia, K.: Understanding changes in the topology and geometry of financial market correlations during a market crash 1–48 (2021)
13. Katz, Y.A., Biem, A.: Time-resolved topological data analysis of market instabilities. Phys. A Stat. Mech. its Appl. **571**, 125816 (2021)
14. Zulkepli, N.F.S., Noorani, M.S.M., Razak, F.A., Ismail, M., Alias, M.A.: Topological characterization of haze episodes using persistent homology. Aerosol Air Qual. Res. **19**(7), 1614–1621 (2019)
15. Musa, S.M.S.S., Md Nooran, M.S., Razak, F.A., Ismail, M., Alias, M.A., Hussain, S.I.: Using persistent homology as preprocessing of early warning signals for critical transition in flood. Sci. Rep. **11**(1), 1–14 (2021). https://doi.org/10.1038/s41598-021-86739-5
16. Gobithaasan, R.U., et al.: Clustering selected terengganu's rainfall stations based on persistent homology. Thai J. Math. **2022**(Special Issue), 197–211 (2022)

17. Tralie, C.J., Perea, J.A.: (Quasi)periodicity quantification in video data, using topology. SIAM J. Imaging Sci. **11**(2), 1049–1077 (2018)
18. Perea, J.A., Deckard, A., Haase, S.B., Harer, J.: SW1PerS: Sliding windows and 1-persistence scoring; discovering periodicity in gene expression time series data. BMC Bioinform. **16**(1), 1–12 (2015)
19. Myers, A., Munch, E., Khasawneh, F.A.: Persistent homology of complex networks for dynamic state detection. Phys. Rev. E **100**(2) (2019)
20. Soliman, M., Lyubchich, V., Gel, Y.R.: Ensemble forecasting of the Zika space-time spread with topological data analysis. Environmetrics **31**(7), 1–13 (2020)
21. Yamanashi, T., et al.: Topological data analysis (TDA) enhances bispectral EEG (BSEEG) algorithm for detection of delirium. Sci. Rep. **11**(1), 1–9 (2021)
22. Graff, G., Graff, B., Pilarczyk, P., Jabłoński, G., Gąsecki, D., Narkiewicz, K.: Persistent homology as a new method of the assessment of heart rate variability. PLoS One **16**(7), e0253851 (2021). https://doi.org/10.1371/journal.pone.0253851
23. Edelsbrunner, H., Harer, J.: Computational Topology. Open Probl. Topol. **II**, 493–545 (2010)
24. Zomorodian, A., Carlsson, G.: Computing persistent homology. Proc. Annu. Symp. Comput. Geom. 347–356 (2004)
25. Perea, J.A., Harer, J.: Sliding windows and persistence: an application of topological methods to signal analysis. Found. Comput. Math. **15**(3), 799–838 (2015). https://doi.org/10.1007/s10 208-014-9206-z
26. Christopher, T., Nathaniel, S., Rann, B.-O.: A lean persistent homology library for python. Open J. 925 (2018)
27. Lim, K.Y., Zakaria, N.A., Foo, K.Y.: A shared vision on the historical flood events in Malaysia: integrated assessment of water quality and microbial variability. Disaster Adv. **12**(8), 11–20 (2019)
28. Lum, P.Y., et al.: Extracting insights from the shape of complex data using topology. Sci. Rep. **3**, 1–8 (2013)
29. Vietoris, L.: Über den höheren zusammenhang kompakter räume und eine klasse von zusammenhangstreuen abbildungen. Math. Ann. **97**(1), 454–472 (1927)
30. Perea, J.A., An application of topological methods to signal **1**(919), 1–34 (2013)
31. Vejdemo-Johansson, M., Skraba, P., De Silva, V.: Topological analysis of recurrent systems. Work. Algebr. Topol. Mach. Learn. NIPS **2**(1), 2–6 (2012)
32. Takens, F.: Detecting strange attractors in turbulence. In: Rand, D., Young, L.-S. (eds.) Dynamical systems and Turbulence, Warwick 1980, pp. 366–381. Springer Berlin Heidelberg, Berlin, Heidelberg (1981). https://doi.org/10.1007/BFb0091924
33. Abdi, H., Williams, L.J.: Principal component analysis. Wiley Interdiscip. Rev. Comput. Stat. **2**(4), 433–459 (2010)
34. Edelsbrunner, H., Letscher, D., Zomorodian, A.: Topological persistence and simplification. Discret. Comput. Geom. **28**(4), 511–533 (2002)
35. Carlsson, G., Zomorodian, A., Collins, A., Guibas, L.J.: Persistence barcodes for shapes. Int. J. Shape Model. **11**(2), 149–187 (2005)
36. Baldi, P., Brunak, S., Chauvin, Y., Andersen, C.A.F., Nielsen, H.: Assessing the accuracy of prediction algorithms for classification: an overview. Bioinformatics **16**(5), 412–424 (2000)
37. Hanley, J.A., McNeil, B.J.: The meaning and use of the area under a receiver operating characteristic (ROC) curve. Radiology **143**(1), 29–36 (1982)

Clustering Stock Prices of Industrial and Consumer Sector Companies in Indonesia Using Fuzzy C-Means and Fuzzy C-Medoids Involving ACF and PACF

Muhammad Adlansyah Muda, Dedy Dwi Prastyo[✉], and Muhammad Sjahid Akbar

Department of Statistics, Faculty of Science and Data Analytics, Institut Teknologi Sepuluh Nopember, Surabaya, Indonesia
dedy-dp@statistika.its.ac.id

Abstract. Fundamental and technical analysis that investors generally use to select the best stocks cannot provide information regarding the similarity of stock price characteristics of companies in one sector. Even though companies are in the same sector, each company has a different ability to earn profits and overcome financial difficulties. So, clustering is done to find the stock prices of companies with the same characteristics in one sector. This research uses data on industrial and consumer sector companies' stock prices because the industrial and consumer sectors are one of the largest sectors in Indonesia. The variables used in this research are open, close, and HML (High Minus Low) stock prices. Several clustering methods that can be used to cluster time series data are Fuzzy C-Means and Fuzzy C-Medoids. In addition, this research also uses several approaches with ACF (Autocorrelation Function) and PACF (Partial Autocorrelation Function), which can handle data with high dimensions and allow the comparison of time series data with different lengths. Based on the highest FS (Fuzzy Silhouette) value, the empirical results show that the two best methods for clustering open, close, and HML stock prices are Fuzzy C-Means and Fuzzy C-Medoids. The clustering results using Fuzzy C-Means are the same for open stock prices and close stock prices data. Meanwhile, there are different clustering results for HML stock price data.

Keywords: ACF · Fuzzy C-Means · Fuzzy C-Medoids · PACF · Stock prices

1 Introduction

The current era of digitalization makes it easier for everyone to invest. Investment is an activity of sacrificing money or other resources today to expect profits in the future. One type of investment that can be an option is stocks. Every investor wants to benefit from the stocks they own. So, it is necessary to consider several methods to choose the right stock to buy. Generally, several methods that can be used to choose stocks are the fundamental analysis and technical analysis approaches. However, these two methods cannot provide information regarding the similarity of the characteristics of the company's stock prices in one sector. One of the advantages of knowing the similarity of the characteristics of the company's stock prices in one sector is being able to avoid losses in one cluster of stocks owned and gain profits in another cluster of stocks. Even though the companies are in the same sector, each company has different capabilities for making profits and overcoming financial difficulties. So that it can be grouped to find out the stock price of companies with the same characteristics in one sector. This research uses data on stock prices of industrial and consumer sector companies because the industrial and consumer sectors are one of the largest sectors in Indonesia. According to [1], the processing industry sector was the most significant contributor to the national GDP (Gross Domestic Product) in the second quarter of 2022, with a percentage of 17.84%.

Stock prices constantly change depending on the supply and demand of stocks [2]. One statistical method that can be used for time series data clustering is time series clustering [3]. The main difference between time series clustering and ordinary clustering is in the unit of observation. One of the clustering methods that can be used for time series data is Fuzzy Clustering. Fuzzy Clustering is a soft clustering technique that allows each object to have more than one cluster with different degrees of membership, while hard clustering assigns objects precisely in only one cluster [4]. Several clustering methods in Fuzzy Clustering include Fuzzy C-Means Clustering and Fuzzy C-Medoids Clustering. The main difference between the two methods is in the centroid calculation. According to [5], Fuzzy C-Medoids overcomes the weakness of Fuzzy C-Means in grouping time series data containing noise.

Several research studies have been done previously in classifying stock prices using Fuzzy Clustering. In previous research, the work [6] examined stock grouping for two different stock markets (NASDAQ and MIBTEL) using Fuzzy C-Medoids Clustering and involving the cepstral function. Furthermore, the researcher [7] examined the daily return index of 30 international stock exchanges and the daily return of the stocks that make up the FTSEMIB index using Fuzzy C-Medoids involving the GARCH model. The authors [8] examined the grouping of 69 stocks from SET (Stock Exchange of Thailand) using Fuzzy C-Means and then selected the optimal portfolio using MOGA (Multi-Objective Genetic Algorithm).

Various approaches have been made to improve grouping results using Fuzzy Clustering. Several approaches that can be referred to are the usage of ACF proposed by [9] and PACF proposed as employed in this research. ACF is a diagnostic tool to check dependencies [10]. In comparison, PACF is a value that shows the relationship between the current time series value and values at a different time point after eliminating the effect of the values between them [11]. The approach using ACF and PACF can handle data with high dimensions and allows for comparing time series data of different lengths. The good results with the ACF approach are shown in the research of [9], which shows that Fuzzy C-Means involving ACF is the best method compared to C-Means and Hierarchical.

Based on the explanation previously mentioned, this research will group the stock prices of industrial and consumer sector companies in Indonesia using Fuzzy C-Means and Fuzzy C-Medoids involving ACF and PACF. The variables used in this research are the stock prices of industrial and consumer sector companies in Indonesia, including open, close, and HML (High Minus Low), with the period used in this research being 3 August 2020 to 3 August 2022. The results of this research are expected to find out the best clustering of industrial and consumer sector companies' stock prices in Indonesia so that investors can buy stocks in different clusters to avoid losses in one cluster of stocks and gain profits in another cluster of stocks.

2 Literature Review

2.1 Fuzzy Clustering

Fuzzy Clustering is a soft clustering technique that can be used to group time series data. Its difference from traditional clustering is that in traditional clustering, objects are grouped correctly only in one cluster, whereas in Fuzzy Clustering, objects can have more than one cluster with different degrees of membership in different clusters [12, 13]. According to [14], the Fuzzy Clustering method is very good at clustering time series data for several reasons. First, the clustering procedure using Fuzzy Clustering does not require a distribution assumption. Second, the Fuzzy Clustering method gives better clustering results than the C-Means method in the real case [15]. Third, grouping using Fuzzy Clustering is computationally more efficient because changes in the value of the degree of cluster membership are less likely to occur in the estimation procedure [15] and are less affected by local optima problems [16]. Fourth, Fuzzy Clustering can show whether there is a second-best cluster that is almost as good as the best cluster, and this cannot be demonstrated by traditional clustering methods [17]. Fifth, Fuzzy Clustering tends to have better sensitivity in capturing the characteristics of a time series. In many real cases, a time series can occur deviations or transitions at any time and, with a standard clustering approach (non-fuzzy), tends to lose the basic structure of the time series [18]. Lastly, Fuzzy Clustering can adapt well to define a time series prototype [18]. This last advantage is possible when the prototype has a time series pattern that tends not to be too different from the observed time series pattern.

Fuzzy C-Means Clustering. Given a data matrix $X = \{x_{it} : i = 1, \ldots, n; t = 1, \ldots, T\} = \{x_i = (x_{i1}, x_{i2}, \ldots, x_{it})' : i = 1, \ldots, n\}$ where x_{it} represents the i-th object observed at time t and x_i represents the i-th object vector. The Fuzzy C-Means Clustering objective function proposed by [19, 20] is formulated in Eq. (1) below:

$$\min : J_m(U; h) = \sum_{i=1}^{n} \sum_{c=1}^{C} u_{ic}^m d_{ic}^2 = \sum_{i=1}^{n} \sum_{c=1}^{C} u_{ic}^m \|x_i - h_c\|^2 \tag{1}$$

where $\sum_{c=1}^{C} u_{ic} = 1$ and $u_{ic} \geq 0$, the u_{ic} is the degree of membership of the i-th object to the c-th cluster, the $d_{ic}^2 = \|x_i - h_c\|^2$ is the squared Euclidean distance between the i-th object and the centroid of the c-th cluster. Then $h_c = (h_{c1}, h_{c2}, \ldots, h_{ct})'$ is the centroid of the c-th cluster where h_{ct} denotes the t-th component of the c-th centroid vector. Furthermore, m is the fuzziness parameter that controls the partition where $m > 1$; when

$m = 1$, it will be obtained by clustering with the standard C-Means method [21]. Using the Lagrange Multiplier method, Eq. (1) can be found as a conditional optimal iterative solution for the degree of membership and the centroid, which is shown in Eqs. (2) and (3) [22].

$$u_{ic} = \frac{1}{\sum\limits_{c'=1}^{C} \left[\frac{\|x_i - h_c\|}{\|x_i - h_{c'}\|} \right]^{\frac{2}{m-1}}} = \frac{\|x_i - h_c\|^{-\frac{2}{m-1}}}{\sum\limits_{c'=1}^{C} \|x_i - h_{c'}\|^{-\frac{2}{m-1}}} \tag{2}$$

$$h_c = \frac{\sum\limits_{i=1}^{n} u_{ic}^m x_i}{\sum\limits_{i=1}^{n} u_{ic}^m} \tag{3}$$

Each centroid summarizes the features of each cluster because it represents the average of the appropriate weights of the observed feature set [4]. The steps for calculating iterative solutions to Eqs. (2) and (3) are shown as follows [22]:

Step 1: Determine the number of clusters c and parameter m and the initial degree of membership matrix $u_{ic}^{(j)}$ ($i = 1, \ldots, n$; $c = 1, \ldots, C$) with $j = 0$.
Step 2: Calculate the centroid using the following Equation:

$$h_c^{(j+1)} = \frac{\sum\limits_{i=1}^{n} u_{ic}^{m(j)} x_i}{\sum\limits_{i=1}^{n} u_{ic}^{m(j)}}$$

Step 3: Calculate the new membership degree with the following equation:

$$u_{ic}^{(j+1)} = \frac{1}{\sum\limits_{c'=1}^{C} \left[\frac{\|x_i - h_c^{(j+1)}\|}{\|x_i - h_{c'}^{(j+1)}\|} \right]^{\frac{2}{m-1}}} = \frac{\left\|x_i - h_c^{(j+1)}\right\|^{-\frac{2}{m-1}}}{\sum\limits_{c'=1}^{C} \left\|x_i - h_{c'}^{(j+1)}\right\|^{-\frac{2}{m-1}}}$$

Step 4: Make a comparison between $u_{ic}^{(j)}$ in Step 1, with $u_{ic}^{(j+1)}$ in Step 3. If the result $\left| u_{ic}^{(j+1)} - u_{ic}^{(j)} \right| \leq \tau$ where τ is a very small positive number, then the iteration stops. If not, then set $j = j + 1$ and go back to Step 2.

Various developments have been made to improve clustering using the Fuzzy C-Means Clustering method. Several approaches to improve clustering performance in the Fuzzy C-Means Clustering method consider ACF and PACF. Clustering using Fuzzy C-Means Clustering involving ACF and PACF is done by replacing x_i with ρ_i for the ACF approach and replacing x_i with ϕ_i for the PACF approach.

Fuzzy C-Medoids Clustering. Fuzzy C-Medoids Clustering overcomes the weakness of Fuzzy C-Means Clustering in clustering time series data with noise [5]. Given a data matrix $X = \{x_{it} : i = 1, \ldots, n; t = 1, \ldots, T\} = \{x_i = (x_{i1}, x_{i2}, \ldots, x_{it})' : i = 1, \ldots, n\}$ where x_{it} represents the i-th object observed at time t and x_i represents the i-th object vector, and given $V = \{v_1, v_2, \ldots, v_C\}$ is the medoid of the c-th cluster. The Fuzzy C-Medoids Clustering objective function proposed by [23] is formulated in Eq. (4) below:

$$\min : J_m(V; X) = \sum_{i=1}^{n} \sum_{c=1}^{C} u_{ic}^m d_{ic}^2 = \sum_{i=1}^{n} \sum_{c=1}^{C} u_{ic}^m \|x_i - v_c\|^2 \tag{4}$$

where $\sum_{c=1}^{C} u_{ic} = 1$ and $u_{ic} \geq 0$, the u_{ic} is the degree of membership of the i-th object to the c-th cluster, d_{ic}^2 is the squared Euclidean distance between the i-th object and the centroid of the c-th cluster, and m is the fuzziness parameter that controls the partition. To obtain the degree of membership can use Eq. (2) by using the centroid $h_c = v_c$ which is denoted in Eq. (5) below:

$$u_{ic} = \frac{1}{\sum_{c'=1}^{C} \left[\frac{\|x_i - v_c\|}{\|x_i - v_{c'}\|} \right]^{\frac{2}{m-1}}} = \frac{\|x_i - v_c\|^{-\frac{2}{m-1}}}{\sum_{c'=1}^{C} \|x_i - v_{c'}\|^{-\frac{2}{m-1}}} \tag{5}$$

Equation (4) cannot be minimized through optimization techniques because the required conditions cannot be derived from the medoid. So, it is necessary to search for the optimal medoid to get the degree of membership with the steps shown as follows [24]:

Step 1: Determine the number of cluster c and the initial medoid value $V^{(j)}$ with $j = 0$.

Step 2: Calculate the degree of membership with the following Equation:

$$u_{ic}^{(j)} = \frac{1}{\sum_{c'=1}^{C} \left[\frac{\|x_i - v_c^{(j)}\|}{\|x_i - v_{c'}^{(j)}\|} \right]^{\frac{2}{m-1}}} = \frac{\left\|x_i - v_c^{(j)}\right\|^{-\frac{2}{m-1}}}{\sum_{c'=1}^{C} \left\|x_i - v_{c'}^{(j)}\right\|^{-\frac{2}{m-1}}}$$

Step 3: Calculate the new medoid $V^{(j+1)}$ with $v_c = x_r$ where r is obtained by the following Equation:

$$r = \operatorname*{arg\,min}_{1 \leq c' \leq n} \sum_{i=1}^{n} u_{ic}^{m(j)} \|x_{c'} - x_i\|^2$$

Step 4: Make a comparison between $V^{(j)}$ in Step 1, with $V^{(j+1)}$ in Step 3. If $V^{(j)} = V^{(j+1)}$, then iteration stops. If not, then set $j = j + 1$ and return to Step 2.

ACF and PACF approaches can be applied to the Fuzzy C-Medoids Clustering method to improve clustering performance. Clustering using Fuzzy C-Medoids Clustering involving ACF and PACF is done by replacing x_i with ρ_i for the ACF approach and replacing x_i with ϕ_i for the PACF approach. The idea to involve the ACF and PACF is motivated by the success of their use in some approaches to building time series models, such as [25–27].

2.2 Fuzzy Silhouette

The important thing that needs to be answered in clustering scenarios is how many clusters exist in the data and how real or good the clustering itself is. This situation means that regardless of the clustering technique used, the number of clusters and the validity of the clusters formed must be determined [28]. The size of the cluster validity is used to obtain the best order of the number of clusters. According to [29], there are several measures that can be used for Fuzzy Clustering; they are MPC by [30], K by [31], T by [32], SC by [33], and PBMF by [34]. However, the research results by [35] show that none of the five indices correctly shows the optimal number of clusters for all the data tested. So, in this research, the best number of clusters was determined from the best FS (Fuzzy Silhouette) value proposed by [36]. The main difference between the FS method and the usual Silhouette is the use of fuzzy partition matrices in the calculations. Given a partition matrix for data $U(X) = [u_{ic}]_{C \times n}$ then FS value can be defined in Eq. (6) below:

$$FS = \frac{\sum_{i=1}^{n} \left(u_{pi} - u_{qi}\right)^{\alpha} s_i}{\sum_{i=1}^{n} \left(u_{pi} - u_{qi}\right)^{\alpha}}, \tag{6}$$

where

$$s_i = \frac{b_{pi} - a_{pi}}{\max\{a_{pi}, b_{pi}\}},$$

with s_i is a Silhouette on the i-th object, a_{pi} is the average distance of the i-th object with all other objects belonging to cluster p, b_{pi} is the average distance of the i-th object with all other objects outside cluster p, u_{pi} and u_{qi} are the first and second largest elements of the i-th column of the fuzzy partition matrix, and α is a weighting coefficient where $\alpha \geq 0, p \in \{1, \ldots, C\}, q \in \{1, \ldots, C\}$, dan $p \neq q$.

3 Methodology

3.1 Data Set

The data used in this research is stock prices of industrial and consumer sector companies in Indonesia obtained from the Yahoo! Finance website. The variables used in this research are open, close, and HML (High Minus Low) of stock prices. The open stock price is the stock price when the stock market opens at 9 AM Western Indonesian Time. Then the close stock price is the stock price when the stock market close at 4 PM Western Indonesian Time. The HML is the difference between the highest and lowest stock prices. The period used for research data is from 3 August 2020 to 3 August 2022. There are 230 companies used in this research, consisting of 47 industrial sector companies and 183 consumer (cyclical and non-cyclical) sector companies. This research does not include companies with unchanged stock prices (sleeping stocks).

3.2 Methods

In this research, the stock prices of industrial and consumer sector companies in Indonesia will be grouped using Fuzzy C-Means Clustering and Fuzzy C-Medoids Clustering with and without involving ACF and PACF. The aim is to find out the best method for clustering stock prices of industrial and consumer sector companies in Indonesia. The first step in the analysis is to do clustering using Fuzzy C-Means Clustering and Fuzzy C-Medoids Clustering with and without involving ACF and PACF, where the fuzziness parameter used in this research is $m = 1.5$. Then calculate the FS value with $\alpha = 1$ to determine the best number of clusters. Finally, determine the best method based on the highest FS value.

4 Results and Discussions

4.1 Simulation Study

In this research, a simulation study was conducted using two scenarios. The first scenario aims to determine the ability of Fuzzy C-Means and Fuzzy C-Medoids with and without involving ACF and PACF for clustering data generated from the same model but with different means. Then the second scenario aims to determine the ability of Fuzzy C-Means and Fuzzy C-Medoids with and without involving ACF and PACF for clustering data generated from different models. The first scenario is the data generated from AR(1) model using the parameter $\phi_1 = 0.75$ with average $(\mu_1) = 60$ and AR(1) model using parameter $\phi_1 = 0.5$ with average $(\mu_2) = 100$, where the model for data generated can be written in Eqs. (7) and (8). Whereas the second scenario is the data generated from the model in Eq. (7) and MA(1) model with parameter $\theta_1 = 0.75$, where the model can be written in Eq. (9).

$$X_t = \delta_1 + 0.75X_{t-1} + W_t, \tag{7}$$

where $\delta_1 = \mu_1(1 - \phi_1) = 60(1 - 0.75) = 15$.

$$X_t = \delta_2 + 0.5X_{t-1} + W_t, \tag{8}$$

where $\delta_2 = \mu_2(1 - \phi_1) = 100(1 - 0.5) = 50$.

$$X_t = W_t - 0.75W_{t-1}, \tag{9}$$

with W_t is residual and $W_t \sim N\left(0, \sigma_W^2\right)$ where $\sigma_W^2 = 1$. The generation data was replicated three times for each model, and the number of observations was 250. Let $m = 1.5$ and $C = 2$, then the results of clustering for each scenario using Fuzzy C-Means and Fuzzy C-Medoids with and without involving ACF and PACF are shown in Table 1 and Table 2.

Table 1. Results of clustering for first scenario.

Model	FCM	FCM-ACF	FCM-PACF	FCMdd	FCMdd-ACF	FCMdd-PACF
AR(1) with ϕ_1 = 0.75	1	2	2	1	1	1
AR(1) with ϕ_1 = 0.75	1	1	1	1	2	2
AR(1) with ϕ_1 = 0.75	1	2	1	1	1	2
AR(1) with ϕ_1 = 0.5	2	2	2	2	1	1
AR(1) with ϕ_1 = 0.5	2	1	1	2	2	1
AR(1) with ϕ_1 = 0.5	2	2	1	2	1	2

Table 2. Results of clustering for second scenario.

Model	FCM	FCM-ACF	FCM-PACF	FCMdd	FCMdd-ACF	FCMdd-PACF
AR(1) with ϕ_1 = 0.75	1	1	1	2	2	2
AR(1) with ϕ_1 = 0.75	1	1	1	2	2	2
AR(1) with ϕ_1 = 0.75	1	1	1	2	2	2
MA(1) with θ_1 = 0.75	2	2	2	1	1	1
MA(1) with θ_1 = 0.75	2	2	2	1	1	1
MA(1) with θ_1 = 0.75	2	2	2	1	1	1

Table 1 shows that the Fuzzy C-Means and Fuzzy C-Medoids are very good for clustering data that have values that tend to be close. Meanwhile, Table 2 shows that the

Fuzzy C-Means and Fuzzy C-Medoids with and without involving ACF and PACF are very good for clustering generation data from different models. These findings show the ability of the Fuzzy C-Means and Fuzzy C-Medoids with and without involving ACF and PACF for clustering data with patterns that tend to be the same.

4.2 Clustering Open Stock Prices

The first step in clustering is determining the best number of clusters based on the FS value. The results of calculating the FS value for clustering open stock prices using Fuzzy C-Means and Fuzzy C-Medoids with and without involving ACF and PACF are shown in Fig. 1. Based on the highest FS value shown in Fig. 1, it can be concluded that the best number of clusters for clustering open stock prices using Fuzzy C-Means without involving ACF and PACF is 3 clusters. Meanwhile, the best number of clusters for clustering open stock prices using other methods is 2 clusters. The Fuzzy C-Means and Fuzzy C-Medoids without involving ACF and PACF are two methods that have the best FS values compared to other clustering methods. The results of clustering open stock prices of industrial and consumer sector companies in Indonesia using Fuzzy C-Means and Fuzzy C-Medoids without involving ACF and PACF are shown in Fig. 2.

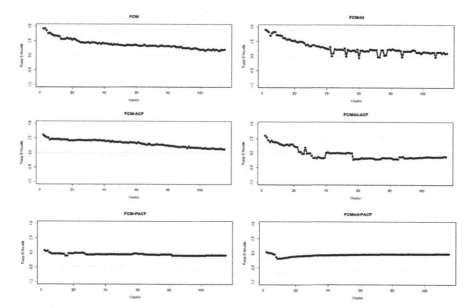

Fig. 1. Comparison of FS values for clustering open stock prices of industrial and consumer sector companies in Indonesia using Fuzzy C-Means and Fuzzy C-Medoids methods with and without involving ACF and PACF.

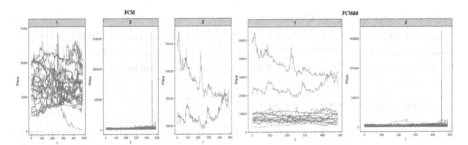

Fig. 2. Comparison of clustering open stock prices of industrial and consumer sector companies in Indonesia using Fuzzy C-Means and Fuzzy C-Medoids.

4.3 Clustering Close Stock Prices

The results of calculating the FS value for clustering close stock prices using Fuzzy C-Means and Fuzzy C-Medoids with and without involving ACF and PACF are shown in Fig. 3.

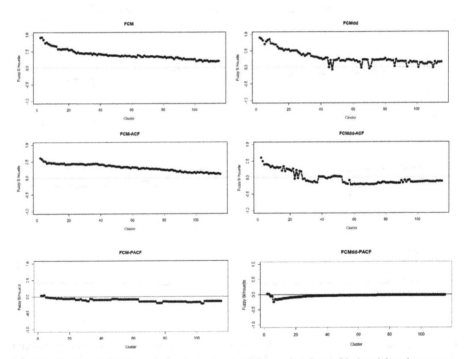

Fig. 3. Comparison of FS values for clustering close stock prices of industrial and consumer sector companies in Indonesia using Fuzzy C-Means and Fuzzy C-Medoids methods with and without involving ACF and PACF.

Based on the highest FS value shown in Fig. 3, it can be concluded that the best number of clusters for clustering close stock prices using Fuzzy C-Means is 3 clusters.

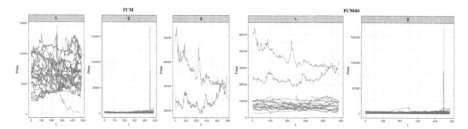

Fig. 4. Comparison of clustering close stock prices of industrial and consumer sector companies in Indonesia using Fuzzy C-Means and Fuzzy C-Medoids.

Meanwhile, the best number of clusters for clustering close stock prices using Fuzzy C-Means involving PACF is 4 clusters and other methods are 2 clusters. The Fuzzy C-Means and Fuzzy C-Medoids without involving ACF and PACF are two methods that have the best FS values compared to other clustering methods. The results of clustering close stock prices of industrial and consumer sector companies in Indonesia using Fuzzy C-Means and Fuzzy C-Medoids are shown in Fig. 4. Figure 4 shows that the results of clustering open and close stock prices are the same using Fuzzy C-Means. Meanwhile, there are differences in the results of clustering open and close stock prices using Fuzzy C-Medoids for PTSP (PT Pioneerindo Gourmet International Tbk), which are grouped in cluster 1 in clustering close stock prices.

4.4   Clustering HML Stock Prices

HML stock prices can be calculated by calculating the difference between the highest and lowest stock prices. Using the same procedure as in previous sections, determine the optimal number of clusters based on the highest FS value shown in Fig. 5.

The best number of clusters for clustering HML stock prices using Fuzzy C-Means is 4 clusters. Then the best number of clusters for clustering HML stock prices using Fuzzy C-Means involving ACF and PACF and Fuzzy C-Medoids with and without involving PACF are 2 clusters. Meanwhile, the best number of clusters for clustering HML stock prices using Fuzzy C-Medoids involving ACF is 15 clusters. Fuzzy C-Means and Fuzzy C-Medoids are the best clustering methods for clustering HML stock prices based on FS value. The results of clustering HML stock prices using Fuzzy C-Means and Fuzzy C-Medoids are shown in Fig. 6.

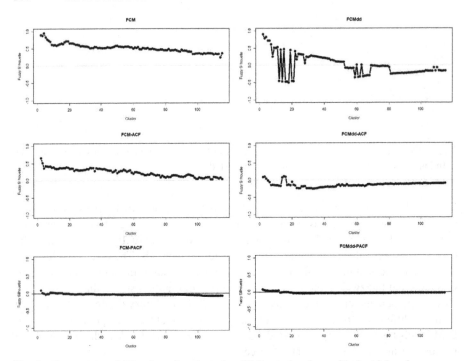

Fig. 5. Comparison of FS values for clustering HML stock prices of industrial and consumer sector companies in Indonesia using Fuzzy C-Means and Fuzzy C-Medoids methods with and without involving ACF and PACF.

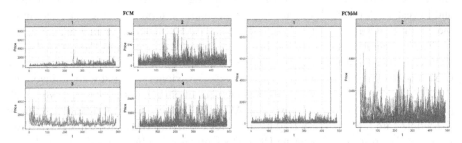

Fig. 6. Comparison of clustering HML stock prices of industrial and consumer sector companies in Indonesia using Fuzzy C-Means and Fuzzy C-Medoids.

4.5 Comparison of Clustering Results

Based on the results of clustering open, close, and HML stock prices using Fuzzy C-Means and Fuzzy C-Medoids with and without involving ACF and PACF, it can be concluded that the Fuzzy C-Means is the best clustering method compared to other methods. The list of companies in each cluster from the results of clustering stock prices using Fuzzy C-Means is tabulated in Tables 3 and 4. The successful implementation of Fuzzy C-Means applied in Indonesian data in the context of clustering of cross-sectional data can be seen in [37].

Table 3. Results of clustering open and close stock prices using Fuzzy C-Means.

Price	Cluster	Stocks
Open and Close	1	AMFG, ASII, HEXA, JECC, SCCO, BRAM, INDR, PTSP, SLIS, SONA, AALI, CPIN, DLTA, FISH, ICBP, INDF, MLBI, SMAR, STTP, TCID, TGKA, UNVR
	2	ABMM, AMIN, APII, ARKA, ARNA, ASGR, BHIT, BLUE, BMTR, BNBR, CAKK, CCSI, CTTH, DYAN, ICON, IKBI, IMPC, INDX, INTA, JTPE, KBLI, KBLM, KIAS, KOBX, KOIN, KONI, KPAL, KRAH, LION, MARK, MFMI, MLIA, MLPL, SINI, SKRN, SOSS, SPTO, TIRA, TOTO, VOKS, ZBRA, ABBA, ACES, ARGO, ARTA, AUTO, BATA, BAYU, BELL, BIMA, BLTZ, BOGA, BOLA, BOLT, BUVA, CBMF, CINT, CLAY, CNTX, CSAP, CSMI, DFAM, DIGI, DUCK, EAST, ECII, ERAA, ERTX, ESTA, ESTI, FAST, FILM, FITT, FORU, GDYR, GEMA, GJTL, GLOB, HRME, HRTA, IKAI, IMAS, INDS, INOV, IPTV, JIHD, JSPT, KICI, KPIG, LMPI, LPIN, LPPF, MAPA, MAPB, MAPI, MARI, MASA, MDIA, MICE, MINA, MNCN, MPMX, MSIN, MSKY, MYTX, NASA, NATO, PANR, PBRX, PDES, PGLI, PJAA, PMJS, PNSE, POLU, POLY, PRAS, PSKT, PZZA, RALS, RICY, SBAT, SCMA, SHID, SMSM, SOFA, SOTS, SRIL, SSTM, TFCO, TMPO, TRIS, TURI, UANG, UNIT, VIVA, WOOD, YELO, ZONE, ADES, AGAR, AISA, ALTO, AMRT, ANDI, ANJT, BEEF, BISI, BUDI, BWPT, CAMP, CEKA, CLEO, COCO, CPRO, CSRA, DAYA, DMND, DPUM, DSFI, DSNG, EPMT, FOOD, GOOD, GZCO, HERO, HMSP, HOKI, IKAN, ITIC, JAWA, JPFA, KEJU, KINO, KPAS, LSIP, MAIN, MBTO, MGRO, MIDI, MPPA, MRAT, MYOR, PALM, PANI, PCAR, PGUN, PSDN, PSGO, RANC, RMBA, ROTI, SDPC, SGRO, SIMP, SIPD, SKBM, SKLT, SSMS, TBLA, UCID, ULTJ, UNSP, WAPO, WICO, WIIM
	3	UNTR, GGRM

Table 4. Results of clustering HML stock prices using Fuzzy C-Means.

Price	Cluster	Stocks
HML	1	AMFG, HEXA, KONI, SCCO, ARGO, BLTZ, MAPA, MASA, MSIN, PTSP, ADES, FISH, KINO, MYOR, PANI, SKLT, SMAR, TCID
	2	ABMM, AMIN, APII, ARKA, ARNA, ASGR, BHIT, BLUE, BMTR, BNBR, CAKK, CCSI, CTTH, DYAN, ICON, IKBI, IMPC, INDX, INTA, JTPE, KBLI, KBLM, KIAS, KOBX, KOIN, KPAL, KRAH, LION, MARK, MFMI, MLIA, MLPL, SINI, SKRN, SOSS, SPTO, TIRA, TOTO, VOKS, ZBRA, ABBA, ACES, ARTA, AUTO, BATA, BAYU, BELL, BIMA, BOGA, BOLA, BOLT, BUVA, CBMF, CINT, CLAY, CNTX, CSAP, CSMI, DFAM, DIGI, DUCK, EAST, ECII, ERAA, ERTX, ESTA, ESTI, FAST, FILM, FITT, FORU, GDYR, GEMA, GJTL, GLOB, HRME, HRTA, IKAI, IMAS, INDS, INOV, IPTV, JIHD, JSPT, KICI, KPIG, LMPI, LPIN, MAPB, MAPI, MARI, MDIA, MICE, MINA, MNCN, MPMX, MSKY, MYTX, NASA, NATO, PANR, PBRX, PDES, PGLI, PJAA, PMJS, PNSE, POLU, POLY, PRAS, PSKT, PZZA, RALS, RICY, SBAT, SCMA, SHID, SMSM, SOFA, SONA, SOTS, SRIL, SSTM, TFCO, TMPO, TRIS, TURI, UANG, UNIT, VIVA, WOOD, YELO, ZONE, AGAR, AISA, ALTO, AMRT, ANDI, ANJT, BEEF, BISI, BUDI, BWPT, CAMP, CEKA, CLEO, COCO, CPRO, CSRA, DAYA, DLTA, DMND, DPUM, DSFI, DSNG, EPMT, FOOD, GOOD, GZCO, HERO, HMSP, HOKI, IKAN, ITIC, JAWA, JPFA, KEJU, KPAS, LSIP, MAIN, MBTO, MGRO, MIDI, MPPA, MRAT, PALM, PCAR, PGUN, PSDN, PSGO, RANC, RMBA, ROTI, SDPC, SGRO, SIMP, SIPD, SKBM, SSMS, TBLA, UCID, ULTJ, UNSP, WAPO, WICO, WIIM
	3	UNTR, GGRM
	4	ASII, JECC, BRAM, INDR, LPPF, SLIS, AALI, CPIN, ICBP, INDF, MLBI, STTP, TGKA, UNVR

5 Conclusions

The simulation study results show that Fuzzy C-Means and Fuzzy C-Medoids without involving ACF and PACF are very good for clustering data with values that tend to be close. In addition, Fuzzy C-Means and Fuzzy C-Medoids with and without involving ACF and PACF are very good for clustering data that have patterns that tend to be the same. The empirical results show that the two best methods for clustering open stock prices, close stock prices, and HML stock prices are Fuzzy C-Means and Fuzzy C-Medoids. Based on the highest FS value, it can be concluded that Fuzzy C-Means is the best clustering method for clustering stock prices of industrial and consumer sector companies in Indonesia. The clustering results using Fuzzy C-Means are the same for open and closed stock prices. Meanwhile, there are some differences in the results of clustering when compared to the results of clustering HML stock prices. This research also showed that clustering with ACF and PACF approaches did not give good results compared to without involving anything.

Acknowledgment. This research is supported by *Deputi Bidang Penguatan Riset dan Pengembangan, Kementerian Pendidikan, Kebudayaan, Riset, dan Teknologi & Badan Riset dan Inovasi Nasional* under the scheme *Penelitian Dasar*, number of contract 008/E5/PG.02.00.PT/2022 & 1506/PKS/ITS/2022. The authors thank DRPM ITS for the support. The authors also thank the reviewers whose comments and valuable suggestions helped improve the quality of this paper.

References

1. BPS: Berita Resmi Statistik. Badan Pusat Statistik, Indonesia (2022)
2. Nair, B.B., Saravana Kumar, P.K., Sakthivel, N.R., Vipin, U.: Clustering stock price time series data to generate stock trading recommendations: an empirical study. Expert Syst. Appl0 **70**, 20–36 (2017). https://doi.org/10.1016/j.eswa.2016.11.002
3. Liao, T.W.: clustering of time series data - a survey. Pattern Recogn. **38**, 1857–1874 (2005)
4. D'Urso, P. : Fuzzy clustering. Handbook of Cluster Analysis, pp. 545–574. Taylor & Francis Group, LLC, Boca Raton (2016)
5. Liu, Y., Chen, J., Shuai, W., Liu, Z., Chao, H.: Incremental Fuzzy C Medoids clustering of time series data using dynamic time warping distance. PLoS One **13**(5), e0197499 (2018). https://doi.org/10.1371/journal.pone.0197499
6. D'Urso, P., De Giovanni, L., Massari, R., D'Ecclesia, R.L., Maharaj, E.A.: Cepstral-based clustering of financial time series. Expert Syst. Appl. **161**, 113705 (2020). https://doi.org/10.1016/j.eswa.2020.113705
7. D'Urso, P., Giovanni, L.D., Massari, R.: GARCH-based robust clustering of time series. Fuzzy Sets Syst. **305**, 1–28 (2016)
8. Long, N.C., Wisitpongphan, N., Meesad, P., Unger, H.: Clustering stock data for multi-objective portfolio optimization. Int. J. Comput. Intell. Appl. **13**(02), 1450011 (2014). https://doi.org/10.1142/S1469026814500114
9. D'Urso, P., Maharaj, E.A.: Autocorrelation-based fuzzy clustering of time series. Fuzzy Sets Syst. **160**(24), 3565–3589 (2009)
10. Cryer, J.D., Chan, K.-S.: Time Series Analysis with Applications in R, 2nd edn. Springer Science+Business Media, LLC, New York (2008)
11. Ke, Z., Zhang, Z.: Testing autocorrelation and partial autocorrelation: asymptotic methods versus resampling techniques. Br. J. Math. Stat. Psychol. **71**(1), 96–116 (2018)
12. Wedel, M., Kamakura, W.A.: Market Segment: Conceptual and Methodological Foundations, 2nd edn. Kluwer Academic Publishers (2000)
13. Kruse, R., Döring, C., Lesot, M.-J.: Fundamentals of fuzzy clustering. In: Advances in Fuzzy Clustering and its Applications, pp. 3–30. John Wiley & Sons Ltd (2007)
14. Maharaj, E.A., D'Urso, P., Caiado, J.: Time Series Clustering and Classification. Taylor & Francis Group, LLC, Boca Raton (2019)
15. McBratney, A.B., Moore, A.W.: Application of fuzzy sets to climatic classification. Agric. For. Meteorol. **35**, 165–185 (1985)
16. Heiser, W.J., Groenen, P.J.F.: Cluster differences scaling with a within-clusters loss component and a fuzzy successive approximation strategy to avoid local minima. Psychometrika **62**, 63–83 (1997)
17. Everitt, B.S., Landau, S., Leese, M., Stahl, D.: Cluster Analysis, 5th edn. John Wiley & Sons Ltd, London (2011)
18. D'Urso, P.: Fuzzy clustering for data time arrays with inlier and outlier time trajectories. IEEE Trans. Fuzzy Syst. **13**(5), 583–604 (2005)
19. Dunn, J.C.: A fuzzy relative of the ISODATA process and its use in detecting compact well-separated clusters. J. Cybern. **3**(3), 32–57 (1974)

20. Bezdek, J.C.: Numerical taxonomy with fuzzy sets. J. Math. Biol. **1**, 57–71 (1974)
21. MacQueen, J.: Some methods for classification and analysis of multivariate observations. In: Proceedings of the Fifth Berkeley Symposium on Mathematical Statistics and Probability, vol. 1, pp. 281-297 (1967)
22. Bezdek, J.C.: Pattern Recognition with Fuzzy Objective Function Algorithms. Plenum Press, New York (1981)
23. Krishnapuram, R., Joshi, A., Yi, L.: A fuzzy relative of the k-Medoids algorithm with application to web document and snippet clustering. In: 1999 IEEE International Fuzzy Systems Conference Proceedings, vol. 3, pp. 1281–1286 (1999)
24. Krishnapuram, R., Joshi, A., Nasraoui, O., Yi, L.: Low-complexity fuzzy relational clustering algorithms for web mining. IEEE Trans. Fuzzy Syst. **9**(4), 595–607 (2001)
25. Suhartono, N.S., Prastyo, D.D.: Design of experiment to optimize the architecture of deep learning for nonlinear time series forecasting. Procedia Comput. Sci. **144**, 269–276 (2018). https://doi.org/10.1016/j.procs.2018.10.528
26. Suhartono, P.D., Saputri, F.F., Amalia, D.D., Prastyo, B.S., Ulama, S.: Model selection in feedforward neural networks for forecasting inflow and outflow in Indonesia. In: Mohamed, A., Berry, M.W., Yap, B.W. (eds.) Soft Computing in Data Science, pp. 95–105. Springer Singapore, Singapore (2017). https://doi.org/10.1007/978-981-10-7242-0_8
27. Prastyo, D.D., Nabila, F.S., Suhartono, M.H., Lee, N.S., Fam, S.-F.: VAR and GSTAR-based feature selection in support vector regression for multivariate Spatio-temporal forecasting. In: Yap, B.W., Mohamed, A.H., Berry, M.W. (eds.) Soft Computing in Data Science: 4th International Conference, SCDS 2018, Bangkok, Thailand, August 15-16, 2018, Proceedings, pp. 46–57. Springer Singapore, Singapore (2019). https://doi.org/10.1007/978-981-13-344 1-2_4
28. Dubes, R., Jain, A.K.: Clustering techniques: the user's dilemma. Pattern Recogn. **8**, 247–260 (1976)
29. Sardá-Espinosa, A.: Time-series clustering in R Using the dtwclust Package. The R Journal **11**(1), 22 (2019). https://doi.org/10.32614/RJ-2019-023
30. Dave, R.N.: Validating fuzzy partitions obtained through C-shells clustering. Pattern Recogn. Lett. **17**(6), 613–623 (1996)
31. Kwon, S.: Cluster validity index for fuzzy clustering. Electron. Lett. **34**(22), 2176–2177 (1998)
32. Tang, Y., Sun, F., Sun, Z.: Improved validation index for fuzzy clustering. In: American Control Conference, Portland (2005)
33. Zahid, N., Limouri, M., Essaid, A.: A new cluster-validity for fuzzy clustering. Pattern Recogn. **32**(7), 1089–1097 (1999)
34. Pakhira, M.K., Bandyopadhyay, S., Maulik, U.: Validity index for crisp and fuzzy clusters. Pattern Recogn. **37**(3), 487–501 (2004)
35. Wang, W., Zhang, Y.: On fuzzy cluster validity indices. Fuzzy Sets Syst. **158**(19), 2095–2117 (2007)
36. Campello, R.J.G.B., Hruschka, E.R.: A Fuzzy extension of the silhouette width criterion for cluster analysis. Fuzzy Sets Syst. **157**, 2858–2875 (2006)
37. Rahayu, S.P., Febryani, S., Kusuma, H.B., Suhartono, Prastyo, D.D.: The approach of Fuzzy C-Means cluster and factor analysis on economic potential mapping of regency/city in east java province. In: International Conference on Science and Applied Science (ICSAS) 2018, Surakarta, Indonesia (2018)

Zero-Inflated Time Series Model for Covid-19 Deaths in Kelantan Malaysia

Muhammad Hazim Ismail[1], Hasan Basri Roslee[1], Wan Fairos Wan Yaacob[1,2] (iD),
and Nik Nur Fatin Fatihah Sapri[3(✉)] (iD)

[1] Mathematical Sciences Studies, College of Computing, Informatics and Media, Universiti Teknologi MARA, Cawangan Kelantan, Lembah Sireh, 15050 Kota Bharu, Kelantan, Malaysia
[2] Institute for Big Data Analytics and Artificial Intelligence (IBDAI), Universiti Teknologi MARA, 40450 Shah Alam, Selangor, Malaysia
[3] School of Mathematical Sciences, College of Computing, Informatics and Media, 40450 Shah Alam, Selangor, Malaysia
nikfatinfatihah@uitm.edu.my

Abstract. The development of zero-inflated time series models is well known to account for excessive number of zeros and overdispersion in discrete count time series data. By using Zero-inflated models, we analyzed the daily count of COVID-19 deaths occurrence in Kelantan with excess zeros. Considering factors such as COVID-19 deaths in neighboring state and lag of 1 to 7 days of COVID-19 death in Kelantan, the Zero-Inflated models (Zero-Inflated Poisson (ZIP) and the Zero-Inflated Negative Binomial (ZINB)) were employed to predict the COVID-19 deaths in Kelantan. The ZIP and ZINB were compared with the basic Poisson and Negative Binomial models to find the significant contributing factors from the model. The final results show that the best model was the ZINB model with lag of 1,2,5 and lag of 6 days of Kelantan COVID-19 death, lag of 1-day COVID-19 deaths in neighboring State of Terengganu and Perak significantly influenced the COVID-19 deaths occurrence in Kelantan. The model gives the smallest value of AIC and BIC compared to the basic Poisson and Negative Binomial model. This indicate that the Zero Inflated model predict the excess zeros in the COVID-19 deaths occurrence well compared to the basic count model. Hence, the fitted models for COVID-19 deaths served as a novel understanding on the disease transmission and dissemination in a particular area.

Keywords: COVID-19 deaths · Count model · Zero-inflated Poisson (ZIP) · Zero-Inflated Negative Binomial (ZINB)

1 Introduction

Coronavirus (CoV) or COVID-19 is an infectious disease that formerly known as severe acute respiratory syndrome coronavirus-2 (SARS-CoV-2). It is the greatest threat to global public health and has given huge impact to the social, economy and country as a whole. As to date, more than 500 million people have been infected while about 6.4

M. Yusoff et al. (Eds.): SCDS 2023, CCIS 1771, pp. 291–302, 2023.
https://doi.org/10.1007/978-981-99-0405-1_21

million of people died worldwide due to COVID-19 (World Health Organization) [1]. It was declared a pandemic by the on March 12, 2020.

Malaysia is not immune to this coronavirus's global spread. As of August, 2020, the Malaysian Ministry of Health (MOH) [2] confirmed more than 4.7 million cases of COVID-19 were recorded with more than 36,085 deaths due to COVID-19. In Malaysia, Selangor recorded the highest number of verified COVID-19 cases. Nevertheless, Kelantan is the state recorded with the highest infection rate [2]. Several actions have been taken to offset the increment of the infected cases. One of the actions is the enforcement of Movement Control Order (MCO) in order to slow down the spread of COVID-19 in communities (18th March to 31st March 2020). According to Jun [3], the first COVID-19 wave ran from January 25 to February 16, 2020, while the second wave ran from February 27 to June 30, 2020. The third wave began on September 8, 2020. The spread of COVID-19 has resulted to healthcare professionals and other front-line employees face huge obstacles in controlling the number of deaths.

Many scientists and researcher are working to help reduce the number of infected cases. Among the effort are by analyzing the data and developed a statistical model to predict the contributing factors that affect the spread of COVID-19 cases. Different models have been used in recent studies to predict the incidence, prevalence and death rate of COVID-19. Among the contribution made are using extended Susceptible-Infected-Removed (eSIR), Susceptible-Exposed-Infected-Removed (SEIR) [4], spatial and temporal analysis spatial and temporal time series mixed-effects GLM model [5] and deterministic epidemiological models focusing on time evolution [6, 7].

In order to describe sequences of observed counts, two well-known probability distributions were used. The Poisson distribution, for example, it is distinguished by its attribute of equal-dispersion, or the equivalence of its mean and variance. If the variance of a random variable is larger than the mean, it is said to be over-dispersed. Second, the negative binomial distribution, which is employed instead of the binomial distribution to represent observed overdispersion in the data. It is a typical choice of probability distribution for unbounded counts with overdispersion. However, in some circumstances, a specified count, generally zero, might appear more frequently than other series counts, and ignoring the frequent occurrence of zero values can lead to overdispersion and biased parameter and standard deviation estimators. Lambert [8] proposed zero-inflated models, in which the distribution is a blend of certain count models, such as the Poisson or the negative binomial, with one that is degenerate at zero, to account for frequent zero values in the data. A number of research contributions have lately arisen in the literature to address the issue of adequate statistical modelling of zero inflation with time series of counts [9].

Hence, the purpose of this study is to develop a prediction model for daily confirmed COVID-19 death by using the zero-inflated model. This study will be conducted using the daily number of COVID-19 death in Kelantan and its neighbouring states.

2   Related Works

In real life, discrete count time series data with an excessive number of zeros have necessitated the creation of zero-inflated time series models. This issue has led to the creation of the zero-inflated count model, which can handle an excessive zero while also allowing for overdispersion in analysis [9]. The zero-inflated model is used to determine whether an individual count outcome is from the always-zero group or from another group, whereas the usual Poisson or Negative Binomial model is used to model outcome in the not always zero groups, which may produce zero or other outcomes. To handle zero-inflated data, the zero-inflated Poisson (ZIP) model can be fitted to the data, while, zero-inflated Negative Binomial (ZINB) model can be applied as an alternative model due to overdispersion. To add, the ZIP model is a variant of the well-known Poisson regression model that allows for an excess of zero counts in the data. According to Lambert [6], the ZIP model can be described as a mixing model for counting data with excess zeros.

The outbreak of coronavirus (COVID-19) has given a significant impact on global health since the virus can cause a sudden death. As a result, the goal of this ecological study was to look into the relationship between different predictors and COVID-19 fatality. In a small case study on New York city reveals that the days-to-peak for infection in neighboring boroughs correlates with inter-zone mobility rather than interzone distance [10]. In addition, the COVID-19 deaths are reported within 7 days after a patient being diagnosed with virus COVID-19 [11]. The spread of the virus become faster within a short of time and worsen the situation more likely to be happened in a densely populated area [12].

A recent study done by Tawiah et al. [13] had applied zero-inflated models as to explore the features of the daily count of COVID-19 fatalities in Ghana. In the partial-likelihood framework, the authors fitted a ZIP autoregressive model and a ZINB autoregressive model to the data. The findings of the study revealed that the dynamic ZIP was able to fit the data better than dynamic ZINB autoregressive model. Meanwhile, Kedhiri [14] also had applied the zero-inflated mixed auto regression model for modelling and forecasting possible trajectories of COVID-19 infections and mortalities using Tunisian data. Daily data on deaths count which comprised from March, 2020 to February, 2021 was used in the analysis. The findings of the study showed that the zero-inflated mixed auto regression successfully account for the excess zero in the data at which the model produce a better fit and resulted to more accurate prediction of COVID-19 deaths in Tunisian data.

3 Material and Methods

3.1 Material

The data used in this study consist of 13 variables which are the daily number of COVID-19 death in Kelantan, the previous 1 to 7 days number of death of observed in Kelantan, the previous day number of deaths observed in neighbouring state which Terengganu, Pahang and Perak, time and population. The term 'lag' in the number of deaths observed in Kelantan and the previous day of neighbouring state is represented as a gap of certain period or the number of previous days. This data was tabulated according to date and all four selected states.

The data covered the period from 17th March 2020 until 14th March 2022 which takes around 721 days or equivalent to 2 years. Thus, the total number of observations used in the study is 721. The COVID-19 death published dataset was obtained from the Malaysian Ministry of Health (MOH) in GitHub website (https://github.com/MoH-Malaysia/covid19-public/blob/main/epidemic/deaths_state.csv) and the population data were obtained from the Department of Statistics Malaysia (DOSM).

3.2   Predictive Models for Count Data

This study aimed to developed predictive model for COVID-19 deaths with excess zeroes in Kelantan, Malaysia. Firstly, the data was fitted with basic count model of Poisson and Negative Binomial model. Then, to account for excess zeros occurrence in the COVID-19 deaths, an application of zero-inflated Poisson model and zero-inflated Negative Binomial model were fitted to the data. The following section describes the statistical models applied in the study.

Basic Poisson and Negative Binomial Count Model. Poisson model is the basic count model which often been applied by researchers as a benchmark model in fitting the count data. This is due to Poisson model suits the statistical properties of count data and it is flexible to be reparametrized into other forms of distributional functions [15, 16]. This model assumes response variable to be independent and follows a Poisson distribution. It specifies that each observed count y_i, is drawn from Poisson distribution with conditional mean of μ_i, given vector X_i for case i. Thus, the density function of y_i can be expressed as:

$$(X_i) = \frac{e^{-\mu}\mu^y}{y!}, y = 0, 1, 2, \ldots \tag{1}$$

$$\ln \mu_i = X'\beta \ o \ \mu_i = e^{X'\beta} \tag{2}$$

where vector X is a set of covariates and β refers to parameter estimates. However, equidispersion assumption hold by Poisson model is always been violated. When the variance of count data exceeds the mean, $Var(y_i) > E(Y_i)$ an issue such "overdispersion" will occur. Due to overdispersion which commonly happened in real data, Negative Binomial model was then applied to the data. The Negative Binomial model introduces a dispersion parameter to solve the issue of overdispersion [9] by allowing the variance of response variable to be greater than its mean. Thus, according to Lambert [8], the density function of Y_i of Negative Binomial model is as follows,

$$f(X_i) = \frac{\Gamma\left(Y_i + a^{-1}\right)}{\Gamma(Y_i + 1)\Gamma\left(a^{-1}\right)} \left(\frac{a^{-1}}{a^{-1} + \mu_i}\right)^{a^{-1}} \left(\frac{\mu_i}{a^{-1} + \mu_i}\right)^{y_i} \tag{3}$$

where the mean and variance of the Negative Binomial model is $E(x_i) = \mu = e^{(x'_i\beta)}$ and $Var(y_i|x_i) = \mu_i + a\mu_i^2$. When $a = 0$, the model turns to Poisson model, and the Negative Binomial model has more flexibility in expressing the correlation between the anticipated value and variation of Y_i. Smaller α indicates that the Negative Binomial model is closer to be a Poisson model.

Zero-Inflated Poisson (ZIP) Model. The model is a hybrid of a Poisson distribution and a degenerate distribution at zero. According to Saengthong et al. [17], the probability mass function for zero-inflated models which correspond to Poisson distribution and Bernoulli distribution has the form,

$$g(x) = \begin{cases} \omega_i + (1 - \omega_i)e^{-\lambda}, & x = 0 \\ (1 - \omega_i)\frac{e^{-\lambda}\lambda^x}{x!}, & x = 1, 2, \dots . \end{cases} \tag{4}$$

where $\lambda > 0 \, and \, 0 < \omega < 1$. Then, the mean and variance of X_i can be derived as follows:

$$E(X_i) = (1 - \omega_i)\lambda_i = \mu_i \tag{5}$$

$$Var(X_i) = \mu_i + \left(\frac{\omega_i}{1 - \omega_i}\right)\mu_i^2, \tag{6}$$

Note that, the marginal distribution of X_i considered as overdispersion, if $\omega_i > 0$.

Zero-Inflated Negative Binomial (ZINB) Model. The ZINB distribution is a discrete distribution that describes the probability of an observed number of failures. This distribution has two different states: the first state has structural zeros ($x_i = 0$) with a probability of ω, while, the second state is having sample zero from Negative Binomial counts ($x_i = 1, 2, \dots$) with a probability of $(1 - \omega_i)$. The ZINB distribution is a mixture of Bernoulli and Negative binomial distribution [17]. Hence, the probability mass function for ZINB distribution is given as follows:

$$g(x) = \begin{cases} \omega_i + (1 - \omega_i)p^r, & x = 0 \\ (1 - \omega_i)\binom{r + x_i - 1}{x_i}p^r(1 - p)^{x_i}, & x = 1, 2, \dots . \end{cases} \tag{7}$$

where the $x = n - r, r > 0, 0 < p < 1 \, and \, 0 < \omega < 1$.

3.3 Model Evaluation

The model performance is being compared using Akaike Information Criterion (AIC), and Bayesian Information Criterion (BIC). By rules of thumb, the smaller the value of AIC and BIC, the better the model. Thus, following Numna [18], AIC and BIC can be computed as follows:

$$AIC = -2 \ln L(\widetilde{\theta}_k) + 2k \tag{8}$$

$$BIC = -2\ln L(\widetilde{\theta}_k) + k \ln(n) \tag{9}$$

where n is a sample size, k is the number of estimated parameters in the models, and $L(\widetilde{\theta}_k)$ is the likelihood of the estimated model.

3.4 Vuong Test

The Vuong test is a non-nested test that compares the estimated probability of two non-nested models [19, 20]. For example, the Vuong test are used to compare the advance zero-inflated count model to the ordinary count model. Let $P_1(Y_i|X_i)$ and $P_2(Y_i|X_i)$ be the probability distribution functions of inflated count model and ordinary count model respectively. The likelihood functions are identical if the models fit the data well. Then, the annotation for Voung test is as follows:

$$m_i = Log\left(\frac{P_1(Y_i|X_i)}{P_2(Y_i|X_i)}\right) \tag{10}$$

3.5 Incidence Rate Ratios

The incidence rate ratio (IRR) was computed in order to determine the correlation between the factor influence with the number of deaths in Kelantan. It is a popular causal metric which mostly used by researchers especially in epidemiological studies that evaluates how a risk factor effects an outcome. Commonly, IRR can be interpreted as: an IRR value of 1.0 indicates no correlation, IRR > 1.0 indicates a positive association, while IRR < 1.0 is vice versa.

4 Result and Discussion

4.1 Descriptive Analysis

Table 1 tabulates a summary statistics for each variables used in the analysis. Based on Table 1, it can be seen that the value of means is smaller than its variance across variables. This could be the initial prove that overdispersion is exist in the dataset. Furthermore, the maximum number of deaths in a day for Kelantan, Terengganu, Pahang, and Perak were about 36, 12, 22 and 28 deaths respectively. This implies that Kelantan had recorded the highest number of deaths in a day followed by Perak, Pahang and Terengganu.

Table 1. Summary statistics

Variable	Mean	Variance
Time	361.000	43380.17
Kelantan_death	1.897	14.212
Kelantan_death_lag1	1.896	14.216
Kelantan_death_lag2	1.890	14.214
Kelantan_death_lag3	1.877	14.100
Kelantan_death_lag4	1.874	14.105

(continued)

Table 1. (*continued*)

Variable	Mean	Variance
Kelantan_death_lag5	1.861	14.039
Kelantan_death_lag6	1.857	14.042
Kelantan_death_lag7	1.852	14.040
Kelantan_population	1,909,983	270,635,401
Terengganu_death_lag1	1.125	4.307
Pahang_death_lag1	1.233	5.626
Perak_death_lag1	2.259	17.423

Figure 1 shows the trend of COVID-19 death in Kelantan from March 24, 2020, till March 14, 2022. Based on the Fig. 1, an increase trend in the death toll from day zero (the day COVID-19 was identified in Kelantan) to roughly at day 574. The incline in the number of deaths in the early pandemic could possibly be related to an increase in the number of active, severe cases and also the lack of movement restriction policy during the peak of pandemic. Next, Fig. 2 shows that the dataset contains a high number of zero counts (no deaths) which make up 66.71 percent of the total time series data. There is no doubt that the numbers show zero inflation. Even if the infection rate is rising, it is important to look into the daily death reports to see if the majority of Kelantan COVID-19 patients have developed pandemic resistance as a result of vaccination or have responded well to the care they received in COVID-19 treatment facilities. Thus, the study applied predictive models for COVID-19 deaths in Kelantan using zero-inflated model to predict the COVID-19 deaths.

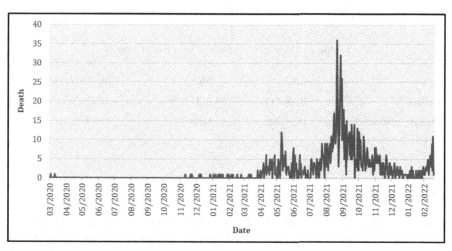

Fig. 1. COVID-19 Deaths Trend in Kelantan

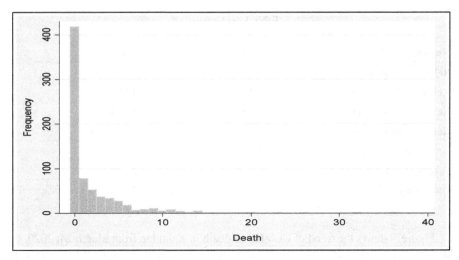

Fig. 2. Excess Zero in COVID-19 Deaths in Kelantan

4.2 Analysis Basic Count Models

In the beginning of analysis, the study starts with the basic count model of Poisson model and Negative Binomial model. Table 2 summarizes the model comparison between basic count model between Poisson model and Negative Binomial model. The result indicates that Negative Binomial model is more suitable and appropriate in fitting the data due to overdispersion issue over Poisson model since Negative Binomial model has the lowest AIC and BIC when compared to the Poisson model, with values of 1839.202 and 1898.75, respectively. For further improvement of model performance in predicting the COVID-19 deaths, the analysis of the study was then continued with zero-inflated count model which the results were revealed and discussed in the next section.

Table 2. Model performance of basic count models

Model	AIC	BIC	Log likelihood
Poisson	2088.711	2143.679	−1032.356
Negative binomial	1839.202	1898.75	−906.601

4.3 Variables Selection

Since there were many variables found to be not significant from both ZIP and ZINB full model, the model was then revised by performing feature selection (see Table 3). The revised model was conducted by removing those insignificant variables using backward elimination procedure to maintain the only significant variables in the model to predict the number of COVID-19 death in Kelantan. As a result, from feature selection that has been conducted, variables such as Kelantan death (lag 1, lag 2, lag 5 and lag 6), Terengganu death (lag 1) and Perak death (lag 1) were selected to be included in the revised proposed zero-inflated model (see Table 4).

Table 3. Full model comparison between ZIP and ZINB

Variables	ZIP		ZINB	
	Poisson	Inflate	NB	Inflate
Time	1.000	-0.006^{*}	1.000	-0.009^{*}
Kelantan_death_lag1	1.021^{*}	-0.174	1.023	-0.029
Kelantan_death_lag2	1.020^{*}	-0.555^{*}	1.021	-0.829
Kelantan_death_lag3	1.001	-0.080	1.004	-0.249
Kelantan_death_lag4	1.004	-0.269	1.010	-0.997^{*}
Kelantan_death_lag5	1.018^{*}	-0.507	1.021	-0.940
Kelantan_death_lag6	1.034^{*}	-0.136	1.038^{*}	-0.126
Kelantan_death_lag7	1.005	0.114	1.014	0.377
Terengganu_death_lag1	1.049^{*}	-0.053	1.058^{*}	-0.314
Pahang_death_lag1	1.002	0.052	1.006	0.272
Perak_death_lag1	1.022^{*}	0.003	1.022^{*}	-0.215
Constant	$9.86 \times 10^{-7*}$	4.072^{*}	$7.97 \times 10^{-7*}$	4.760^{*}
Vuong	7.040	–	6.550	–
AIC	1794.864		1691.648	
BIC	1904.8		1806.164	

* Significant at $\alpha = 0.05$.

Table 4. Parameter estimation for selected variables

Variables	Coef	Std. Err	T	P > t	[95% Conf. Interval]	
Kelantan_death_lag1	0.216	0.035	6.10	<0.001	0.146	0.285
Kelantan_death_lag2	0.159	0.035	4.58	<0.001	0.091	0.228
Kelantan_death_lag5	0.134	0.034	3.94	<0.001	0.067	0.200
Kelantan_death_lag6	0.305	0.035	8.75	<0.001	0.236	0.373
Terengganu_death_lag1	0.138	0.049	2.84	0.005	0.043	0.234
Perak_death_lag1	0.082	0.029	2.86	0.004	0.026	0.138
Constant	0.031	0.094	0.33	0.738	-0.153	0.216

4.4 Model Comparison between Reduced Zero-Inflated Models

Reduced Zero-Inflated Poisson (ZIP(R)). The summary result of analysis on the model comparison between reduced zero-inflated Poisson model (ZIP(R)) and reduced zero-inflated Negative Binomial model (ZINB(R)) is portrayed as in Table 5. Based on Table 5, all the selected variables were found to be significant in count model (p-value ($P < 0.05$)). Nevertheless, only Kelantan_death_lag1 and Kelantan_death_lag6 were found to be insignificant in inflated model. This indicates that the current number of COVID-19 deaths in Kelantan are likely to be influenced by the number of COVID-19 deaths recorded in a previous 1,2,5, and 6 days in Kelantan and the previous 1-day number of COVID-19 deaths in Terengganu and Perak. For the purpose of model comparison, AIC and BIC values of ZIP(R) model were computed about 1802.999 and 1867.128 respectively. The significance of Vuong test with p-value ($P < 0.05$) indicates that the ZIP(R) model is also preferred over ZIP (see Table 3). Next, due to overdispersion issue and excess zeros count in COVID-19 deaths data, the study was then applied ZINB(R) model and the model performance was being compared to ZIP(R).

Reduced Zero-Inflated Negative Binomial (ZINB(R)). Similar to results obtained from ZIP(R) model, it was found that the number of COVID-19 deaths in Kelantan can be predicted based on the number of COVID-19 deaths occurred in previous 1,2,5, and 6 days in Kelantan, the previous 1-day number of deaths in Terengganu and Perak. The Vuong test on ZINB(R) model also shows a significant value for this model. The high value of Vuong Test on ZINB(R) model (9.540) (see Table 5) compared to ZINB full model (6.550) (see Table 3), which indicates ZINB(R) model shows a better improvement than ZINB full model in analyzing the data. Based on Table 5, the values for AIC and BIC for ZINB(R) model were about 1702.314 and 1771.024 respectively. In comparison, the best model in predicting the COVID-19 deaths in Kelantan was ZINB(R) model since this model recorded the smallest value of AIC and BIC over AIC and BIC values computed in ZIP(R) model. From the best model obtained, it can be interpreted as the number of COVID-19 deaths recorded in the past 1, 2, 5 and 6 days in Kelantan were likely to influence the current number of COVID-19 deaths in Kelantan by 2.9%, 2.7%, 2.7% and 4.4% respectively. Meanwhile, the study also managed to find out that the number of COVID-19 deaths of neighbouring state of Kelantan also show a significant result in contributing to the number of COVID-19 deaths in Kelantan. For instance, the current number of COVID-19 deaths in Kelantan significantly be influenced by the previous 1-day of number of COVID-19 deaths in Terengganu and Perak by 5.6% and 2.2% respectively. Surprising, Terengganu reported a high percentage in contributing the number of COVID-19 deaths in Kelantan. This serves as significant evidence that the number of COVID-19 deaths in neighbouring state surround Kelantan could potentially influenced the number of COVID-19 deaths recorded in Kelantan.

Table 5. Reduced Model Comparison between ZIP (R) and ZINB (R)

Variables	ZIP(R)		ZINB(R)	
	Poisson	Inflate	NB	Inflate
Kelantan_death_lag1	1.024*	0.789	1.029*	0.800
Kelantan_death_lag2	1.023*	0.314*	1.027*	0.260*
Kelantan_death_lag5	1.021*	0.412*	1.027*	0.291*
Kelantan_death_lag6	1.037*	0.859	1.044*	0.800
Terengganu_death_lag1	1.050*	0.581*	1.056*	0.489*
Perak_death_lag1	1.021*	0.654*	1.022*	0.653*
Constant	$9.45 \times 10^{-7*}$	13.197	8.06×10^{-7}	12.730
Vuong	11.320	–	9.540	–
AIC	1802.999		1702.314	
BIC	1867.128		1771.024	

* Significant at $\alpha = 0.05$

5   Conclusion and Future Work

The main objective of this study was to fit zero-inflated models such ZIP and ZINB models in order to investigate prominent factor that influence COVID-19 deaths in Kelantan. Firstly, the trend analysis of COVID-19 deaths in Kelantan from March 24, 2020, till March 14, 2022 showed a rise as the infection rate, active cases and severe cases are continued to rise from day zero to day 574. In addition, the study revealed an overdispersion issue and excess of zeros count in the data. The application of zero-inflated negative binomial model towards the COVID-19 deaths in Kelantan data was found to be a better model than zero-inflated Poisson model in predicting the number of COVID-19 deaths in Kelantan. The findings of the study revealed that the current number of COVID-19 deaths in Kelantan mostly be influenced by previous number of COVID-19 deaths of previous 1,2,5 and 6 days. Interestingly, the number of COVID-19 deaths in Terengganu and Perak were statistically significant in influencing the number of COVID-19 deaths in Kelantan at which the highest percentage was contributed by Terengganu. This study managed to prove that the neighbouring state factor potentially influenced the current number of COVID-19 deaths in Kelantan. For future study, this study can be extended using other contributing factors such as vaccination rate and also death cases which cover the whole daily COVID-19 death cases in Malaysia. Eventually, this provides new insight in understanding this disease and the local authorities can plan for the effective strategies in reducing COVID-19 deaths.

Acknowledgement. The registration fee is funded by Pembiayaan Yuran Prosiding Berindeks (PYPB), Tabung Dana Kecemerlangan Pendidikan (DKP), Universiti Teknologi MARA (UiTM), Malaysia. Special thanks to School of Mathematical Sciences, College of Computing, Informatics and Media, Universiti Teknologi MARA for supporting this research project. We are also would like to express our gratitude to Ministry of Health for the data used in the study. We are also grateful to the Editor, the Associate Editor and anonymous referees for their insightful comments and suggestions.

References

1. World Health Organization (WHO): World Health Organization Coronavirus Disease (COVID-19). https://covid19.who.int. Last accessed 20 Sep 2022
2. Ministry of Health Malaysia: COVIDNOW in Malaysia. https://covidnow.moh.gov.my/. Last accessed 15 Oct 2022
3. Jun, S.W.: Movement Control Order Not a Lockdown. Malay Mail (2020)
4. Hamzah, F A., Lau, C., Nazri, H., Ligot, D.V., Lee, G., Tan, C.L.: CoronaTracker: World-wide COVID-19 Outbreak Data Analysis and Prediction. Bull World Health Organ. 19 (2020)
5. Giuliani, D., Dickson, M.M., Espa, G., Santi, F.: Modelling and predicting the spatio-temporal spread of Coronavirus disease 2019 (COVID-19) in Italy. BMC Infect. Dis. 20, 700 (2020)
6. Liu, Y., Gayle, A.A., Wilder-Smith, A., Rocklöv, J.: The reproductive number of COVID-19 is higher compared to SARS coronavirus. J. Travel Med. 27, taa021 (2020)
7. Kucharski, A.J., et al.: Early dynamics of transmission and control of COVID-19: a mathematical modelling study. The Lancet Infect. Dis. 20(5), 553–558 (2020)
8. Lambert, D.: Zero-inflated poisson regression, with an application to defects in manufacturing. Technometrics 34(1), 1–14 (1992). https://doi.org/10.1080/00401706.1992.10485228
9. Wan Yaacob, W.Y., Lazim, M.A., Wah, Y.B.: A practical approach in modelling count data. In: Proceedings of the Regional Conference on Statistical Science 2010, vol. 2010, pp. 176–183 (2010). http://instatmy.org.my/downloads/RCSS'10/Proceedings/17P.pdf
10. Roy, S., Ghosh, P.: Factors affecting COVID-19 infected and death rates inform lockdown-related policymaking. PLoS ONE 15(10), 1–18 (2020). https://doi.org/10.1371/journal.pone.0241165
11. Yuan, X., Xu, J., Hussain, S., Wang, H., Gao, N., Zhang, L.: Trends and prediction in daily new cases and deaths of COVID-19 in the United States: an internet search-interest based model. Explor Res Hypothesis Med. 5(2), 1–6 (2020). https://doi.org/10.14218/ERHM.2020.00023
12. Provenzano, S., Roth, S., Carozzi, F.: Urban Density and Covid-19. London School of Economics and Political Science, London (2020)
13. Tawiah, K., Iddrisu, W.A., Asosega, K.A.: Zero-Inflated time series modelling of COVID-19 deaths in Ghana. J. Env. Public Health 2021, 1–9 (2021). https://doi.org/10.1155/2021/5543977
14. Khedhiri, S.: Statistical modeling of COVID-19 deaths with excess zero counts. Epidemiol. Methods 10(s1), 20210007 (2021). https://doi.org/10.1515/em-2021-0007
15. Colin Cameron, A., Trivedi, Pravin K.: Essentials of count data regression. In: Baltagi, B.H. (ed.) A Companion to Theoretical Econometrics, pp. 331–348. Blackwell Publishing Ltd, Malden, MA, USA (2003). https://doi.org/10.1002/9780470996249.ch16
16. Shankar, V., Mannering, F., Barfield, W.: Effect of roadway geometrics and environmental factors on rural freeway accident frequencies. Accid. Anal. Prev. 27(3), 115–123 (1995)
17. Saengthong, P., Bodhisuwan, W., Thongteeraparp, A.: The zero inflated negative binomial – Crack distribution: some properties and parameter estimation. Songklanakarin J. Sci. Technol. 37(6), 701–711 (2015)
18. Numna, S.: Analysis of Extra Zero Counts using Zero-inflated Poisson Models, (57), 3 (2009)
19. Vuong, Q.H.: Likelihood ratio tests for model selection and non-nested hypotheses. Econom. Soc. 57(2), 307–333 (1989)
20. He, H., Zhang, H., Ye, P., Tang, W.: A test of inflated zeros for Poisson regression models. Stat. Methods Med. Res. 28(4), 1157–1169 (2019). https://doi.org/10.1177/0962280217749991

Author Index

Printed in the United States
by Baker & Taylor Publisher Services